Dance Legacies of Scotland

Dance Legacies of Scotland compiles a collage of references portraying percussive Scottish dancing and explains what influenced a wide disappearance of hard-shoe steps from contemporary Scottish practices.

Mats Melin and Jennifer Schoonover explore the historical references describing percussive dancing to illustrate how widespread the practice was, giving some glimpses of what it looked and sounded like. The authors also explain what influenced a wide disappearance of hard-shoe steps from Scottish dancing practices. Their research draws together fieldwork, references from historical sources in English, Scots, and Scottish Gaelic, and insights drawn from the authors' practical knowledge of dances. They portray the complex network of dance dialects that existed in parallel across Scotland, and share how remnants of this vibrant tradition have endured in Scotland and the Scottish diaspora to the present day.

This book will be of interest to scholars and students of Dance and Music and its relationship to the history and culture of Scotland.

Mats Melin is a lecturer at University of Limerick, Ireland. He has worked and performed extensively in Angus, Sutherland, the Scottish Highlands, the Hebrides, Orkney, and Shetland, promoting Scottish traditional dance in schools and communities.

Jennifer Schoonover is a dancer and choreographer. She teaches movement principles, improvisation, dance pedagogy, and dance modalities including Cape Breton Step, Ceilidh, Highland, and Scottish Country dancing.

Dance Legacies of Scotland
The True Glen Orchy Kick

Mats Melin and Jennifer Schoonover

LONDON AND NEW YORK

First published 2021
by Routledge
2 Park Square, Milton Park, Abingdon, Oxon OX14 4RN

and by Routledge
52 Vanderbilt Avenue, New York, NY 10017

Routledge is an imprint of the Taylor & Francis Group, an informa business

© 2021 Mats Melin and Jennifer Schoonover

The right of Mats Melin and Jennifer Schoonover to be identified as authors of this work has been asserted by them in accordance with sections 77 and 78 of the Copyright, Designs and Patents Act 1988.

All rights reserved. No part of this book may be reprinted or reproduced or utilised in any form or by any electronic, mechanical, or other means, now known or hereafter invented, including photocopying and recording, or in any information storage or retrieval system, without permission in writing from the publishers.

Trademark notice: Product or corporate names may be trademarks or registered trademarks, and are used only for identification and explanation without intent to infringe.

British Library Cataloguing-in-Publication Data
A catalogue record for this book is available from the British Library

Library of Congress Cataloging-in-Publication Data
Names: Melin, Mats, author. | Schoonover, Jennifer, author.
Title: Dance legacies of Scotland : the true Glen Orchy kick / Mats Melin and Jennifer Schoonover.
Description: Abingdon, Oxon ; New York, NY : Routledge, 2021. | Includes bibliographical references and index.
Identifiers: LCCN 2020038144 (print) | LCCN 2020038145 (ebook) | ISBN 9780367489472 (hardback) | ISBN 9781003043607 (ebook)
Subjects: LCSH: Clog dancing--Scotland--History. | Step dancing--Scotland.--History. | Dance--Scotland--History. | Scotland--Social life and customs.
Classification: LCC GV1646.S35 M45 2021 (print) | LCC GV1646.S35 (ebook) | DDC 793.3/209411--dc23
LC record available at https://lccn.loc.gov/2020038144
LC ebook record available at https://lccn.loc.gov/2020038145

ISBN: 978-0-367-48947-2 (hbk)
ISBN: 978-1-003-04360-7 (ebk)

Typeset in Bembo
by KnowledgeWorks Global Ltd.

Contents

List of figures	vii
List of tables	ix
Foreword	x
Introduction	1
1 'I wish I had it in my power to describe to you': introductory observations on Step dance and its place in Scotland	12
2 From regional variations to standardisation of vernacular dance	27
3 *Na brògan dannsaidh/*The dancing shoes: foot anatomy, footwear, and body posture	41
4 Gaelic references and continental European connections	55
5 From Hornpipes to High Dances: historical terms and overlapping usage	67
6 Hyland step forward: eighteenth-century accounts	77
7 A few more flings and shuffles: nineteenth-century accounts, 1800–1839	100
8 Aberdeenshire to the Hebrides: nineteenth-century accounts, 1840–1899	131
9 Breakdown: twentieth-century accounts	162
10 *An t-Seann Dùthaich*: dancing in the Scottish diaspora	184

vi *Contents*

11 First-hand Step dance encounters and recollections
in Scotland from the 1980s to 2016 collected by Mats Melin   199

12 Weaving the steps to the music   211

13 Echoes and reflections   230

Appendix—Tune examples as given in the text   239
Bibliography   243
Index   257
    General 257
    Dance titles 261
    Song/tune titles 264
    People 265
    Places and languages 270

Figures

0.1	Map of Scotland	10
1.1	An illustration showing the catch out (a) and the catch in (b) in the treepling motif, from Flett, *Traditional Dancing in Scotland*, 1985: 262	13
1.2	The White Cockade/*An Chocàrd*	16
3.1	Modern soft leather ghillie pump	47
3.2	Shoe with hardwood tip and heel	48
3.3	Dancing in bare feet	49
3.4	Dandy clogs for dancing	51
3.5	Painting (detail). *A Highland Dance*. David Allan (*c.* 1780). Original in National Galleries of Scotland	52
3.6	Sword dancer wearing hard-soled shoes with buckles. Artist unknown. Chicago, The Regan Printing House, 1910	53
6.1	McGill's Hornpipe Steps, 1752	81
6.2	McGill's Gige Steps, 1752	82
6.3	*The Dance on Dun-Can*, Thomas Rowlandson. Picturesque Beauties of Boswell, Part the Second, 1786	84
6.4	Illustration in Faujas de Saint-Fond (1799: 301) showing the interior of Dalmally's Blacksmith, MacNab's house in 1784	94
7.1	Extract of prices for dance tuition given in Thomas Wilson, *An Analysis of country dancing…*, 1811	100
7.2	An engraving showing Country dancing, Scotch Reels, and Quadrilles coexisting on a dance floor by J. Shury, from Thomas Wilson's 1816 3rd edition of the *Companion to the Ballroom*	101
7.3	Guillard notation of *aisig-thrasd* 1989: 25	108
7.4	Guillard notation of kick step 1989: 25	109
7.5	Guillard notation of expanding Peacock's minor (half-bar) step into a single (one-bar) step 1989: 26	109
8.1	Mr Robert Owen's Institution, New Lanark, 1825. *Quadrille Dancing*	135
8.2	Single and double treble counting exampled in 2/4 and 4/4 time	137

viii   *Figures*

8.3 *Gille Calum* by R.R. McIan, 1848   144
8.4 A member of the Scottish dance company *Dannsa*: Step dancer
     Sandra Robertson performing the *Smàladh na Coinnle*
     at Crear, Argyll   148
8.5 Sword Dance diagram, McIntyre-North, 1880   155
9.1 Dancing to the piper at a fair in Campbeltown, Argyll *c.*1900
     (SLA 58.35.26)   164
9.2 Hebridean dancing at South Uist Games, 1920s   171
9.3 Extract from Dancie Reid's notebook. Example of treble
     description   173
9.4 Extract from Dancie Reid's notebook. Description of the first
     step of the Flowers of Edinburgh   174
9.5 Members of Drumalban Dance company performing a Scotch
     Reel, at a Scottish Traditions of Dance Trust conference,
     Stirling, 2003   180
10.1 Sunday afternoon ceilidh at the MacLean farmstead in
     Washabuck in the late 1940s or early 1950s   185
11.1 Fearchar MacNeil, Isle of Barra, 1990   200
11.2 Anna Bain, Sheila McKay, Maggie Moore, and Sandra
     Robertson. Photo taken at Step Dancing Seminar,
     Dingwall, 1997   203
11.3 Shetland Folkdance in 1995 dancing a four-couple
     Shetland Reel   208
12.1 Hard shoes with heels are shown in this illustration
     of doing the backstep in the Highland Fling taken from
     D.R. MacKenzie's *National Dances of Scotland* ([1910], 1939
     reprint edition), page 34   212
12.2 Illustration shows difference between a triple and a treble   214
A.1 'Minuet' from James Oswald's 1745 *Caledonian Pocket Companion*   239
A.2 'Go to Berwick, Johnnie' from Angus MacKay's 1857
     Tutor for the Highland Bagpipe   239
A.3 '*Gille Crubach anns a' Ghleann*/Miss Drummond of Perth' from
     Angus MacKay's 1857 *Tutor for the Highland Bagpipe*   240
A.4 '*Tuloch Gorm*/Tulloch Gorum' from Angus MacKay's 1857
     Tutor for the Highland Bagpipe   240
A.5 ''*S truadh nach bu leis &c.*/Oer the Hills and Far Awa' from
     Angus MacKay's 1857 *Tutor for the Highland Bagpipe*   241
A.6 'College Hornpipe' from James Stewart Robertson's 1884
     Athole Collection   241
A.7 'Over the Water to Charlie/*Null air an Uisge gu Tearlach*' from
     Angus MacKay's 1857 *Tutor for the Highland Bagpipe*   242
A.8 'Flowers of Edinburgh' from James Stewart Robertson's 1884
     Athole Collection   242

Tables

12.1 Some examples of common dance and music structural
       segmentations   226
12.2 Some common structures of a selection of named percussive
       dances   227

Foreword

My first thought on reading this book was how much I wished it had existed when I was conducting my master's degree research on Step dance back in 2015. Mats and Jen have collected numerous disparate sources, unearthed some buried treasures, and present all their findings within a framework of perceptive interpretation. I am deeply grateful to them both for bringing this knowledge into all our hands (and feet!).

As a teenager, it was something of a surprise to me to learn of the debate surrounding the origins of percussive Step dancing in Scotland. Growing up in Scotland in the 1990s and early 2000s, I attended various *fèisean* and learned percussive Step dancing alongside *clàrsach* and Gaelic song. In those early years, I was vaguely aware of a connection to Nova Scotia and the Gaelic diaspora, but I never questioned the 'Scottishness' of the style.

As mentioned in Chapter 13, I am among a 'new wave of indigenous Scottish Step dancers' who benefitted from the reintroduction of percussive Step dance from Cape Breton in the 1980s and 1990s. Since I grew up with the tradition, that reintroduction felt relatively seamless. The Cape Breton steps complemented my growing knowledge of Gaelic music and song, and I stomped and shuffled enthusiastically around the kitchen floor to the rhythm of fiddle tunes and *puirt a beul*.

Later, however, I relived the surprise of earlier Cape Bretoners who, having been invited to share their Scottish ancestors' steps in the motherland, were told by some that their style was 'Irish.' According to these critics, percussive Step dance did not have a historical presence in Scotland at all.

The authors of this book are certainly not alone in challenging this viewpoint, but the examples they have collected are particularly helpful in painting a fuller picture. Building on the work of Margaret Bennett, Michael Newton, and many others, they show how significant channels of cultural influence existed between Scotland and the rest of Europe, in addition to those between Scotland and Ireland. Their research offers ample evidence of the independent existence and development of percussive Step dance in Scotland.

This is particularly vindicating for Gaels in both 'the Old Country' and the diaspora, who have long maintained this connection through their knowledge of genealogy and the intergenerational transmission of their culture. For centuries, Scottish Gaels have been forced to tolerate ignorant and belittling suggestions that their culture is coarse, barbaric, or simply a poor imitation of Irish traditions (*i.e.* Trevor-Roper in Hobsbawm, 1983). In contrast, this book offers examples of how the Scottish percussive dance tradition has developed richly, distinctly, and with its own set of aesthetic markers.

Combining examples from over three centuries of dance development, the authors provide compelling historical evidence of the widespread presence of percussive Step dance in Scotland. Indeed, although the style is now most commonly associated with Gaelic-speaking communities, it is shown here to have been popular in many other parts of the country as well.

We can now more clearly see the path of this developing tradition: meandering, wide-ranging, adaptable, at times suppressed or re-directed, but continuous, nonetheless. Its development has been shaped by factors of emigration and environment, morality and memory, fashion, standardisation, and serendipitous connections prompting new growth and revitalisation.

Mats's and Jen's passion for dance and dance scholarship is evident throughout their work, and their book draws on years of meticulous research and practical involvement in the art form. It is a labour of love, and I hope it will inspire many more lovers of dance in their learning and expression. *Dance Legacies of Scotland* does much to reconnect contemporary iterations of percussive Scottish dancing with their earlier origins, but the onward path of the tradition remains unknown. As the authors point out, 'a dance is only alive during an act of it being performed by a human being, who makes choices and becomes an embodied interpretation of the material.' May we shape it with care and creativity.

Happy dancing!
Màiri Britton
Antigonish, Nova Scotia
July 2020

Introduction

The disappearance of hard-shoe Step dancing in Scotland—from dancing masters to dance organisations

Scottish dancing has been celebrated for its high spirit and energy, and dance stands out as a striking feature of Scotland's cultural fabric throughout recorded history. In the 1800s, a complex network of dancing masters spanned the country and filled a demand for dance education that reached through all social classes. However, in the early 1900s, Scottish dancing traditions were seen as being in danger of extinction.

Two separate groups emerged to preserve and resurrect Scottish dances. Both groups aimed to create wider platforms for dances signifying Scottish identity and culture. One, the Scottish Country Dance Society, was formed in 1923, founded by Ysobel Stewart of Fasnacloich and Jean Milligan. As the Girl Guide Commissioner for Argyll, Mrs Stewart specifically wanted to teach group dances associated with Scotland, as opposed to the English dances promoted by the Girl Guiding organisation in the twenties.[1] The Society began publishing books of dance instructions, offered summer classes, and worked steadily to standardise technique and teaching objectives. From the inception of what is now known as the Royal Scottish Country Dance Society (RSCDS),[2] Scottish Country dancing intended to assert Scottishness. Today that expression of Scottish identity has a global reach; the RSCDS has over 150 branches on six continents.

The other group was the Scottish Official Board of Highland Dancing, which, from the outset of its formation in 1950, intended to standardise competitive dancing. Dance competitions had long been features of Scottish sporting and cultural gatherings known as Highland Games, but in the forties, irregular judging prompted action to make the competitions more objective and fair. Now titled the Royal Scottish Official Board of Highland Dancing (RSOBHD),[3] this organisation intended to define what constituted Highland dancing as well as establish itself as the worldwide authority governing that definition. The RSOBHD published judging criteria in its textbook, *Highland Dancing*, in 1955. The introduction remarked on a 'general neglect of Scottish culture which has prevailed, until recently, in all

2   *Introduction*

four Scottish universities,' and complained that 'Highland Dancing has been largely ignored by learned men.' This textbook remains in print, in an eighth edition, and continues to set the rules for a majority of Highland Games held around the world. The RSOBHD promoted selected versions of dances from competitive Games' cultural traditions, at the expense of Highland dance steps and legacies that didn't make it into their textbook.[4]

These organisations have shaped global perceptions of Scottish dancing, and along the way, they have influenced what footwear dancers use. Both encourage wearing soft-soled dance shoes. Their publications suggest that flexible leather-soled slippers lacing crisscross atop the forefoot be worn for Scottish dancing: the RSOBHD mandates 'Black Highland dancing pumps'[5] and the RSCDS shows similar footwear in the *Won't You Join the Dance?* manual.[6] The prevalence of the soft shoe in Scottish dance styles is a recent development, however. an issue not widely understood by modern-day practitioners of Scottish Country and Highland dancing.

Before 1900, hard-soled shoes, often embellished with silver buckles, were worn for Highland dancing competitions. Dancers sported dress shoes for social dancing throughout Scotland before and in parallel to the rise of the RSCDS style. Highland dancing pumps, today colloquially known as 'ghillies,' have been manufactured only since the very late 1800s. There were so few professional Games dancers who wore Highland dancing pumps around the turn of the century that, according to dancing master D.G. MacLennan, 'there was only one shop in all Scotland where these shoes could be obtained.'[7] This specialised shoe came to be adopted widely by Highland dancers in the early 1900s, and thereafter by the Scottish Country Dance Society in the 1920s. The soft-shoe techniques promoted since 1920 are recent innovations.

Before 1900, dancing across Scotland was quite varied, and did not conform exclusively to practices published by the RSCDS and RSOBHD. Dancing exhibited individuality and reflected stylistic hallmarks unique to certain areas. Written odds and ends can be patched together to reveal a wide group of practices that existed simultaneously and sometimes occurred only in isolated areas—some reflecting influences from earlier dancing masters, and some not. A patchwork of studied and vernacular dance forms covered Scotland; these forms were not homogenous. One of these practices has stood out in particular interest to us: percussive dancing, where the movement of the body generates dynamic rhythm. Percussive dancing had been widespread through Scotland but *has* veered towards the brink of extinction in the twentieth century. To help shine a light on this practice, in this book, we have compiled any and all references we could find depicting percussive dancing from Scottish legacies.

Some of the material included in this book had been uncovered by previous researchers, and some of it we dug up independently. We have filled in some background information to provide context for the historical references. To emphasise the diversity in cultural practices, we have left variant spellings as we found them to share the distinct flavours colouring the primary sources, and to allow the original writers to express themselves in the unique ways they initially did. We included any original italic formatting and emphases placed by these writers The fluidity of orthography encountered in these passages reflects diversity in perceptions, and helps to form an impression of pre-standardised cultural experiences.

Percussive dancing in Scotland was actively suppressed when some influential dancing masters promoted genteel dance fashions. However, passages admonishing dancers for shuffling and snapping show us that it happened frequently enough to garner active disapproval in line with societal aesthetic shifts. Those quotations will speak for themselves later on.

The source material in this book

Most of the early references in this study come from English-language sources, with quite a number of them written by observers and explorers unfamiliar with Scottish culture. In this process, the act of seeing, and perhaps the effect of being seen, can be an active component of the situation described. Some comments can come off as derogatory or stereotyped to our eyes today. Writers' cultivated worldviews often coloured their descriptions. Few of the detailed depictions come from people native to the country, and so outsiders' biases can be discerned in many accounts. Even Scottish Lowland commentators display lack of understanding of the Gaelic-speaking world in descriptions of the Highlands and Islands. Each reference is important in that it provides information about a time we can no longer see for ourselves, but it is also important to consider the inherent limitations and biases of each source sharing that information.

Folklore, consisting of traditional beliefs, customs, stories, dances, and other transmissions of a community passed down through generations by word of mouth, itself is 'intimately related to power relations in society, to economic factors, to public institutions and to academic disciplines,' as James Porter summarises Christopher Tilley's characterisation of the discipline.[8] Even orally transmitted legacies informing the cultural practices of dancing are embedded with biases and subjectivity. Porter particularly cautions about the lens of tartanry, or 'the cult of tartan as a symbol of identity,' when looking critically at accounts of Scottishness. He leans on Angus Calder's definition of tartanry as an 'ideological means by which "a Union of practical convenience became a Union of irrational love and tears, sublimated in militarism, tartanry, royalism, and, eventually, imperialism"' which has morphed into a twentieth-century 'debased culture of sentimentality.'[9] Porter suggests that the duty of a folklorist is 'to ensure that cultural representation, like cultural identity itself, is seen as a process, and not as a reified, idealized view of the past.'[10] Instead of the word 'folklore,' Porter suggests using 'the term "discourse" because it implicitly rejects the idea of folklore as solely a product of communal imagination or individual aesthetic sense.'[11] In this investigation, accounts from a wide variety of locations and sources show the far-reaching practices of percussive dancing across Scotland. We look through a wide lens in a spirit of discourse with an ethnochoreological perspective.

Dance as a discipline can carry a loaded set of cultural assumptions itself. Dance artist and theoretician Rudolf Laban described this when he wrote,

4   *Introduction*

'We all think that we observe actions in others with sufficient accuracy to be able to understand and assess the people we observe, but in reality, we are influenced by factors which distract us from what we actually see. Preconceived ideas, biased opinions, too-lively an imagination or too-ready censure, all obscure the only data we have—a person's movement as it was performed without reference to its result.'[12] One must consider the partialities behind the source of any comments being made, while at the same time reading any objective content contained.

British dance anthropologist Theresa Jill Buckland also cautions us not to apply personal sensory perceptions in analyses and reconstruction of historical dance forms, pointing out that 'problems exist with such approaches, not the least of which is the often unrecognized projection of a universalist notion of the body.'[13] This caution may equally be applied to broadly sweeping rules shaping the perceptions of watching dancers in earlier times as well as today.

Even though some writers claim to categorise Scottish dancing as a whole, we cannot allow any one of these passages to be viewed as representing practices of every area of Scotland. On the other hand, some writers particularly note regional variants. Colonel Thomas Thornton was aware that different regions had different styles, and labelled one movement he observed 'the true Glen Orgue [Orchy] kick.' Born in London, and finishing his education at Glasgow University, Thornton applies a label categorising this step as being 'true' from the perspective of an outside observer. Whether a dancer from Glen Orchy at that time would also have categorised the 'kick' as 'true' to that area remains obscure, but that Thornton identified the step as being notable there is nonetheless valuable information.

One aspect of nineteenth-century Scotland is important to understand, even in all its ugliness: a deep-growing conflict of values and ideologies between Anglo- and Scoto-phone Scots and the people of Gaeldom. The Gael was frequently depicted as 'lazy' and a member of an inferior race, an expression and extension of a longstanding prejudice. Scottish historian Thomas M. Devine tells us the:

> [a]rticulate Lowland attitudes to the Highlands in the Victorian era were profoundly ambivalent, and varied in tone and emphasis over time. On the one hand, romantic Highlandism had made the region a fashionable tourist destination for the elites of British society [...] But there was also a much darker side to Lowland perceptions which became increasingly dominant and influential during the famine years. One of the first published works arguing for an innate inferiority of the Celtic race was John Pinkerton's *Dissertation on the Origin and Progress of the Scythians or Goths* of 1787. [...] Even if the views of Pinkerton and his ilk were shared by only a small intellectual minority in the eighteenth century, they still helped to lay one of the key foundations for the later flourishing of racist thought: the assumption that the Celt was inferior to the Anglo-Saxon. In Scotland, this distinction came to be seen by some as a racial

divide between the Highlands and the Lowlands. In the first half of the nineteenth century, race became an even more central part of medical and scientific research. [...] The Teutonic-Celtic distinction was further refined, the former associated with industriousness, a strong work ethic and enterprise, the latter with indolence, sloth and dependency. [...] the economic failures in the Highlands came to be explained by some as a result of Celtic inadequacy rather than a consequence of environmental constraints [...] The famine crisis made these views even more influential. [...] What had emerged then, by 1848–9, were irreconcilable differences between the traditional values of Gaeldom and the prevailing ideologies of contemporary capitalism, improvement and social morality.[14]

This topic is explored in greater detail in Devine's book, as well as in the writings of James Hunter.[15] Shades of this prejudice, sadly, persist today in Scottish politics and press, particularly in relation to the Gaelic language. This bias lacks fundamental understanding and respect towards a way of life, culture, and language. This perception of inferiority is not only directed towards Gaelic culture; it has been directed towards dancers who picked up steps in the home environment or village by association-based dancers in eastern, central, and Lowland Scotland.

The observers' viewpoints and their terminology

In this collection, we compile many observers' accounts of events they witnessed and later described in text. Some allusions to dance practices come through poems and songs both in English and Gaelic. Actual dancers' thoughts, feelings, words, or terminology are largely absent. A few notebooks and ballroom guides contain terminology for dance motifs, but how much the published terminology relied on active usage and how much instead reflected publishing conventions of the time, to encourage wider readership or sales, is unclear today.

In dance notebooks, we get a privileged look at the personal words and expressions of particular individuals, be they dance teachers or pupils. What their handwritten terminology specifically reflects is a matter of some conjecture. When a notebook was kept by a pupil, such as Frederick Hill in Alford in 1841, we can assume that his notes were significantly influenced by the words his teachers used. A lot of detective work and guesswork is required in deciphering and analysing these notes. One of Hill's notes gives the instruction 'Beat time.' Although we do not know what part of the body was beating time, we can tell that it was making sound.

Biases held by researchers can affect how they view and present the material they find. Dance historian George Emmerson includes many descriptions of hard-shoe dancing in his book, yet repeatedly discounts that percussive dancing in hard shoes was a common practice. His dissent in this area seems unfair and strange. However, Emmerson was active with the RSCDS, which, as noted

6 Introduction

earlier, promotes wearing soft-soled shoes for dancing. He wrote a number of books marketed particularly to RSCDS practitioners, and was the devisor of *Sauchie Haugh*, a popular Scottish Country dance. While we owe a great deal to Emmerson for his prodigious research, his 1972 tome, *A Social History of Scottish Dance*, exhibits a bias against the practice of percussive footwork in Scotland. Emmerson's later writings reflect a greater degree of comfort accepting hard-shoe dancing as common practice, including this passage from *A Handbook of Traditional Scottish Dance*: 'Stepping in social reels was by no means confined to the southwest of Scotland but was also reported in the West Highlands.'[16]

It is also important to question and consider the biases present in the backgrounds of researchers who published steps they collected in Scotland. In many sources these dance notators apply an *etic*, or outsider, perspective of words and terminology, which may draw assumptions or apply prejudices not native to the home culture. Seldom are words shared that were used by the informants, which would provide insider, or *emic*, knowledge of that event.[17] D.G. MacLennan, Jack McConachie, Thomas Flett, and Frank Rhodes all notated dance steps from areas to which they were not native. Flett and Rhodes made meticulous notes using numbered foot positions borrowed from Highland dancing to reflect nuances regarding individual foot placement displayed by each informant. Even though the informants may not have used foot position numbers themselves, the notators' aim was to reflect accuracy in their movement notations. Accuracy was not important to MacLennan, who altered material to better suit his own standards. This, in itself, does not take away from the quality of the dances he recounts, but it is important to know that MacLennan changed the steps.[18] Descriptions of dances must be read critically to determine whether dance notators present material with integral faithfulness to the original, or whether ulterior motives are at work.

We don't know if the informants appreciated or agreed with these notations, nor do we have full details of how they recalled and embodied the dances they shared. Informants may not have had words for movements, may not have volunteered to share the words they used, or their words just may not have been noted down. These researchers' publications become primary sources, to be interpreted in turn by readers. If that same researcher teaches subsequent learners in person, as Tom Flett did, some of the original ways can be transmitted aurally or kinaesthetically, a more historical transmission mode. In our later chapter presenting onomatopoeia, words that reflect the sound of an action in their sounds and syllables, of certain terms within Highland dancing terminology, we present motif names that have been passed down through oral transmission that we feel are embedded with percussive dance rhythms and qualities.

What types of questions prompted this study?

Our investigation of percussive dancing in Scotland resulted from a multitude of interconnected questions put to a broad spectrum of material. Upon finding any reference relating to dancing in Scotland, the first thing we asked ourselves was: Could the described dance occurrence be classified as 'percussive' and in what way? What biases and backgrounds did the observers of these instances have or exhibit? Did observers objectively describe what they saw, or did they embellish their stories to evoke some reaction? What else could be learned by researching the terminology used by these writers, and, by extension, other commentators, of these Scottish dance event descriptions?

Regarding the descriptions found in these sources, what terms now associated with particular styles of dance may have had other meanings in the past? Did words' meanings from various languages or dialects shift in translation to modern English? How did terms used for dancing vary from one geographical area to another? Was dance terminology used by Gaelic speakers in Scotland and Canada? Do words used for dance have layered, underlying connotations that resonate with a certain group of practitioners only? Did the commentators use words that today connote percussive dance but did their usage in fact signify something else?

Were movement motifs that seem identical from a mechanical point of view perceived as being different, due to different names placed on them in separate areas, or stylistic differences layered over the dancing, such as outward rotation of the legs? What terminology, spoken or written, can be understood as describing percussive movement motifs? How do the influences of what surfaces are danced on (soil, stone, wood, *etc.*) and footwear is worn (bare feet, hard-soled shoes, soft-soled shoes) affect motif usage, and their descriptions, as physical situations change?

Through an ongoing spirit of searching, asking these questions along the way, we compiled the material included in this book to illustrate the percussive dancing legacies of Scotland.

Our journey begins

The references in this volume are only snapshots of dance legacies from *only* the individuals encountered. Our findings can be seen as a patchwork quilt incorporating carefully collected snippets. Some of the people featured are named, such as teachers, performers, and individuals who kept notebooks that survive and are accessible. Others are nameless performers who inspired observers to write about them at certain points in time. Dancers were influenced or taught by dancers before them and influenced others in turn by performing. A considerable shift away from this natural form of transmission through observing, listening, and embodying material[19] occurred when dance organisations created rules and regulations on how people should dance. Thus, individuals' choices and legacies were diminished in favour of the unified preferences of leaders of standardising organisations. The power and legacy of the individual dancer is still strong in Cape Breton Island, Canada, as an example, where percussive dancing practices have been fostered in the *Gàidhealtachd*.

Some of the accounts we include have been quoted before in other research into Scottish dancing. We aim to shine a particular light on these

8   *Introduction*

commentaries. We have also uncovered passages, via search engines in online databases and newspaper archives, which have not, to our knowledge, been previously considered in Scottish dance history research.

We connect Scottish dance to historical British, Irish, and pan-European dance developments, so a few ground-breaking and far-reaching aesthetic and choreographic innovations from these areas are included to show how they influenced Scottish dancing. In fact, dance commentary in Gaelic-language source material reveals direct cultural exchange between the remotest parts of Scotland and the European continent in the seventeenth and eighteenth centuries. Our search for references regarding sounds made by dancing on wooden floor surfaces has yielded constructive results. The impacts of Continental trends, innovations, fashions, instrumentations, and choreographies as well as the importance of the Continental dancing masters on Scottish dancing cannot be overlooked.

The authors

Mats Melin learned Scottish Country and Highland dancing in Stockholm, Sweden, from the age of 12 through his local RSCDS branch and its affiliated dance group, the Caledonian Dancers. In his teens, Mats travelled to Scotland on numerous occasions to explore solo and social dancing in the West Highlands and the Hebrides, and styles from Orkney and Shetland. Between 1995 and 2004 he was Traditional Dance Development Officer for four Scottish Council areas: Shetland, Sutherland (later part of Highlands Council), Angus, and Perth and Kinross. He researched all he could about Scottish social dances, going to rural dance halls where dancing did not necessarily reflect the formal class structures he encountered in organisation-run classes in Scotland, Sweden, and further afield in Canada and New Zealand.

In 1992, Mats encountered Harvey Beaton, who was teaching Cape Breton Step dancing in the Isle of Skye. This fuelled Mats's interest in the percussive dance memories in Scotland. On occasion, Mats was actively discouraged from researching this area, and was told that it would be futile to search for percussive Step dance in Scotland because it was 'never' part of the tradition. Mats studied for an MA in Ethnochoreology at the University of Limerick in Ireland under Dr Catherine Foley and applied the methods of this discipline to doctoral fieldwork in Cape Breton Step dancing in 2012. As a result, in 2015, his book *One With the Music: Cape Breton Step Dancing Tradition and Transmission* was published. Since then, through Lorg Press, he has published *A Story to Every Dance: The role of lore in enhancing the Scottish solo dance tradition* (2018), and *Hebridean Step Dancing: The legacy of nineteenth-century dancing master Ewen MacLachlan* (2019). Teaching and lecturing at the University of Limerick's Irish World Academy of Music and Dance prompted him to start writing this volume, adding new data to what he had begun collecting in the early1990s.

Jennifer Schoonover has been trained as a Scottish Country dancer and Highland dancer in the United States. She is a member of the RSCDS, Boston Branch, and is a fully certificated teacher under that organisation. She also holds an Associate Membership in Highland dancing with the British Association of

Teachers of Dancing, affiliated with the RSOBHD. While still new to Scottish dance styles, Jen travelled to Cape Breton Island in Canada in the hope of interacting with what she perceived to be a home culture for the Highland dance styles she was learning. Jen quickly learned that the dance style deeply rooted in Scottish Gaelic culture around Cape Breton Island is in fact a Step dance modality rather different from the forms she had been taught were traditional practices. Jen has learned Cape Breton Step dance through attending social dances and from a number of different teachers in Cape Breton. In 2017, she apprenticed with two Boston-based Cape Breton Step dance master artists: Mary MacGillivray and Judy McKenzie. Jen also teaches modern and creative dance, regularly teaching courses in dance pedagogy aligned with Laban Movement Analysis principles at Bridgewater State University in Massachusetts.

Mats and Jen were introduced to one another through Colin Robertson, an independent researcher who is a former proprietor of the Scottish National Dance Company and a retired dancer and teacher. The three of us share an interest in the history of Scottish dancing, as well as in the widespread misrepresentations of historical dance practices of Scotland. Jen has a background as a copyeditor, and helped edit some of Mats's other writings. When Mats shared an early draft of some of the material in this book, Jen had lots of interest and suggestions, and this larger book collaboration grew from that.

We have enlisted the help of a number of other people in preparing the document you're reading now: Dr William Lamb, Senior Lecturer in Celtic and Scottish Studies at the University of Edinburgh; Howard Lasnik, Distinguished Professor of Linguistics at the University of Maryland and Scottish Country dancing tutor *extraordinaire*; Chris Metherell of the Instep Research Team; Heather Sparling, Professor of Ethnomusicology at Cape Breton University; Jason Beals, Simon Pfisterer, and Iain MacDonald of Glenuig, who generated music notation included in this book; dancer and Scottish Gaelic instructor Màiri Britton, who helped clarify some translations and allowed us to include some of her work; and Scottish Gaelic scholar Michael S. Newton, who graciously reviewed and suggested improvements on our chapter including his scholarship. We are also deeply grateful to Yves Guillard, Dr Margaret Bennett, and Allister MacGillivray for kindly granting us permission to include quotations from their works. We wish to thank the National Galleries of Scotland, the Irish Traditional Music Archive, the New Lanark Trust, Edinburgh City Libraries, Live Argyll Libraries, John MacLean, Finn Harper, Jane (Flett) Harrison, and Lindsay (Flett) Smith for allowing us to include their illustrations.

We'd also like to offer some serious gratitude to family and friends who have supported us along the way. Jen's dear spouse Jason Beals offered important support by helping with digital images and music notation in this publication, and supported Jen with unwavering patience and reassurance. Eleanor and Jasper Beals made motivational posters encouraging Mom to make time to write. *Tapadh leibh!* Mats wishes to thank Emma, his wife and soul mate, for always supporting and encouraging his work, and likewise his three children, Solveig, Ingrid, and Magnus, for their support and understanding of the processes of writing and research.

We both wish to dedicate this work to Colin Robertson, who offered tremendous encouragement throughout the process of writing this book, including proofreading, suggesting insightful points to consider, and sharing resources. Without Colin, this partnership might never have happened.

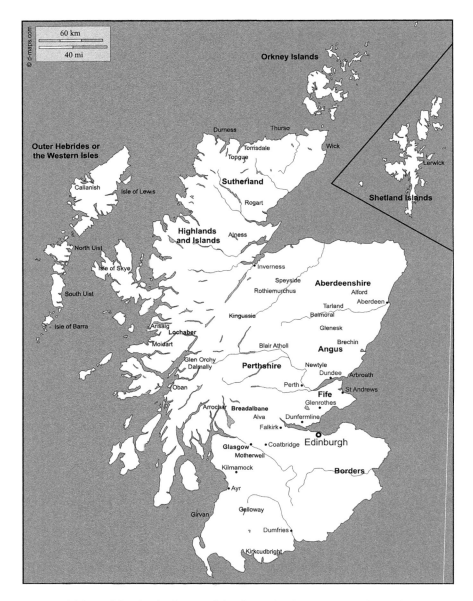

Figure 0.1 Map of Scotland—Some of the Scottish place names and significant areas mentioned in this book

Source: https://d-maps.com/m/europa/uk/ecosse/ecosse59.

Notes

1. https://www.rscds.org/about/history/founders [Accessed 20 February 2020].
2. Bestowed the title 'Royal' in 1951.
3. Bestowed the title 'Royal' in 2019.
4. The much smaller organisation, the Scottish Official Highland Dancing Association (SOHDA), was set up in the 1947 and strove to achieve similar goals to the RSOBHD but with a perspective of including more varied step legacies.
5. RSOBHD 1955: 83–85.
6. Milligan 1985: 11–15.
7. Flett 1985: 14.
8. Porter 1998: 1.
9. Porter 1998: 2.
10. Porter 1998: 10.
11. Porter 1998: 1.
12. Laban 1963: 99.
13. Buckland 2011: 15.
14. Devine 2011: 116–118.
15. Hunter 2010.
16. Emmerson 1995: 14.
17. The *emic/etic* distinction comes from linguist Kenneth Pike who stated that we should 'attempt to discover and to describe the pattern of that particular language or culture in reference to the way in which the various elements of that culture are related to each other in the functioning of the particular pattern' (1954: 8). The *emic/etic* distinction is used by many dance anthropologists and ethnochoreologists as a theoretical basis to distinguish between what is significant to the culture itself, the insider, or *emic*, perspective, and what the outsider, or *etic*, perspective sees as significant to that culture.
18. See Melin 2019a.
19. See Melin 2015.

1 'I wish I had it in my power to describe to you'

Introductory observations on Step dance and its place in Scotland

At the outset, we wish to share two observations that inspired us and provided guiding lights for our research. These glimpses of dancing practices from within Scotland reflect characteristics that stood out as remarkable in the late eighteenth and early nineteenth centuries, but are remarkably absent from modern-day perceptions of Scottish dancing. Shuffling, the making of rhythmic sounds on the ground with the feet, was seen as the main thread running through Scottish dancing by Colonel Thomas Thornton, who visited Glen Orchy in Argyllshire in the late eighteenth century.

> They were dancing a country-dance when we entered. The company consisted of about fourteen couple, who all danced the true *Glen Orgue kick*. I have observed that every district of the Highlands has some peculiar cut; and they all shuffle in such a manner as to make the noise of their feet keep exact time.[1]

In Aberdeen, around that same time, advice that dancing master Francis Peacock wrote down emphasised individuality, personal style, and improvisation: '… you have it in your power to change, divide, add to, or invert, the different steps described, in whatever way you think best adapted to the tune, or most pleasing to yourself.'[2] Historical records show that dancers in Scotland made sound and made up steps. Descriptions from earlier times depict an interactive, inventive dance form incorporating audible rhythms. Literary references reveal a history of percussive dancing in Scotland that has been disregarded over the past hundred years.

The clattering, extemporaneous forms recounted by witnesses and practitioners from times past bear little resemblance to today's lists of officially sanctioned soft-shoe step sequences. If you take a Highland or Scottish Country dance class today, common cues are 'be light on your feet' or 'no scraping the floor.' Improvisation is out of the question on competitive platforms in Scotland because RSOBHD and SOHDA dancers performing steps not described in the textbook disqualify themselves from events. Only in the theatrical Sailor's Hornpipe and Irish Jig can elements of intentionally percussive footwork be seen on these platforms today. Clearly, Scottish dancing traditions have evolved significantly since the early 1800s.

Treepling

Thomas M. (Tom) and Joan F. Flett, who researched Scottish dancing in the 1950s, pointed out that percussive dance customs were still recalled at that time. They stated, in their 1964 seminal publication *Traditional Dancing in Scotland* that

> the art of 'treepling' in social dances—the art of beating out the rhythm of the music with the feet—is one of the lesser-known features of Scottish dancing that has now almost entirely disappeared. So far as we know, treepling steps were performed by men only, and were usually confined to Country Dances, though they were also occasionally used in Reels.[3]

This treepling movement motif, depicted in Figure 1.1, also made its way into a number of Scottish solo Step dances: the Earl of Erroll and the Flowers of Edinburgh recorded in Aberdeenshire; the First of August danced in the Hebrides; and the Flowers of Edinburgh and Over the Hills and Far Away preserved by the Gillis family in Cape Breton Island, Canada; the motif even persists in the competitive Sailor's Hornpipe.

In dance studies, the term 'motif' refers to a sequence of movements forming a unit similar to the way a sequence of letters creates a recognisable word. A motif can repeat within dances and span dances within a style. The treepling

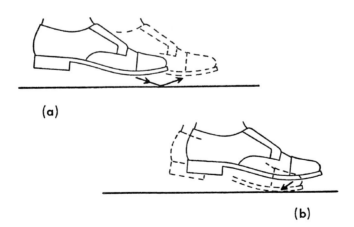

Figure 1.1 An illustration showing the catch out (a) and the catch in (b) in the treepling motif, from Flett, *Traditional Dancing in Scotland*, 1985: 262

Source: Image used with kind permission by Jane (Flett) Harrison and Lindsay (Flett) Smith.

14   *'I wish I had it in my power'*

motif consists of a step on one foot, a catch out and a catch in with the other foot, and a step to transfer weight. The word 'catch' refers to a swipe on the floor away from ('catch out') or towards ('catch in') the body. The treeple, or triple, takes its name from the three movements occurring between the pulse of stronger downbeats made by the supporting foot: the two catches out and in, together forming a motif some dancers call a shuffle; followed by a third movement, a light, brief step onto that foot. Dancers would 'treeple it' through social figures such as petronella and poussette 'with the men's tacketty boots rattling away.'[4] The Fletts' research highlights that treepling had been a very popular dance step before the time of their interviews.

What do we mean by 'dance?'

We start by looking critically at some crucial terms at the heart of our study. Dance can be defined essentially as any expressive movement. It is important to remember that European labels for and conceptions of 'dance' are not universal. The term 'dance' often comprises 'music, dance, games, instruments, festivals, and so on within one word [and this] is not all that uncommon.'[5] Dance may form part of different kinds of rituals though it need not be a ritual in itself. According to Chambers dictionary the word 'dance' has its etymological origin in Europe in the Old High German (*c.* 500–1050 AD) word *dansón*, meaning 'to stretch' or 'to drag,' and has evolved through the Old French (*c.* fourteenth century) *danser, dancer,* and the Middle English (late twelfth to late fifteenth century) *dauncen, daunsen.*[6]

The term 'dance'[7] entered Scottish Gàidhlig as the verb *dannsadh* or the nouns *dannsa, damhsa,* and *danns* and in Irish Gaeilge as *damhsa.*[8] In Scottish and Irish Gaelic, there are other words referring to dancing: in Scottish Gàidhlig, *ruidhle* (to reel, an imported Germanic word) is used to indicate a pathway of travelling; in Irish Gaeilge, *rince* (ring, also of Germanic origin) is used interchangeably with *damhsa.*[9] It is not unusual that a society may have several words for dance to reflect different contexts, as, for example, in Spanish, where *danza* is a ritual activity while *baile* refers to secular dance.[10]

When studying dances of various cultural heritages, ethnochoreologists strive to view material with a neutral, impartial perspective, and define the varied technical forms of dance found around the world as humanly organised movement systems. In the dance legacies of Scotland, an element that gets emphasised in the organisation of movement is the synchronising of motifs to align with musical rhythms. Dancers employ rhythmic step patterns in social and performance situations. Dancing was so highly and widely valued in Scotland in the nineteenth century that an honorific title emerged for male dancing masters: 'Dancie.'

In Scottish Gàidhlig, the phrase *gabh danns* (give a step, literally 'take a dance') is used to encourage the act of dancing, as well as *danns* for 'dance' and *a' dannsa* or *a' dannsadh* for 'dancing.' 'Steps' are *ceumanan.*[11] Cape Breton Scottish Gàidhlig teacher and singer Goiridh Dòmhnallach shared that the term for Step dance prior to the 1970s was simply '*danns*' because there was no need to distinguish it from anything else.[12] When Cape Breton Step dancing classes were advertised at *Sabhal Mòr Ostaig* in the Isle of Skye, Scotland, in the early 1990s, the label given was *dannsa-ceum,* highlighting the Gàidhlig words for both 'dance' and 'step.' On 9 March 2015, *BBC Alba* broadcast a programme exploring Cape Breton and Scottish Step dancing called *Faram nam Bròg,* translated as 'In Their Steps' (literally, percussion of the shoes), a description included in the song *Sabhal Iain 'ic Ùisdein.* Another term in Gàidhlig refers to kicking dancing, or *dannsa breabaidh,* which may be connected to the Glen Orchy [Orgue] kick Thornton mentioned. The word 'kick' may suggest kicking the ground with the heel or toe of the foot.

Differing usage and meanings of the term 'step'

The term 'step' is of interest in itself as it has several different meanings. All of these meanings intertwine and are used regularly by dancers and teachers to refer to different aspects of Step dancing. It is used to label the form, as Step dancing; as a verb to perform steps; to refer to the rhythmic length of an instance of dancing; and to refer to varied motifs and units, as in the phrase 'the step is repeated on each foot' or as in 'this dance consists of six steps' or that you have 12 steps to choose from. It can also indicate a specific transference of weight.

In mechanical terms, a 'step' on to one foot indicates that a transfer of weight occurs from one foot to the other without a moment of elevation; the body maintains contact with the floor while the weight is being transferred from foot to foot. This can be contrasted with terms signifying aerial transference of weight: the term 'hop' refers to a moment of elevation from one foot, suspension of the body in the air with no point of contact to the ground, followed by a landing on that same foot; a 'spring' is also a movement of elevation, but takes off from one foot and lands on the other. A 'step' can be taken onto a specific part of the foot: contact with the ground can occur on the ball; heel; half point, where the pads of the toes support the weight; or the whole foot. The term 'step' in this mechanical sense does not necessarily indicate a level of noise made by the foot; it can be light and gentle, strong and forceful, or any gradient in between depending on the effort applied.

Another definition of the word 'step' concerns a choreographic and structural unit, a movement motif pattern or *enchainment.* This meaning of the word 'step' refers to a combination of movements fitting into a specific design as a unit to delineate movement ideas in the context of a longer dance. In composed solo dances, a 'step' is commonly eight bars long, illustrated in musical notation in Figure 1.2, in reel (4/4) and jig (6/8) time, and four bars in strathspey (4/4) time. A step commonly has the same length as the part of the music it coordinates with, and is seen as a choreographic component, or module. Each step is comprised of smaller motifs that are combined into longer phrases. Reel- and jig-time 'steps' often exhibit a segmentation giving a characteristic motif for the

16   'I wish I had it in my power'

The White Cockade
An Chocàrd

March   Trad

Figure 1.2 The eight-bar A part of The tune The White Cockade/*An Chocàrd*, a tune used for the dance The First of August in South Uist, illustrating the step length. The step would be repeated on the other foot to A repeat of this A part. Step repeat structures in this dance can be seen in relation to eight bars of music. There are characteristic motifs on bars 1 and 2 and bars 5 and 6 in each step in this dance, and then are motifs that occur, repeating, in *every* 'step' on bars 3 and 4, and bars 7 and 8. While categorised here as a march, the White Cockade alternately can be labelled as a Scotch measure, polka, quickstep, or reel. Fluidity of dance and tune labels is a subject explored in greater depth by Egil Bakka.[13] This version of the tune was sung to Mats in *canntaireachd*/chanting by renowned piper Rona Lightfoot as being the local South Uist version of the tune and has been notated by Iain MacDonald of Glenuig

first two bars, another motif for the third and fourth bars, a repeat of the first motif on bars five and six, and then a closing motif, sometimes called a close or a break, on bars seven and eight. There are exceptions to this design, but this structure is common. This structure also occurs in strathspey-time steps with each segment being just one bar in length. The 'step,' having been danced once, often is repeated, symmetrically, on the other side to a repeat of the same part of the accompanying tune. A series of 'steps' following this pattern are then combined in various ways to form a named 'dance.' This segmentation and variants thereof are further discussed in Chapter 12. This second meaning of the word 'step' describes the organisational structure of dances and is applied to dances done in both soft and hard shoes.

In improvised, orally transmitted Step dancing, this usage morphs to refer to motifs of varying lengths. In the current Cape Breton style, a 'step' can refer to a shorter motif repeated on alternating sides or on the same side a number of times, not always danced in a symmetrical fashion. Motifs exist that occur for three-quarters of a bar or one-and-a-half bars, creating a driving syncopation in repetition. Some 'steps' are longer choreographic units, and span two, three, four, or even eight bars in length before being repeated. Individual dancers may improvise or choose not to repeat the same sequence exactly on each side. What a 'step,' its length, and any symmetrical repeat means becomes a more fluid concept within improvisational modalities; yet, the word 'step' is commonly used when describing and sharing motifs in vernacular styles.

The term 'Step dance' has yet another meaning. It also can signify that dancers make sounds with their feet through 'stepping' or 'tapping' (as in Tap dance). In fact, Kenneth Burchill in his 1938 book *Step Dancing* defines the term Step dancing as 'the expression of rhythm by means of feet.'[14] Within Scotland, the term 'Step dance' can mean different things depending on context and cultural location. Sometimes the word reflects a combination of these two meanings. Titled dances, such as the Hebridean First of August and the Cape Breton *Dannsa nam Flurs*/Flooers [Flowers] o' Edinburgh, are both percussive in nature and contain sequences of choreographic 'step' units. 'Step dance' as a label is worthy of careful attention, as it does not have one discrete definition.

The term 'Step dancing' in some areas, like the Angus District, used to refer to *all* solo dances that involved learning a string of 'steps,' *e.g.*, Highland Fling, Sword Dance, Hornpipes, or Jigs. 'Are ye going tae the step dancing?' in Angus and Dundee, then, meant, 'are you going to the dance class?' Newspaper adverts in Northeast newspapers between the 1880s and 1930s also report performances of Step dances, where, when named, refer equally to Highland Flings, Sword Dances, and Hornpipes. The earliest Scottish newspaper account of Step dancing we have found announced George Roberts 'step dancing' at a Dundee Music Hall event in the *Dundee Courier* on 2 March 1886.

What signifies 'percussive dance'?

The word 'percussion' has evolved from Latin, a noun defined as 'a beat, strike' in a musical sense. In dance, 'percussive' generally indicates an emphasis on sounds created by a dancer's feet striking, brushing, or tapping different ground surfaces, creating a particular soundscape. 'Percussive' does not always infer that hard-soled shoes need to be worn, nor does it require that one must dance on a wooden surface, to create a particular sound. Percussive sounds can be produced by a dancer in bare feet or soft shoes on different surfaces to good effect. Ethnochoreologist and Irish dance researcher Catherine Foley draws the percussive dance family tree this way:

> [...] the percussive dance family is broad and manifests itself in a multiplicity of forms including: dance forms that concentrate on audible footwork patterns; hand clapping dances; or those that use any of the body, or indeed, the whole body to create different, audible, rhythmic percussive patterns.[15]

It is important to keep in mind that the whole body of a dancer can create sound in dancing, instead of concentrating on footwork only. Hand clapping, featured in children's games and accompanying songs finishing the process of waulking the cloth in the Highlands, provides an example of body percussion not relying on footwork. Clapping has endured in a number of Highland

18   *'I wish I had it in my power'*

and Scottish Country dances. Snapping fingers is another way sounds can be made by parts of the body other than feet.

Snapping and clapping

A percussive practice once noted widely in Scotland was snapping of the fingers. Even Bonnie Prince Charlie, to divert his melancholy after the battle of Culloden, danced a Highland Reel to the accompaniment of mouth music, and 'skipped so nimbly, knacking his thumbs and clapping his hands.'[16] Snapping features frequently in writings of the early 1800s as a regular and appropriate contribution to social dancing in Scotland, as portrayed in this passage from the 1815 novel *Clan-Albin* where an older woman watches a dance, 'snapping her fingers in time with the lively strathspey.'[17]

Englishman Thomas Wilson, dancing master for the King's Theatre Opera House in London, was vigorously opposed to the practice. In that very same year, 1815, he complained that 'Snapping the fingers, in Country Dancing and Reels, and the sudden howl or yell too frequently practised, ought particularly to be avoided, as partaking too much of the customs of barbarous nations.' In a footnote, Wilson conceded that these customs were 'Introduced in some Scotch parties as partly national with them.'[18] Wilson's footnote indicates that at least one Scot had defended this practice, asserting that yelping enthusiastically, or heuching, as this practice is termed in Scots, was customary back home.

Snapping of the fingers was so identified with Scottish dance practices that it became a signifier of the Highlander stereotype. Londoner Sarah Green typified, somewhat ungenerously, a dancer from the Highlands taking 'such pains with his steps' and working 'so hard with his legs, feet, and arms, not to mention the continual snapping of his fingers, that it is fatiguing to see him' in her satirical 1824 book *Scotch Novel Reading, or Modern Quackery*, that poked fun at the craze for novels set in Scotland.[19]

Heuching, percussive beating, and snapping are ways dancers engage in a real-time feedback loop with musicians and other dancers. The practice of snapping and clapping in time with music, observed in the mid-eighteenth century in Scotland, predates the era of the Quadrille in England and Scotland. The Quadrille emerged in France in the late eighteenth century and had its heyday in England in the early nineteenth century. In the era of the Quadrille, with large numbers of dancers on the floor accompanied by a relatively small number of musicians, it became important for dancers not to make extra noises so that the music could be heard, and danced to, by all. Wilson's request to refrain from snapping on dance floors coincides with and is likely an extension of the burgeoning of the Quadrille's popularity in the United Kingdom and Ireland.

Today, snapping has been completely silenced in twentieth-century Highland dance practices, having evolved into an abstract hand position. Whenever a Highland dancer's hands are not placed in fists at the waist, they are poised to be ready to snap, with the thumb touching the first knuckle joint of the middle finger. Since standardisation of Highland styles, dancers' fingers continually hold this shape, never releasing the tension that would result in audible snaps were the fingers to follow through. The only sounds that competitive dancers' hands are permitted to make anymore are the resounding claps signifying changes to quick time in the Sword Dance and the *Seann Triubhas*. A few remnants of keeping time survive in some Scottish Country Dances, such as Princess Royal and Prince of Orange. All sounds made by dancers seem to have been actively silenced by dance masters under the influence of London aesthetics, treepling and shuffling included. The Lowe brothers, prominent dancing masters and fashion setters, with an influence on Queen Victoria and the Royal family both in Scotland and England, discouraged 'rattling and shuffling' in the mid-nineteenth century.[20] Dancing venues came to be seen as places for practicing manners and interacting with higher classes, and percussive elements in the dancing became actively disapproved of in ballrooms.

In the non-standardised Reeling social dance style, however, snapping and clapping endure and occur frequently. An example of this happens in the set and turn corner figure; dancers set with two *pas de Basque* steps, then usually clap hands before turning each other. Some dancers snap fingers whilst dancing, or, in the Eightsome Reel, stand still and clap hands in the centre while the seven other dancers circle round and back around the soloist.

Though we have shown the popularity of snapping and clapping in Scotland, hand and body percussion are not unique to this region only, and occur in multitudes of dances across Europe. The Norwegian solo dance *Halling,* Balkan dances, Hungarian solo dances, the German *Schuhplattler*, and Flamenco dancing in Spain are just some examples. In many places, this type of expression forms an integral part of the movement's iteration. The following lines from Catherine Foley also help define the term percussive:

> Percussive dancers use acoustic space and, through the use of the body and sounds created by the body, they embody the music rhythmically, dynamically and percussively [...] percussive dancers are more than percussionists; they are dancers who explore and interpret an acoustic world through their world of sound and gesture. In so doing, sound and gesture become one within the dancer's body, and although percussive dancers perform to and are inspired by music they also make their own music.[21]

The notion of what constitutes a percussive dancer should not be limited by a conception of sound alone. A percussive dancer is seen as well as heard. A percussive dancer is 'not only aware of the dynamics of sound that they create with their bodies but they are also aware of the importance of the world of gesture with its visual dimension.'[22]

Must footwork be audible to be perceived as being percussive? In this book, we share accounts of Scottish dancing making sounds in various types

20 *'I wish I had it in my power'*

of footwear and with hands and voices. However, dance portrays rhythm visually and kinaesthetically as well as aurally. Given this idea, can:

> a dancer present a visual kinetic rhythmic pattern that is not audible but that maps, traces, or alludes to a rhythmic sound through the kinetic realm and still be considered percussive? Or must a percussive dancer wear shoes and produce culturally-specific body movements that take up the acoustic space, rhythmically and sonically, as in language? […] The notion of a 'percussive dancer' is a western concept and one that is not shared by all cultures. And although we in the West may allude to cultures as having percussive dances, the cultures themselves may not perceive, or indeed, categorize these dances in the same way. Equally, we may categorize a dancer as a percussive dancer, but how does the dancer categorize him/herself?[23]

It would be interesting to know if the dancers described by Thornton would have categorised their own dancing as primarily percussive, or if that effect was more notable from an outsider's perspective. Mats has explored similar ideas regarding transmission and embodiment within the Cape Breton Step dance tradition.[24] Any percussive dancing mode, however, involves reflecting rhythmic structures and musical phrases to enhance the music through dynamic motif choices and sometimes, syncopations, making the sounds part of the music. Both the music and the environment of the moment help a dancer decide what notes to emphasise sonically and visually. Even without musical accompaniment, one can perform to an internalised and embodied music.

Placing Step dancing in Scotland within a wider European dance context

Any occurrence of percussive Step dance in Scotland should not be seen in isolation, but should be considered in context within a wider view of British, Irish, and pan-European forms of vernacular dance featuring percussive sounds made by dancers' feet. The pervasive influence of European dancing masters must be understood as having a crucial role in the dissemination and development of this type of footwork across Europe, including Scotland.

A hundred years ago, 'Step Dance' was, in the words of Cecil Sharp in 1911, 'the most popular folk dance at the present time, […] a standing proof of the capacity of the village dancer to create and execute extremely complex and intricate movements.'[25] Because Step dance was so popular and widespread, Sharp deliberately avoided documenting it. Film footage of competitive Clog dancing from the late 1800s taken in London survives, and provides a glimpse of this quick, precise, and playful form.[26] That the winner of that self-proclaimed 'World Championship' hailed from Glasgow is of particular relevance to our study. The standard of percussive dancing in Scotland in the late 1800s was high.

Tom and Joan Flett, mentioned earlier as Scottish dance researchers, also researched Step dance in England and noted many affinities there to practices in Scotland, particularly in dance masters' repertoires. The Fletts studied Step dance traditions in Lakeland[27] in particular; others have investigated Step dancing from other regions and legacies.[28] Step and Clog dancing endure across England and Wales to this day as a specialised dance culture. Though today regional labels are often applied to styles of Clogging or Step dancing, these styles stem from families, teachers, and individuals. While there were regional specialities, Step dancing crossed borders.

From a global perspective today, Step dancing tends to be associated with Ireland. This happens particularly where percussive dancing is not a local custom. In Ireland, on the other hand, there is widespread awareness that Step dancing stems from a traditional, as opposed to a nationalistic, dance practice. In the twenty-first century, percussive footwork is given many regional stylistic labels, such as *Sean nós*, North Kerry, and Clare Battering. Some other styles are referred to as 'traditional' or 'old traditional.' Variants are associated with particular dance teachers or vernacular performers, current and past. Attributing stylistic traits to teachers or dancers persists in usage; regional labelling has appeared more recently.[29]

The disappearance of percussive dance practices in Scotland in the twentieth century has led to misunderstandings regarding the origin of Cape Breton Step dancing in Canada. Although dance scholar Frank Rhodes found only limited memories of hard-shoe styles in use in Scotland in the 1950s, he recorded percussive versions of iconic Highland dances surviving in Cape Breton, including the Fling, *Seann Triubhas*, and the Flowers of Edinburgh, during his 1957 visit there.[30] Oral history recounts that these percussive dances surviving in Cape Breton came from Scotland along with emigrants from Morar. The structures of these percussive versions made it clear to Rhodes that they were connected to the Games' versions; furthermore, they shared movement motifs with dances extant in Scotland, although performed with different guiding aesthetic principles by the 1950s. Recent books on Gaelic piping by John G. Gibson suggest that Step dancing in Cape Breton also stems from an established vernacular tradition of percussive dance in Scotland.[31]

Percussive Step dance styles across the United Kingdom and Ireland share many common movement and motif combinations. The most striking differences are seen in how the steps are performed in relation to the different tunes preferred in different areas. Some unique movements may predominate in certain areas, but the processes of stepping are often similar. Differences between motifs can be slight: for example, how a 'shuffle' is executed—what part of the foot strikes the ground, when in relation to the music this occurs, and whether it is an isolated ankle action or one involving the whole leg. Percussive dance in the British Isles and Ireland can be understood as one family of dancing, though that family has many local dialects forming its expression.

22 *'I wish I had it in my power'*

Labelling dancing

Every single individual who dances embodies unique aspects. We must consider how we typify and categorise Scottish dancing as well as how we place dancing in the Scottish context.

Classification of dance styles, percussive or otherwise, often involves assigning geographical signifiers or labels, such as Hebridean, Highland, Lancashire, North Kerry, Connemara, Cape Breton, or Ottawa Valley, to name but a few, to set them apart and to distinguish them from each other. This type of labelling leaves out the individuals who actually embody the material unless a sub-qualifier such as a dancer individual 'x' or family 'y' gets added. Though geographical identifiers help draw distinctions between dancing styles, they are more accurate when used in combination with specific attributions about whom the sources, the actual people who dance or danced that way, are or were.

The regional identification of local styles is a relatively new phenomenon and has emerged to categorise music in the 1970s and dance in the 1980s.[32] When Cape Breton Step dancer Harvey Beaton was asked in 2007 if he could recall when he first became aware of the term 'Cape Breton Step dancing' being used, he found it difficult to pinpoint a specific time, but said that it was possibly with the increase in formal teaching and workshop demand abroad. He mentioned that when he was growing up, it was simply called 'dancing.'

The label 'Hebridean Dancing,' however, seems to have appeared much earlier, around 1926. It first appeared in the *Oban Times* on 14 August 1926. This regional identification may have been introduced by D.G. MacLennan, who adjudicated the South Uist Highland Games in 1925 and saw dances performed there that he had never seen before.[33] Dancer Fearchar MacNeil, who learned these dances as a child in the Isle of Barra in the Western Isles, first encountered the label 'Hebridean Dance' in 1935 and had never heard the dances referred to in this way before then.

The term 'Highland' creates an assignation of this dancing style to a particular geographical area of Scotland, even though some dances labelled as Highland dances may not have originated in the Highlands at all. Just as the 'Irish Jig' competed at Highland Games has its roots in a theatrical stereotype, some of the dances defining Highland dancing today may have originated in staged depictions of Highlanders. Written documentation of the Highland Fling as a performance dance appears in London and Edinburgh before the dance is documented in the Highlands.[34] The popularity of the play *Rob Roy* in the 1820s in Edinburgh,[35] with a Highland Fling in Act 3, probably bolstered the popularity of the dance and informed how dancing masters taught it. Furthermore, the Highland Fling was taught by dancing masters throughout the British Isles, not just ones in Scotland.

The term 'vernacular,' generally used in relating to a language or dialect, can also refer to a dance style shared by the common people living together in a country or geographical region. Though this distinction denoting popular usage among a distinct community is useful information, the term 'vernacular' glosses over the individual performers embodying the dancing, situating them as an anonymous generality. 'Legacy' may be a more useful and accurate term. 'Legacies' of individual dancers' expressions can be observed so that we can recognize each dancer's influence.

Tradition or legacies?

When we refer to legacies, we wish to honour the individual dancers who embodied the instances of percussive Step dancing collected in this book. This respect for individuals' approaches to dancing is of central importance in how we view the material. We examine all accounts of Step dancing legacies we have been able to locate, as well as critique the lenses through which these instances of dancing were seen and reflected.

Dancing legacies evolve through various processes of transmission and interpretation, and changes can be made by students of the individuals, by observers, and by the performers themselves over time. We prefer the concept of legacy to tradition. To us, legacies allow for a wider spectrum of aural, visual, and kinaesthetic forms and perceptions of what constitutes percussive dance informed by individuals' preferences and abilities. This sense of legacies accommodates connected vernacular dancing practices happening in relation to each other while reflecting individual expressions, as opposed to there being one standardised dance form and one idealised technique.

In contrast to our viewpoint, many, if not most, textbooks on Scottish dance present material as a singular 'tradition.' In some cases, there is an underlying assertion that this tradition is static, as in 'this is how we have always done it,' implying authority. William Cameron's pre-RSOBHD textbook implies rules without stating what they are when he writes that 'new variations and steps are continually being invented and are accepted as correct as long as they are authentic and are in their own original traditional category.'[36] This implies that there are parameters defining a universal 'authentic' correctly Scottish way, and an 'original traditional category.' One may question how these terms are defined; however, this ambiguity helps shape a mindscape that these states, even if not explained, exist, and that a dancer must rely on someone else's authority in determining correctness. British dance anthropologist Theresa Jill Buckland, who has outlined complexities, problems, and ambiguities relating to authenticity and cultural memory of long-lived dances, points out that any given set of performers within a tradition makes choices that define their 'authentic tradition.'[37] As a case in point, Cameron's philosophy does not respect local variations and individual expression. Shortly after Cameron's writing, Highland steps became standardised, dancers were prohibited from inventing steps for competitive platforms, and the Highland dance 'tradition' became even more controlled.

24 *'I wish I had it in my power'*

This development reflects Eric Hobsbawm's later typifying of the ways national identities are bolstered when 'existing customary traditional practices' get 'modified, ritualized and institutionalized for the new nationalistic purposes.'[38] However, institutionalised traditions evolve, too; in 2018, the RSOBHD added reintroduced 'steps and movements from the past' to the latest edition of the textbook 'to challenge our current generation, and those going forward, yet still preserve our history, culture, and traditions from past generations.'[39] Historical step motifs were returned or added to the textbook to expand the list of steps sanctioned for competitions.

Even when an author makes an attempt to show a variety of legacies, researchers must be on guard for any undisclosed biases or preferences informing the material. D.G. MacLennan's 1950 book about Highland dancing, on the one hand, acknowledges and gives descriptions of examples of 'older ways' of dancing. On the other hand, MacLennan neglects to divulge that the versions of the 'Hebridean' dances he gives are his own arrangements, and that he embellished and changed the dances he said he saw dancers performing in South Uist in the mid-1920s.[40] Acknowledging an awareness of various legacies does not ensure integrity of research.

The singular word 'tradition' implies one cohesive body of knowledge. Vernacular dance in Scotland should be seen as a multitude of parallel 'legacies,' and also, and perhaps most importantly, these legacies should not be seen as static in any way but rather constantly evolving along with the human bodies that perform them. Legacies relate to processes informed by individual expressions and preferences relative to customary dance practices, whereas a tradition focuses on an envisioned, external ideal of dancing.

Discussions about the definition of tradition as a concept are numerous.[41] Some definitions that work well for Scottish dance include one by American folklorist Henry Glassie: 'tradition is the means for deriving the future from the past and then define tradition, once again, as volitional, temporal action [...] History, culture, and the human actor meet in tradition.'[42] Glassie's definition envisions a tradition as an ongoing process, not static. But, as another American folklorist, the late Bert Feintuch argued, 'tradition is a social and academic construct standing for and resulting from an on-going process of interpreting and reinterpreting the past.'[43] Musician and ethnomusicologist Mike Anklewicz[44] states that he is more comfortable using the word 'historical' rather than 'traditional' 'to avoid the academic and ideological burden the term 'tradition' has come to bear,'[45] when referring to music or dance styles of the past. Using the word 'historical' allows us to discuss a plurality of styles of the past without 'subscribing to a hegemonic concept of a singular "tradition."'[46] A good way of looking at 'tradition' when reading this book is, as Spalding and Woodside put it, always being 'work-in-progress.'[47]

The word 'tradition' is used very sparingly in the definition of intangible cultural heritage prepared by the United Nations Educational, Scientific, and

Cultural Organization (UNESCO). Part of the definition of UNESCO's convention for the safeguarding of *Intangible Cultural Heritage* reads:

> The 'intangible cultural heritage' means the practices, representations, expressions, knowledge, skills – as well as the instruments, objects, artefacts and cultural spaces associated therewith – that communities, groups and, in some cases, individuals recognize as part of their cultural heritage. This intangible cultural heritage, transmitted from generation to generation, is constantly recreated by communities and groups in response to their environment, their interaction with nature and their history, and provides them with a sense of identity and continuity, thus promoting respect for cultural diversity and human creativity.[48]

The UNESCO definition highlights human creativity, transmission from generation to generation, and communities and individuals responding to the environment and changes around them. This definition incorporates fluidity and change in its core.

The references to percussive Step dancing in Scotland and the Scottish diaspora that we have found generally exhibit a sense of diversity and creativity on the part of the dancers adapting to changing environments, fashions, and contexts around them at a given time. Within these passages, we also track shifts in Scottish dance aesthetics away from individuality in expression, variation, and improvisation and towards standardisation and homogeneity of technique. Within Scotland, dancing masters, and, later, organisations governing dance genres, emerged that successfully promoted 'refined,' ballet-inspired aesthetics. In the process, they created revised and 'improved' versions of 'traditional,' or, perhaps more accurately, vernacular dancing. A nuanced understanding of terms such as 'traditional' and 'vernacular' helps us to read the historical references we list in this book with greater sensitivity.

Notes

1. Thornton 1804: 238.
2. Peacock 1805: 98.
3. Flett 1985: 260.
4. Flett 1985: 260.
5. Royce 2002: 9.
6. s.v. 'dance' Chambers Dictionary, 1993.
7. The term 'dance' in French is *danse*; in Danish, Dutch, Norwegian, and Swedish *dans*; Spanish and Italian *danza*; and in German *tanz*.
8. Newton 2019.
9. The following words are all referring to dance or dancing in some way: *Ridhil*, see also *rìghil, rìghle, rìghleachan* equals the word Reel; *rìghil* means to dance a reel. *Rinc*, or ring means to dance, or hop; and *ringeach* (*ringtheach*, *-eiche*) is dancing; as is *ringeadh*. The word *ringeal* is a circle or sphere, and finally *ringear* means dancer. All entries were found in Dwelly's *Illustrated Gaelic to English Dictionary*, (1901) 1988.
10. Royce 2002: 10.

11. Scholar Heather Sparling mentioned to us in personal communication that usage of these phrases likely originates within the twentieth century.
12. Dòmhnallach 2010.
13. Bakka 2001.
14. Burchill 1938: xi.
15. Foley 2008: 47.
16. Forbes 1895: 109.
17. Johnstone 2003 [1815]: 56.
18. Wilson 1815: 267.
19. Green 1824: 2; 139–140.
20. Lowe 1831: 1–10.
21. Foley 2008: 55.
22. Foley 2008: 54–55.
23. Foley 2008: 48.
24. Melin 2015: 246–252.
25. Sharp 1911: 10.
26. This footage from the Huntley Archives depicting a specially filmed presentation of a Step dancing competition in London, England, is available for viewing here: https://www.youtube.com/watch?v=p-dtk7WwqBE [Accessed 8 December 2018].
27. Flett 1979.
28. Suggested websites with information on English Step and Clog dancing: www.instep.co.uk has a wide range of information including the Flett manuscript collection; independent researcher Chris Brady offers various articles on: http://chrisbrady.itgo.com/dance/stepdance/trad_step_dancing.htm. [All accessed December 2016].
29. See Foley 2001, 2007, 2012, and 2013; and Ni Bhriain 2006, 2008, and 2010.
30. Flett 1996: 199–203.
31. Gibson 1998, 2005, and 2017.
32. Quigley 2008.
33. Melin 2019a: 34.
34. Melin 2018: 14–15.
35. https://www.gla.ac.uk/myglasgow/library/files/special/collections/STA/articles/national_drama/index.html [Accessed 2 May 2020].
36. Cameron 1951: 3.
37. Buckland 2011: 1–16.
38. Hobsbawm, Eric. (1984). Introduction: Inventing Traditions. In Eric Hobsbawm and Terence Ranger (Eds.), *The Invention of Tradition*. Cambridge: Cambridge University Press.
39. Royal Scottish Official Board of Highland Dancing 2018: v.
40. Melin 2019a.
41. Anklewicz 2012: 89.
42. Glassie 2003: 192–3.
43. Feintuch 1993: 192.
44. Anklewicz 2012.
45. Anklewicz 2012: 97.
46. Anklewicz 2012: 86.
47. Spalding and Woodside 1995: 249.
48. UNESCO's Convention for safeguarding of the Intangible Cultural Heritage: https://ich.unesco.org/en/convention and https://ich.unesco.org/en/performing-arts-00054 [Accessed 19 July 2017].

2 From regional variations to standardisation of vernacular dance

The impacts on dancing by dancing masters and the emergence of dance organisations

In 1964, the Fletts noticed a widespread misperception, that the Scottish 'National Dances,' meaning Reels and Country dances, 'were regarded as being on a different plane from ordinary ballroom dances' such as the Polka, Mazourka, Waltz, La Varsovienne, or Schottische.[1] That mindset has become more entrenched in the twenty-first century, as social dancing in the RSCDS style and competitive Highland dancing within the RSOBHD and SOHDA frameworks, because they adhere more rigidly to specific aesthetics, are seen as being superior to forms like Old-Time Social dancing, Ceilidh dancing, Reeling, or the more recently, introduced percussive Step dancing. The Fletts, however, pointed out that in the early 1950s,

> as far back as living memory extends, Reels and Country Dances were regarded as being on exactly the same footing as Square and Circle Dances. Moreover, in common with all the other social dances which were in current use, Reels and Country Dances were taught by professional dancing-teachers in the normal course of their classes. [...] It is essential to realise also just how thoroughly the teachings of professional dancing-teachers permeated the structure of social dancing in Scotland, for before 1914 most young people in Scotland attended dancing classes at some time or other.[2]

Dancing masters adapted material they taught as fashions changed, and before their era ended, some incorporated modern ballroom dances such as the Quickstep, Slow Foxtrot, and Tango.[3] They also taught varied forms of dances with the same titles. Dancing masters Huat and Taylor taught distinctive versions of the Marquis of Huntly's Highland Fling in the mid–1800s,[4] and several variants of popular Country dances such as Duke of Perth, Jacky Tar, and Quadrille Country Dance were taught by different dancing masters in different locations.[5] The influence of dancing masters plus a strong sense of community kept various parallel dance practices on equal footings. Different

28 *Standardisation of vernacular dance*

types of dances were regarded as equally valid. Solo dancing was also an integral part of the local gesturescape.[6]

In rural and island communities where the Reel was the main, or, in some places, the only social dance, improvisational footwork and a percussive soundscape encouraged a degree of variation and innovation and enriched social interaction.

> It might be thought that only the use of a considerable variety of setting steps would give interest to an evening of Reels, but this was not so. In the warm intimate atmosphere of a crowded croft kitchen, with the noise of the dancing bouncing back off the walls and the low ceiling—the loud 'heuchs', the crack of finger and thumb, the thud of the dancers' feet, and, above all, the inspiriting music of the fiddle—it did not really matter how many or how few steps one knew, for the joy in dancing a Reel under these conditions was not the pleasure obtained from intricate stepping, but the sheer joy of vigorous rhythmic movement to exciting music.[7]

The Fletts indicate that many dancing masters did not obsess over precise placement of feet in steps but tended to prioritise spatial relationships within social dances so that each pupil would be at the right place at the right time.[8] Emphasis on footwork likely varied according to students' capabilities and teachers' objectives. While technical discipline may not have been emphasised every moment, dancing masters had large repertoires of solo dances, choreographed new dances, and modified existing dances to suit their tastes, or to suit pupils' capabilities. The trademark of a good dancing master was an ability to encourage and enliven students to perform in a musically neat and tidy manner. Scottish dance historian George Emmerson also pointed to the 'enjoyment of technique' as motivation for learners.[9] Fieldwork by Mats Melin in the late 1990s elicited memories of dancing masters, such as Dancie Reid of Newtyle in Angus, down on hands and knees placing pupils' feet in correct positions. Reid, among others, was also remembered for rapping a pupil over the ear with a fiddle bow if the pupil did not perform a step satisfactorily. Many dancing masters had large classes, sometimes of a hundred pupils or more, so perfecting steps may not always have been at the top of the agenda. Recollections and archival film footage (see Chapter 9, 1915) both indicate that the earlier technique exhibited looser flow than the Scottish dance forms currently promoted. Many dancing masters adjusted what material they taught, including Angus dance master Dancie John Reid, after he joined and taught for the RSCDS in the 1930s and 1940s.[10]

In her book *Pointed Encounters*, Anne McKee Stapleton categorises key differences between the ways Scottish and English dancing masters of the early nineteenth century sought to teach dancing by comparing dance manuals of the time. Scottish dancing masters focused 'on the importance of egalitarian education, adaptability, and personal expression.' In contrast, English dancing masters, through the 'rhetoric of science, math, and law [...] emphasise mastery and control.'[11] The waves of standardisation affecting Highland and Scottish Country dancing in the twentieth century followed this 'English' model particularly regarding control: rulebooks and prescribed steps were promoted and dancers within organisations were expected to follow directions. Highland dancers today would be disqualified in competition if they were to create and present unique steps for the Fling, Sword, or Reels, though that is precisely what nineteenth-century dancers did to showcase their distinctive abilities. A little more flexibility, slightly more in line with the 'Scottish' model Stapleton categorised, is still allowed within the New Zealand Academy and some Australian Highland dancing organisations such as the Victorian Scottish Union.

The twentieth-century promotion of controlled standards for dance styles labelled Scottish has resulted in widespread generalisations that such practices served and serve as unifying, signifying threads for disparate groups of people across Scotland. Just as the geography of Scotland has fostered wide variation in language, many dialects of dance practices have coexisted over the course of Scottish history. Care must be taken *not* to consider one's own norms as the only norm at the expense of ignoring other normal practices. An open mind considers these differences more equitably. The 'other' is often seen as strange until it becomes familiar.

A wave of standardisation surged throughout the United Kingdom as American dances became popular in the late nineteenth and early twentieth centuries. The Glasgow-based British Association of Teachers of Dancing (BATD) was the first standardising association and remains the 'oldest national organisation of dancing teachers in Britain.'[12] J.D. McNaughton, in his presidential address to the BATD in 1914, outlined concerns about widespread confusion regarding popular dances of the day. However, another objective of standardisation was economic stability, partly for dance teachers, and partly for the governing body itself. Dance anthropologist Theresa Buckland points out that 'ready-made dances, new choreographies annually authorised by the teaching organisations, ensured a committed clientele who, following the same rhythm and pathways, could be packed in greater numbers into the hall.'[13]

In her research on dance in Aberdeenshire over the past 200 years, Patricia Ballantyne recently studied factors that contributed to the standardisation of Scottish dancing. Ballantyne identified a number of themes that influenced the shift towards governing bodies: reaction, either to an earlier change or a perceived *status quo*; authority, through licensing and certification; commercialism driving higher expectations of professionalism; authenticity, promoted through backstories; learning in educational, as opposed to social, situations; opinions on the parts of dancers and musicians; and revivalist sentiments.[14] The success of the organisations regulating Scottish dancing seems to reflect that there was fertile ground for the standardisation efforts.

Incorporating balletic lines and motifs into Highland dancing

Around the same time that the BATD was formed, a Ballet-influenced dance aesthetic for solo Highland dancing started to take hold among a few prominent Highland dancers in the 1880–1890s period. This shift has not been widely documented but was investigated by New Zealand Highland dancer Kim Whitta. In his 1982 thesis *Scottish Highland Dance: Tradition and Style*, Whitta discusses the difference between standardising and stabilising the solo Highland dance tradition. He describes a meeting of minds between the MacLennans and the McNeills, two Edinburgh-based dancing-teacher families, which initiated a shift in the Highland dance aesthetic of the time. Donald G. MacLennan, who studied Ballet under the famous Danish *Maître de Ballet*, Alexander Genée, alongside his older brother William MacLennan, came to an agreement 'to improve the standard of Highland Dancing' with the McNeill family, who also had experience of Ballet technique.[15]

Around this time, William MacLennan was viewed as having been the epitome of piping and Highland dancing. His untimely death in 1892 did not prevent him from leaving his mark on Highland dancing history, which included incorporating virtuosic Ballet motifs. The inclusion of the *entrechat* into the Highland repertoire can be attributed to William MacLennan.[16] His Ballet teachers included Enrico Cecchetti and Maestro Barratti.[17] He featured frequently at the top of Highland Games' results lists for both piping and dancing; competitors began to copy his movements to try to garner higher placings themselves.

Whitta quotes from a document written by the founder of the New Zealand Academy of National Dancing, Inc., Mr I.D. Cameron, resulting from meetings with D.G. MacLennan, who was visiting New Zealand, where these 'improvements' to Highland dancing were discussed:

> This resulted in many refinements being introduced into the art: snapping fingers, shouting during the performance (whoofing) were removed during the performance and also improvements in the dance (steps) were introduced. The long steady influences of the French courts were introduced.
>
> During this period, special interpretation of the dances were introduced by both schools of dancing (the M[a]cLennans and the McNeills), but the 'famous William M[a]cLennan's outstanding qualities as the world recognized authority were acceptable to both schools of thought.'
>
> 'The McNeills,' says Mr Cameron, 'produced a number of outstanding dancers: Neil Cameron, a master who trained many dancers of that day was one. Others also were produced and from their training they were encouraged to introduce their own interpretation of the dance, based on the basic foundations. This introduced the era of the individual dancer who set his own sequence of steps and timing and the Masters who were later to establish their own schools and standards, to be found in many

parts of Scotland at the time. This produced some confusion of thoughts which resulted 'in a conference held in Edinburgh on 2 April 1925—the aim of the conference being to preserve the traditional style free from incorrect innovations.' The rules which were adopted as a standard by the conference were primarily formulated by D.G. MacLennan, Edinburgh, direct representative of the dancing of his brother the late William M[a]cLennan, who was universally recognised as the foremost exponent of his time, and whose style was followed—then and in later years—by such well-known dancers as—John McNeill, Edinburgh; John McKenzie, Glasgow; Charles McEwan, Edinburgh and J.A. Pirie, Aberdeen.[18]

Another influential dance teacher with Ballet training was London-based George Douglas Taylor, who also studied under Cecchetti. Highland dance teachers of this era possibly felt that, with their experience and prominence, they should lead others to adopt changes to stabilise and enhance the Highland dance tradition. D.G. MacLennan claimed, 'that not only should you know the history and tradition and changes in a dance; but it is an added advantage to be able to dance the changes when demonstrating.'[19]

After the 1925 conference, a few different organisations materialised 'to preserve the traditional style free from incorrect innovations.' The New Zealand Academy of Highland and National Dancing was the very first and was formed in 1945. Two organisations in Scotland itself, the 1947 SOHDA and 1950 RSOBHD, were latterly formed to promote and govern Highland dance competitions. When they included William MacLennan's late-nineteenth-century balletic innovations in their syllabi, they vetted these as Highland dancing motifs.

The result we see today is a competitive dance form performed using turn-out and *demi-pointe* with elevation, strength, and linear shape being among the most valued attributes. In short, the ideals of a very few, very influential individuals created a path of development away from qualities previously valued, including audible beating and shuffling, inverted footwork, and staying close to the floor. Instead, higher elevation, pointed footwork, soft landings from jumps, double-beat highcuts, and *entrechats*, movements aligned with balletic ideals of continental European stages, became prized in Highland dance organisations. The era of the individual dancer, such as William MacLennan, with freedom to express individuality and innovate or improvise, ended, and was replaced by association-based rules and regulations with centralised aesthetic and technical guidelines.

A trend starting in the nineteenth century and continuing into the twentieth saw dancing masters produce lighter, graceful solo dance arrangements for young ladies, in contrast to the stronger, assertive Highland dance routines exclusively for males. This trend likely reinforced gender roles and perhaps reflected movement that was compatible with the clothing and corsets women wore in Victorian times. This shift should not be confused with a stereotypic perception that women inherently and exclusively 'should' perform

32 *Standardisation of vernacular dance*

in a lighter, smoother manner. A romantic ideal of the female as a light, otherworldly, and fairylike being emerged along with aesthetic ideals portrayed in staged Ballet performances. Susan Au connects this list of attributes to the single most important influence on nineteenth-century Ballet, the aesthetic philosophy of Romanticism, which shaped Ballet's modern identity:

> The point technique, or dancing on the tips of the toes; the bouffant skirt called the tutu; the desire to create an illusion of weightlessness and effortlessness; and the association of the female dancer with ethereal creatures of fantasy, such as sylphs and fairies [...] significantly, most of these characteristics apply solely to the female dancer, for in the course of the century the male dancer suffered a crushing loss of prestige.[20]

Of course, not all these ideals filtered down to local dancing masters or the sharing of more vernacular dance forms. Looking at Highland and Scottish Country dancing aesthetics of today, however, the romantic ideal of ethereal anti-gravity exertion endures.

Another issue affecting the shift in gender of participants in Scottish dancing in the twentieth century is that many Scottish men did not return home from military service. Many pipers and dancers, for example, were killed in the First or Second World Wars. As a result, many women's Scottish Country dance groups were set up, often through the Women's Rural Institute. Many more women than before began teaching dance and started competing in Highland dance. Solo dances gradually shifted from being performed predominantly by men and boys to being performed predominantly by girls and women. As the century progressed, the majority of participants in competitive dancing shifted from adult dancers to children. A child typically weighs less than an adult, which may have affected a shift in aesthetic towards lighter styling, and may also have contributed towards the disappearance of complex percussive steps from dances.

Shifts in social dancing aesthetics

The refining process of Scottish Country dancing from 1923 onwards is reasonably well documented: the Fletts in their 1950s research and Emmerson in his 1972 book discuss and analyse aspects of this. RSCDS dance manuals, co-founder Miss Jean C. Milligan's publication *Won't You Join The Dance*,[21] and Milligan's biography *Dance With Your Soul*[22] all claim alignment with ideals of Ballet.

> The whole performance of Scottish Country or Ballroom Dancing shows markedly the influence of the French Court, and its technique is closely allied to that of Ballet, so popular then and always in France.[23]

Milligan's publication uses four of the five basic Ballet foot positions as a starting point. She attributes a Scottish lineage to the skip change of step motif by connecting it to Aberdeen dancing master Francis Peacock's 1805 description of the 'Kemshoole'/*Ceum Siubhail*, and qualifies that 'all Scottish steps require strength, agility and endurance, with the addition of much grace and poise.'[24] However, she also writes that 'the origin of Scottish Dancing was the French Ballet and even today in the Basque Country they speak of the Scottish steps.'[25] Without questioning the inconsistency within these statements, Miss Milligan set a particular tone regarding technique leaning towards Ballet, an aesthetic still favoured by the Society. The earlier adoption of balletic techniques and motifs that were incorporated in Highland dancing may have also influenced the developing RSCDS style.

It should be noted that the adoption of technique has been selective, and that neither Highland dancing nor Scottish Country dancing is direct expressions of Ballet. Ballet dancers generally keep heels on the floor unless turning on *demi-pointe* or stepping on *piqué*; Highland and Scottish Country dancers keep heels off the floor at all times while dancing. The influence of the resulting shape aspects of Ballet, such as pointed toes and feet and outward rotation of the legs, has been enormous; other aspects of the process of balletic technique, such as lowering the heels to the floor when landing, or practising *barre* exercises to strengthen muscles of the feet and legs, have been ignored.

As we have seen, MacLennan and Milligan made changes to dancing that have resulted in a new view of what is 'traditional' in Highland and Scottish Country dancing. It is worth looking critically at an instance of Jean Milligan's use of the word traditional. She claims that a step, if not performed correctly, 'loses its distinction and its traditional appearance becomes blurred and smeary.'[26] While ethnochoreologists see tradition as a work in progress, Milligan's use of the word 'traditional' indicates adherence to technique and shape. One step, in particular, became set in a method that several people felt was not at all traditional.

One of those people was Ysobel Stewart, the other RSCDS co-founder, who grew up in the landed Campbells of Inverneill and Ross family home of Inverneill House near Ardrishaig in Argyll and participated in social dancing in her youth. In the 1950s, she confided that she was 'always sorry to see the flick which has been adopted by a number of Scottish Country Dancers. The Pas de Basque was dignified and quiet and could be performed as quietly in heavy walking shoes as in rubber soled ones.'[27] The 'flick,' or *jeté,* at the end of the *pas de Basque* had not been common in the dancing Mrs. Stewart had observed while growing up. As an aside, we note that she associates 'dignified' with quiet; percussive traditions were sometimes associated with lower social classes.

Another was dancing master D.G. MacLennan who publicly criticised the RSCDS interpretation of the *pas de Basque* motif promoted at that time and to this day:

> The old style of movement as taught by all the well-known teachers was more *gliding* than the '*Jumpy*' manner of to-day; and the eternal pas de basque step now used for 'poussette' was never seen [...] 'Pas de Basque' is described in books as 'spring on to Right to side (1), bring Left heel up

34 *Standardisation of vernacular dance*

to Right instep, and transfer weight on to it (2), beat Right (3) *and extend Left* to *left side* (4).' That is very wrong, and I have heard of candidates for an exam. certificate losing marks for not answering according to the pre-scribed formula. Anyone who has learned this simple step from a dancing master knows that it *finishes* with closed feet; and the weight should *not* be transferred to front foot (at 2); that is the cause of so much 'bobbing' of head and body seen to-day.[28]

MacLennan further suggested that the *'pas bas'*/low step was the original setting step he had observed in pre-standardised Scottish Country dancing. He thought that teachers who didn't know French confused the terms, and considered the *'common* pronunciation of this technical term, "pas de *bas,*"' to be bad French.[29] The *pas de Basque* motif taught in Ballet travels on the second step; in the Scottish motif, the second step closes to the supporting foot.[30] The pronunciation 'pah deh bah' MacLennan described persists in usage by some RSCDS and RSOBHD teachers when referring to the *pas de Basque.* MacLennan himself actively participated in a stylistic shift towards balletic aesthetics in Highland dancing before its standardisation, and so it is interesting to observe his criticism of the RSCDS in the early 1950s.

To provide resonances with Scottish cultural identity, Scottish Country and Highland dancing teachers tell fanciful stories about how certain aspects of the dances signify Scotland or historical events to bolster dances' nationalist symbolic resonances. National identity is seen as being celebrated by partici-pating in the dancing. The modern formation Double Triangles is an exam-ple: RSCDS teachers aver that the stretched arms of first couples with corner dancers evoke the design of the Scottish Saltire flag. Double Triangles was not, however, specifically a Scottish formation. In 1815, Double Triangles was described by English dancing master Thomas Wilson as first couples danc-ing figure-of-eight tracks around their corners.[31] The method the RSCDS uses today was devised in the twentieth century and subsequently has been inserted, inaccurately, into interpretations of historic dances.[32]

Part of the RSCDS mandate, intended to provide support for a form seen as being endangered in the 1920s, was to document dances, which were carefully named and described using unified steps and figures, with diagrams on how to execute the dances. However, documentation was quickly supplanted by inter-pretations of historical manuscripts with newer styling applied. The publication of source manuscript dates within these dance directions has encouraged them to be seen as fixed entities going back hundreds of years.[33] When depictions of dancing from the past are researched, to understand them more accurately, we must take into account changes these practices have undergone.

The argument is not being made that the RSCDS style is wrong in itself; far from it. Scottish Country dancers around the world have developed inno-vations that continue to evolve in a distinctive dance culture. The issue of nationality relates to our study, however, because the RSCDS has branded itself as Scottish dancing nationally and globally, influencing a generalised perception that dancing across Scotland has been this way for hundreds of years. The RSCDS style is, in fact, modern.

The promotion of RSCDS dances as 'traditional' has inspired a number of researchers to question this. The Fletts started out as Highland and RSCDS dancers and went on to conduct in-depth research of dancing in Scotland and England. English cryptanalyst and Scottish dancer Hugh Foss wrote articles and booklets critical of RSCDS dance manuscript interpretations. Hugh Ansfrid Thurston (1922–2006), another English World War II cryptographer as well as a mathematics professor and RSCDS dancer, also researched historic dance practices.

Thurston considered arm positions to be a more recent addition to Scottish dancing. He noted that an observer of late-eighteenth-century dancing, Edward Topham, was struck by the absence of arm movements in Scots' dancing, and pointed out that Aberdeen dancing master Francis Peacock assigned no arm positions to his steps. Thurston identified that dancing in Nova Scotia conformed to these descriptions.[34] He remarked, 'the style and technique of the reel to at least 1805, then must have been different from the style in use in Scotland today [1950s]. In fact, the descriptions fit Irish dancing (as seen today) rather better than Scottish.'[35]

To learn more about vernacular dance legacies in Nova Scotia, Thurston reached out to Angus L. MacDonald (1890–1954), who was Premier of Nova Scotia at that time. Angus L., as he was popularly known, was born in a small family farm at Dunvegan in Inverness County, Cape Breton Island, of mixed Acadian and Scots Highland parentage. He described a reel he remembered from growing up:

> the most common dance was the 'Reel of Four' or 'Scottish Reel' (or as it was sometimes called, the 'Four hand Reel'). In this reel two couples faced each other, and as the violinist or piper struck up the strathspey, the lady crossed in front of her partner in time to the music, and continued until she reached the spot formerly occupied by the other couple. Here she turned to face her partner, and, the other couple having proceeded similarly, the four persons began their steps—the men standing back to back, each man facing his partner. After a few steps in this position, the four again executed a sort of march, in time to the music. This time the ladies returned to their original positions and the men again stood back to back, but now the men faced their opposite partners. This performance was repeated normally, I should say, until each man and each woman had faced each other twice. Then the musician broke into a reel, and the dancers changed their steps accordingly, but the process of circling round was repeated for the reel in the same way as for the strathspey. There was very little use of the hands in this form of dance. Sometimes, during the reel part of the dance, a man and woman would cross their hands and execute the step in that position, but this was not always done. Sometimes, too, a man would link his right arm to the left arm of the lady and they would execute a turn or two.

Beyond the occasional crossing or linking of arms that I have mentioned, the dance was entirely a matter of footwork. There was no use of the arms as one sees today in the Highland fling or Seann triubhas.[36]

MacDonald's observation that 'the dance was entirely a matter of footwork' seemed significant to Thurston. Thurston saw dances such as the Earl of Errol and the King of Sweden as remaining examples of 'what was once the prevalent style.'[37] Thurston pointed to Cape Breton Island as a place where the older form of dance migrated to from the late eighteenth century onwards.

> Although nowadays one finds the familiar Highland fling, sword-dance, and *Seann triubhas* taught in Nova Scotia, fifty years ago [about 1900] they were uncommon, and dancing in the old style can still be seen at the highland games at Antigonish and the *Mod* in Cape Breton.[38]

Thurston may have been referring to percussive solo dances, such as *Dannsa nam Flurs*/Flooers of Edinburgh being danced at the Antigonish Games, as some Scottish percussive solo dances were still remembered in 1957 when Frank Rhodes visited Cape Breton. It is also possible that the dancers who won medals at these Games improvised their step combinations. In either case, the focus was on the footwork. Thurston again quoted Angus L. MacDonald who wrote 'the most highly-thought-of dancers are those who hold the body from the waist up quite stiffly and rely entirely on the use of their feet and legs. The use of the arms is not considered good dancing.'[39]

The dancing MacDonald described is a style practised in communities with a prevalence of Scottish Gaelic speakers. It's been suggested that emigrant groups uphold home cultural practices rigorously to maintain a connection to the places they left. It's likely that Cape Breton dancing reflects Scottish dance practices predating the wave of standardisation that swept over Scottish dance forms in the twentieth century. Due to the popularity of standardised styles, though, today, percussive Step dancing is generally not seen as Scottish. RSCDS and RSOBHD dancing are often labelled as being 'traditional' though, as we have illustrated, both styles emerged in the twentieth century.

What is deemed 'Scottish' dance?

There have been hard-lined and derogatory points of view expressed by some 'authorities' of standardised Scottish dance and music forms regarding Step dancing practices of Nova Scotia and Maritime Canada and their connection to Scotland. When the Gaelic College at St. Ann's, situated in north-eastern Cape Breton, opened in 1939, it was not set up to preserve the local Scottish Gaelic culture, which Step dancing was part of. Its aim was to promote 'tartanism.'[40] Teaching the Gaelic language was initially part of the curriculum; language instruction was subsequently scaled back.[41] Instead, imported Scottish arts and crafts were taught. It quickly became mandatory for children attending summer courses to wear kilts to all classes.

Local versions of 'Highland dances,' such as the Fling, *Seann Triubhas*, and Sword Dance, in Cape Breton predate the Gaelic College's founding. These dances were known in various areas around Cape Breton and taught in Sydney Mines before Gaelic Mod dance competitions began to be held at the Gaelic College in 1939.[42] The Fling and *Seann Triubhas* from the Gillis family legacy, notated by Frank Rhodes, were, in fact, percussive.[43]

Importantly, however, when the Gaelic College began offering classes in Highland dance, they imported teachers from outside Cape Breton to teach the standardised forms taking shape in Scotland at that time, as opposed to the local versions. Notably, J.L. MacKenzie was brought in from Scotland to teach RSOBHD steps and technique. Scottish Country dancing, a dance form unknown in Cape Breton until it appeared at the Gaelic College, also began to be offered for adults. Due to the College's promotion of these outside styles of dance as 'Gaelic tradition,' doubts began to appear within local communities regarding the Scottish Gaelic origins of Step dancing. In 1957, Frank Rhodes observed these doubts, yet was convinced that Cape Breton dancing had roots in Scotland:

> When the solo dances taught by the dancing-masters began to be forgotten, extemporised stepping of a form similar to that used in the Cape Breton Island Reels came to be used in place of the solo dances in exhibitions and competitions, so that until very recent years the dancing on these occasions was quite dissimilar in style to that seen on similar occasions within living memory in Scotland. The discrepancy in style was not widely appreciated in Cape Breton Island until in 1939 the Gaelic College at St. Ann started teaching modern Highland Games dancing together with some of the Country Dances published by Royal Scottish Country Dance Society and some of the dances collected by Mrs. Mary Isdale MacNab of Vancouver. Since then many people in Cape Breton Island have doubted the Scottish origin of the stepping, and either have considered it to be an importation from Virginia or have attributed it to the French settlers from Louisburg or later to non-Scottish immigrants. While all these factors may have had some influence on the present-day style, it is certain that the roots of the step dancing lie in the solo dances and Reel steps which were brought from Scotland in the early nineteenth-century.[44]

Some of the Gaelic College teachers imported from Scotland were dismissive of the local Step dance tradition. One of them was the late piping instructor, Seumas MacNeill (d. 1996), who was the director for the College of Piping in Glasgow for nearly 50 years. Seumas's strong opinions on teaching and fingering techniques form the fundamentals of the College of Piping Tutor book series, prepared by MacNeill and Thomas Pearston. MacNeill may be most recognised in worldwide piping circles for his contributions to the *Piping Times*. This monthly magazine about piping was produced almost single-handedly by Seumas from its beginning until his death.[45] MacNeill's monthly editorial was always erudite, topical, and

38 *Standardisation of vernacular dance*

frequently controversial, and could lead to many a lively discussion among the piping fraternity.

MacNeill wrote an editorial in the *Piping Times* in 1995 describing a mid-twentieth-century interaction between the influential RSOBHD champion and teacher J.L. MacKenzie and Cape Bretoners. Some Cape Breton dancers showed MacKenzie their steps and suggested that their local form of dancing had come from the old country though they understood it had died out there since then. MacKenzie laughed at their suggestion and countered with his own assumption that the steps must have come from Ireland, reasoning that Canadians would be apt to mix up the cultural practices. We do not know whether the dancers shared that the dance form was rooted in Scottish Gaelic speaking communities, and we wonder whether it would have made a difference if they had.

Cape Breton Step dance started being promoted in Scotland around 1992,[46] prompting MacNeill's editorial, where he went on that 'in Scotland some people are trying to claim that step dancing did originally come from here, although there is not the slightest shred of evidence to support this.'[47] Research into historical descriptions of Scottish dancing shows that there is evidence to support this. The assertion MacNeill and MacKenzie put forward, that percussive Step dancing was not done in Scotland, was false: eyewitness accounts of dancing in Scotland describe dancers making sounds with their feet.

In the course of that interaction, MacKenzie also demonstrated an 'early form of the Highland fling where the legs were spread evenly apart and the two feet thumped flatly on the floor simultaneously.'[48] It strikes us that the word 'thumped,' which MacNeill used to describe MacKenzie showing the 'early' Fling, indicates percussive dancing and seems to connote disdain for that style in relation to the newer, quieter version of Highland promoted at that time. While the 'spread' was indeed an earlier Fling motif, outlined in MacLennan's 1952 book,[49] the depth of historical knowledge J.L. MacKenzie had beyond that regarding the background of Highland dancing otherwise would have been limited to a few commonly given stories and fallacies perpetuated in Highland dancing instruction as to origins for the dances. The RSOBHD textbook preface of 1955 admits their lack of knowledge regarding the history of Highland dancing.[50]

MacNeill's passage illustrates a particular mindset regarding what 'correct' Scottish dancing is: one, which scholar Michael Kennedy in his Gaelic Nova Scotia impact study says, belongs to self-appointed 'improvers' to mediate Gaelic culture, who assume that these particular art forms are easily learned because they are regarded as 'simple.' Moreover, Kennedy indicates that there has been a stereotypical belief that 'carriers of Gaelic tradition were simply not very bright—and certainly not as intelligent as the "improvers"'—in this case, the instructors from the College of Piping. MacNeill's portrayal of Cape Bretoners as wrong, and erroneous claim that Scottish Gaelic communities did not know the difference between Irish and Scottish culture, summarily dismissed an extensive body of orally transmitted knowledge detailing the history and evolution of Scottish culture in Nova Scotia.[51]

Eventually, the Gaelic College added Step dancing and fiddling to their course offerings, taught by local dancers and players, in the 1978 summer programme.[52] Gaelic language classes were reinstated around the same time. In December 2011, there was a public debate on the role of Highland dancing at the Gaelic College, but classes in Highland dance remain part of the course offerings.[53]

Shared vernacular percussive dance legacies

We can see how public perception of what constitutes Scottish dancing has been affected and widely shaped by organisations promoting Highland and Scottish Country dancing. Even though other forms of dance, such as Ceilidh and Old-Time dancing, are practised in various locations, they are sometimes viewed as lesser, or not as technically advanced.

It is not surprising then, that when Cape Breton Step dancing was being promoted as a Scottish-origin form of Step dance around Scotland in the 1990s, it was often greeted with suspicion, or seen as Irish dance, by the public.[54] Since the global success of the 1994 show Riverdance serves as a reference point for most people, percussive dance gets categorised as being in the Irish domain. Turning this perception on its head, our publication provides a compendium of references to percussive Step dancing in Scotland, not as isolated occurrences, but as commonplace and shared vernacular dance practices and legacies. Dancing masters taught percussive dances throughout all levels of society when fashions dictated. Certain forms in common vernacular use concentrated more in some places than others.

Notes

1. Flett 1985: 6–7.
2. Flett 1985: 7.
3. Flett 1985: 11.
4. MacFadyen and MacPherson 2009: 71–73.
5. Flett 1985: 244–253.
6. Gesturescape as a term is concerned with the construction and shaping of world-views within local contexts and from different perspectives that flow and change over time between places and people. It concerns itself specifically with thought about, and the embodied knowledge of, movement. Mats Melin first coined the term gesturescape in 2012 when he was searching for an encompassing and appropriate term to describe the many layers of awareness of the movement environment observed, one that went beyond practitioners' awareness of the physical act of dancing itself encapsulate wider awareness, thinking, and imagination concerning this dance style in relation to familiar everyday movements.
7. Flett 1985: 3.
8. Flett 1985: 25.
9. Emmerson 1972: 263.
10. Melin personal archive.
11. Stapleton 2014: 64.

40 *Standardisation of vernacular dance*

12. Buckland 2011: 90.
13. Buckland 2011: 188.
14. Ballantyne 2016: 11–12.
15. Whitta 1982: 43.
16. MacLennan 1952: 27.
17. MacLennan 1952: 85.
18. Whitta 1982: 43–44.
19. Whitta 1982: 49.
20. Au 1997: 45.
21. Milligan 1982 revised edition.
22. MacFadyen and Adams 1983.
23. Milligan 1982: 9.
24. Milligan 1982: 9.
25. Milligan 1982: 5.
26. Milligan 1982: 20.
27. Correspondence between Mrs. Stewart and T.M. Flett in 1964. https://insteprt. co.uk/wp-content/uploads/2020/02/JTF_Correspondence_Folder-Y_16_Ysobel-Stewart-of-Fasnacloich-1964_Redacted.pdf [Accessed 29 February 2020].
28. MacLennan 1952: 74–75.
29. MacLennan 1952: 75.
30. These two clips show the differences between the Ballet *pas de Basque*: https://www. youtube.com/watch?v=aQh9-lIqYZY and the Scottish Country dancing *pas de Basque*: https://www.youtube.com/watch?v=_tj6iXEpQyk [Accessed 20 February 2020].
31. Wilson 1815: 130.
32. For examples of nationalistic stories about Highland dances, see Melin, 2018.
33. Morrison 2003 and 2004.
34. Thurston 1984: 33.
35. Thurston 1984: 33.
36. Thurston 1984: 32–33.
37. Thurston 1984: 57.
38. Thurston 1984: 57–58.
39. Thurston 1984: 58.
40. McKay 1992: 37. See also Kennedy 2002: 246–252.
41. Kennedy 2002: 248, 249.
42. MacArthur 2012.
43. Rhodes 1985; Gibson 1998 and 2005.
44. Rhodes 1985: 273.
45. Obituary, Glasgow Herald, 6 Apr. 1996: http://www.heraldscotland.com/news/ 12046997.Seumas_MacNeill/ [Accessed 29 December 2016].
46. Melin 2005.
47. MacNeill 1995: 16–17.
48. MacNeill 1995: 16–17.
49. MacLennan 1950 (1952): 45–46.
50. Melin 2018.
51. Kennedy 2002: 217. Kennedy also offers a tongue-in-cheek scenario where all the Irish teach the Scots settlers to Step dance, even in time signatures unknown in Ireland, only to abandon the Scots to get on with it (Kennedy 2002: 216).
52. Kennedy 2002: 249.
53. Letters to the press with accompanying comments on the matter. http://www.whats-goinon.ca/2011/12/letter-to-the-editor-the-end-of-an-era-at-the-gaelic-college/ [Accessed 12 February 2012]. This information is no longer available online.
54. Melin 2005, 2006, 2012a, 2013a, and 2013b.

3 *Na brògan/dannsaidh/*The dancing shoes

Foot anatomy, footwear, and body posture

In this chapter, we focus our attention to the dancing feet and how they are described in the texts we analyse. Furthermore, we look at footwear and dancing surfaces and how they affect the dancing sounds. Interestingly, heels are mentioned particularly in early references to Scottish dancing. Toe-and-heel steps, where the toes and heels get touched to the floor in punctuated, emphasised gestures, are notable motifs in Highland dancing. Some steps perceived as 'older' in the Cape Breton Step dance tradition involve heel beats or accented heel touches that create a particular soundscape and a distinctive visual appearance.[1] The Merriam-Webster Dictionary gives the definition of toe-and-heel as an intransitive verb meaning to do Tap dancing or jigging.

Anatomy of the foot

Movement of and attention to the heel suggests spatial and rhythmic punctuation, as the heel consists of just one tarsal bone, the largest in the tarsal group and in the entire foot. The size and shape of the calcaneus, the heel bone, drives a weighted, direct placement of the heel in pedestrian strides. In contrast, the forefoot consists of a complex network of muscular tissue, 26 bones, and 33 joints, including: five metatarsal bones; fourteen phalanges; plus the two sesamoid bones under the big toe joint.[2] Springs and landings done on the forefoot exhibit sequential transfers of weight, moving successively through the joints, allowing dancers to reduce sound and impact on landing.

Motion of a heel can only exhibit simultaneous flow because the calcaneus consists of one bone and is not in itself jointed. If weight is transferred on to it, balance occurs on one point of contact, as opposed to the forefoot where many bones and muscles actively shift to maintain equilibrium. Muscular and fascial tissue emanates from the calcaneus under the sole of the foot and up the back of the calf. The calcaneus, talus, and tarsal bones together create a joint that tends to function as a hinge, but the heel bone itself does not intrinsically possess capacity for successive or undulating movement. While a landing from a moment of elevation onto the forefoot can accommodate a gradual weight transfer where it is possible to elongate, diffuse, or soften the sound of impact, transfer of weight onto the heel cannot achieve this; it

42 *The dancing shoes*

happens in a definite, distinct single moment. References to heels in dancing may indicate staccato moments of accent and direction emphasising shape and rhythmic definition.

Footwear

Footwear is an important subject to consider, given that different shoe types can limit movement of the feet, elevate the heels, and accentuate sounds made in contact with a floor. People across Scotland wore varied types of footwear at different points in time. The Fletts felt that this matter was of extreme importance because footwear changes the relationship of the feet with any dancing surface. The type of footwear worn can hinder how closely the feet can be placed together in closed foot positions. To consider how footwear may have affected dancing, we give an overview of shoes customarily worn in different regions of Scotland over the course of the past several centuries.

Footwear in the Highlands historically

Observers describe various forms of footwear, including none at all. Highland men and women in the eighteenth century frequently went barefoot in summer and winter. This may have been true in other parts of Scotland as well, but the point was made regularly about Highlanders at this time. Highlanders' lives were documented in English at this point in history by a number of high-profile publications, such as Johnson's and Boswell's travelogues. Life in the Highlands and Islands was presented along the lines of being foreign or unknown to English speakers. This sort of documentation survives in travel writers', former military officers', and engineers' publications, as well as records of parish priests and provosts from different locations around the country.

When the Highlanders did wear shoes, they were what in Gaelic were called *brògan tionndaidh*/turned shoes, or 'pumps,'[3] usually made from deerskin and fairly rough-and-ready. A pump refers to a shoe upper with a low-cut vamp, leaving the top of the arch exposed, which may have a high, low, or, as in *brògan tionndaidh*, no heel. The word *bròg* is Gaelic for shoe and comes from the Old Norse word '*bròk*' meaning 'leg covering.'

In *A Description of the Western Islands of Scotland*, detailing his 1695 journey, Martin Martin wrote: 'The shoes antiently wore, were a piece of the hide of a deer, cow or horse, with the hair on, being tied behind and before with a point of leather.'[4] Martin gives further details: 'the generality now wear shoes, having one thin sole only, and shaped after the right and left foot, so that what is for one foot will not serve the other.'[5]

Highlanders also wore taller footgear: leather boots of untanned skin, laced up to just below the knee. These were called *cuaran*, according to John MacKay, who elaborated, 'It was much in the style of the sandals worn by Eastern [European] nations. It is this that gave rise to the term 'Roughfooted Scots.' '*Feumaidh fear nan cuaran èiridh uair roimh fhear nam bròg.*' (The man with

The dancing shoes   43

the sandals must rise an hour before the man with the shoes).'[6] Alexander Nicolson referred to this same proverb/*seanfhacal*, adding that 'the lacing of the "cuaran" was a tedious affair.'[7]

Captain Edward (sometimes given as Edmond) Burt, an engineering agent serving with General Wade, was sent to Inverness from about 1724–1728 as a contractor. His often blunt descriptions, published first in 1754, illustrate life at that time. With regards to the Highlanders' shoes Burt's Letter XXII states:

> [...they] are often barefoot, but some I have seen shod with a kind of Pumps, made out of a raw Cow-hide, with the Hair turned outward, which being ill-made, the Wearer's Foot looked something like those of a rough-Footed Hen or Pigeon: these are called Quarrants, and are not only offensive to the Sight, but intolerable to the Smell of those who are near them (187) [...] By the way, they cut holes in their brogues though new made, to let out the water when they have far to go, and rivers to pass; this they do to prevent their feet from galling [becoming sore].[8]

Rev John MacRury (1843–1907) from Benbecula, the established minister of Snizort, also documented material culture of the Highland people. In 1901, MacRury recalled the days of his childhood about 1850:

> People spent very little money in those days on footwear (*caiseart*). Usually the women went barefoot until the snows and frosts of the winter came. But going to church on Sunday, or at any other time when they had to go away from home, they would put on their shoes. I have often seen young women going to church, he says, with their shoes tucked in their oxters until they got near the church. Then they would wash their feet and put on their shoes. One would seldom see a man who had come of age going barefoot. But when they came home from work they would take off their shoes. On the other hand, young lads would never normally wear shoe or bonnet until they had grown to their full size (*gus am biodh iad uiread 's a bhitheadh iad*). That left them strong, healthy and hardy. [...] The shoes which people wore in those days had two names—*brogan Gallda* (Lowland shoes) and *brogan Gaidhealach* (Highland shoes). Lowland shoes were made of Lowland leather or Highland leather, with a hempen shoe-lace (sreing chainbe) and roisin (ròsaid) just as shoemakers makes shoes nowadays. [...] Highland shoes were made shoes made with Highland leather, tied by a thong.[9]

As recently as 1895, Provost Alexander Ross of Inverness described brogues continuing to be made individually by their own wearers:

> The making of brogues was a matter of some importance, and it was not unusual, before starting on a journey, for the Highlander to sit down

and make his brogues. These were simply rough leather uppers sewed to the soles without welts or strips of leather, which, in our modern shoes, are considered necessary for attaching the soles to the upper leather, and which enables the shoemaker to produce the highly-finished article now made. The old brogue-maker began by sewing the sole to the upper leathers (which he had previously shaped) by means of a long thong or lace, and when he had done so he turned the shoes, while still soft, outside in, thus concealing the sewing and producing the finished article. These brogues were not meant to be water-tight, but simply as a protection, and their duration was not great. [...] The making of Highland brogues is now quite a thing of the past, and they are rarely met with, and few know how to make them. Some years ago I tried to get specimens of the common brogues as made by the country people, and had two specimens made in Lochaber. [...] The brogue is of the rudest description and could not stand heavy wear. The material is brown untanned leather, and the shape is the ordinary form of tie shoe, sewn with leather thongs, and certainly far from being watertight. Thread and rosin were formerly unknown to the Highlander, and thongs of seal skin to sew the brogues were highly prized.[10]

This early footwear was the same as described by Martin Martin and Captain Burt earlier.[11] Generally, stiff-soled and heeled shoes were not worn in the Highlands through the 1700s.

Footwear in the Lowlands historically

In urban areas and the central and Lowland regions, the shoes worn were rather different from the brogues and *cuaran* of the Highlands. Men generally wore shoes, while most women and children even of higher classes went barefoot, especially in summertime. Regarding the Highland tradition of walking barefoot, Londoner Thomas Morer observed in 1689, when visiting the Highlands as an army chaplain to a Scottish Regiment fighting for William of Orange, that this tradition was 'founded upon ancient law, that no males should wear shoes till they were 14 years of age, that they might be hardened for the wars.'[12]

Occasions, when both men and women would have worn shoes in the 1700s, would have been going to church on Sundays and holidays, and during frosty or snowy weather. 'Even at that,' George Emmerson writes, 'the women particularly seemed so unaccustomed to their shoes that they hobbled as they walked, and usually, in going to kirk on Sunday, carried their shoes until they came within sight of the church. Likewise, housewives travelling to town would walk barefoot to the environs, and then would wash their feet and don their shoes and stockings.'[13] Ladies' shoes were fashioned of floral brocade, and soled with leather.

By the 1750s, men wore shoes made of morocco or leather, with buckles and medium-height heels. Silver buckles make quite an impression in the following vignette from Allan Cunningham's 'The Ploughman' published in 1825:

> The bonniest sight I ever saw
> Was by the brig of Johnstone,
> For 'midst a rank of rosie queans
> I saw my dearie dancin':
> Snow white stockings on his legs
> And siller buckles glancin'
> A gude blue bonnet on his head,
> And O, but he was handsome![14]

At the end of the 1700s, shoes became a status symbol among all classes of people, especially in urban areas. Dancing slippers, with or without small heels, became fashionable footwear at assemblies. Pupils of the itinerant dancing masters seem to have worn whatever shoes they had for dance classes.

The 1800s saw the use of low-heeled and flat shoes in assembly and ballroom dancing for both sexes in both Europe and America. This footwear encouraged a tendency to slide or walk through dances, as they were made of thin leather, and had long openings across the top of the feet with no lacings or buckles over the arches to hold the shoes on. Sometimes ladies would add ribbons attaching to the sides of the shoe to tie around the ankles and help hold the shoes on. When attending formal dances, one would change into these special dancing slippers after arriving. In the countryside, people could not afford dedicated dance shoes, so they wore their best everyday shoes for dancing. Members of higher classes had enough disposable income to devote to special shoes for dancing. Dancing slippers began to signify refinement and economic status. Emmerson gives us the following observation regarding this adoption of dance shoes:

> In due course, one can see it was considered a mark of refinement for males to wear dancing slippers and hence in the usual confused way, this fashion came to be regarded by the common people as an affectation. Thus, even today, it has been reported from parts of Scotland and Nova Scotia that males have shown a marked disinclination to wear gillies when they are introduced to Scottish country dancing.[15]

Here, Emmerson may be editorialising somewhat, suggesting an excuse for why dancers might not want to wear the Highland dancing pumps we might infer he himself preferred. This disinclination may have instead reflected a cultural preference on the part of dancers in these areas to wear everyday shoes for dancing.

46   *The dancing shoes*

In the rural districts of the late 1800s and early 1900s, many Scottish men wore ordinary outdoor shoes or boots, including tackety, hobnailed, boots. Elsewhere, black patent leather dancing shoes were worn for classes and balls. Girls of both countryside and town wore the lightest shoes they could afford, with moderately high heels of about an inch or so. This resulted in men wearing rather stiff and unyielding footwear while ladies' footwear was more flexible. Heels and rigid soles prevent excessive pointing of the toes and would have hindered men from rising high up on the balls of the feet.

Footwear used by dancers

The Fletts describe types of shoes typically worn by dancers in Scotland before the 1920s as 'black patent leather dancing shoes' for the men, with an alternative of 'ordinary outdoor shoes or boots,' while ladies and girls wore 'light shoes with moderately high heels.'[16] This echoed dance master D.G. MacLennan's recollections of dancing. In 1947, MacLennan complained about the modern fashion of wearing Highland dancing pumps for social dancing:

> Another matter that should be discouraged is the wearing of solo dancers' stage pumps—heel less, thin-soled. These 'slippers' were never worn by anybody in a ballroom, as they are bad for flat feet and fallen arches.[17]

As standardising organisations gained ground in Scotland, there was a shift towards dancing on the balls of the feet and pointing the toes. This was made possible by a transition away from wearing patent leather, heeled shoes to wearing soft-soled dancing pumps. The light Highland dancing pump, or ghillie, as it is sometimes referred to, shown in Figure 3.1 is now commonly worn both for Country dancing as well as for Highland. Prior to the First World War, dancing pumps were worn only by professional Highland Games dancers. D.G. MacLennan of Edinburgh remembered that, in his youth, there were so few people wearing these Highland dancing pumps, 'that there was only one shop in all Scotland where these shoes could be obtained.'[18] In 1891, competitors at the Braemar Highland Games were depicted scathingly by a Londoner as performing 'dances which consist mainly in snappings of the fingers, and insane efforts to scratch the bare knee of one leg with the heel of the shoe worn on the opposite foot.'[19] Shoes with heels were usually worn in Highland competitions prior to 1900.

The development of the soft dancing pump is still going on, with supple leather uppers hugging the foot for a sleek profile. The 'soft' pumps of the early 1900s appear stiff in comparison. Today Highland dancers buy shoes a few sizes too small and stretch them very tightly around the feet. Ghillies differ from Ballet shoes in that leather is not gathered beneath the toes. The use of the half-point position, where slight weight is placed on the pads of

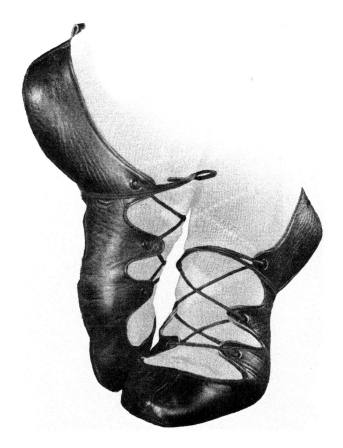

Figure 3.1 Modern soft leather ghillie pump

Source: Photo used with kind permission by C. Robertson.

the first, second, and third toes, is uncomfortable over gathered leather. The on-the-leg and closed foot positions promoted in Highland dancing today rely on the ghillies' crisscrossing laces across the top of the foot to hold the shoe on.

The word 'ghillie,' pronounced 'gillee,' now frequently used to refer to this kind of shoe does not follow Gaelic orthographic rules. The 'h' after the 'g' is out of place because lenition should only occur after an article, as in *a' ghille/* of the boy, pronounced 'ah yill-yeh.' English speakers likely spell this word this way to indicate an assumed Gaelic flavour. The Gaelic word for shoe is *bròg* as mentioned above, and the word *gille* means boy or male servant. This style of laced pump has earned its ghillie name through an association of Highlanders as workers and servants of Highland chiefs. The *Oxford English*

Dictionary (OED) gives the following usage as starting around the mid-1700s: 'gillie-wetfoot *n. Obs.* (also in adapted form **gillie-casflue**) [a rendering of Gaelic *gillecasfliuch*, < *cas* foot + *fliuch* wet.] a contemptuous name among Lowlanders for the follower of a Highland chief; *spec.*, the servant who carried the chief across a stream.' The OED also shows that the use of the word 'gillie' to refer to a shoe dates from the 1930s, coinciding with the rise of the RSCDS and early standardisation of Highland Games dancing.

Today, people who engage in Old-Time Social dancing, Ceilidh dancing, Reeling, and percussive Step dancing in Scotland wear comfortable ordinary outdoor shoes or leather-soled shoes with small heels like the shoe in Figure 3.2, in accord with the longer-standing practice of wearing ordinary or dress shoes for dancing. The disappearance of evening shoes from Scottish Country dancing influenced the disappearance of percussive treepling in Country dances such as Petronella, the Flowers of Edinburgh, and Jacky Tar. In a 2009 letter to the editor of *Scottish Country Dancer* magazine, the late Bill Clement, past chairman of the RSCDS, pointed out that 'we do not need to go back to the 18th or 19th century to find people dancing in outdoor shoes.' He shared observations from RSCDS examiner Winnie Wadsworth, that 'the ladies and gentlemen all wore proper evening shoes' at a party at Holyrood, and that 'their dancing did not suffer in any way.' Clement bemoaned that 'the Society does not encourage members to dance in heeled shoes at a ball,'[20] and felt that 'we are losing a Scottish tradition.'[21]

Competition and displays inspire dancers to determine what shoes are suitable for performing. Social and impromptu dancing takes place in whatever shoes happen to be worn at the time, and footwear can be removed if the shoes are not suitable for Step dancing. Indeed, barefoot dancing is relevant to our investigation and was depicted. Allan Ramsay's *Tea Table Miscellany* provides one example in 'bonny singing Bess/Wha dances barefoot on the green.'[22] The painting *A Piper and His Lassie*, by Sir William Allan (1782–1850), shows a girl dancing barefoot while a male musician wears shoes.[23] Dancers of the Scottish peasantry likely danced barefoot during both the eighteenth and nineteenth centuries.

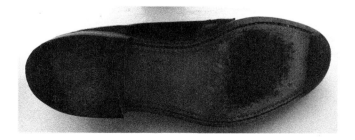

Figure 3.2 Shoe with hardwood tip and heel
Source: Photo © M. Melin.

The dancing shoes 49

Figure 3.3 Dancing in bare feet
Source: Photo © M. Melin.

Percussive Step dancing does not exclude dancing in bare feet, as depicted in Figure 3.3. Sounds made by the feet can range from soft, light shuffling, and scraping sounds to crisp, sharp noises to low, heavy thudding sounds, with a full range of sonic textures in between. All of these qualities interrelate in percussive dancing. In addition, a wider range of sound textures can be created on different surfaces. As an example, sand can be sprinkled on the floor and a dancer can create special audible effects, as in the Sand Jig or Sand Dance that many Scottish dancing masters taught. A large range of soundscapes can be associated with specific types of Step dancing. There is no problem producing percussive sounds with bare feet on various surfaces, such as stone, soil, sand, or wood. If the ground is hollow beneath flagstones or floorboards, good sound textures can easily be produced with enhanced resonance. Sounds that can be generated by barefoot Step dancing can be just as eloquent as sounds made by different types of shoes on different surfaces.

Dance scholar Màiri Britton shares her research and thoughts on barefoot and shod dancing in her unpublished paper *Bùird is Bròdan* of 2016. She writes that while most people in the Highlands and Islands could afford at least one pair of work boots or shoes, which were noted for clattering on or off dance floors:

> Some continued to dance with no shoes, such as Peter MacDonald recorded in 1952 talking of his dancing school days as a boy in Invermoriston.[24] References in puirt-à-beul, however, indicate that the concept of dancing

50 *The dancing shoes*

shoes was by no means alien to the Highlands during the nineteenth and twentieth centuries. One such example is '*Cha dèan na brògan dannsaidh an gnothaich idir idir dhomh,*' which is a complaint about the inadequacy of a certain pair of dancing shoes.[25] It can be dated at the latest from 1879, due to its inclusion in the Gaelic song collection *An t-Òranaiche,*[26] but could be older. Another example is '*Sabhal Iain 'ic Ùisdein*'[27] which mentions 'Ruidhle nam Pòg,' a kissing dance examined in depth in Flett.[28] The line '*A' cluinntinn faram nam bròg*' [hearing the racket of the shoes] indicates not only that shoes were worn for dancing, but they produced a particularly audible sound, similar to the shuffling noted by Colonel Thornton.[29]

Certainly what may be gleaned from the evidence above is that a variety of both social and solo dances were performed with different shoes to produce different percussive effects during the eighteenth through twentieth centuries, and we should therefore be wary of creating too absolute a dichotomy between soft- and hard-shoed approaches. Instead, it may be helpful to take a rather more holistic approach, imagining a soundscape of various combinations of shoes and surfaces, a variety that can still be witnessed today. Bare feet can produce considerable sound in certain contexts, and even when the feet are not audible the dance may still be considered 'percussive' in the way it is experienced by the body of the dancer and in the 'mind's ear' of the observer.[30]

Just as several languages are spoken in Scotland, several dance styles were and are danced. Even when dancing in a shared form, dancers will make different sounds depending on where they are dancing, on what they are dancing, what they are or aren't wearing on their feet, and how they respond rhythmically. A wide range of sounds and practices is natural in dancing encompassing self-expression.

Dance posture—upright or leaning forward

The posture of a Step dancer is another aspect worth considering. Many commentators on European Step dance assume that it employs an upright posture enabling certain types of movements to be efficiently performed by the feet. Both Appalachian dance scholar Phil Jamison and jazz historian Marshall Stearns[31] point out differences noted by several sources between African and European dance posture. Jamison contrasts the way an African dancer moves bare feet against naked earth in a crouched body position to the way a European dancer keeps an upright body position and wears hard-soled leather or wooden shoes or clogs, such as in Figure 3.4, on wooden floors, 'with the dancer's weight on the balls of the feet.'[32] Stearns elaborates:

> [...] African style is often flat-footed and favors gliding, dragging, or shuffling steps. [... and] is frequently performed from a crouch, knees flexed and body bent at the waist. The custom of holding the body stiffly

Figure 3.4 Dandy clogs for dancing
Source: Photo used with kind permission by C. Robertson.

erect seems to be principally European. [… and] places great importance upon improvisation […] allowing freedom for individual expression.[33]

Since the Scottish forms of Step dancing, historical and current, are part of a much larger family of percussive dancing spanning across the British Isles and Ireland these observations above are beneficial to our understanding of percussive dance embodiment. Some current Irish Step dance forms favour a vertical upper body, with the main percussive movements performed by the balls of the feet. These characteristics also can be seen as favoured aesthetic preferences of some Cape Breton Step dancers, for example. However, this does not give the whole picture of what is encompassed within Step dancing posture in these geographical areas. Many Irish *Sean nós* dancers lean the upper body slightly forward to allow the core weight of the body to shift backwards, enabling the execution of heel-battering steps, which take weight and make sounds with the heels, and use the arms in a swinging fashion or lifted position. In Cape Breton Island, a favoured upper-body aesthetic is to dance tall and upright, yet some dancers lean forward. This may be viewed as an individual trait or style but it is part of the accepted practices.[34] Cape Breton dancers use the hip and knee joints of the working leg while increasing flexion of the supporting leg slightly to enable the heel and toe to connect with the floor during the 'shuffle' movement. The upper body stays relatively upright in a relaxed manner. The current improvisational Step dancing style in Scotland

52 *The dancing shoes*

Figure 3.5 Painting (detail). *A Highland Dance*. David Allan (*c.* 1780). Original in National Galleries of Scotland. Used with kind permission. Both the men and the women wear low-heeled, buckled brogues in this dance scene, set in the Blair Atholl area. One man leans forward while the other arches up and slightly back. Arm positions of the dancers are not uniform. The bodily alignment of the woman on the far right resembles a posture commonly seen among Cape Breton Step dancers today

"Gillie Callum" or Sword Dance.

Figure 3.6 Sword dancer wearing hard-soled shoes with buckles. Artist unknown. Chicago, The Regan Printing House, 1910

Source: Permission kindly granted by the Francis O'Neill Collection, Irish Traditional Music Archive, Dublin.

is highly influenced by the Cape Breton Step dancing style with an upright and relaxed body position, while the various soft-shoe options, particularly under RSCDS- and RSOBHD-promoted aesthetics, strongly favour a light and upright body stance usually exhibiting a large degree of control.

These few examples show that within Step dancing forms, upright body stance is not universal. Looking at the painting of Scottish dancing in Figure 3.5 by David Allan from the 1780s, various body stances are seen in action. In an illustration not included in this book, in David Hume's (1891) *Imperial History of England*, captioned as the *National Dance of the Highland Clansmen*, the dancers' focus downward suggests that great attention is being paid to their footwork. That stance also recalls the body and head alignment used by dancers performing a Sword Dance, depicted in Figure 3.6.

Upper-body positioning does influence the execution and flow of steps. When Isle-of-Barra dancer Fearchar MacNeil danced, he had an upright, loose upper-body stance, allowing his body to sink on bended legs. This posture facilitated light and graceful transitions of weight. There are many variables in Step dancing. Wearing hard-soled shoes with low heels affects style and stance, particularly in comparison with dancing barefoot. A depiction of one dancer cannot be taken to typify the posture of a geographical area; stance is highly individual. Modern aesthetic preferences emphasising upright verticality of the body and efficiency in movement should not bias our perceptions of past practices and descriptions.

Notes

1. Melin 2012a and 2015.
2. The number of bones in the forefoot and their shapes can vary slightly from person to person.
3. Mackay and Macleod 1924: 100.
4. Martin 1713: 207.
5. Martin 1713: 207.
6. Mackay 1924: 100.
7. Nicholson 1882: 184.
8. Burt 1876: 185.
9. MacilleDhuibh 1993.
10. Ross 1974: 31–33.
11. Brogue, brog—a Highland 18th-century shoe of untanned hide with the hair turned outwards, stitched with leather and tied before and behind with a thong; now a heavy shoe, especially decorated with a distinctive pierced pattern along the seams. From Scottish Gaelic *bròg*. [*The Concise Scots Dictionary* and Dwelly's *Illustrated Gaelic to English Dictionary*].
12. Morer 1702: 14.
13. Emmerson 1972: 262.
14. Cunningham 1825: 322.
15. Emmerson 1972: 263.
16. Flett 1985: 14.
17. MacLennan 1952: 75.
18. Flett 1985: 14.
19. Dancing 1891/1984: 40.
20. Footage of dancers wearing high heels on the White Heather Club television programme is at: https://www.youtube.com/watch?v=jyLXjPdBKEA [Accessed 2 March 2020].
21. RSCDS 2009.
22. Ramsay 1794: dedication, iii.
23. Image accessible: https://www.the-athenaeum.org/art/full.php?ID=163840 [Accessed 2 March 2020].
24. Tobar an Dualchas SA1952.139.A5. http://www.tobarandualchais.co.uk/gd/fullrecord/23236/10;jsessionid=24AA73A4CE50B3268F5016A4EB73323E [Accessed 20 May 2017].
25. SA1956.32.B12. http://www.tobarandualchais.co.uk/en/fullrecord/84582/4;jsessionid=44A74593C74D416AA2BA8984970BA358 [Accessed 20 May 2017].
26. Mac na Ceardadh 1879.
27. SA1952.074.1. http://www.tobarandualchais.co.uk/gd/fullrecord/92544/1/LuckyDip [Accessed 20 May 2017].
28. Flett 1964: 41–45.
29. Flett 1964: 6–7.
30. Britton 2016: 4–7. See also Melin 2015: 104.
31. Jamison 2015; Stearns 1994 [1968].
32. Jamison 2015: 130.
33. Stearns 1994: 15.
34. Melin 2017.

4 Gaelic references and continental European connections

Chluinnte faram nam bròg[1]—the clatter of their boots!

Recent research into Gaelic-language source material, that has until recently been widely ignored by researchers, supports rethinking historical timelines of the Scottish dance traditions. In his 2013 article *'Dannsair air ùrlar-déile thu': Gaelic evidence about dance from the mid-17th to late-18th century Highlands*, Celticist Michael Newton shows that Gaelic oral and textual sources describe frequent interactions between people of the European mainland and the Highlands of Scotland. These interconnections made a strong impact on the dance practices of the Gaels. While Continental influences on Scottish dance traditions had been outlined earlier by both the Fletts and Emmerson, many of the Gaelic sources in Newton's article had not been previously examined. Newton focuses on 'interpreting and contextualizing how music and dance traditions were adopted and adapted in Gaelic society,'[2] and he singles out French courtly dance customs that, in his view, influenced dance in the Highlands.

Dance develops across the European continent

While Lowland Anglophone cultural influences seeped into the Highlands from the early seventeenth century onwards, European customs also influenced the Highlands and Islands. Many sons of Highland families, particularly Catholic ones, were sent to be educated on the Continent, primarily to France, Spain, and Italy. As they became acquainted with European norms, customs, and languages, learning about courtly dance practices would have been natural.[3] As Jennifer Nevile summarises in 'Dance in Europe 1250–1750,' 'not only were specific choreographies, dance steps, and dance styles common to more than one country, so too were attitudes to dancing shared across geographic areas, and over long periods of time,'[4] and she continues:

> [d]ance music also travelled with the musicians who played it, as dance musicians lived and worked in more than one country: many of the best wind-band players in Italy in the fifteenth century were German. In the mid-sixteenth and seventeenth centuries Italian musicians, like

56 *Continental European connections*

Jean-Baptiste Lully, and dance masters travelled to the French court to live and work. The presence of dance tunes from the repertory of one country that are recorded in manuscripts or printed books from another country is also an indication of the international nature of the dance practices during this period[5] [...] The duties of the dance master were also standard throughout the period and across Europe. Acquiring expertise in dancing meant acquiring a bodily agility, an elegance in posture and manners, and the correct and necessary presence and address.[6]

Ethnochoreologist Catherine Foley traces some stylistic characteristics of Irish Step dancing to the Continental European development of technique in dancing, enabled and shaped by particular material conditions:

Italy led in the field of professional dancing masters, and although France would dominate the development of ballet, Italy led in matters of technique (as the writings of Caroso and Negri show[7]), where virtuosity was the preserve of male dancers. During the early Renaissance in Italy, much attention was paid to footwork that was facilitated by the marbled floor of the palace courts. [...]

During the sixteenth century, corsets (for both males and females), ruffs or stiff collars, swinging cloaks and a novelty of the 1570s—heels on the shoes—assisted in shaping the dance aesthetic of the high Renaissance. Corsets precluded torso movements, and ruffs forced the head to remain in an upright position; consequently, the dance aesthetic and technique of the sixteenth century focused on footwork, performed with precision, dexterity and somewhat great speed. The introduction of heels on shoes allowed for these foot movements to be audible.[8]

Ingrid Brainard further elaborates that Negri's 1602 treatise *Le gratie d'amore* 'contains some of the most difficult steps of the high Renaissance and is packed with an enormous amount of technical detail, [...] foot crossings, [...] beats, [...] and vigorous stamps. The last were the chief ingredient of the *canario* [...] and coincident with the advent of shoes with heels, [...] which allowed the Spanish flavour of the dance to become audible.'[9] A little over ten years earlier, in 1589, Thoinot Arbeau published his *Orchesographie* where foot and leg positions and gestures are described and illustrated, and, according to Foley, are show affinities 'with basic Irish step dance positions and gestures.'[10]

The canary, or, in Spanish, *canario*, was a sixteenth- to eighteenth-century dance in 3/8 or 6/8 meter first published in Febritio Caroso's 1581 *Il ballerino*. It depicted a fiery wooing, and was marked by rapid heel-and-toe stamps, noisy sliding steps that partners used to advance and retreat, and distinctive music. In this time period, the *canario* was sometimes identified as a *gigue* due to its lively and showy nature.'[11] Canaries were popular throughout Europe.

George Emmerson[12] has outlined religious developments and aspects of dance during this era in Lowland Scotland in his 1972 *Social History of Scottish*

Dance. While he portrays dance at the Scottish court in England in depth, he only briefly acknowledges the influence of the French Court and the establishment of its new academy, created to stop the perceived declining standards of dance. King Louis XIV of France was a staunch supporter of that academy, the *Académie Royale de Danse*, established in 1661 under his auspices. It had 13 dancing masters entrusted to seek perfection in the art of dance. Subsequently, the number of dancing masters on the European circuit increased significantly, as localised academies were established to develop and maintain standards and to control dance, dancing, and dance masters.[13]

Given that the influence of the French court was so strong, it is important to look at what influenced the French court itself. Italian and Spanish musicians and dancers were dominant there. Dance historian Jennifer Nevile points out that 'the first significant treatises on dancing were written in Italy' in the sixteenth and early seventeenth centuries.[14] She continues:

> It was in this atmosphere of immense attention to the dance that kings of France, Louis XII and François I, learned to appreciate dancing in the Italian manner. [...] It was mainly through the Italian dancing masters that princes and their courtiers throughout Europe learned to dance [in the sixteenth century. [...] The habit of employing Italian dancing masters in France was supplemented by the presence of Italian instrumentalists at the French Court. Charles IX in particular augmented their number, spending large sums on the best violins from Milan and Cremona, and encouraging violin players and lutenists to come to his court in order to satisfy his great love of music and dancing. [...] By the reign of Henri III, seventy-six percent of violin players were Italian, and of professional dancers one hundred percent.[15]

The bonds between royal courts through marriage encouraged wide cultural exchange and influence. Even the 'Italian dance technique was enriched by the Spanish dance influences.'[16] There was a pan-European culture of court dance, which influenced dance in general as court ideals caught on in other levels of European societies. Courts did not reflect dance ideas indigenous to their kingdoms, but, rather, reflected cross-cultural élite aesthetics.

In the early seventeenth century, Raoul Auger Feuillet (1700 and 1704), Michel Gaudrau (*c.*1714), and F. Rousseau (*c.*1725) published notations for theatrical virtuoso dances:

> Performed for a kinesthetically attuned audience, these virtuosities were not stressed by preparations and conclusions, rather, they were merely slipped into the rhythmic flow of the dance; an expert dancer should make Baroque dance appear very easy. In fact, the performance of Baroque dance is exceptionally demanding because of its subtle textures of movement and the highly developed rhythmic interplay between dance and music. It requires an inherent nobility of presence and motion,

58   Continental European connections

an unfaltering rhythmic sense, intellectual dexterity, quick and precise footwork, a strongly cantered balance and control, and a keen awareness of spatial configuration.'[17]

What Wendy Hilton describes above could easily be attributed to percussive Step dance as we find it in its many forms today. It is not too far-fetched to suspect a strong link between these aesthetic ideals, forged by the high standards of formal instruction and passed down from one dancing master to the next, and what have survived as core aspects of good Step dancing.

Both Emmerson in 1972 and Foley in 2013 describe the flow of communication of Continental European dance practices as having filtered across to London, Dublin, and Edinburgh. John Weaver (1673–1760), who translated Feuillet's *Chorégraphie*, theoretical dance descriptions using Feuillet's own system of dance notation, as *Orchesography or the Art of Dancing* in London in 1706, was a London dancing master who, with other dancing masters in England, helped promote and propagate the European standards. Dance practices also spread to remoter parts of rural Scotland and Ireland through wealthy landowning families' connections to the Continent.

The type of dance that Gaels who interacted with foreign courts would have been exposed to in the 1600s and 1700s would have been the courtly and theatrical Minuet and its precursor, the *Courante*. Almost all Minuet accompaniment is phrased in series of two 3/4 measures, sometimes notated as one measure of 6/4. Dance music frequently contains strains of eight or sixteen measures, or an eight-measure strain followed by one of twelve. The origin of the Minuet is obscure, writes dance historian Wendy Hilton,

> but the scores of Jean Baptiste Lully (1632–1687), which contain some ninety pieces titled menuet, indicate that the rhythm was used increasingly during the 1600s and soon predominated. The *menuet ordinare* superseded Louis XIV's favourite dance, the *courante*, and remained the most popular ballroom *danse à deux* (couple dance) in aristocratic society until the years following the French Revolution in 1789.[18]

The Minuet had enormous social significance. Even those who did not particularly enjoy dancing were expected to practice the Minuet until they could dance it with ease and, as Rameau frequently stressed, without affectation.[19] The various *pas des menuet* consist of four changes of weight/steps and different motions—a *plié*/bending of the knees, followed by an *élevé*/a rise, or a straightening of the knees—together called *mouvement*. The *mouvement* provides the characteristic rhythmic accents within the dance, which usually coincide with the musical downbeats. A *pas de menuet* always starts on the right foot and takes two measures of 3/4 time. The various steps can be performed either with or across the musical bars or phrases.[20]

As the popularity of the Minuet and the versions of it that evolved over time grew and dispersed to other layers of society, ideas that were part of the dance, such a couple performing a duet, distinctive travelling patterns, and steps crossing musical phrases resulting in syncopated rhythmic interplay in contrast to melodies, emerge as accepted and familiar choreographic conventions. These ideas affected how other dances developed and emerged in parallel to the Minuet.

Over time, the Minuet morphed into a vernacular form of dance in many areas, such as Scandinavia.[21] In Scotland and England, the Minuet receded in popularity at the beginning of the nineteenth century, after having been the most important dance in polite assemblies in Scotland in the eighteenth century. Emmerson details the Minuet's demise in detail. Importantly, Emmerson suggests that the Strathspey Minuet mentioned in publications and playbills in the eighteenth century is, in fact, the same as the Strathspey Reel, which later becomes the Strathspey in the Highlands.[22] This could be another instance of court and assembly dancing filtering into vernacular usage.

Even though the courtly Minuet may not have been a percussive dance by design, it was performed in hard-soled heeled shoes on wooden floors. Some vernacular versions of the Minuet surviving today, in Finland, for example, include both hand clapping and foot stomps to mark rhythm and figure changes.[23] In 1776, Topham described Scots 'galloping' a Minuet, which he states is locally called 'a *straspae*.' 'Nothing of the minuet is preserved, except the figure; the step and the time most resemble an hornpipe.'[24] Did he mean the Scottish Strathspey Minuet was faster, or that the dancers were clomping or thumping on the floor, or perhaps both? Topham's hornpipe comparison seems to suggest something percussive being performed. (See Chapter 6 for further details.)

References to dancing in Gaelic sources

Michael Newton's study of Gaelic sources highlights that there was frequent, ongoing contact between the Gaelic-speaking Highlands and the Continent. Some of these connections were established through education: some Gaels training for the Catholic priesthood attended seminaries at Valladolid in Spain; St. Lô, Coutances, or the Scots Colleges in France; or Rome in Italy. Others found their way to the Continent via the Jacobite or Royalist movements, or by participating in the Continental wars of the seventeenth and eighteenth centuries. Exposures to European customs in high-social-status contexts extended cultural influences, including dance, to the Highland élite, which would naturally become assimilated into local cultural expressions among the general Highland population. As both Newton and Nevile indicate, the spread of these social dances was simultaneous with and possibly responsible for the introduction of the fiddle to Gaelic culture in both Scotland and Ireland by the mid- to late-seventeenth century. Instrumentation, dance music, and dance practices combined together as an interconnected, but fluid and reconfigurable 'package' influenced these regions, argues Newton.[25]

60 *Continental European connections*

While there was resistance to this change, writes Newton, a poem from 1693 places these new fiddle and dance practices at the court of Iain Breac MacLeòid of Dunvegan where both the 'accomplished and precise' movements of these dances and the French influence are highlighted:

> *an déidh ceilearadh beòil*
> *dannsa oileanach ordail suas*
> *le fear-bogha 'nan còir*
> *chumail modha ri pòr an cluas.*

> After voices had been lifted up in song,
> they took the floor for dancing, accomplished and precise,
> with one who wielded a bow near at hand to make the measure
> sound in their ear.[26]

A metaphor in a song from 1715 envisions women dancing on wooden floors in the Clanranald chieftain's mansion house in South Uist, alluding to his French and Italian contacts and experience abroad on the Continent. Dancing was portrayed at the great Highland houses throughout wintertime and at military camps in Europe from this period[27] as well as in a number of other early- to mid-eighteenth-century examples. Newton's research shows the important role dance played in the social interactions of the élite and how the élite's status was reinforced through association with the Continent.[28] Two examples of dancing portraying percussive properties of dancing are of particular interest to our study.

The first is the literary motif borrowed into the eighteenth-century Gaelic panegyric code as expressed in the phrase '*dannsair air ùrlar-déile thu*'/you are a dancer on a wooden-plank floor, which Newton elaborates on:

> By the second quarter of the eighteenth century, the formula *Dannsair air ùrlar-déile thu* '(You are) a dancer on a wooden-plank floor' (and variations thereof) became somewhat common in the set of stock images and phrases used by Gaelic poets for praising their subjects, fitting easily into the élite characteristics of their subjects and their noble rank in Gaelic society [...] These new dance forms (and poetic phrases which depict them) are a reflection of, and rely upon, a particular form of material culture found only in élite habitations: wooden floors. In these recurrent oral formulae, *ùrlar-déile/ùrlar-clàraidh/bordaibh*, all indicating wooden flooring, appear in association with the dance, demonstrating not only the refined manners of the dancers as an aspect of their aristocratic background and training, but also the material signs of wealth in the form of domestic architecture [...] in addition] some texts imply that the wooden floor is a better resonator for percussive dance effects.[29]

The key idea here is the perception that better dancing and better sounding dancing would be achieved on wooden floor surfaces. This idea must have made its way to the peasantry, which, at the time, would have been limited to packed soil or stone floors. The peasant class did not have ready access to hard-soled shoes, which later evolutions of percussive dance, from the late eighteenth century onwards, have made into a prerequisite for dancing on wooden floors. As mentioned previously, percussive footwork should not be dismissed entirely in light of the absence of hard-soled shoes. Dancing sounds can be achieved in bare feet and in soft-soled shoes on both dirt and stone floors. Stamping newly laid dirt floors flat for the annual refurbishing of barns required a community effort in Shetland. Dancing on flagstones in the Black Isle in Scotland and Step dancing on stone floors by stone-masons in Ireland are other examples of percussive dance on non-wooden surfaces.[30]

In Ireland, Tyrone-born Irish writer and novelist William Carleton (1794–1869) describes dancing on wooden floors and half-doors in his novel depicting tenant farmers:

> While the usual variety of Irish dances—the reel, jig, fling, three-part-reel, four-part-reel, rowly-powly, country-dance, cotillion, or cut-along (as the peasantry call it), and minuet [...] The dance in Ireland usually commences with those who sit next the door, from whence it goes round with the sun. In this manner it circulates two or three times, after which the order is generally departed from, and they dance according as they can [...] At the dance we are describing, however, there was no dissension; every heart appeared to be not only elated with mirth, but also free from resentment and jealousy. The din produced by the thumping of vigorous feet upon the floor, the noise of the fiddle [...][31]

This account of dancers taking turns around the room resembles an account of dancers in north Sutherland in Chapter 11.

Dancing on the half-door shows up in a nineteenth-century Scottish Gaelic song created by *Iain Mac-Dhughaill*/John MacDougall, from Ardgour near Inverlochy. The song is '*Dan-Gheall: Do Chomh-chruinneachadh nan Gàidheal ann an Glascho, sa' bhliadhna 1858, a' nochdadh gach buannachd a tha 'sruthadh o'n cùisean-gheall 's o'n cluichibh*/Prize-song, to the Gathering of the Gaels in Glasgow in the year 1858, showing each victory flowing from the prize-competitions and from the games,' sung to the tune '*Tha mi a'm' chadal 's na duisgear mi.*' The sixth verse[32] describes dancing at the gathering.

> *Na dannsaireach fileanta,*
> *Sgiobalta, lùthmhor,*
> *Gur taitneach air ùrlar, 's gur boidheach iad:*
> *'S gu'm faicear na h-uaislean*
> *A bualadh am bas*
> *An àm gluasad an cas air a' chòmhla dhoibh;*
> *A' freagradh le mire*

62   Continental European connections

Do phongaibh an inneil
An ceileir bu bhinne na'n smeòrach leinn—
Ceòl caithreamach pìoba,
Gun dith no gun uireasbhuidh

The elegant/flowing dancers,
Neat, strong,
Delightful on the floor, beautiful:
And the gentlemen are seen
Clapping their hands
When it's time for them to move their feet on the door;[33]
Responding merrily
To the beats of the instrument
Music sweeter than the music of the thrush—
The lively music of the pipe,
Without defect or want

The qualities of neatness and strength are highly appreciated, and the relationship between the music and footwork is praised in this song. These same core concepts remain at the heart of Step dancing in Cape Breton.[34] The poetic trope of the smooth wooden dance surface continued in usage, too, in Gaelic poetry and song in Cape Breton, where immigrants' houses were predominantly built of wood, plentiful in the area. The popular, twentieth-century *Òran do Cheap Breatainn* by Dan Alec MacDonald recounts, '*Dhannsamaid air ùrlar réidh, Gur e "Cabar Feidh" bu mhath leinn*'/we would dance on a smooth floor, and *Cabar Feidh* would be our favourite.[35] MacDonald lived in Framboise, Richmond County, with forebears from North Uist, and was recognised as 'the premier Gaelic bard in Cape Breton at the time of his death in 1972.'[36]

Another Iain MacDhughaill song depicting dancing is titled *Do Mhor ni'c 'Illeathain*. *Nighean do Alasdair Mac 'Illeathain a bh'ann an Arasaig*/To Sarah MacLean, a daughter of Alexander MacLean, Arasaig. Verse six and the second half of verse seven[37] read:

Bu ghrinn leam air ùrlar thu
Le mùirn air do chuir suas;
Gu h-éibhinn, eutrom, ionnsuichte,
Neo éisleineach, brisg, dlùth-cheumach,
Neo-mhearachdach 's gach cùrsa dheth,
'S glan tionndadh anns gach cuairt;
A' freagradh fonn nam pong ro-lùghar,
'S a' chruit-chiùil ri fuaim.

'N uair ghlacadh tu 'm piano
Bu ghàirdeachas do m' chluais—
Gu ceòlmhor, éibhinn, stòlda, ceutach,
Anns gach beus thug buaidh.

Neat you were to me on the floor
Joy made you spring up;
Delightfully, light, cultured,
Spirited, clever, close-stepping,
Correct in each turn of it,
And crisp turning in each round/whirl
Answering so energetically the music of the beats
While the violin was playing.

When you'd take to the piano
'T was a pleasure to my ear—
Musically, delightful, steady, comely,
In each element you won.[38]

Neatness comes across here as a core attribute to good dancing, where stepping is close to the floor and full of energy and drive. 'Answering' the music suggests that the dancing was audible.

Yet another song attributed to Iain MacDhughaill popular with Gaelic singers today is *Na Brogan Dannsaidh*/The Dancing Shoes.[39] This song, set to the strathspey 'The Braes of Tullymet,' portrays a disastrous pair of shoes that caused blisters, broke, and prevented dancing!

Another Gaelic song from the mid-1800s depicting Step dancing was shared by John Gibson. The song was written by John MacIntosh, whom Gibson describes as 'a Brae Lochaber man who died in Glasgow in 1852.'[40] *An Tàillear mac Gill-Eathain*/The Tailor MacLean song also draws on the dancer on the boards image: "'*S grinn an dansa air thu air clàiridh, 'S bìnn leam starraraich do dha chois*'/Neat the dancer you are on the boards, melodious to me the pattering of your two feet.[41]

Ditties sung to keep time for dancing for which we don't have dates of origin sometimes internally refer to dancing. We are reminded by the *port a beul* lyrics for *An Oidhche Bha na Gobhair Againn*/The Night We Had the Goats, that footwear for dancing was not always needed or preferred. On this night that the goats visited, a little party was inspired, and '*Fhuair sinn aran agus leann, 's dhanns sinn gu furanach. Fhuair sinn aran agus leann, 's dhanns sinn gun bhrògan*'/we got bread and beer, and we danced welcomingly, we got bread and beer, and we danced without shoes.[42] Another instance of noisy dancing is mentioned in the *port a beul* lyrics *Ruidhleadh an Gille Cam*[43]:

Ruidhleadh an gille cam,
'S e mo roghainn air na th' ann,
Ruidhleadh an gille cam,
'S aighearach a' dhòighean.

'S cuireideach na casa cam
Tè mu seach 's a null 's a nall,
'S cuireideach na casa cam
'S bragadaich nan òrdag.[44]

The crippled boy reels
It's my choice he is
The crippled boy reels
His ways are joyful

The crippled legs are frisky
One after the other here and there
The crippled legs are frisky
And the toes are clacking.

'Òran a Chriosamas Tree'/Song of the Christmas Tree portrays foot tapping using different vocabulary: '*Bha faram chas is bualadh bhas*'/there were tapping feet and clapping hands. A dancer is described in this way:

> *Saoil nach e MacLeòid bha tapaidh—*
> *Thilg e sheacaid ghorm dheth,*
> *Gun d' leum a beò nuair chual' e 'n ceòl*
> *Aig tòiseachadh na seirbheis;*
> *E air a chois cho luath ri dreag,*
> *A' breabadaich 's a' stamasan,*
> *Is lias is fallas air a sgall*
> *'S e dannsa 'Tulach Gorm' dhaibh.*

> Do you not think MacLeod was bold?
> He threw off this blue jacket
> He leapt up when he heard the music
> At the start of the proceedings;
> He was on his feet as fast as a shooting star,
> Kicking and prancing,
> His bald head shining and sweating
> As he danced Tulloch Gorm for them.[45]

Another *port a beul* describing tapping is *Peigi Chaluim*: '*Thug sinn fead air "Gille Calum" 's brag air "Jack-a-Tar"*'/we gave a whistle to *Gille Calum* and tapped to Jacky Tar. *Peigi*/Peggy, who was attending a ball, went on dancing: '*Ghèarr i figearan le casan/'S gaileagan le làimh*'/she cut figures with feet/and snaps with hands.[46]

Looking back into history for details about steps, Newton presents another early direct reference to Step dancing in Scots Gaelic culture focusing more specifically on footwork:

> [a]nother poem by *Raonaid nighean mhic Néill MacDonald* about a visit to Skye in the late eighteenth century describes the action of beating the feet on wooden floors to produce a percussive effect, possibly the first reference to step dancing in Scottish Gaelic literature:

Far am biodh na fleasgaichean
A' breabadh air an ùrlar;
'S pìob mhór nam feadan bras ann
Ri caismeachd air gach taobh dhiubh.

Where the lads would be kicking on the floor; and there would be the great bagpipe of the lively chanters playing to the procession on each side of you.[47]

Newton's findings strongly suggest a strong cultural infusion from Europe was assimilated into Gaelic culture as a whole and that it influenced the Gaelic élite. The limitations of cultural memory, combined with selective research neglecting Gaelic expressions, such as songs, stories, and music, has largely bypassed these fragments of dance history up until now. These glimpses of European modes of dancing filtering into Gaelic Scotland are worthy of further investigation.

None of the Gaelic examples cited provide specific details as to the exact manner of the dancing. The references to French influences emphasise the material status marker of wooden floors. The poems may depict aspirations the Highland élite had towards such ideals, as opposed to precise replication of the fashions of the Continent. The seventeenth-century French court favoured a dance style that was more subdued and refined than that of the previous century, when high leaps and showing off by male dancers were hallmarks of the Galliard.[48] Some percussive footwork elements are suggested in the descriptions of seventeenth-century French court dancing, as are refined, economised movements. May we perhaps read between the lines quoted by Newton to envision an amalgamation of existing Gaelic dance ideals with an aspiration to the foreign court ideals? This would promote a useful political image, indicating that the Highland élite were in close contact with the Continental élite. Further research into early Gaelic dance aesthetics and influences may shed more light on these topics.

Notes

1. 'The clatter of their boots' a line from the strathspey port-a-beul *Sabhal Iain 'ic Ùisdein* (The Campbells of Greepe 2011: 284).
2. Newton 2013: 49.
3. Newton 2013: 52.
4. Nevile 2008: 25.
5. Nevile 2008: 25.
6. Nevile 2008: 26.
7. Cesare Negri—*Le gratie d'amore* (1602); and Fabritio Caroso—*Il ballerino* (1581) and *Nobiltà di dame* (1600, 1605).
8. Foley 2013: 39–40
9. Brainard 2004: 338.
10. Foley 2013: 40.

66 *Continental European connections*

11. Sutton 2004: 50–51.
12. Emmerson 1972: 57–81.
13. Astier 2004: 3–5; Rineheart 2017: 65–79.
14. Nevile 2008: 97.
15. Nevile 2008: 97–98.
16. Ivanova in Magri 1988: 35.
17. Hilton 2004: 344.
18. Hilton 2004: 431. Hilton adds 'Michael Praetorius wrote in *Terpsichore* (1612) that the minuet was a descendant of the dance called 'Branle de Poitou,' and Pierre Rameau expressed the same opinion in *Le maître à danser* (1725).'
19. Hilton 2004: 431.
20. Hilton 2004: 432.
21. Biskop 2015.
22. Emmerson 1972: 175.
23. Biskop 2015.
24. Topham 1776: 70–71.
25. Newton 2013: 52.
26. Newton 2013: 53.
27. Newton 2013: 54–56.
28. Newton 2013: 56–63.
29. Newton 2013: 56–57.
30. Melin 2006.
31. Carleton 1852: 341.
32. Mac-Dhughaill, 1860: 24–25.
33. Còmhla may refer to either a door or a half-door.
34. Melin 2015.
35. Creighton and MacLeod 1964/1979: 49–50.
36. Fergusson 1977: 182.
37. Mac-Dhughaill 1860: 30.
38. Translations for both of the Iain Mac-Dhughaill song excerpts are based on Gibson 2017: 46 and 42, with a few changes suggested by Màiri Britton and Michael Newton.
39. Sinclair 1879: 261–263.
40. Gibson 2017: 53.
41. Gibson 2017: 53.
42. Mhàrtainn 2000: 8.
43. A recording of Katerine Dix singing this song is at: http://www.tobarandualchais. co.uk/fullrecord/63170/1 [Accessed 28 July 2017].
44. Mhàrtainn 2000: 64.
45. Campbell 2013: 194–195.
46. Campbell 2013: 166–167.
47. Newton 2013: 69.
48. Beck-Friis *et al.* 1998: 68–69.

5 From Hornpipes to High Dances

Historical terms and overlapping usage

Overlapping methods of labelling music and dance forms morphed gradually over time, so a term used in the late-eighteenth century meant something different than what it means today. Disentangling terminology can be challenging; depending on perspective, preferences, and vocabulary, one observer can describe one instance of dancing quite differently than another observer would. Regarding Step dances, terms such as Scotch Measure; Single, Double, or Triple Hornpipe; High Dance; *Pas Seul*; Rant; and Reel have been applied to various concepts that have shifted over the course of the past 200 years.

Scottish measure

A class of dance tunes known as Scottish, Scots, or Scotch measures appears in print around 1699 onwards, notably published by John Playford, as well as by other music compilers. This suggests that the tune type became popular for dancing in the seventeenth century. Prior to this, music publications in England used the label 'Scots tunes' to categorise melodies such as 'Dumbarton's Drums' and 'Flooers o' Edinburgh.'

The English composer Henry Purcell (1659–1695), mainly remembered for his English-style Baroque music, composed 'Scotch tunes' in 1687 and 1690 that imitated the Scottish measure. According to the Fletts,[1] at one point in time the label Scotch measure was used to denote a distinct tune type. The tempo and character of historical Scotch measures, which also includes 'The White Cockade' and 'Highland Laddie,' are up to conjecture. By the late-eighteenth and early nineteenth centuries, this class of tunes comes to be labelled a double hornpipe, pointed to by Emmerson as the 'progenitor to those tunes we call hornpipes today.'[2] Alastair J. Hardie, in *The Caledonian Companion*, writes that Scotch measures are 'distinguished by a use of anacrusis and a stressing of the first three quavers of the bar and tempi can vary from a leisurely crotchet [quarter note] at 100–108 beats per minute (bpm) to a lively crotchet at *c.* 120 bpm.'[3] Hardie also notices that 'the rhythmic structure of the Scots measure often hints of the [duple-time] hornpipe of over a century later.'[4]

68   *From Hornpipes to High Dances*

What the term Scotch measure signifies is further complicated by statements made by William Stenhouse, who was the editor of James Johnson's *The Scots Musical Museum* after Johnson died around 1820. He assured his readers that, regarding 'Flowers of Edinburgh [...] The editor is creditably informed that the tune only became a fashionable Scottish Measure (a sort of hornpipe so called) about the year 1740.'[5] Stenhouse seems to use the terms Scottish measure and hornpipe in a musical sense, while other writers use Scottish/Scotch/Scots Measure to indicate a dance, as in 'to tread a measure.'[6] Further quoting Joan Flett's online paper on *Hornpipes in Scotland*:

> Charles Stewart [c. 1799–1801], who was musician to Mr. Strange, a well-known Edinburgh dancing master; gives a classification of the different types of hornpipe. He has a section of 'treeble hornpipes' all in common time, a section headed 'double hornpipes' which are in 9/8 time and 'single hornpipes' which are all in 6/4 time.[7] William Stenhouse in his *Illustrations* to the *Scots Musical Museum* noted 'The Dusty Miller.' 'This cheerful old air is inserted in Mrs. Crockat's Collection in 1709, and was, in former times, frequently played as a single, hornpipe in the dancing-schools of Scotland.' He later notes, 'These old tunes – Wee Totum Fogg – The Dusty Miller – Go to Berwick Johnnie – Mount your Baggage – Robin Shure in Har'est – Jocky said to Jenna, etc., etc., have been played in Scotland, time out of mind, as a particular species of 'the double hornpipe.'[8]

From a musical perspective, prior to the mid–eighteenth century, hornpipes or double hornpipes in England and Scotland were syncopated triple-time tunes in 3/2, 6/4, 3/4, or 12/8 time signatures. These tunes had regular four- and eight-bar phrases, usually subdivided into two-bar units. The peculiar jerky quality of the melodic line and the limping gait of the rhythm are due to frequent use of syncopation and an alternating of faster- and slower-moving rhythms.[9] For an example of music in this rhythm, see the 9/8 melody 'Go to Berwick, Johnnie' in the Appendix.

Hornpipe

We have seen the shift of labels moving from Scots measure to hornpipe. The etymology of the English term 'hornpipe' or 'hornpype,' according to Janis Pforsich, is:

> [...] Middle English and may be derived from the Saxon or Germanic word hoerner ('horn'). It was first used by the English, or Anglo-Saxons, to name the dance and its accompanying music. It is also the name of a particular style of rural shepherd's reed pipe, often crafted from animal horns, with a reed mouthpiece and an inflated skin bag. There are numerous regional names for the instrument. The Irish Gaelic word, used by

some traditional musicians, is *cornphíopa*, from the Latin for 'horn,' *cornu*. In Scotland's Lowlands the word is *stoc'n horn*. Some authorities give the Scots Gaelic term as *damhsa* (or *dannsadh*) *gradcharach* (literally, 'dance of the sudden whirls'), but this term is not used by dancers. Gaelic-speaking people have generally adopted the English word hornpipe to describe their dances and music of this type.[10]

Pforsich's translation of *grad[-]charach* does not agree with the definition given by Edward Dwelly's revered dictionary as 'nimble,' 'quick,' or 'agile.' Though all these adjectives could be appropriate adjectives to describe the footwork featured in a Hornpipe, turning does not seem to be indicated in Dwelly's definition. The word for Hornpipe given in Malcolm MacLennan's Gaelic dictionary is like the term given by Pforsich, *dannsa grad-charach*.[11]

The hornpipe as a tune category may have originated in the borderlands between Scotland and England.[12] The standard repertory of the Northumbrian smallpipes includes numerous triple-time hornpipes. Border songs and tunes of the triple-time character, such as 'Dusty Miller' and 'Go to Berwick Johnnie,' and nursery tunes such as 'Dance to Y'r Daddie' or 'Wee Totum Fogg,' illustrate the lighthearted and rhythmic character of the triple-time hornpipe. Henry Purcell's second-most frequent dance form is the triple-time hornpipe, which, as a result, is often referred to as the Purcellian hornpipe.

In the mid-eighteenth century, the common or duple-time hornpipe emerges. This class of hornpipes is now referred to as the 'Jacky Tar,' which is in 4/4 or 2/4 time. As Janis Pforsich elaborates:

> with staccato eighth-note runs punctuated by stresses on the second and third beats in a bar at regular intervals. This 'pom-pom' rhythm also ends the phrase, so in combination with the cadential point of arrival on the first beat, the phrase ends 'pom-pom-pom.' The 'College Hornpipe,' firmly embedded in the contemporary mind as the 'Sailor's Hornpipe,' is the quintessential example.[13]

However, both Scotch measures and hornpipes tend to end phrases with three accented beats as outlined above. An alternate way to distinguish between tune types sees a Scotch measure, such as the 'White Cockade' or the 'Flowers of Edinburgh,' as having an accent structure emphasising beats 1, 2, and 3 of each bar of music, while a hornpipe, including the 'College Hornpipe' mentioned above, emphasises beats 1, 3, and 4 through the phrase before it closes on the pom-pom-pom. The very personal experience of how to categorise rhythmic patterns in relation to musical notation seems open to some interpretation as we see later in this chapter. Regardless, these dance and tune types are closely related, historically.[14] For examples of music in these rhythms, see the Appendix.

Hornpipes gained popularity on the stage, with dancers embellishing the close stepping of the traditional form with technical prowess and characterisation. Emmerson's research[15] lists many historical performers of Hornpipes. Regardless of the time signature of the music danced to, often these dances were called Hornpipes. On playbills, Hornpipes often took the name of the person or character performing the dance on stage. Scottish-themed plays featuring Hornpipes and other dances labelled as Highland or Scotch became popular and were performed by both men and women. As Ballet grew in popularity in the British Isles, it influenced the form these dances took on stage, including the Hornpipes. The late-nineteenth and early twentieth centuries see this influence enduring in the form of the Sailor's Hornpipe competed at Highland Games. The pointed toes in the footwork and the '*ailes de pigeon*,' also known as highcuts, are inspired by Ballet. It is interesting to note that neither sailor nor other comic or character dances on stage were associated with the Hornpipe before 1740. One of the first occurrences was 'A Hornpipe in the Character of a Jacky Tar' billed at Drury Lane Theatre in London in May 1740. After this date, the association between the stereotypical British sailor 'Jacky Tar' and the Hornpipe dance becomes a regular feature of theatre playbills by the 1760s.

In Scotland, Step dances, such as the *Seann Triubhas*, were labelled 'Double Hornpipes' in eighteenth-century Scotland,[16] even though music associated with these dances today get labelled as either reels or rants, *e.g.* 4/4 or 2/4 tunes. The tune commonly associated with the *Seann Triubhas*, 'Whistle o'er the Lave o't,' is now characterised as either a rant or strathspey, both in 4/4 time. William H. Grattan Flood has noticed this same tune was also a seventeenth-century Irish air called 'Maggie Pickens.'[17]

The use of the word Hornpipe may sometimes indicate that the dance referred to is a solo dance. Emmerson explains that within Scottish Step dancing, the term Single Hornpipe was applied to dances and music of the triple-time signature, while Double Hornpipe meant Step dancing to a rant,[18] such as the duple-time 'Soldiers' Joy.' In fact, terms in use from the mid-eighteenth century, such as the now obscure High Dance and *Pas Seul*, were used alongside the term Hornpipe by dancing masters to identify solo dances.

The Sword Dance, also known as *Gille Chaluim*, gets labelled as a Hornpipe or a High Dance in different sources. Sir John Graham Dalyell, in his *Musical Memoirs of Scotland*, calls 'Ghille Challuim' a '*High Dance* or *pas seul*.'[19] Robert MacLagan, in unpublished notes for his 1901 book *Games and Diversions of Argyleshire*, labels both *Gille Caluim* and *Bonaid Ghorm*/Blue Bonnets as Hornpipes. Today we would not categorise title tunes for either of these dances as hornpipes.[20] In fact, the Fletts point out that while John MacTaggart's (1824) description of dancing masters includes them teaching the *Seann Triubhas*, Hornpipes, and the Highland Fling, that:

> The word 'hornpipe' here does not mean that the dances mentioned were all danced to tunes in hornpipe rhythm or that they were all of 'beetling' type. By 1820 the term 'High Dance' had dropped out of use and 'Hornpipe' was being used to denote a solo performance.[21]

Although Hornpipe begins to be used to denote a solo dance in southern areas at this time, High Dance continued to be widely used to categorise solo dances in other parts of Scotland through the nineteenth century, as we will present later in this chapter. Hornpipes were sometimes associated with dancers' names, such as Miss Gayton's Hornpipe, taught in Scotland by Joseph Wallace.[22] It should be noted that Miss Esther Jane Gayton was not a Scottish dancing student but rather was a professional dancer on the London stages in the early nineteenth century. Lord Byron referred to her in his 1808 poem 'English Bards and Scotch Reviewers,' as 'bound'ing before 'marquises' and 'dukes' at Drury Lane.[23]

Hornpipe stepping was not only a solo practice; it became incorporated in Country dances throughout the British Isles, although, similarly to the practice of treepling, it came to be considered vulgar in the more select assemblies.[24] The nineteenth-century *Lowes' Ball-Conductor* casts percussive stepping in the Country dances in a negative light in its advice to dancers:

> [...] there is more of a Gentleman's breeding observed in conducting his partner down a [Country] dance [...] than some seem to be aware of, and it would be well of if some Gentlemen would give a little more attention to their partner's mode of stepping, and not drag them along as if by force, whilst they themselves are capering, rattling, or shuffling their feet in the rudest manner. Such barbarism must be disgusting to every person accustomed to more cultivated conduct, and cannot please any but such as are equally rude with those who are guilty of it.[25]

Clearly, the Lowe brothers did not approve of this style of dancing. More detail will be given regarding their influence on Scottish dancing fashions in our compilation of references to dancing in the nineteenth century.

As a musical distinction, after about 1830, the term 'hornpipe' was regularly applied to common time 4/4 tunes. Prior to that, it was generally, though not exclusively, the case that a 'single hornpipe' was a tune in 3/2, 'double' was in 9/8 time, and 'treble' like a modern 4/4 hornpipe.[26] Today, when English musicians play 4/4 hornpipes for Clog dancing, they subdivide each bar into triplets rather than quavers and thus evoke a particular feel, or swing, in the music.

High Dance

High Dance as a term seems to have come into use initially to denote dances involving energetic, elevated steps, in contrast to the gliding steps of *Basse*, or low, Dances of the sixteenth century. This label came to be used regularly in Scotland to indicate a set of dance moves performed solo. The term High Dance may have been used by Scottish dancing masters in naming dance arrangements made for children of the Scottish gentry. The term is found with various names affixed to it, such as 'Miss Robertson's High Dance,'

72   *From Hornpipes to High Dances*

'Mr Keith's Favorite High Dance,' 'Miss Ann Cockburn's Fancy High Dance,' and 'Miss Honeyman of Armadale's High Dance' in music collections from the late-eighteenth and early nineteenth centuries.[27] In an advertisement helping to show what characterised High Dances from nearby Northumberland, dance master Mr Duncan Mac Gibbon performed several High Dances 'with great Dexterity' at a Ball in Hexham.[28] Coordination, agility, and intricacy seem indicated by the word 'dexterity.'

Edinburgh newspaper notices incorporating this term appeared in February 1745 for Monsieur Froment's Ball at Baillie Fife's Close in Edinburgh, which announced that 'several High Dances will be performed.'[29] Later in Edinburgh, in 1772, it was announced that Signora Marcoucci, of Italian extraction in name at least, would be teaching 'all manner of dancing' including 'high dances and country dance-steps.'[30]

An Aberdeen dancing master advertised a long and varied list of the dances he could teach in 1782: 'PLAIN, DOUBLE, and FIGURE minuets, the minute de la cour, the coupe and princess royals new minute, he likewise teaches great variety of Cotillons, hornpipes, and high dances, as also proper steps for dancing reels and country dances all in the most fashionable taste.'[31] Mr Fraser, teacher of dancing, was promoting his lessons to 'the nobility, gentry, and citizens of Aberdeen.' Hornpipes and High Dances were differentiated from each other in this list, though both terms may have referred to solo or performance dances.

In 1783 in Banff, Mr Isaac Cooper, 'Music Master,' declared he had spent time in Edinburgh the previous summer studying music and dance. He offered classes in such dances as the 'minuet de la Coer, the Prince of Wales Minuet, the Davonshire Minuet, and a variety of Cotillions and Allemandes, and several new high dances.'[32]

Mr Fraser, 'Teacher of Dancing,' announced to 'the Ladies and Gentlemen of Edinburgh, and neighbourhood,' that he has moved to 'A Large Room in the middle of Warriston's Close, Luckenbooths; [...] where he teaches the Minuets, High-Dances, and Hornpipes in the most fashionable and approved taste. The Cotillions being now the most fashionable Country-Dances in all polite assemblies.'[33] Though we are not certain that this was the same Mr Fraser previously teaching in Aberdeen in 1782, it is quite possible.

In Edinburgh, in 1795, James Scott taught 'The Minuet, High Dances, &c, &c. A variety of Steps for Country-dances, Strathpseys, and Cotilions.'[34] Later, in Edinburgh in 1817, Mr Moffat invited the public to his 'Ball on Thursday 3rd April in Dale's Room, 40, Prince's Street' where 'High Dances will be over by ten o'clock, when Public Dancing commences.'[35] In 1832, the following report of dancing in Inverkeithing in Fife appeared:

> Mr James Pollock, resident teacher of dancing at Leith, has been exercising his profession at this place with considerable success having, besides his large public school, been employed privately in several families of the most respectable country gentlemen of his vicinity. On the 21st ult. he

From Hornpipes to High Dances   73

concluded his labours for the season with a very fine Ball attended by upwards of 120 individuals, including his scholars. Dancing began with minuets, high dances, and hornpipes, to which succeeded quadrilles in French perfection, gallopades, German waltzes, including the beautiful attitudes and figures displayed in the semi-barbarous mazourkas, concluding with a variety of gymnastic exercises. The company present were highly pleased with the performances in general—but that chastened gracefulness which distinghuishes Mr Pollock's method of dancing was particularly admired, and his own unassuming and gentlemanly manners has secured him the good opinion of all classes in this quarter.[36]

We know that Aberdeenshire dancing masters in the 1840s used the term High Dance for solo dances of varied time signatures, including 3/2 hornpipes, 4/4 hornpipes, Scotch measures, and 6/8 jigs, because High Dance is used to identify the solo dances detailed in Frederick Hill's personal notebook.[37] Mr Ranald Macgregor, professor of dancing in the Strathspey region, closed his season's session at Cromdale with his pupils' Ball at Balmeanach on Monday 11 November 1850. 'The Highland fling, as danced by the young lads, and the high dances by the young girls were beautifully performed.'[38] In this instance, High Dances were associated with female performers.

A Mr M'Intosh also appeared in the Strathspey area in 1852, teaching music and dance in Grantown [on Spey], and his finishing Ball at Advie featured

> a succession of reels, strathspeys, country-dances, quadrilles, &c, which were performed with grace and elegance. Several of the females executed the high dances very creditably. The Reel of Tulloch was danced by four young ladies in fine style, and was particularly admired by the spectators, as were also the sword dance, Highland fling, &c., which were performed by some of the young men with true Highland spirit, fully supporting the ancient fame of Strathspey in the light fantastic art.[39]

'High dances' and 'step dances' were still featured in Brechin in 1871 in a description of Mr Fettes's class ball.[40] Whether the label used by the observer is Hornpipe or High Dance, one can generally understand that these terms refer to solo dances, to which additional explanations may hint at particular specifics or characteristics.

Pas Seul

Another label applied to solo Step dancing was the French term *Pas Seul*/solo step. *Pas Seul* may refer to a light, graceful style of presentation but does not rule out the possibility of a dance being percussive.

For example, in Montrose and Aberdeen dancing master Archibald Duff's publication *Choice Selection of Minuets; favourite airs, hornpipes and waltzes etc.*,

74 *From Hornpipes to High Dances*

published in Edinburgh in 1812, there are a number of arrangements of tunes which seem to have been devised to accompany dances that may also have been arranged by him for his pupils. Of these dances, most are in three parts, like *Pas Seul Miss Jane Forbes*, which was comprised of 'Pomposo' in 4/4, then 'Slow—Bonny Jean of Aberdeen,' and finally 'Presto—Speed the Plough.' Among other dances included we find *Miss Eliza Low's High Dance, Carleton House High Dance, Pas Seul danced by Miss Margaret Burnett of Leys*, and *Pas Seul danced by Miss Francis Urquhart*. These arrangements were usually made up by selections of reels, strathspeys, jigs, and airs in 2/4 and 9/8 time.

Dance master Robert Lowe's advertised assembly in Glasgow in 1830 featured *Pas Seuls*: 'every style of DANCING presently fashionable, including the MAZOURKA, as performed at the Court of St. Petersburgh, and also at London by Mons. GUYNEMER, which Mr. Lowe's Pupils will introduce, as they have been first in presenting every fashionable Dance to the inhabitants of Glasgow for some years past. Mr Lowe's Pupils will also, as usual, exhibit some of the higher exercises—Minuets, Gavottes, *Pas Seuls,* Pas de Deux, &c.'[41]

In the same year, 1830, Edinburgh dance master W. Smyth published *A Pocket Companion for Young Ladies and Gentlemen containing Directions for the performance of Quadrilles, Scotch, English, Irish, French, and Spanish Country Dances, Reels, &c, &c* in Edinburgh. In his introduction to the Quadrille section he states:

> It is now agreed upon by almost every person in the polite world, that there is no kind of Dancing so well fitted for Society as the Quadrille, wherein the pas seul, pas de deux, or Dancing by individuals and couples, are occasionally introduced; which admits of breathing time, and gives full opportunity for conversation, to those of the set who are disengaged [...] By means of the pas seul, &c, an anxious yet politely conducted contention for the palm of superiority, is kept up by the rival Dancers, which gives infinite interest to the whole. That these Dances may be well performed, it is necessary to accompany the music as closely as possible, and therefore a good musical ear is of greatest importance. The peculiar feature of Quadrille dancing is, smoothness and softness.[42]

These examples show that dancing masters used the term *Pas Seul* to describe a wide variety of solo stepping. It is quite plausible that the character of the stepping in these cases was of a softer nature, as both Lowe and Smyth were promoting smooth, refined dance fashions.

Reels and Rants

While we have looked at the overlap of musical and dancing terms related particularly to solo dancing, words relating to social dancing also migrate to denote time signatures. The word Reel has been used to describe travelling patterns of various forms in dances in Scotland since the sixteenth century.[43] Pathways of Reels may reflect the task of spooling rope or thread, portrayed by Alexander Ross in the phrase 'hae the yarn reel'd' in his song 'Woo'd and Married an A.'[44] The earliest portrayal of the Reel given by the Oxford English Dictionary (OED) is by Alexander Montgomerie's 1585 poem Flyting with Polwart depicted as 'raveld the reill,' with raveled indicating a confused tangling. Reels can occur in circular form, where dancers go single file around the same circle, or in other forms incorporating weaving patterns where dancers pass alternating shoulders, making a series of curves around each other. Often Reels involve a structure alternating between travelling and dancing on the spot.[45] This word has also evolved to refer to tune types in 2/4 or 4/4 time signature. The pattern of a Reel may be danced to music in hornpipe, rant, strathspey, jig, or reel time. Another feature of some Reels is a change in tempo, most often from strathspey to reel time. Like terms such as hornpipe or step, the word has been applied to a number of things resulting in overlapping meanings.

According to Mary Anne Alburger, the word rant, 'when used as a [tune] title, is almost always associated with the name of an individual or a group of men [...] Although the word comes from Old Dutch [*ranten*, meaning 'talk nonsense or rave'], there may be some overlapping meaning with the Gaelic, where *rann* means verse, and *ran* a melancholy cry.'[46] There may also be a possibility that the name could have been derived from the precursor to the Minuet, the Courant/*Courante*, which refers to running.

The OED gives a chiefly Scottish use for the word Rant as a lively dance tune and traces usage back to 1656. While the term Rant appears frequently in titles of contemporary Scottish Country dances, there is no specific step or definition differentiating Rants from Reels. A Rant step and dance type endure in Northumbrian dancing practices.

Terms outlined in this chapter show up occasionally in references to dancing included in the following four chapters. The terms Hornpipe and Reel, particularly, show up frequently in references to dancing in Scotland in the eighteenth century, where we are headed next.

Notes

1. Flett 1993.
2. Emmerson 1988: 122.
3. Hardie 2005: 24.
4. Hardie 2005: 24.
5. Stenhouse 1839 [*c*. 1820].
6. Flett 1993.
7. Historical Music of Scotland. http://www.hms.scot/fiddle/source/233/ [Accessed 20 March 2019].
8. Flett 1993.
9. Pforsich 2004: 376.
10. Pforsich 2004: 375.
11. MacLennan 1979 [1925]: 470.

12. Emmerson 1972: 206.
13. Pforsich 2004: 376.
14. Emmerson 1972: 157; 208–222.
15. Emmerson 1972.
16. Emmerson 1972: 206.
17. Grattan Flood 1927: 261.
18. Emmerson 1972: 207.
19. Dalyell 1849: 104.
20. Flett 1993.
21. Flett 1996: 8.
22. Flett 1993, 1996: 151.
23. Byron 1898: 347–348.
24. Pforsich 2004: 377.
25. Lowe 1831: 162–163.
26. Flett 1996: 11.
27. Flett 1993: 4.
28. *Newcastle Courant*, Saturday 27 April 1734.
29. *Caledonian Mercury,* Tuesday 12 February 1745.
30. *Caledonian Mercury*, Saturday 28 March 1772.
31. *Aberdeen Press and Journal*, Monday 14 January 1782.
32. *Aberdeen Press and Journal*, Monday 11 August 1783.
33. *Caledonian Mercury*, Monday 13 June 1785.
34. *Caledonian Mercury*, Saturday 26 December 1795.
35. *Caledonian Mercury*, Saturday 29 March 1817.
36. *Edinburgh Evening Courant*, Saturday 6 October 1832.
37. MacFadyen and MacPherson 2009: table of contents.
38. *Elgin Courant, and Morayshire Advertiser*, Friday 22 November 1850.
39. *Elgin Courant, and Morayshire Advertiser*, Friday 26 November 1852.
40. *Stonehaven Journal*, Thursday 23 March 1871.
41. *Glasgow Herald*, 17 December 1830.
42. Smyth 1830: 10–11.
43. Emmerson 1972: 151–152.
44. Ross 1778: 163.
45. Flett 1985: 133.
46. Alburger 1983: 217–218.

6 Hyland step forward

Eighteenth-century accounts

Eighteenth-century Scotland, experiencing social transformations and enlightenment

Eighteenth-century Scotland was in the middle of 'the Age of Transformation,' as prominent Scottish historian T.C. Smout labels the period spanning 1690–1830.[1] The country saw many fundamental changes, including England's absorption of Scotland's parliamentary identity through the Act of Union in 1707. Scotland experienced upheaval in the two failed Jacobite risings in 1715 and 1745–1746, and, in the aftermath, faced repercussions towards Highland culture resonating to this day. Increased contact with Europe and England influenced shifts away from older kinship-based clan systems and dramatic changes in land ownership across the country. The period cemented the 'change in character of the Lowland landowner from that of a military magnate with strong feudal loyalties and antipathies to that of a peaceful member of the British landed classes.'[2] Furthermore, the end of the American War of Independence in 1783 coincided with the 'astounding expansion of the cotton industry based on applications in several different parts of Scotland of the new factory technology of Lancashire,'[3] that heralded a departure from past economic structures. The industrial sector grew quickly.

The century saw migration that pulled the traditional fabric of Scottish society in several directions. About twenty percent of the population spoke Gaelic, dialects of Scots were widely used, and English was beginning to become more commonplace. Standard English was the language of religion, education, and government, and it became a socially prestigious jargon adopted by upwardly mobile middle classes. It was a time of migration, with Gaelic-speaking Highlanders moving to the Lowlands and growing urban centres in the central belt; others began emigrating to North America and other emerging colonies. Smout summarises the social groups in action during the century in this way:

> The landowners, who in the Lowlands stood at the head of society when the great agrarian changes were made, and the farmers and peasants who followed or assisted them when these changes came about; the Highlanders, whose world was shattered and changed by political as well

as by economic factors; the middle classes of the towns, who provided so many of the merchants, entrepreneurs and inventors of the first phase of the industrial revolution; and […] the emergent class of industrial workers who formed the first true industrial proletariat in society.[4]

Division of wealth deepened between landowners and merchants and those who had next to nothing. Furthermore, Scottish education entered a golden age in the late eighteenth century, while, according to Smout, it was equally a golden age of Scottish cultural achievement.[5] In the latter category, Scots excelled particularly in painting, architecture, poetry, and novels. Robert Burns, Sir Walter Scott, James Boswell, Allan Ramsay, James Hogg, and John Galt are examples of prominent Scottish writers from this time.

The eighteenth century was the era of the Scottish Enlightenment, characterised by an outpouring of intellectual and scientific accomplishments, effects of which spread far beyond Scotland's borders. Within Scotland, the Enlightenment was characterised by a comprehensive empiricism and practicality, where the chief values were improvement, virtue, and practical benefit for the individual and society as a whole. As Smout, again, concludes:

> The golden age of Scottish culture was achieved largely by the Lowland middle-class with the approval and patronage (but not the initiative) of the landed classes, against a complex background of historical change— of economic change enabling Scotland better to afford her culture, of educational change in her universities and schools, and of psychological change in the attitude of society towards its own aspirations.[6]

Dance in Scotland comprised various forms existing in parallel to each another and spanning social, linguistic, and religious borders. In the Highlands and Islands, the social dances of the time documented by the Fletts and Rhodes were mainly Reels and Dramatic Jigs.[7] The growing, largely urbanised middle class and landed gentry were engaged in attending public assemblies, appearing first in Edinburgh and then spreading to other burghs and towns. Public halls and house parties became familiar events in the principal burghs until, by the 1770s, it was possible for Topham to say that, 'I do not know any place in the world where dancing is made so necessary a part of polite education as in Edinburgh.'[8]

Dances featured at assemblies were Minuets, Country Dances, and Reels. The square Set dance, the *Cotillon*, arrived in Edinburgh after 1780, but 'was never more than a novelty in Scotland,' according to Emmerson.[9] Edward Topham named the Reel as the Scots' favourite dance in 1775.[10] The Minuet was Aberdeen dancing master Francis Peacock's favourite dance, by his own account. By the mid-1780s, Minuets had disappeared from the Edinburgh assemblies.[11] The latter half of the century seems to have offered fertile ground for the numerous dancing masters and dancing teachers that emerged throughout the burgh.[12]

Notably, Emmerson points out that there was a severe decline in attendance of the Edinburgh Assembly Rooms in 1783 that did not pick up again until 1798.[13] This dip coincides with the 'Laki haze' as it is known across Europe. This sulphurous haze followed a massive volcanic eruption in Iceland and reportedly caused thousands of deaths in Europe throughout 1783 and the winter of 1784. This catastrophe also may have been a contributing factor in triggering the French Revolution in 1789, through failed harvests, and increasing poverty and famine.[14] The Laki eruption triggered weather pattern changes in North America, and the following years saw severe winter conditions and storms in Scotland. Milder weather returned in 1789. Such a seismic event, affecting all aspects of life in Scotland, in the direct path of ash fall from the eruption, must have influenced the dance and music cultural practices included in Emmerson's research.

The dancing master profession emerges, and many names of dance teachers are listed in census records. The profession grew in importance and social standing over time. Around the middle of the century in Edinburgh were dance masters by the names of MacQueen and Downie, alongside Frenchmen Pierre Lamotte and Antoine LePicq. Later on, dance masters by the names of Martin and Barnard were teaching, and even the famous James Harvey d'Egville from England and Italian Giovanni-Andrea, later Sir John Andrew Gallini came to Scotland to teach dancing. David Strange, who taught in both Ayrshire and Edinburgh between 1760 and 1788, had studied dancing with some famous figures: Signor Gallini in London; Maltere, who taught the French royal family, in Paris; and a member of the celebrated Vestris[15] dancing family.[16] D'Egville, who had been at the King's Theatre in London, advertised classes in 'Scotch Reels, Highland Flings and all Caledonian steps' in both Edinburgh and Glasgow.[17] Both Johnny McGill and James Gregg taught dancing in Ayrshire before 1761. In Aberdeen were A. Duff, who published *Country Dancing made plain and easy* in 1764, and Francis Peacock, who died in 1807. Archibald Duff, born *circa* 1770 possibly in Aberdeen, taught dancing and music in Montrose, and later taught dance in Aberdeen after Peacock's death. John Lowe, born in Kincardineshire in about 1765 was a dancing master, violinist, and composer at Marykirk.

Now that we have a sense of the Scotland of this century, we will list historical accounts mentioning percussive footwork and pertinent dancing practices.

Charlotte Brereton, Epistle from Scotland, 1742

Raised in Wrexham in Wales, Charlotte Brereton served as a governess for a well-to-do Scottish family. She wrote poems for the *Gentleman's Magazine*. A poem written in the form of a letter from Scotland describes an average day in the life of her occupation, including the following lines:

> Or if gaily disposed, we dance a Scotch Reel
> In which how you'd stare at each nimble heel.[18]

80   *Hyland step forward*

Dancing in the Reel required fancy footwork and skilful ability. Singling out heel work is notable from a percussive perspective. As described earlier, the calcaneus is a single bone, and contact of the heel with any given surface creates a more sudden, punctuated sound than the forefoot tends to make. Since the heels are nimble here, they are moving quickly and adroitly, as the word connotes speed and rhythmic flexibility.

The rhythmic metre for this couplet is set up by a series of anapaests and iambs creating a 6/8 rhythm. The lines reflect dance music structure, as if the couplet reflects four bars of music. Although the Reel is the dance mentioned, the author portrays a rhythm we categorise as a jig today.

Mr John McGill, dancing master, Girvan, Ayrshire, 1752

A frequent contributor to the *Notes and Queries* publication, 'a certain W.J. which [the Fletts] believe to be William Jerdan of Dunse,'[19] shared a glimpse of Step dance terminology used in 1752:

> the dancing master of a southern Scottish town wrote out manuscript instructions for his pupils, of whom my father was one: and a copy is now before me which may suggest some musical and other minor matters relating to the amusements of our progenitors, curious enough for a notice in 'N.&Q.' It is entitled 'The Dancing Steps of a Hornpipe and Gigg.' As also Twelve of the Newest Country Dances, as they are performed at the Assemblies and Balls. All Sett by Mr. John M'gill for the use of his school, 1752. [...] I do not know that the dancing instructions for sixteen steps in the hornpipe, and fourteen in the gigg, would be very intelligible now-a-days; seeing that in the former, the second, third and fourth steps are 'slips and shuffle forwards,' 'spleet and floorish (?florish) backwards,' 'Hyland step forwards,' and there are elsewhere directions to 'heel and toe forwards,' 'single and double round step,' 'slaps across forward,' 'twist round backwards,' 'cross strocks aside and sink forward' 'short shifts,' 'back hops,' and finally, 'happ forward and backward' to conclude the gigg with éclat.[20]

Arguably, the terminology is not conclusive evidence that these steps were decidedly percussive, but 'shuffle,' 'slaps,' and 'heel and toe' all connote some level of sound generation and fancy footwork. Emmerson, in his article on *The Hornpipe* from 1970, asserts that the dancing master concerned 'was undoubtedly the celebrated Girvan fiddler Johnnie McGill.'[21]

A manuscript, now held in the RSCDS Archives in Edinburgh,[22] likely dates from around the same time, if indeed it is not the actual manuscript referred to in *Notes and Queries*. It was given to that organisation in the mid-1970s after a clear-out of a solicitor's office in Dumfries. A few spelling differences occur in the handwritten document from the typeset account in *Notes*

Hyland step forward 81

Hornpipe

1 _Slip and bait Round_
2 _Three Slips and Shuffle forward_
3 _Split and Florish backward_
4 _Hyland Step forward_
5 _Florish and Shuffle backward_
6 _Hop off forward_
7 _The Slow Back Step backward_
8 _Three Steps aside and Shuffle forward_
9 _Duble Back Step backward_
10 _Heel and Toe forward_
11 _Flird and Bait backward_
12 _Single and Double Round Step_
13 _Flird aside forward_
14 _Single and Double Flirds backward_
15 _Slipaside forward_
16 _Twist Round Backward and Shuffle forward_

Figure 6.1 McGill's Hornpipe Steps, 1752

and Queries above. The manuscripts for the Hornpipe (Figure 6.1) and Gige (Figure 6.2) entries are typed here for clarity.

Alexander Ross, 1768

Alexander Ross was born in 1699 in Aberdeenshire. His family were farmers, but he went on to work as a tutor, and later took a position as a headmaster in Lochlee, Angus. His long poem in Scots titled _Helenore, or the Fortunate Shepherdess_, first published in 1768, includes a scene at a wedding where one of the party 'knack'd his thumbs and sang.' After that, some dancing is described:

> ... the dancing neist began,
> And thro' and thro' they lap, they flang, they ran:
> The country dances and the country reels,
> With streecked arms bobb'd round, and nimble heels.[23]

Gige

1 *Two hops aside and Sink forward*

2 *Split and Sink backward*

3 *Hyland Step forward*

4 *Single and Duble step backward*

5 *Cross Strocks aside and Sink forward*

6 *Duble step backward*

7 *Short Strocks forward*

8 *Back hop backward*

9 *Trips aside forward*

10 *Back Twist Backward*

11 *Flird forward*

12 *Duble baits aside backward*

13 *Short Steps round*

14 *Single hops up and down the floor with a florish*

_____ *at the foot* _____

Figure 6.2 McGill's Gige Steps, 1752

Again, heels provide a convenient rhyme with reels, and are notable features of the dancing. Heels are described as nimble again, forming a convention used to signify or typify Scottish dancing. The rhythm created by iambic pentameter in this poem reflects simple metre.

Another song attributed to Ross shows even more boisterous dancing. 'The Bridal O't' was written to the tune of 'Lady Lucy Ramsay,' and the song ends describing dancing:

> For dancing they gae to the green,
> And aiblins to the beatin o't:
> He dances best that dances fast,
> And loups at ilka reesing o't,
> And claps his hands frae hough to hough,
> And furls about the feezings o't.[24]

Highlighted here are the sounds of clapping and encouragement for the boisterous birling, jumping, and beating. As the words lean towards alliteration of the letters 'h' and 'f,' the singer would mimic a breathlessness that would be brought on by such exercise.

Robert Fergusson, Edinburgh, 1772

The Edinburgh poet Robert Fergusson (1750–1774) also drew special attention to heels in one stanza of his poem 'The Daft Days,' about the Christmas holiday season:

> For nought can cheer the heart sae weel
> As can a canty Highland reel;
> It even vivifies the heel
> To skip and dance:
> Lifeless is he wha canna feel
> Its influence.[25]

Attention focused on the heels of a dancer again suggests fancy footwork, a component of Step dancing. The 'eel' rhyme gets extended in this poem, with reel and heel further rhymed with *weel*/well and feel. This stanza evokes an ongoing, repetitive rhythm of iambs, reflecting the simple metre categorised as reel time today. The first two lines reflect four bars of reel-time music. The rhythm gets interrupted near the end in the shorter lines with just two iambs each, reflecting forced pauses where the subject becomes more philosophical. In this poem, the heel is 'vivified,' brought to life, specifically by the canty, Scots for cheerful and invigorating, music associated with the Highlands.

Boswell and Johnson in the Hebrides, 1773

James Boswell (1740–1795) was a Scottish biographer and diarist born in Edinburgh. He is best known for his 1786 biography of the English literary figure Samuel Johnson, who was born in Lichfield, Staffordshire in 1709 and died in 1784. On 6 August 1773, 11 years after first meeting Boswell, Johnson set out to visit his friend in Scotland. Johnson's account of the trip, *A Journey to the Western Islands of Scotland*, portrayed social problems and struggles that affected the Scottish people, and celebrated many unique facets of Scottish society.

Descriptions of dancing are found in Johnson's book and in Boswell's *Journal of a Tour to the Hebrides*. On Wednesday, 8 September 1773, Boswell described an evening of dancing where he and Johnson were entertained by *Macgillichallum*, the MacLeod Laird of Raasay, off the Skye coast, after having just arrived by boat.

> It was past six o'clock when we arrived. [...] Soon afterwards a fiddler appeared, and a little ball began. Rasay himself danced with as much spirit as any man, and Malcolm bounded like a roe. Sandie Macleod [...] made much jovial noise.[26]

This dancing party was a raucous, noisy event. Samuel Johnson described the same occasion: 'the carpet was then rolled off the floor; the musician was called, and the whole company was invited to dance, nor did ever fairies trip with greater alacrity.'[27]

Two days later, Boswell attended another evening dance despite a day of strenuous exercise:

> Though we had passed over not less than four-and-twenty miles of very rugged ground, and had a Highland dance on the top of Dun Can, the highest mountain on the island, we returned in the evening not at all fatigued, and piqued ourselves at not being outdone at the nightly ball by our less active friends, who had remained at home.'[28]

Figure 6.3 shows a caricature of Boswell and Mr Malcolm M'Cleod dancing a jig on a hilltop.

Figure 6.3 The Dance on Dun-Can, Thomas Rowlandson. Picturesque Beauties of Boswell, Part the Second, 1786

Source: In public domain through Open Access. Original in the Metropolitan Museum, NY.

Regarding local dancing practices, Boswell noted that 'they dance here every night. [...] There seemed to be no jealousy, no discontent among them; and the gaiety of the scene was such, that I for a moment doubted whether unhappiness had any place in Rasay.'[29]

Mr Boswell and Johnson continued their travels through the Hebrides. On Saturday, 2 October 1773, having returned to Skye, they met Mr James M'Donald, factor to Sir Alexander M'Donald of Sleat, who invited the two travellers to Sir Alexander's house at Armadale. Boswell wrote:

> In the evening the company danced as usual. We performed, with much activity, a dance which, I suppose, the emigration from Sky has occasioned. They call it 'America.' Each of the couples, after the common involutions and evolutions, successively whirls round in a circle, till all are in motion; and the dance seems intended to shew how emigration catches, till a whole neighbourhood is set afloat. [...] We danced to night to the musick of the bagpipe, which made us beat the ground with prodigious force.'[30]

Boswell's phrase 'made us beat the ground' may suggest that the rowdy, lively dancing happened outside. He credits the bagpipe accompaniment as the influence inspiring stronger beating than usual. According to Boswell, culture in Skye was permeated with music and dancing.

Edward Topham, Edinburgh, 1774–1775

Englishman Major Edward Topham (1751–1820), born in York, was a journalist and playwright. Sometime after 1769 he travelled the continent for 18 months before spending six months in Scotland (1774–1775) with his former schoolfellow Sir Paul Jodrell.[31] In 1776, he published observations from this visit in *Letters from Edinburgh, 1774 and 1775, containing some Observations on the Diversions, Customs, Manners, and Laws of the Scotch Nation.*[32]

Topham's descriptions are continuously critical, opinionated, and frequently derogatory regarding how Scots danced, and compare Scottish dancers to English, French, Spanish, and Swiss dancers he had previously observed. Occasionally he expresses some level of admiration for their dancing skills. He begins by saying 'if you have been informed the Scotch dance well, I beg that you will retain your favourable opinion of them, without asking mine; for, on this point, I am by no means partial to them.'[33] In Letter XXXIII from Edinburgh, labelled 'On the Scotch Dances,' he writes:

> The dances of this country are entirely void of grace; which appears to me to be the first principle, unless we consider it, as the Savages do, merely as an exercise. [...] The general dance here it is a Reel, which requires that particular sort of step to dance properly, of which none but people of the country can have any idea. All the English whom I have seen attempt it, were very deficient in their imitations; and though the

86 *Hyland step forward*

Scotch were too polite to laugh at them, they saw and felt the ridicule of grown gentleman learning to dance.

[…] The Scotch admire the Reel for its own merit alone, and may truly be said to dance for the sake of dancing. I have often sat a very wearied spectator of one of these dances, in which not one graceful movement is seen, the same invariably, is continued for hours. How different is this from the Allemande! A Scotchman comes into an assembly room as he would into a field of exercise, dances till he is literally tired, possibly without ever looking at his partner, or almost knowing who he dances with. In most countries the men have a partiality for dancing with a woman; but here I have frequently seen four gentlemen perform one of these Reels seemingly with the same pleasure and perseverance as they would have done, had they had the most sprightly girl up for a partner. The Reel is the only thing which gives them pleasure: if the figure is formed, it appears, no matter with what; and they give you the idea, that they could, with equal glee, cast off round a joint stool, or set to a corner cupboard. […] Another of the National dances is a kind of quick minuet, or what the Scotch call a *Straspae*. We in England are said to walk a minuet: this is galloping our minuet. […] In this [minuet] of the Scotch, however, every idea of grace seems inverted, and the whole is a burlesque: nothing of the minuet is preserved, except to figure; the step and the time most resemble an hornpipe—and I leave you to dwell upon the picture of a gentleman full-dressed, and a lady in an hoop, lappets, and every other incumbrance of ornament, dancing an hornpipe before a large assembly.[34]

Topham reveals that he is familiar with the fashionable dancing of the times when he contrasts the Reel dancing of the Edinburgh assembly with the Allemande and the Strathspey with the Minuet. His description portrays Scottish dancing as fast and boisterous compared to fashionable dancing. The word 'galloping' evokes the rhythmic sound making of a horse's gait. That men can dance a Reel together, without having female partners, is to him a foreign concept.

The dancing of Reels and further allusions to Hornpipe steps are mentioned in Letter XLII, 'On the Assemblies public and private':

Besides minuets and country dances, they in general dance reels in separate parts of the room; which is a dance that every one is acquainted with, but none but a native of Scotland can execute in perfection. Their great agility, vivacity, and a variety of hornpipe steps, render it to them a most entertaining dance; but to a stranger, this sameness of the figure makes it trifling and insipid, though you are employed during the whole time of its operation; which, indeed, is to reason why it is so peculiarly adapted to the Scotch, who are little acquainted with the attitude of standing still.

Hyland step forward   87

> Allemands and Cotillons are neither admired nor known in public companies in this city. Those ladies who have seen them danced in Paris or London are under willing to introduce them, well knowing how little calculated they are for the meridian of their country.[35]

That Topham seems to get bored with the 'sameness' of the figures danced in the Reel helps us identify the repeating pattern of reeling, a travelling figure alternating with dancing in place, comprises this dance, though it is not clear if travelling was in a circle or a figure of eight pattern. We can also infer that dancing occurred through the entirety of the figure, not only while staying in place but also during the travelling, since his comments describe dancers 'employed during the whole time of its operation' as the Scots are 'little acquainted' with standing still.

From a percussive dance point of view, his comments relating to steps he observes in the Reels are of great interest. He compares them to Hornpipe dancing, with which he seems quite familiar. In Topham's Letter XLI, written after having attended one of the numerous dancing masters' finishing balls in Edinburgh, he remarks on what he, or possibly the dancing master, calls High Dances:

> At these balls the children dance minuets, which would be very tiresome and disagreeable, as well from the badness of the performance as from the length of time they would take up, were they regularly continued, but the dancing-masters enliven the entertainment by introducing between the minuets their high dances (which is a kind of double hornpipe) in the execution of which they excel perhaps the rest of the world. I wish I had it in my power to describe to you the variety of figures and steps they put into it. Besides all those common to the hornpipe, they have a number of their own which I never before saw or heard of; and their neatness and quickness in the performance of them is incredible; so amazing is their agility, that an Irishman, who was standing by me the other night, could not help exclaiming in his surprise 'that by Jesus he never saw children so handy with their feet in all his life.'
>
> The motion of the feet is indeed the only thing that is considered in these dances as they rather neglect than pay any attention to the other parts of the body; which is a great pity, since it would render the dance much more complete and agreeable, were the attitudes of the hands and positions of the body more studied and understood by them. From the practice of these high dances, one great advantage is derived to the young men, in giving prodigious powers to their ankle and legs; but I cannot say it is an ornamental advantage either to them or to the ladies; as it makes them too large in those parts for the proportion of the rest of the body, and takes off that fine tapering form which is so essential to real beauty.[36]

Can we detect a change in Topham's opinion on Scottish dancing, having become more accustomed to it over time? Topham confidently declares that

88 *Hyland step forward*

these 'high dances' resemble what he calls a 'double hornpipe' and that the dancers have a wide variety of steps at their disposal. Improvisation of steps might be inferred here, given the striking originality of steps 'never before saw or heard of.'

As the Fletts point out, it is 'quite likely that at least some of step dancing still known today was derived from stage dancing of the late seventeenth and eighteenth centuries.'[37] In 1802, Irishman John Harden observed a dancing school in Bowness, in Cumbria, a county in Northwest England adjacent to Scotland, where he noted 'the rasp of dancing school fiddle and the clatter of the sturdy footed youth,' words which indicate percussive Step dancing in action.[38] Topham observes that the Scots have steps he is not familiar with, but that are of similar style to something he has observed. They appear quick and neat. There is little upper body or arm movement and the emphasis is placed predominantly on footwork. Can we infer that, when he observes a lack of 'attitudes of the hands and positions of the body more studied and understood' and that 'they rather neglect than pay any attention to the other parts of the body,' perhaps dancers maintained an upright posture with hands held loosely by the sides? If so, that would suggest that the posture so common among various Step dance styles today was also common back in the late eighteenth century.

That solo dances from rural and Highland areas found their ways into urban dancing masters' schools, and also into Lowland assembly rooms in Edinburgh, has been detailed by both Emmerson and the Fletts.[39] A detail to note in Topham's remarks, however, is that these High Dances were so highly evolved, that he, and other contemporary English observers, such as James Hall and Thomas Garnett, compared them to the English dancing they knew.[40] Indeed, Garnett recalled his visit to a dancing master's ball, featuring Niel Gow playing fiddle, at an Inn in Dunkeld in early August 1798:

> In the evening there was a dancing-school ball in the inn, to which we were politely invited, and where we had the again an opportunity of hearing Neil Gow, and observing the superiority of the highlanders to our countrymen in dancing; some of the children whom we saw dancing this evening, would have cut no disgraceful figure on the stage.[41]

The *Caledonian Mercury* 26 December 1795 newspaper advertised dancing classes in Edinburgh run by James Scott, which invited 'Ladies and Gentlemen to be taught at their own lodgings The Minuet, High Dances, &c, &c and a variety of steps for Country-dances, Strathspeys, and Cotilions.' Just a year earlier, on 22 November 1794, the *Dublin Evening Post* advertised Mr Dempsy's classes, having 'returned from Scotland [...] most fashionable Reels and Highland Strathspeys, as performed in Edinburgh and London.' He also taught the Minuet and the Cotillion 'if required.' In fact, Williamson's *Directory for the City of Edinburgh, Canongate, Leith, and Suburbs* from 1774–1775 lists the following dancing masters, without giving details of what they taught:

Boswell, David, dancing-master, Broad Wynd, Leith
Fraser, William, dancing-master, Royal Arch Lodge
Le Picq (Pique), Antoine, dancing-master, Skinner's Close
M'Donald, James, dancing-master, Blackfriars Wynd
Middlemist, Robert, dancing-master, Carrubber's Close
Sealey, Joseph, teaches dancing, Foulis's Close
Strange, David, teaches dancing, Toderick's Wynd

Emmerson describes that, in the eighteenth century, English stages featured many dances with Scottish themes or names. These *entr'actes* of the London theatres from the beginning of the 1700s onwards are assumed to have been creations of professional stage dancers of the time.[42] Even though created for the stage, can we also assume that that they were derived from or inspired in part by traditional High Dances? Or, were they created with some stereotypical ideas of what names such as Scotch Measure, Lilt, and Reel, and, later, Strathspey and Fling, were supposed to look like? Giovanni-Andrea Gallini[43] in his 1722 *Treatise on the Art of Dancing* suggests borrowing Scottish dance, music and costume ideas for theatrical performance. After referring to the Scotch Reel as danced by the 'Highlanders in North-Britain,' he writes that:

[…] nothing can be imagined more agreeable, or more lively and brilliant, than the steps in many of the Scotch dances. There is a great variety of very natural and very pleasing ones. And a composer of comic dances, might, with great advantage to himself, upon judicious assemblage of such steps as he might pick out of their dances, form a dance that, with well adapted dresses, correspondent music, and figures capable of a just performance, could hardly fail of a great success upon the theatre.[44]

Famed Aberdeen dancing master Francis Peacock commented '[t]his dance [the Reel], indeed, admits of so great a variety of natural and brilliant steps, as seldom fail to please.'[45] Despite that, these *entr'acte* song and dance interludes fell out of favour during the nineteenth century.

Topham reports little-to-no arm movements by writing that 'they rather neglect than pay any attention to the other parts of the body,' while performing intricate footwork resembling a 'double hornpipe.' This observation may reflect unmet expectations: subtle arm movements suitable for dancing in a crowded room may have looked small in comparison to the theatrical and caricatured percussive Hornpipes in use on English stages. Stage Hornpipe footwork is presumed to be closely related to the traditional Hornpipe dancing of the late eighteenth and early nineteenth centuries. Emmerson, in his

90 *Hyland step forward*

1970 article on the *Hornpipe* points out the popularity of the Hornpipe on the stages:

> Sailors' dances were familiar among numerous other character or comic dances on the 18th-century stage; but the practice of distinguishing hornpipes seems to suggest that these 'Sailors' Dances' were not necessarily hornpipes [tune type]. [... For example] at Covent Garden, April 1755, we notice 'in the sailors' dance by desire will be introduced a hornpipe by Poitier.' Poitier, whose son and daughter also danced, was French. [...] Again, at Covent Garden (May 1765) we find—'A new hornpipe by Miss Snow in character of a sailor,' which was repeated once or twice, and then disappears from the bills. Meantime hornpipes—with no allusion to sailors—are billed with somewhat increasing regularity.[46]

What are labelled as Hornpipes in these stage playbills may not necessarily have been danced to what we now refer to as a common-time 'hornpipe' tunes but may have been danced to jigs, Scotch measures, or triple-time hornpipes in 3/2, 6/4, or 9/8 time, as presented in Chapter 5. These 'hornpipes' were regular fare in Scottish dance schools of the eighteenth century, alongside the Highland Reel and, in the urban centres of fashion, the Minuet, according to Emmerson.[47]

> 'Stepping' in social dancing was certainly familiar in the Scottish West and Lowlands in the late 18th and in the 19th centuries. Indeed, hornpipe 'stepping' was familiarly employed in Country Dances wherever these were enjoyed in the British Isles, although it was regarded as vulgar in the more select assemblies. [...] In every community in which 'stepping' was enjoyed there were occasions for the solo dancer to exhibit his prowess [...]. Improvisation was a feature of every good exponent's performance, but most of the steps were pre-conceived and were identified by names [...].[48]
>
> The theatrical dancer was not likely to be content to limit himself to the close stepping of the traditional hornpipe dancer, and we must not be surprised, therefore if the theatrical hornpipe grew to embrace the embellishing contributions of trained dancers. Sir John Gallini writes in 1772 [...] that dancers from France and Italy studied hornpipe dancing in England and introduced it to continental audiences with great success [...].[49]

Step dancing similar to what Topham portrayed in a demeaning tone thus came to be popular in those places, setting the fashions he contrasted to Scottish dancing.

Thomas Thornton, Dalmally, North Argyll, 1786

Englishman Colonel Thomas Thornton (1747 or 1750–1823 in Paris, France) was a contemporary of Topham. He became an ardent sportsman and during his tour of the northern and western Scottish Highlands in 1786 he engaged in hunting, shooting, fishing, and hawking.[50] During the tour Thornton describes in his book *A Sporting Tour through the Northern Parts of England and Great Part of the Highlands of Scotland,* published in London in 1804, he attended a dancing master's ball held at the Dalmally Inn on 9 October 1786, in clan Campbell's North Argyll, where he was staying at the time:

Dalmally

Here we found a most excellent inn: indeed, much superior to what it was when I was last here, though I then thought it a very good one, and passed in it some pleasant days, rendered additionally so, by the party I was then with giving a ball, which was the first time I had seen Highland Dancing.

While supper was getting ready, having heard the sound of music, and understanding it was a dancing-master's ball, in consequence of the harvest-home, I made the landlord introduce us to him. So goodly a scene, and so motly a set, exceeded anything I had before met with. They were dancing a country-dance when we entered.

The company consisted of about fourteen couple, who all danced the true *Glen Orgue kick.* I have observed that every district of the Highlands has some peculiar cut; and they all shuffle in such a manner as to make the noise of their feet keep exact time. Though this is not the fashionable style of dancing, yet, with such dancers, it had not a bad effect.

But I shall never forget the arrogance of the master; his mode of marshalling his troops, his directions, and other manoeuvres were truly ridiculous; he felt himself greater than any adjutant disciplining his men, and managed them much in the same manner.

The scholars having done, sat down, when, from the closeness of the room, and the great *pains* they had taken to warm themselves, though, no doubt, greatly fatigued before with the hard labour of the day, we were very desirous of retiring as expeditiously as possible, requesting their acceptance of some whiskey-punch to drink their landlord's health, Lord Breadalbane, but were not permitted, till we had seen a specimen of the master's talents, who was requested to dance a hornpipe.

After having made several apologies for his want of pumps, &c. *pour les forms,* he ordered his fiddler, in a very dictatorial style, to play his favourite tune, and from a shelf, tumbled down a pair of Highland brogues, in which he soon stood on the floor and began his essay.

The eyes of the scholars were all upon him, and, at every extraordinary exertion they showed signs of their perfect approbation, by loud plaudits: and, if he did not dance the correct taste of Vestris, he at least cut some capers which that self-conceited performer would have found it difficult to imitate.

From the causes already mentioned, which by no means subsided, but rather increased, we were heartily glad when he had finished. But it gave

92   *Hyland step forward*

me great pleasure to see these poor people as innocently amused, and to observe with what spirit they danced, after the fatigues of the day, which evidently proved the strong inclination the Highlanders have for this favourite amusement. How much more rational is this conduct than that of our labourers in England, who, in their way, would be intoxicated and riotous? We sat down to a plentiful, neatly-served supper, and having tasted nothing since breakfast, devoured all before us.[51]

The remark that this is not the 'fashionable style' of dancing marks an emerging divide where some styles of dancing begin to be seen as high-class and fashionable, or viewed as rustic and lower-class. Even though Clog dancing continues to be presented on urban stages after this date, a shift away from emphasising the percussive soundscape and towards favouring visual effects begins.

Thornton shared important observations. First of all, he called the dancing he sees 'Highland dancing,' the same label Boswell uses for the dance he enjoyed with M'Cleod on Dun Can, and an early use of this specific term. Then Thornton described manners he has come to associate with dancing masters directing their Finishing Balls; he clearly does not approve of the dancing masters' uppity 'airs.' If Thornton knew of the term 'high dance,' he did not use it here. Why did Thornton point out the dancing master's excuses for not wearing dancing 'pumps?' Did the dance master feel that, in the presence of an Englishman, he needed an excuse to explain why he danced in Highland brogues, rather than in fashionable assembly room pumps? This incident, where the dancing pumps cannot be located, is curious. The dancing master almost seemed to require an excuse to wear Highland brogues for dancing instead of soft shoes.

The 'loud plaudits' suggest that the local crowd was accustomed to cheering on dancers. Thornton points out that the audience is appreciative and knowledgeable in watching skilled dancing in action. While observing dance is a spectator sport, this audience of 'scholars' takes an active role in watching, listening, and thinking about the dancing. This may contrast with the more distant, passively observed, proscenium stage dances of London and Paris. In Dalmally, a dialogue occurs between dancers and observers. The dancing garners sharp observation to detail, and elicits responses when it succeeds.

The assessment of the dancing master's solo Hornpipe exhibition by Thornton is critical, but betrays some admiration as well. Comparing this dancing master to Auguste Vestris was praise indeed. Auguste Vestris (1760–1842) was a celebrated French dancer, dubbed '*le dieu de la danse*'/the god of dance, a popular title bestowed on the leading male solo dancer of each generation at the *Paris Opéra*. Vestris later trained both August Bournonville and Marie Taglioni.

The identity of the unnamed dancing master is a mystery. The only music and dancing teachers recorded as teaching in the vicinity of Argyllshire in the first centralised Scottish Census of 1841 are Duncan Mackay from Campbeltown, born in 1781 and listed as a Teacher of Dancing, and John Downie from Kilmartin, born in the same year and listed as Teacher of

Music. Both of these gentlemen would have been too young to be the dancing teacher described by Thornton. No teachers listed in the 1841 census were born in the early 1760s or earlier. This dancing master could have come from another district; however, the limitations of the census information make it impossible to identify who the dancing master could have been at that time.

Other information about dancing masters, however, comes to us through the research of Gaelic scholar Michael Newton. Two dancing masters were listed among subscribers to editions of poetry: one published by Donnchadh *Bàn* Mac an t-Saoir in 1790 listed a Mr Archibald Macintyre, dancing master based at Easdale, south of Oban in Argyll; Coinneach MacCoinnich's 1792 *Orain Gaidhealach* listed James Fraser, dancing master at Kenmore.[52] It is not specified whether this refers to the Kenmore south of Inverary or the Kenmore near Aberfeldy, but as many other subscribers are from the Blair Atholl area, the latter is suggested. In the 1792 *Orain Gaidhealach*, three other subscribers noted as fiddlers, James Finlayson of Cromarty, James Cameron of Karr, and James Gow of Kincraigie were listed among other musicians. These fiddlers may have taught dancing as well. Furthermore, in the subscribers' list for Patrick McDonald's *Collection of Highland Vocal Airs* of 1784, a Fort William dancing master Mr Andrew Laughlan appeared as did a musician, Mr John M'Nichol of Glenurchy [*sic*]. An unnamed dancing master was listed among the occupations of residents on the Duke of Argyll's Lands in Oban and was included as a member of the Masonic Lodge in 1791,[53] and potentially also could have been the Dalmally dancing master.

French travel writer Barthélemy Faujas de Saint-Fond described his own journey through Scotland in his 1799 *Travels in England, Scotland and the Hebrides*. He recounts, in his first volume, how he met 28-year-old Gaelic-speaking schoolteacher Patrick Fraser, who held two paid posts in Dalmally in 1784: teaching in the local school in Dalmally; and giving private lessons to the local innkeeper's many children. In addition, these children had a writing teacher and a dancing master who 'came every year from a distance to spend some months at his [the innkeeper's] house, exclusively occupied in giving the lessons.'[54] Sadly, no name was given. The descriptions make it clear that Dalmally was a Gaelic-speaking environment at that time. Schooling occurred in both English and Gaelic, and writing and dancing were emphasised as important areas of study. Faujas de Saint-Fond noted that the Highlanders he saw only spoke 'in the Celtic language' and the fact that the innkeeper 'could speak a little English' reinforces this statement.[55] We wonder who the innkeeper was; no name was given. Cross-referencing traveller and philanthropist John Knox's experience of the Dalmally Inn in 1786, however, provides a further glimpse of his character

> [...] a commodious inn at this place [Dalmally] is rented at 6*l.* and the window-tax amounts to 4*l.* 10*s.* This disproportion arises from the well-judged munificence of the proprietor, who thus, almost at his own expence, accommodates travellers with descent lodgings.[56]

Figure 6.4 Illustration in Faujas de Saint-Fond (1799: 301) showing the interior of Dalmally's Blacksmith, MacNab's house in 1784. Note that the women are barefoot while the men wear shoes

Source: Image in public domain.

Faujas de Saint-Fond described the Highlanders he observed in Dalmally, and also represented in an illustration in Figure 6.4, as wearing wrap-around plaids, blue bonnets on their heads, and on their feet, 'shoes, which in general, each makes for himself, in a coarse but stout manner ... tied with strings of leather; this kind of shoes are known by the name of *brogues*.'[57]

The innkeeper hosting this Finishing Ball 'was in easy circumstances,' according to Faujas de Saint-Fond in 1784.[58] The hospitality offered at his establishment, only two years prior to Thornton's visit, was notable, suggesting the proprietor took great care in maintaining his accommodations:

> [the inn ...] its elegant appearance in so wild and unfrequented a situation astonished us. The threshold of the door, and the stairs were sourced and strewed with fine shining sand; the dining-room was covered with a carpet; the beds were neat and good; and the landlord was a worthy man.[59]

Was the carpet on a wooden floor or did it cover a dirt floor? As a man of apparent means, one may speculate that his inn could have had a wooden floor that helped to amplify the sounds of the feet in Thornton's description. We have found no images of Dalmally Inn, built by architect Ludovic Picard on behalf of Lord Breadalbane and, along with other construction in the area, completed in 1780–1781.

Hyland step forward   95

What distinguished the 'Glen Orgue [Orchy] kick' precisely is unknown, and, as with so many other steps special to various districts, that information may have passed away with its exponents. However, several common Strathspey and Reel steps in the Cape Breton Step dancing tradition use a 'kick step' motif where the heel or the ball of the foot sweeps forward and strikes the ground. It is not too farfetched to connect steps that have remained in continuous use in Cape Breton Gaelic-speaking communities since the early 1800s to what Thornton saw in *Gàidhealtachd* Scotland. The Gaelic phrase *dannsa breabaidh,* means 'kicking dance,' and was used in Kingussie to denote Step dancing. What characterised the dancing master's solo Hornpipe, what distinguished his capers, and what his favourite tune was may be lost to the annals of time.

It is clear that Thornton had seen similar noise-making 'shuffles' in other areas of the Highlands. He noted that these shuffles kept exact time, to music, we presume. Does that mean that dancers improvised steps to fit the melody, or did Thornton merely indicate that they kept good timing? Even though he approved of what he saw in its particular context he was likely more accustomed to upper-class, fashionable society. His description affirms the vigorous nature of the dancing and that it was a favourite pastime of the Highlanders even after a long working day. It is a great pity that Welshman Thomas Pennant, who travelled through similar areas as Thornton did in 1769, did not take note of any dancing he may have seen.[60]

Thornton's keen sportsman's eyes spotted dancers keeping time in an earlier entry in his book. On a blustery 18th of September, Thornton went to Pitmain [House], near Kingussie in Strathspey and Badenoch, to attend a 'Highland Festival' by the clan MacPherson.

At five o'clock dinner was announced, and each gentleman, with the utmost gallantry, handed in his tartan-drest partner. The table was covered with every luxury the values of Badenoch, Spey, and Lochaber could produce [...] When seated, no company at St. James's ever exhibited a greater variety of gaudy colours, the ladies being dressed in all their Highland pride, each following her own fancy and wearing a shawl of tartan; this, contrasted by the other parts of the dress, at candle-light, presented a most glaring *coup d'oeil.* [...]

The ladies gave us several very delightful Erse songs, nor were the bagpipes silent; they played many old Highland tunes; and, among others, one, which is, I am told, the test of a piper's abilities; for, at the great meeting of the pipers at Falkirk, those who cannot play it, are not admitted candidates for the annual prize given to the best performer. After the ladies had retired, the wine went round plentifully, but, to the honour of the conductor of this festive board, every thing was regulated with the utmost propriety, and, as we were in possession of the only room for dancing, we rose the earlier from table, in compliance with the wishes of the ladies, who in this country, are still more keen dancers than those of the southern parts of Britain.

96   *Hyland step forward*

> After tea, the room being adjusted and the band ready, we returned; and, minuets being, by common consent, exploded, danced, with true Highland spirit, a great number of different reels, some of which were danced with the genuine Highland fling, a peculiar kind of cut.
>
> It is astonishing how true these ladies all dance to time, and not without grace; they would be thought good dancers in any assembly whatever.[61]

This passage reveals a community aware of dancing fashions coming from London. After a certain amount of time and wine, the controlled, slow, and orderly fashionable dances were democratically 'exploded.' The atmosphere in the room went from 'utmost propriety' to boisterous and unleashed as dancing shifted to native local reels.

Since the ladies were commended on their ability to keep time to the music, obviously this aspect stood out to Thornton. The notable 'step' in this reel was 'The genuine Highland fling,' and Thornton's repeating phrase, 'a peculiar kind of cut,' may signal that both these labels he applied, 'Glen Orchy kick' and 'Highland fling,' identified iconic movement motifs.

In the introduction to the 1896 edition of Thornton's book, Herbert Maxwell shared that Sir Walter Scott was a severe critic of Thornton's work. Scott felt Thornton gave too many minute details about each episode and hunting exploit for the book to be engaging.[62] If Thornton's style suffered from his being an accurate and detailed observer, his abilities to fully and accurately describe situations are valuable for historical research. In our case, we wish he had been even more detailed in his dance observations.

James Currie, Southwest Scotland, 1790s

James Currie's writings about the 'Scottish peasantry' come from Currie's contextualisation of Robert Burns's life. Dumfriesshire native James Currie (1756–1805) was a physician and was the son of a minister in Annandale. Currie met Burns in Dumfries in 1792, later undertook to publish Burns's writings, and subsequently published his anthology in four volumes in 1800. There is no exact date ascribed to these observations but we can place them in the 1780s–1790s:

> That dancing should also be very generally a part of the education of the Scottish peasantry will surprise those who have only seen this description of men; and still more those who reflect on the rigid spirit of Calvinism, with which the nation is so deeply affected, and to which this recreation is strongly abhorrent. The winter is also the season when they acquire dancing, and indeed almost all their other instruction. They are taught to dance by persons generally of their own number, many of whom work at daily labour during the summer months. The school is usually a barn, and the arena for the performers is generally a clay floor. The dome is lighted by candles stuck in one end of a cloven stick, the other

end of which is thrust into the wall. *Reels, strathspeys,* country dances, and *hornpipes* are here practised. The jig, so much in favour among the English peasantry, has no place among them. The attachment of the people of Scotland of every rank, and particularly of the peasantry, to this amusement, is very great. After the labours of the day are over, young men and women walk many miles, in the cold and dreary nights of winter, to these country dancing-schools; and the instant that the violin sounds a Scottish air, fatigue seems to vanish, the toil-bent rustic becomes erect, his features brighten with sympathy; every nerve seems to thrill with sensation, and every artery to vibrate with life. These rustic performers are indeed less to be admired for grace, than for agility and animation, and their accurate observance of time. Their modes of dancing, as well as their tunes, are common to every rank in Scotland, and are now generally known.[63]

Currie's comments on the general place and importance of dance in Scotland are valuable, but his inclusion of Reels, Strathspeys, and Hornpipes and the importance of the 'accurate observance of time' flag the possibility that percussive dance was happening. Timing is always important with regards to dancing, but that Currie chose to single out the difference between steady timing and studied 'grace' appears significant.

Dannsa breabaidh—the kicking dance

Some terms and phrases that suggest percussive and kicking footwork in the eighteenth-century accounts are *nimble heels, shuffle, heel and toe forward, slaps across forward, vivifies the heel, beat the ground, Hyland and hornpipe steps, kick, feet keep exact time,* and *accurate observance of time.* Mr A. Duff's 1764 *Country Dancing made plain and easy* publication includes a travelling step, consisting of a series of 'step-hops' from foot to foot forward, commonly referred to today as skipping, as well as a setting or footing step, described as a 'step-hop backwards,' known today as a 'hop-backstep' or 'backstep with a hop.'[64] This type of step can be made more or less percussive depending on how strongly or lightly the feet relate to the dancing surface. Other Scottish music and Country dance publications outline the spatial pathways for figures and interactions between dancers and couples but provide no step descriptions beyond 'footing.'[65]

Emmerson's history of the dancing of the eighteenth century shows who attended the gatherings, who danced, organised, and taught the dances, and shows that Minuets, Country Dances, and Cotillions were popular, but cannot completely detail the specific steps and figures involved. Interpretation of the Country Dance manuals of the era remains informed guesswork. This will change somewhat when we shift our attention to Francis Peacock's 1805 publication, in which he looks back on his observations of the eighteenth century and gives more detailed descriptions of footwork motifs.

98   *Hyland step forward*

Notes

1. Smout 1990.
2. Smout 1990: 195–196.
3. Smout 1990: 195–196.
4. Smout 1990: 197.
5. Smout 1990: 197.
6. Smout 1990: 483.
7. Flett 1985 and 1996.
8. Emmerson 1972: 87. Topham, Letter xli [1776].
9. Emmerson 1972: 146.
10. Topham, Letter xli, 1776.
11. Emmerson 1972: 99.
12. Emmerson 1972: 100.
13. Emmerson 1972: 100.
14. The Laki eruption in Iceland 1783–1784. The sulphurous 'Laki' haze is reported to have caused thousands of deaths in Europe throughout 1783 and the winter of 1784. In Great Britain, the summer of 1783 was known as the 'sand-summer' due to ash fallout, and it has been estimated that about 23,000 British people died from the poisoning in August and September 1783. In France, a sequence of meteorological extremes included a harvest in 1785 that caused poverty for rural workers, accompanied by droughts, bad winters and summers, including a violent hailstorm in 1788 that destroyed crops. This in turn contributed significantly to increasing poverty and famine that presumably contributed towards triggering the French Revolution in 1789. The growing season temperature in NW Europe was generally low in the years following the Laki eruption until 1794. The global cooling following the Laki eruption in Iceland 1783–1784 was felt worldwide. (http://www.climate4you.com/ClimateAndHistory%201700-1799.htm#1783-1784:%20 The%20Laki%20eruption%20in%20Iceland) [Accessed May 27 2017].
15. Possibly Marie-Jean-Augustin Vestris, known as Auguste Vestris (1760–1842) or perhaps more possibly his father Gaétan (Gaetano Apolline Baldassarre) Vestris (1729–1808) the Florence-born French ballet master who made his debut at the Paris *Opéra* in 1749.
16. Emmerson 1972: 114–115.
17. Emmerson 1972: 114–115.
18. Brereton 1742/1990: 189.
19. Flett 1993.
20. *Notes and Queries,* Vol. 12, 1855: 159.
21. Emmerson 1970: 19.
22. McGill's manuscript can be seen on the RSCDS website at: https://archive.rscds. org/index.php/mcgill-manuscript [Accessed 28 April 2020].
23. Ross 1778: 132.
24. Chambers 1829: 495.
25. Fergusson 1785: 118.
26. Johnson and Boswell 1985: 253.
27. Johnson and Boswell 1985: 74.
28. Johnson and Boswell 1985: 255.
29. Johnson and Boswell 1985: 261.
30. Johnson and Boswell 1985: 327.
31. Topham background according to introduction of reprint of extracts by William Brown, publisher, Edinburgh, n.d. vii–viii.
32. The 1776 edition is available online on Google Books: http://books.google.ie/books/about/Letters_from_Edinburgh.html?id=1HZbAAAAQAAJ&redir_esc=y [Accessed 4 July 2014].

33. Topham 1776: 76.
34. Topham 1776: 67–71.
35. Topham 1776: 157–158.
36. Topham 1776: 149–150.
37. Flett 1979: 19.
38. Flett 1979: 4.
39. Emmerson 1972: 83–123; Fletts 1985: 1–30.
40. James Hall's (1807) book is titled *Travels in Scotland, by an Unusual Route*. He describes dancing at a country wedding as 'all kinds of rural mirth going on, some at reels, others at country dances, minuets, fandangoes, highland capers, &c.' on pages 300–301.
41. Garnett 1811 Vol 2: 74. http://books.google.ie/books?id=ZSY-AQAAMAAJ&p-g=RA1-PA1&dq=thomas+garnett+tour+through+the+highlands&hl=en&sa=X-&ei=qc62U7PxLajY7AaDp4HYCA&ved=0CD4Q6AEwAQ#v=onep-age&q=dance&f=true [Accessed 15 June 2014].
42. Emmerson 1972: 125–129.
43. Giovanni-Andrea Gallini (born 1728 in Florence, Italy, and died 1805 in London) was a dancer, choreographer and later impresario and opera manager in London.
44. Gallini 1772: 184–185.
45. Peacock 1805: 83.
46. Emmerson 1970: 22–23.
47. Emmerson 1970: 12–13.
48. As is exemplified by the step names given by McGill earlier.
49. Emmerson 1970: 20–21.
50. Further information about Colonel Thornton can be found in the Dictionary of National Biography, 1885–1900, Volume 56, by John Goldworth Alger. http://en.wikisource.org/wiki/Thornton,_Thomas_%281757-1823%29_%28DNB00%29 [Accessed 5 July 2014].
51. Thornton 1804: 238–239.
52. Newton 2015: 11 https://www.academia.edu/12364911/Keeping_it_Reel_The_Origins_of_the_Reel_in_a_Scottish_Gaelic_Context [Accessed 20 June 2019].
53. Morrison 2015: 139.
54. Faujas de Saint-Fond 1799: 281–282.
55. Faujas de Saint-Fond 1799: 266.
56. Knox 1787: 15–16.
57. Faujas de Saint-Fond 1799: 268.
58. Faujas de Saint-Fond 1799: 281.
59. Faujas de Saint-Fond 1799: 270.
60. Pennant 2000 [1771].
61. Thornton 1804: 171–172.
62. Thornton 1896: xiii.
63. Burns and Currie 1806: 13–14. These notes were also reproduced in the Edinburgh Magazine (1800: 32–33) and in American travel writer John Melish's publication (1812: 427–428).
64. In modern competitive Highland dancing these are referred to as 'retirés' or 'retiré skips.'
65. Robert Bremner's 1761 *Second Collection of Scots Reels or Country Dances … and Proper Directions to each Dance*; John Walsh's *24 New Country Dances for the Year 1718*; Dundee dance master David Young's *Duke of Perth Manuscript* of 1734; and the *Castle Menzies Manuscript* of 1749.

7 A few more flings and shuffles
Nineteenth-century accounts, 1800–1839

Nineteenth-century European influence on Scottish dance

As we prepare to view accounts of the nineteenth century, it is worth noting that the early publications will more accurately reflect observations based in the later part of eighteenth century. This particularly applies to descriptions by Alexander Campbell and Francis Peacock in 1804 and 1805. It is also important to remember that these passages are only static snapshots of dancing that was alive and evolving.

During the late eighteenth and early nineteenth centuries, there was an active exchange of dances and fashions particularly between France, England, and Scotland. One of the fashions pertinent to this study was the popularity of Scottish dances in London. Sometimes it is difficult to tell whether Scottish dance steps and practices originate in Scotland or in London, where Scotch dances were all the rage. Examples of this can be seen in the list of dances excerpted from Thomas Wilson's 1811 price list in Figure 7.1. Wilson's price list includes many titles categorised as Scottish dances or motifs today.[1]

	L.	S.	D.
Shantruse	4	4	0
Scotch Minuet	3	3	0
Highland Fling	3	3	0
Irish Comic Dance	3	3	0
Broad-sword Hornpipe	5	5	0
Ground Hornpipe	4	4	0
Irish and Scotch Reels, with the original Scotch and Irish Steps	4	4	0
Tambourine Hornpipe	4	4	0
Rifle Hornpipe	5	5	0
Strathspey Minuet	4	4	0

Figure 7.1 Extract of prices for dance tuition given in Thomas Wilson, *An Analysis of country dancing …*, 1811

Figure 7.2 An engraving showing Country dancing, Scotch Reels, and Quadrilles coexisting on a dance floor by J. Shury, from Thomas Wilson's 1816 3rd edition of the *Companion to the Ballroom*. Note the piper sitting down, playing for the Highland Reel dancers in the foreground left

Source: Image in public domain.

An illustration in his 1816 *A Companion to the Ball Room* in Figure 7.2 shows three of the dance types enjoyed in London at the time: a Country dance set; a Quadrille set; and a Foursome Reel grouping complete with kilted dancers and a piper.

In 1816, the Quadrilles, imported from France, were first danced publicly in Edinburgh. Other dances from the continent followed, and, with the help of the dancing masters' classes and advertisements, became new favourites in ballrooms and rural dance halls alike. The Lancers and Caledonian Quadrilles, followed by Polkas, Mazurkas, Waltzes, German and Highland Schottisches, Two Steps, and their many derivatives entered the social dance scene at all levels of society. In some places Minuets remained a while longer, and Highland Reels also lived on in vernacular dance.

The nineteenth century was marked by the collapse of the Spanish and Napoleonic empires and by growing influence of the British and Russian Empires and the United States. In Scotland, the 50-year period from 1780 to 1830 was significant, according to T.C. Smout:

> The social and economic stagnation of a peasant society was banished; the industrial and agrarian revolution since 1780 had committed her not merely to being an industrialised society but also to becoming a society where rapid and accelerating social change was the normal condition of life.[2]

102 *A few more flings and shuffles*

The processes of economic change were manifold, and not without their problems. Neither the nostalgia for the past reflected in literature nor revivals of religious puritanism could halt them. The Industrial Revolution continued; the textile industries were followed by coal and iron. Later in the century, steel, shipbuilding, jute, tweed, and high-yield farming succeeded, changing the Scottish economic landscape fundamentally. Unbelievably complex social problems arose, influenced by quick urbanisation. Burgh infrastructures were inadequate, resulting in overcrowding, housing problems, low wages, long hours, and widespread alcohol abuse.[3] In 'some ways the biggest change in the decades before 1830 had been Scotland's tendency to become more British and less specifically Scottish.'[4] The talented intelligentsia was drawn away from Scotland to London and beyond, helped by the ease of railway transport and communication via the telegraph. Other segments of Scottish society left the country altogether.

The very complex and multiplicitous reasons for migration of Scots during the early nineteenth century are detailed by Scottish historian T.M. Devine in his 2011 book *To the Ends of the Earth, Scotland's Global Diaspora 1750–2010*. The Scottish Clearances occurred intermittently over a span of about one hundred years, from the 1760s up until the late 1850s, with emigrants dispersing to many overseas destinations. Movement patterns of hundreds of thousands of people are also recounted from rural to urban centres in search of work, partly due to the Highland Clearances, because of economic factors and landowner profit priorities, and partly due to the mid-century famine period. Later in the century, Lowland emigration, plus an immigration of 205,000 Irish and tens of thousands of people of Jewish, Lithuanian, and Italian descent, as well as other ethnicities from south of the Border into Scotland, changed the demography of the country fundamentally.[5] Writers of the time were aware of the many changes occurring in Scottish life ways, with some writing specifically to document customs they believed should be preserved for posterity. Our first reference in this chapter comes from this sort of documentation.

Alexander Campbell, Highlands, 1804

In his lengthy footnotes to his poem *The Grampians Desolate*, Alexander Campbell included a description of one of the pantomimic dances of the Highlands. The *Damhsa an Chleoca*/cloak dance, involves two characters, a gentleman and a servant. The characters enter a party or scene as if they have just arrived from a trip. Then,

> He all at once stops, throws off his mantle, plaid, or cloak, and away his staff, affecting at the same time considerable emotion; his servant, who is by, picks up the cloak and staff, and puts on the one, and places the other in his hand, endeavouring at the same time to quiet his master, who

seems to be pacified, and foots it away again to the same tune, till he tires, and throws away his mantle and staff again; which his man takes up, and presents them as before; repeating the same several times, till at last the servant recollecting that he has a letter, he pulls it out of his pocket, and offers it to his young master, who says he is unable to read, owing to a phlegmon on his posteriors, which marvellously affects his eye-sight![6]

Today much Scottish dance is presented in a proud and serious way, but earlier dances got a lot of mileage out of humour. The cheeky, naughty undertones here relate a dance style more down to earth than the highly controlled motifs and serious presentation we have come to associate with Scottish dance today. Campbell did not say precisely where he saw this dance nor did he explain what he meant by 'foots it away.' It is tempting to connect this 'footing' to A. Duff's 1764 description of the 'hop-backstep.' Other dramatic or pantomimic dances Campbell recounted in this publication were *Damhsa nam Boc*/dance of the buck or billygoat, *Fidh an Gunn*/weaving or knitting of the gown, and *Crait an Dreathan*/the wren's croft. The Fletts researched other pantomimic or mimetic actions of various songs, dances, and games in their 1956 article *Dramatic Jigs in Scotland*, but they did not discuss percussive aspects of the steps featured in the dances.

Alexander Campbell was born in 1764 in Tombea, Loch Lubnaig and died in abject poverty in Edinburgh in 1824. He was a musician and writer of miscellaneous works. Campbell recounted further dance descriptions later, as will be glimpsed in his 1815 account below.

Francis Peacock, Aberdeen, 1805

In 1805, the Aberdeen dancing master Francis Peacock (1723–1807) published his book, *Sketches Relative to the History and Theory, but more especially to the Practice of Dancing.* Peacock had been a dancing master in Aberdeen for many years when his book was published. According to G.M. Fraser's notes in *Aberdeen Street Names* of 1911:

> In the year 1742, some influential inhabitants of Aberdeen represented to the Town Council 'that the town was at great loss for want of a right dancing master to educate their children.' After a certain amount of thought, the Council resolved to advertise for a suitable person, and two candidates presented themselves to show their qualifications to the Magistrates, in front of a crowd of gentlemen and ladies in Trinity Hall.
>
> James Stuart, of Montrose, was found to be better at dancing and teaching, and he was employed; but it seems he was unsatisfactory, for in 1746 the council resolved to advertise again for 'a person of sober, discreet and moral character.' They soon got a letter from Mr John Dawney,

104 *A few more flings and shuffles*

dancing-master in Edinburgh, recommending as suitable a Mr Francis Peacock. Apparently he suited the council, and on Valentine's Day of 1747 they made Mr Peacock, then twenty-three, the official and sole Dancing-Master of Aberdeen during his good behaviour, agreeing to pay him seven shillings sterling per student per month, together with some money to organise the music.[7]

Peacock retained this monopoly until 1790. According to Colin Russell,[8] Francis Peacock was a native of Edinburgh; there is also a school of thought that he was born in England. His parents and the location of his birth are so far unknown. It is clear from his writing that he was familiar with Edinburgh life. According to the 18 April 1857 *Aberdeen Herald and General Advertiser*:

> He was very hospitable, and the principal inhabitants of the town were often his guests. A few individuals who were his pupils are still living, and recollect upon him opening his balls when nearly eighty years of age. The ball used to commence at four o'clock in the afternoon, and sometimes continue till four o'clock next morning.

Peacock died shortly after his book about dancing was published, in Aberdeen, on 26 June, 1807, at the age of 84. Peacock's descriptions of Reel steps are thus informed by a span of almost 60 years as a dancing master.[9] One may argue that Peacock's London dance training with Desnoyer, Glover, and Lally, and his standing as a prominent dancing master influenced his descriptions. He was known to have favoured the Minuet over the Country Dances that became popular in the second half of the eighteenth century.

> His principal aim as a teacher of dancing was to develop in his pupils an ability to move with dignified and confident elegance. He considered this to be an asset not just in the ballroom, but [also] in life generally.[10]

We can judge the manner of his conduct in classes from the account of a contemporary and pupil, Alexander Jaffray, in whose *Recollections of Kingswells, 1755–1800* is found a description of the experience of attending Peacock's classes in 1770 when Jaffray was 15 years old:

> I attended the established dancing school of the city. The master was Mr Peacock, a really scientific professor. He was, of course, an excellent master, but stern and severe when a dull pupil came under his hands. I went through the minuet, but very indifferently, and declined exhibiting at the Ball, finding myself unequal to the task. The only part I took any pleasure in was the country dancing practised once every week. I declined attending school after the first three months; tired of the practice of dancing, of which in after years I became very fond.[11]

It is said that he charged two guineas per term for his classes and that on some level he dismissed footwork and figure technique stating, 'as for the jigging part, and the figures of dances, I count that little or nothing better, than as it tends to perfect graceful carriage.'[12]

According to Peacock's own remarks, his position in Aberdeen gave him a good observation point for different steps used throughout the Highlands:

> Our Colleges draw hither, every year, a number of students from the Western Isles, as well as from the Highlands, and the greater part of them excel in [Reels ...] some of them, indeed, in so superior a degree that I, myself, have thought them worthy of imitation.[13]

Peacock applied Ballet terminology, a lingua franca for dance at the time, in only three of his explanations of Reel steps, to describe some actions that lift the body into the air. His descriptions provide us with the earliest written instructions of Scottish dance steps, all of which have Anglicised Gaelic names. Whether they were current names in use in the Highlands or adapted by Peacock to make his work sound more exotic or authentic is a matter of debate. Peacock was likely not a Gaelic speaker and if coming from either Edinburgh or England he would not have grown up with the language. He admits as much:

> it may be proper, first, to premise, that I have used my best endeavours to ascertain their Gaelic names, and have reason to think I have been successful in my enquiries. And here I am prompted by gratitude to acknowledge my obligations to a literary friend, (well versed in the Gaelic language) who has obligingly favoured me with the etymology of the terms, or adopted names, of the steps I am about to describe.[14]

We do not know from whom he learnt these particular steps or who gave him their names. Peacock's 'literary friend' may have been the Lochaber-born Ewen MacLachlan/*Eòghann MacLachlainn* (1775–1822) a Gaelic scholar and poet known for his translations of ancient classical literature into Gaelic, his own Gaelic verse, and his contributions to Gaelic dictionaries. MacLachlan was the librarian to University and Kings College at Aberdeen from 1800 to 1818 and listed as a subscriber to Peacock's book. That Peacock employed Gaelic spelling for some steps, such as *aisig-thrasd* and *fosgladh*, while others, such as kemshóole and kemkóssy, were given in an Anglicised form, may point to a shift away from Gaelic usage to English or urbanised usage at the time. Modifiers applied before the step names, such as 'Minor Kemkossy,' 'Single Kemkóssy,' and 'Double Kemkóssy,' reflect English grammar, not Gaelic. The steps Peacock listed are:

1 Kemshóole,⋆ or Forward Step.—This is the common step for the promenade, or figure of the Reel. It is done by advancing the right foot forward, the left following it behind: in advancing the same foot a second time,

106 *A few more flings and shuffles*

you hop upon it, and one step is finished. You do the same motions after advancing the left foot, and so on alternately with each foot, during the first measure of the tune played twice over; but if you wish to vary the step, in repeating the measure, you may introduce a very lively one, by making a smart rise, or gentle spring, forward, upon the right foot, placing the left foot behind it: this you do four times, With this difference, that instead of going a fourth time behind with the left foot, you disengage it from the ground, adding a hop to the last spring. You finish the promenade, by doing the same step, beginning it with the left foot. To give the step its full effect, you should turn the body a little to the left, when you go forward with the right foot, and the contrary way when you advance the left. ★Or, according to its established orthography, Cèumsiubhail, from Cèum a step, and siubhal, to glide, to move, to go on with rapidity.

2 Minor Kemkóssy, † Setting or Footing Step.—This is an easy familiar step, much used by the English in their Country dances. You have only to place the right foot behind the left, sink, and hop upon its then do the same with the left foot behind the right. †Cèum-coisiche, from Cèum, a step, and Coiseachadh, to foot it, or ply the feet.

3 Single Kemkóssy, Setting or Footing Step.—You pass the right foot behind the left to the fifth position, making a gentle bound, or spring, with the left foot, to the second position; after passing the right foot again behind the left, you make a hop upon it, extending the left toe. You do the same step, by passing the left foot twice behind the right, concluding, as before, with a hop. This step is generally done with each foot alternately, during the whole of the second measure of the tune.

4 Double Kemkóssy, Setting or Footing Step.—This step differs from the Single Kemkóssy only in its additional number of motions. You pass the foot four times behind the other, before you hop, which must always be upon the hindmost foot.

5 Lematrást, ‡ Cross Springs.—These are a series of Sissonnes. You spring forward with the right foot to the third or fifth position, making a hop upon the left foot; then spring backward with the right, and hop upon it. You do the same with the left foot, and so on, for two, four, or as many bars as the second part of the tune contains. This is a single step; to double it, you do the Springs, forward and backward, four times, before you change the foot. ‡From Lèum, a leap, a spring, and Trasd, across.

6 Seby-trast, ‖ Chasing Steps, or Cross Slips.—This step is like the Balotte. You slip the right foot before the left; the left foot behind the right; the right again before the left, and hop upon it. You do the same, beginning with the left foot. This is a single step. ‖From Siabadh, to slip, and Trasd, across.

7 Aisig-thrasd, § Cross Passes.—This is a favourite step in many parts of the Highlands. You spring a little to one side with the right foot, immediately passing the left across it; hop and cross it again, and one step is finished; you then spring a little to one side with the left foot, making the like passes with the right. This is a minor step; but it is often varied

by passing the foot four times alternately behind and before, observing to make a hop previous to each pass, the first excepted, which must always be a spring, or bound: by these additional motions, it becomes a single step. §From Aiseag, a pass, and Trasd across.

8   Kem Badenoch, a Minor Step.—You make a gentle spring to one side with the right foot, immediately placing the left behind it; then do a single Entrechat, that is, a cross caper, or leap, changing the situation of the feet, by which the right foot will be behind the left. You do the same beginning with the left foot. By adding two cross leaps to three of these steps, it becomes a double step.

9   Fosgladh,★ Open Step.—Slip the feet to the second position, then, with straight knees, make a smart spring upon the toes to the fifth position; slip the feet again to the second position, and do a like spring, observing to let the foot which was before in the first spring, be behind in the second. This is a minor step, and is generally repeated during the half, or the whole, measure of the tune. ★An opening.

10 Cuartag,† Turning Step.–You go to the second position with the right foot; hop upon it, and pass the left behind it; then hop, and pass the same foot before.—You repeat these alternate passes after each hop you make in going about to the right. Some go twice round, concluding the last circumvolution with two single cross capers. These circumvolutions are equal to four bars, or one measure of the tune. Others go round to the right, and then to the left. These, also, occupy the same number of bars. †From Cuairt, a round, a circumvolution.

These are an association of different steps, and which are necessary to add variety to the dance. For example: you may add two of the sixth step (Seby-trast) to two of the third (Single Kemkóssy.) This you may vary, by doing the first of these steps before, instead of behind; or you may add two of the second step (Minor Kemkóssy) to one single Kemkóssy. These steps may be transposed, so that the last shall take the place of the first. Again, two of the sixth step (Seby-trast) may be added to the fourth step, (Double Kemkóssy) in going to either side.

Another variety, much practised, is to spring backward with the right foot instead of forward, as in the fifth step, and hop upon the left; then spring forward, and again hop upon the same foot, and add to these two springs, one single Kemkóssy, passing the right foot behind the left. You do the same step, beginning it with the left foot.[15]

Importantly, Peacock's Gaelic names for step motifs have never, so far as we are aware, occurred in any Gaelic-language dance descriptions prior to or contemporary with Peacock's publication. This list, however, has been copied many times over, in the same order, by other writers in English without citing Peacock as the source, including James Logan, Rudolph Radestock, and Edward Scott. It also appeared in a 1969 Gaelic-language book by Calum MacLeoid about Scottish settlers' activities in Nova Scotia.[16] MacLeoid omitted any Anglicised spellings, and appended what seem to be direct translations of English-language Highland dance terminology of the twentieth century: *ceum-cùil*/backstep; *gearradh-àrd*/highcutting; and *gearradh-dùbailte*/double cutting; and then he adds *seatadh*/setting and *bruithcath*/dirk or duelling dance. MacLeoid's additions are incongruous; backsteps, highcuts, and double cuts are names for specific motifs, as are Peacock's original list of step names; however, setting refers to a structural component of social dancing, and the Dirk Dance was a specific dance.

The Reel steps Peacock described have been interpreted in varied ways by the Fletts in 1985; Yves Guillard in 1989; Anne Daye in 1997; and Patricia Ballantyne in 2016. More information about these steps is hosted by the University of Aberdeen on the James 'Scott' Skinner website.[17] Peacock's *'Sketches'* can be accessed online at the Library of Congress and the University of Aberdeen's Scott Skinner websites.[18] Depending on the point of view taken, Peacock's movement descriptions can be interpreted on a scale ranging from percussive to silent in nature. For example, the minor, single, and double kemkóssy steps all exhibit rhythms and body relationship patterns existing in Cape Breton strathspey steps,[19] English Step dancing,[20] and old-style Irish Step dancing.[21] *Ceum-coisiche* is translated by Peacock as a 'Setting or Footing' step, although 'pedestrian' or 'walking' would be an alternate translation of *'coisiche.'*[22] As Peacock mentions, the minor step described was common in English Country dances and in Scotland. Today, this same step motif is referred to as a backstep-with-a-hop, hop-backstep, or Shetland backstep.[23]

French dancer and dance scholar Yves Guillard connected Peacock's steps to Cape Breton Step dance motifs. He provided a Labanotation example, below in Figure 7.3, for the step *aisig-thrasd*, translated in Peacock's book as 'Cross Passes,' also translatable as 'ferry across.'[24]

Guillard indicates he feels this step is 'extremely lively and quick, and [that] it evokes the quotation by Topham about the Reel: "They will sit totally unmoved at the most sprightly airs of an English country dance; but the moment one of these tunes is played, [...] up they start, animated with new life, and you imagine they had received an electric shock, or been bit by a tarantula."'[25]

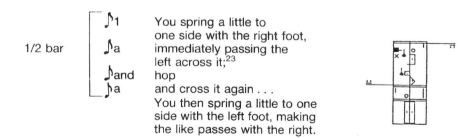

Figure 7.3 Guillard notation of *aisig-thrasd* 1989: 25

Source: Used with kind permission by Y. Guillard.

Count 1	Hop on LF.
Count &	Brush RF forward, making a beat with the ball or heel of the RF as the foot moves forward.
Count 2	Hop on LF.
Count &	Brush RF backward, making a beat with the ball of the RF as the foot moves backward...

Figure 7.4 Guillard notation of kick step 1989: 25

Source: Used with kind permission by Y. Guillard.

Guillard, furthermore, identified a similarity between the *aisig-thrasd* and the Cape Breton 'kick step' mentioned in connection to the 'Glen Orchy kick' earlier in this book, expressed in Labanotation in Figure 7.4. This motif was described by Frank Rhodes in 1957, and remains in common use today:

Rhodes wrote that this strathspey step: '[...] can also be danced alternately on right and left feet, the first count then being a spring from one foot to the other. In this case the emphasis is placed on the first count in each bar, and the rhythm is similar to that of the pas de Basque.'[26] Guillard noted that Peacock gave another version of the step and provided an interpretation of that step in Labanotation shown in Figure 7.5:

> This is a minor step; but it is often varied by passing the foot four times alternately behind and before, observing to make a hop previous to each pass, the first excepted, which must always be a spring, or bound: by these additional motions, it becomes a single step (Peacock 1805: 94–95).[27]

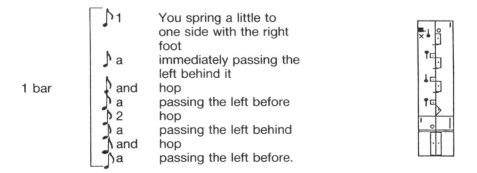

Figure 7.5 Guillard notation of expanding Peacock's minor (half-bar) step into a single (one-bar) step 1989: 26

Source: Used with kind permission by Y. Guillard.

110 *A few more flings and shuffles*

These examples show how a percussive approach could be indicated by Peacock's descriptions. Guillard's research recognises this by linking the Cape Breton movement material to that of Peacock's description.

Peacock's book does not mention any of the now standardised Highland dances such as the Highland Fling, Sword Dance, or *Seann Triubhas*. Despite that, both Isobel Cramb in 1953 and Emmerson in 1972 suggested that Peacock could have been the devisor of the Step dance Earl of Erroll. Their reasoning was that Peacock dedicated his 1762 music book to James Hay, the fifteenth Earl of Erroll, a great patron of the arts who resided at either New Slains Castle, near Peterhead, or Dalgetty Castle, near Turriff in Aberdeenshire.[28] The tune 'The Earl of Erroll' has been attributed to Peacock. However, the Earl of Erroll dance includes frequent repetition of the Treble motif, notably absent from Peacock's book. The music for the Earl of Erroll is a Double Hornpipe and the structure of the dance as reconstructed from Frederick Hill's notebook involves a step danced first on the right side and then repeated on the left, common in most Scottish Step dances.

Emmerson further suggested that Double Hornpipes such as the Earl of Erroll and the King of Sweden could have been featured at the Edinburgh assemblies that Topham attended. Ayrshire-born Edinburgh dancing master David Strange and Peacock appear to have known each other, so it is possible they shared dance repertoire.[29] If these dances existed in Edinburgh, then, based on Topham's comments, a percussive nature would be suggested, as opposed to the way these dances have been interpreted since the 1950s. While we do not have enough facts to conclusively prove these suggestions, percussive interpretations of these steps would be valid from an historical perspective. For instance, the step called lematrást is described as a *sissone*, a word indicating a movement of elevation springing off two feet then landing on one foot. While *sissone* is a term used in Ballet, it does not necessarily follow that the pattern of springing was done with balletic styling of pointed toes and soft landings. There are no other convenient words in English or Gaelic that indicate this type of jump, and the term may simply be useful in defining starting from two feet and landing on one. Springs made from two feet to one foot or vice versa can be made in a way that beats the floor and keeps time, as well, and a step of this nature has been shared in Cape Breton legacies.

Putting the possible percussive nature of the steps aside for a moment, perhaps two other statements of Peacock's are worth highlighting to finish. The first lies within his opinion on the ability of the Highlander to dance their Reels:

> The fondness the Highlanders have for this Quartett, or Trio, (for it is either one or the other) is unbounded; and so is their ambition to excell in it. This pleasing propensity, one would think, was born with them, from the early indications we sometimes see their children shew for this exercise. I have seen children of theirs, at five or six years of age, attempt, nay

even execute, some of their steps so well, as almost to surpass belief. I once had the pleasure of seeing, in a remote part of the country, a Reel danced by a herd boy and two young girls, who surprised me much, especially the boy, who appeared to be about twelve years of age. He had a variety of well chosen steps, and executed them with so much justness and ease, as if he meant to set criticism at defiance. Circumstances like these plainly evince, that those qualities must either be inherent in the Highlanders, or that they must have an uncommon aptitude for imitation.[30]

Peacock was impressed by what seemed to him a natural-feeling musicality and ability of the Highlanders to dance 'inside' the music with great flow of movement 'with justness and ease.'

Another statement deals with a dancer's latitude to improvise and make up individual step and movement combinations. At the very end of his chapter on Scotch Reel steps, Peacock gave examples of ways they could be varied, combined, and altered. He closed by writing:

In short, without particularising any other combinations, I shall only add, that you have it in your power to change, divide, add to, or invert, the different steps described, in whatever way you think best adapted to the tune, or most pleasing to yourself.[31]

Peacock encouraged dancers to make the steps their own, to make up new combinations, and to alter steps, and for dancers to listen to what the music encourages them to do. He suggests that the individual dancer should be creative! In fact, most dancing masters and good dancers do this naturally, as D.G. MacLennan echoed a century later. Invention is a mechanism that can keep dance traditions invigorated and constantly refreshed. Processes of natural creativity and change within Scottish dancing only stopped when Scottish dance associations were formed and set down rules governing what is correct and what is wrong within dance styles.

Elizabeth Grant Smith, Rothiemurchus, 1802–1813

Elizabeth Grant was born in Edinburgh in 1797. She wrote her now famous diaries and journals in the 1840s whilst living in France. In her *Memoirs of a Highland Lady*, Elizabeth Grant described her own experiences learning dances, which she recounted studying at quite a young age at the family estate at Doune House in Rothiemurchus near Aviemore in Speyside. 'I read well at three years old, had long ballads off by heart, counted miraculously, danced heel and toe, the Highland fling, and Highland shuffle, and sang, perched upon the table, ever so many Scotch songs, 'Toming soo ze eye' and such like, to the amusement of the partial assembly.'[32] She described the dancing in a bit more detail a few years later:

112 *A few more flings and shuffles*

> A dancing-master taught us every variety of wonderful Highland step—that is, he taught me, for William never could learn anything, though he liked hopping about to the fiddle—and we did 'Merrily dance the quaker's wife' together, quite to the satisfaction of the servants who all took lessons too, in common with the rest of the population, the Highlanders considering this art an essential in the education of all classes, and never losing an opportunity of acquiring a few more flings and shuffles. The dancing-master had, however, other most distinguished pupils, the present Duke of Manchester and his elder sister, Lady Jane Montague, who were then living in our close neighbourhood with their grandmother, the Duchess of Gordon.[33]

Her descriptions draw attention to the fact that learning dancing was highly valued throughout all classes in Highland Society. The next passage gives a little more detail about what she learned:

> We children sometimes displayed our accomplishments [...] in a prominent manner, to the delight, at any rate of our dancing master. Lady Jane was really clever in the Gillie Callum and the Shean Trews, I little behind her in the single and double fling, the shuffle and heel-and-toe step. The boys were more blundering and had to bear the good-natured laugh of many a hard-working lad and lass, who, after the toil of the day, footed it neatly and lightly in the ball-room till near midnight.[34]

Grant enjoyed observing the differences among dancers, which she shared in this rather newsy, gossipy account:

> The first strathspey was danced by my father and Mrs Macintosh; if my mother danced at all, it was later in the evening. My father's dancing was peculiar—a very quiet body, and very busy feet, they shuffled away in double quick time steps of his own composition, boasting of little variety, sometimes ending in a turn-about which he imagined was the fling; as English it was altogether as if he had never left Hertfordshire. My mother did better. She moved quietly in Highland matron fashion, 'high and disposedly' like Queen Elizabeth and Mrs Macintosh, for however lightly the lasses footed it, etiquette forbade the wives to do more than 'tread the measure.' William and Mary moved in the grave style of my mother; Johnnie without instruction danced beautifully; Jane was perfection, so light, so active, and so graceful; but of all the dancers there, none was equal to little Sandy 'afterwards Factor' the son of Duncan Macintosh, but not of his wife.[35]

While Grant didn't see an ending 'turn-about' as being a characteristic of the Fling, it became a repeating motif that survives today. Possibly she had been taught by her dancing master to see certain dance styles as being 'Highland' fashion. Here is an account of another ball that provides contrast to the previous passage by being a bit more down to earth:

> We delighted in the Floaters' ball, so large a party, so many strangers, some splendid dancers from Strathspey, the hay-loft, the straw-loft, and the upper floor of the threshing-mill all thrown open en suite; two sets of fiddlers playing, punch made in the washing-tubs, an illumination of tallow dips! It is surprising that the floors stood the pounding they got; the thumping noise of the many energetic feet could have been heard half a mile off.[36]

Though Grant's accounts more frequently focus on descriptions of personalities than on footwork details, these passages describing dances do ultimately build a well-rounded description of varying dance scenarios in Scotland in the early nineteenth century.

Anne McKee Stapleton points out that both Grant and Susan Sibbald saw finger snapping at dances as 'a delightful, heartfelt manifestation of Scottish spirit and pride,'[37] at this time, despite some dancing masters' wishes to quell it. Sibbald experienced dancing in the Borders region around the same time described in Grant's memoirs. Sibbald described a local doctor at a dance as 'spinning round the room and cracking his fingers, "Highland Fling," "Pigeon Wing," and "Cut the Buckle" all performed most wonderfully.'[38]

Grant did not mention her dancing master by name but drops hints as to his other pupils, which gives us a geographical spread from Doune House in Rothiemurchus to Gordon Castle near Fochabers. In the 1841 census records, dancing master Adam Myren, whose name is sometimes given as Miren or Meino, who was born about 1782 and based in Mortlach in Banffshire, appears a likely candidate, in terms of both age and location, to have taught around the early 1800s at these estates. Other possible candidates could have been John Cruickshank, born about 1780 in Fyvie, or Lewis Douglas of Dallas in Morayshire, born around 1786.

Charlotte, Lady Wake, Harviestoun, near Alva, 1813

Charlotte Murdoch Tait was the daughter of Crauford Tait of Harviestoun, near Alva in central Scotland, and was born on 9 June 1800. In 1822, she became the wife of Charles Wake, spent her married life in Derbyshire, Worcestershire, and Northamptonshire, and travelled frequently with her husband on the Continent. Charlotte retained lively graphic and amusing impressions of her childhood, and her memoirs describe life in Scotland and of Edinburgh society in the beginning of the nineteenth century. She died in Pitsford, Northamptonshire in 1888.

In *The Reminiscences of Charlotte, Lady Wake*, Charlotte recalled the dancing at a harvest home, or kirn, at Harviestoun, her family home, occurring when she was 13 years old:

114   *A few more flings and shuffles*

At Harviestoun the kirn always took place in a very large building, a sort of barn loft [...] innumerable were the visits made to the buffet by the panting couples, who for a brief space broke away from the dance at the upper end. Fast and faster still, each foot kept that wonderful time, of which none who have not witnessed real Scottish dancing can form the faintest idea. It is a wild enthusiasm that almost seems like a regulated delirium, while every limb answers to the marvellous music of the Scottish reel and Highland strathspey. Feet stamping, fingers snapping, eyes as it were on fire, heads thrown back, while shouts mark the crisis of the dance, it must have been seen to be imagined. Great was the admiring astonishment of the English guests, intense the delight of the young ones. The young ladies danced with the shepherds and the various working-men belonging to the estate, and the gentlemen with the country lasses, till all were so tired that they were obliged to withdraw.[39]

In a letter written on 2 September 1864, she described a trip to the Isle of Arran:

On Tuesday at 10 A.M., by special invitation of the lieutenant commanding H.M. steamship on this station, we went with a large party to Arran, a good day its mountains and lake showing well, and all things most agreeable. Luncheon on deck Brodick Bay and the Duke of Hamilton's castle and garden looking their best. A little delay at Arran, for two of the party made us later than we expected. Still all was prosperous. Tea on deck, dancing sailor's hornpipe, reels, quadrilles.[40]

She also recalled that Lady Menzies was an extremely good dancer, 'particularly distinguishing herself in the Highland reel' at the assemblies and balls of Edinburgh around 1862.[41]

Alexander Campbell, North Uist, 1815

The Special Collections at the University of Edinburgh Library houses musician and field-collector Alexander Campbell's '*A slight sketch of a journey made through parts of the Highlands and Hebrides; undertaken to collect material for Albyn's Anthology, by the Editor; in Autumn, 1815.*' Campbell observed the relationship between *puirt a beul* song and dance:

While at Lochmaddy [...] I witnessed for the first time, persons singing at the same time as they dance: and this is called dancing to port-na-beul, being a succedaneous contrivance to supply the want of a musical instrument. This effect is droll enough; and gives an idea of what one might conceive to be customary among tribes but little removed from the state of Nature. What renders the illusion more probable is the mode in which these merry Islanders perform the double exercise of singing and dancing—thus the men and women sing a bar alternately; by which they preserve the accent and rhythms quite accurately—the effect is animating: and having words correspondent to the characters of the measure—there seems to be a 3-fold species of gratification arising from the union of song and dance—rude, it is confessed—but such as pleases the vulgar; and not displeasant to one who feels disposed to join in rustic pleasures, or innocent amusement.[42]

We particularly note that the relationship of the dancer's movement to the song rhythm stood out enough to warrant an entry in Campbell's journal. Since he finds the 'amusements' of the Highlanders both 'rustic' and 'innocent,' we wonder what dancing he encountered growing up in Edinburgh. Had he taken dance classes in connection with his music studies, or had he attended assemblies that Topham described? Had he met or attended classes with Martin, Barnard, d'Egville, or Gallini, all teaching in Edinburgh at the time? These questions cannot be answered by Campbell's short passage, and he did not elaborate further on the call and response singing he heard, nor did he describe physical details about the dancing. Other observations he made regarding Dramatic Jigs were mentioned earlier in his 1804 passage.

Letter to the Highland Society, Edinburgh, 1817

In their article recounting early Highland Dancing competitions organised by the Highland Society, held in Edinburgh from 1784 to 1844, the Fletts share this vignette of a letter from an anonymous critic addressed to Henry MacKenzie, the Society secretary, dated 14 July 1817:

> Having been informed that you are a member of the Highland Society under whose patronage the Competitors in Highland Music hold their annual exhibition—I beg leave to suggest to you (as a man of taste), that the dances which accompany the music are susceptible of a very simple and obvious improvement—viz. by lighting the lamps in front of the Stage, in place of introducing light from the window on the side of the Stage opposite to the audience, as at present. At present only the dark side of the dancers is visible, without the smallest variety of shade. In consequence the limbs of the dancers resemble, to my fancy, those of the black-legged highland sheep when collected together [...] and their monotonous appearance together with the clattering noise produced, do [...] detract [...] from the true effect of that highly energetic dance [...] There is just one other point [...] that on account of the manner in which the light is introduced, the expose limbs of the dancers are some-times exhibited to view in a manner altogether superfluous, and highly offensive to every Lady of correct taste and feeling—and not a little so, to some of the other sex, who may not perhaps be entitled to express themselves according to their true sensations on the subject.

116 *A few more flings and shuffles*

> Were this matter, Sir, properly regulated, I am satisfied that many of the fair would think it no offence to attend the exhibition, which is not the case at present. And the increased attendance would far more than repay the additional charges of wax candles and lamps.

The Fletts suggested that the 'reference to "the clattering noise produced" by the dancers [...] indicates that they wore hard shoes.'[43] While Emmerson objected, writing 'one can scarcely claim, however, that the practice was traditional,'[44] the frequency with which shuffling and keeping time with the music is mentioned in seventeenth- and eighteenth-century accounts shows that the wearing of hard shoes with heels and effective time keeping in them was indeed widespread.

Edinburgh Theatre-Royal Playbill, 1821

The inclusion of Hornpipes as *entr'actes* for theatrical productions was very common during the eighteenth and nineteenth centuries throughout the United Kingdom. One performance on 4 June 1821 at the Theatre Royal, Edinburgh, for example, included a 'National Pas Seul' by Miss Nichol, and a 'Hornpipe in Fetters' by Mr Stanley as *entr'actes* for the comedy *The Clandestine Marriage*.[45] Listed as an attraction later that week was a 'Highland Reel' accompanying the play *The Heart of Midlothian*.[46] Theatrical culture helped share ideas of what signified Highland dancing in the central and southern areas of Scotland.

The Hornpipe in Fetters was categorised as a 'Scotch Dance' in the early 1800s.[47] The dance was often used as an *entr'acte* dance between the final acts of John Gay's *Beggar's Opera*, which occurs just before the audience finds the antihero MacHeath in jail.[48] When G. Barstow danced a Hornpipe in Fetters, it was categorised as a 'Clog Hornpipe,' as described in the next section.

Edinburgh Dramatic Review, 1822–1825

Playbills reprinted in the *Edinburgh Dramatic Review* in the 1820s provide snapshots of the vibrant theatre scene in Edinburgh at that time. Dances were presented as *entr'actes* between scenes or plays, and sometimes were incorporated into the plays themselves. There are many references to hornpipes of varied sorts and 'Scotch' dances. Following a production of *The Bride of Lammermoor* at the Theatre-Royal Edinburgh in 1822, in an abrupt shift of mood, a Miss Nicoll performed a 'Skipping Rope Pas Seul.' Commentary on her performance enthused that 'After the play, Miss M. Nicoll performed a Skipping-rope Pas Seul very prettily and was unanimously encored.'[49]

A dance performed at the Caledonian Theatre in the early 1820s was a 'Clog Hornpipe in real Fetters' at the Caledonian Theatre, helping to illustrate that the Fetters Hornpipe was specifically percussive.[50] It was performed for the benefit of Mr G. Bristow by Mr Bristow himself, identified as a 'clown,' who kicked off the evening with an 'Astonishing Flight from the Stage to the Gallery and back again to the Stage' followed by his 'Admired Comic Dance of ROLEY POLEY.'

A Misses Eyres' benefit featured variety in its presentation of national dances: the Guaracha, *Seann Triubhas*, and Fling.[51] Dances in national characterisations that drew on stereotypes were popular and rather typical in this period. Many 'national dances' went on to be included in dancing masters' repertoires across the United Kingdom. It is impossible to tell if these dances were accurate representations of multicultural dance traditions or theatrical renderings of emerging national stereotypes, or somewhere between the two. Miss Mary Eyre also surfaces in information we present regarding the 1826 *Extraordinary Dance Book T B.* as having danced Milanie's Hornpipe in Edinburgh in 1821.

Celtic Melodies, Highlands, 1823

An anonymous printed collection in the National Library of Scotland with the title *Celtic Melodies* consists of two volumes of music with labels such as 'Cainntearachd,' 'Pipe Reel,' and 'Cainntearachd, or Porst a beale.' This collection has not been reprinted. *Celtic Melodies* was published by Robert Purdie in Edinburgh. According to Will Lamb, who provided the entry,[52] the date '19 June 1823' is written in pencil on the collection, presumably by pipemaker David Glen (1853–1916). The first number contains a significant passage on page 34:

> This Reel does famously for the Highland way of dancing. It must appear very droll to a stranger. The right foot is first put down, the left drawn up on a level with it, the right foot advanced again, and a kind of bob or curtsey for the fourth movement, this is not done smoothly but thumped through telling every step, the setting is the same, perhaps with the addition of a few side kicks to finish, just as you or I would finish with a 'Jetté et Assemblee?' But the lads brogue it so heartily, and the maidens trip it so neatly, that it is a question whether it is not more animated, than the half sailing, half sleeping, and half walking of the higher classes.

This personal, handwritten message clearly shows that early nineteenth-century dancers coexisted with slight variations in styles of dancing; and that these different styles pertained to dancing the Highland Reels. The writer's use of terminology to describe the differences is telling: French terms are used for the 'half sailing, half sleeping, and half walking of the higher classes' while the familiar thumps and, again, 'kicks,' are used to describe alike the hearty 'brogueing' of the lads, and the neat tripping of the ladies. It is not certain that the upper-class dances referred to were done in Scotland, but it is clear that the dancing 'telling every step' is the 'Highland way of dancing.'

118 *A few more flings and shuffles*

John MacTaggart, Kirkcudbright and Galloway, 1824

A portrayal of the percussive hornpipe treepling or trebling taught by a rural dancing master is found in John MacTaggart's *The Scottish Gallovidian Encyclopedia,* published in London in 1824. MacTaggart's account describes the syllabus of a rural dancing master from the South West Lowlands, probably in MacTaggart's native countryside of Kirkcudbright and Galloway around 1820:

> Commonly the first step dancing masters teach their pupils [...is] Peter a Dick's Peatstack, [...] performed by giving three *flegs* with the feet, and two stamps with the heel alternately; [...] the noise the feet make seems to speak [...] *Peter a Dick, Peter a Dick, Peter a Dick's Peatstack* [...] When the scholars become tolerable at *beetling it,* they are next taught to fleup through the side-step, then *Jack on the Green, Shawintrewse,* and other *hornpipes,* with the *Highland Fling,* mayhap; these dances all got pretty well by the feet in the *first month,* with sketches of *foursome,* eightsome reels and some country dances; but if the scholars attend the *fortnight* again of another *month,* they proceed at great length into the labyrinths of the art.
>
> *A light heel'd souter* is generally the dancing dominie; he fixes on a barn in some *clauchan* to show forth in; he can both fiddle and dance, at the same time; he can cut double quick time, and *trible Bob Major;* he fixes on, and publishes abroad when his *trial night* is to come on, so the young folk in the neighbourhood doff their *clogs,* and put on their *kirk-shoon,* these being their *dancing-pumps;* off they go to the trial, which, if it be a good turn-out, he tries no more, but begins teaching directly; if not, he has a second, and even a *third* trial; [...]
>
> They learn the 'Flowers of Edinburgh,' mayhap; *Sweden* and *Belile's Marches,* with other hornpipes, and country dances many; such as *Yillwife and her Barrles—Mary Grey—The Wun that shook the barley,* &c. with the famous *Bumpkin Brawley;* yes, and they will even dare, sometimes to imitate our Continental neighbours over the water, in their *waltzing, alimanging,* and *Cotillion trade;* ay, and be up with the Spaniards too, in their *quadrilles, borellos,* and *falderalloes* of nonsense; so out-taught, they become fit to attend *house-heatings, volunteer* and *masonic-balls,* and what not.[53]

Beating out the rhythm to 'peter dum dick' was still well known in Dunbartonshire in the 1930s, according to George Emmerson, who himself practised on the 'clappers.'[54] Here is a clear description of the rhythm made by the feet and some often-overlooked information regarding the footwear worn for dancing: either clogs or Sunday-best church shoes. The text connotes that Highland Fling is the name of a step, rather than a dance, and the Seann Triubhas is labelled a Hornpipe. MacTaggart's account indicates that other well-known Hornpipes of the time were the Flowers of Edinburgh and the Sweden March, which may be the dance also called the King of Sweden. He named other steps in use, such as 'trible' and 'cut double quick time.' What the latter signifies remains a question. 'Trible' or treeple/triple/treble, on the other hand, survives into modern use in Scottish dancing. Fleg was defined by MacTaggart as 'a swinging blow with the foot;' the 1987 *Concise Scots Dictionary* explains it as 'a severe blow, a kick.' Emmerson additionally detailed flegs as 'flutterings with a swinging step.'[55] The word fleup, wrote MacTaggart, means 'broad feet,' while Emmerson offered a further suggestion that 'to *fleup* means to dance without lifting the feet, probably shuffling, or trebling (or tripling).'[56] It is possible the word could be a variant of the percussive dance term flap.

Some caution may be warranted when considering John MacTaggart's depiction and his spelling of terminology. In the *Edinburgh Magazine* volume of October 1824, the editors are scathingly critical about the accuracy of much of his work, claiming that many terms are made up or altered to be claimed as coming specifically from Galloway, when, according to them, most were commonly used throughout Scotland and England.[57] Whether this criticism was justified would need further investigation. We can assume that his descriptions accurately depict dancing practices, even if his vocabulary could not be specifically traced to Galloway as a source.

Allan Cunningham, South-west Scotland, 1825

The Dumfriesshire poet Allan Cunningham was born in Keir in 1784 and died in London in 1842. His father had been a neighbour of Robert Burns, and Allan himself became a friend of the self-taught rural bard James Hogg, 'the Ettrick Shepherd.' He was a hard-working writer and editor who collected old ballads and stories. In Volume One of his four-volume work *The Songs of Scotland,*[58] Allan Cunningham described two dramatic folk dances. One, called the Wooing of the Maiden, was a comic dance—'a representation uniting the fourfold qualities of acting, dancing, music, and song'—that must have provided entertainment at weddings, harvest homes, and other festivities. A couple costumed to look like characters entered the barn to the strains of the tune 'The Wooing of the Maiden.' 'They advanced to the middle of the floor beating time to the tune, and smiling upon each other, and mimicking the appearance of delight and joy.'[59] The woman, dressed as an old maid, sang of 'the charms of opulence,' which was countered by the young man's song showing contempt for riches. The woman took umbrage with this and:

> strode round the floor with the stride of an ogress, and shivered all her finery with anger and pride as a fowl ruffles its feathers. Her lover seemed by no means desirous of soothing her; he mimicked her lordliness of step, and the waving of her mantle, and stepped step by step with her and the music round the floor.[60]

120 *A few more flings and shuffles*

After that, the man summoned other dancing partners from amongst the spectators to render the opulent woman jealous.

Another of the pantomimic dances described by Cunningham was to the tune 'Rock and the Wee Pickle Tow.' Cunningham's account tells that the dance depicts the sober themes of thrift and industry, revolving around a 'staid and thrifty looking dame' winding thread. Around her dances a 'joyous middle-aged man, somewhat touched, it may be, with liquor: he holds a candle in his hand, and dances with her round the floor, beating accurate time all the while to the music.' After the two characters have sung about first pleasure and then repentance, the man attempts to set the woman on fire with the candle, and the music 'grows fast and furious ... while the woman eludes him with great activity, and all the while the music and the feet echo to each other.'[61]

Cunningham's reminiscences provide glimpses of a pantomimic Dramatic Jig tradition not widely seen today, that included dances such as the *Damhsa an Chleoca*/cloak dance described by Alexander Campbell and the *Cailleach an Dùdain*/Old Woman of the Milldust, depicting a tragi-comic death and resurrection scenario. In the author's attempt to paint as clear a scene as possible, his descriptions of the feet beating in exact time with the music show us that this effect was consistently performed, noticed by observers, and used to dramatic effect. The geographical location of where these dances were once performed was not specifically identified.

Interestingly, as a finishing note, Cunningham also touched upon the stern religious attitudes of the church towards dancing:

> During the continuance of this unwholesome system of kirk discipline, dancing was accounted a profane amusement; men were rebuked for listening or moving; to the sound of any music save that of psalmody; and those who wished to learn this ancient and forbidden art were obliged to go in private and enjoy it with the terror of kirk-rebuke before them. I remember when the sons of a venerable and strict Cameronian stole out secretly every evening to a dancing school; but I have always had a suspicion that the old worthy was aware of this backsliding of his offspring; and it was remarked, that in his prayers, which were exceedingly long and curious, he sought grace for those who 'foolishly flang on a floor, and who leaped, and danced, and bent the knees (which should bend only to Him above) to a musical idol of wood and thairm [fiddle string].'[62]

Nathaniel Hazeltine Carter, Inveroran, Glen Orchy by Loch Tulla, 1825

In *Letters from Europe, comprising the Journal of a Tour through Ireland, England, Scotland, France, Italy and Switzerland*, American travel writer Nathaniel H. Carter, who was born September 17, 1787 in Concord, New Hampshire, and died in December 1829, described his experiences in the Highlands of

Scotland. He described hearing Gaelic songs sung by his hosts, a Campbell and a McGregor at 'Ballahulish' one evening. On the following night, the 6th of October, at Inveroran by Loch Tolla he wrote:

> Another lonely little inn, by the side of a noisy water-fall within a few yards of the door, afforded us a dish of tea, and a pillow for the night. Duncan M'Intosh, whose name and lineage suggested the proud appellation of *Rex*, and whose integrity presented stronger claims to the title than some who wear it can boast, had sufficient influence with the landlord and his family, consisting of half a dozen lassies, and as many yellow-haired laddies, to get up for our evening entertainment not only another musical party, but a dance. Mine host, whose face had been converted by whiskey into a fine piece of bronze, held the light: an inmate of the tavern played the fiddle, but was unfortunate at the outset in snapping one of the strings: while the rest of the party formed sets, and with naked feet on the naked floor, went through with the various dances of the country,
> 'Where hornpipes, jigs, strathspeys and reels,
> Put life and mettle in their heels.'[63]

This quotation, unattributed lines from Robert Burns's poem *Tam O'Shanter*, relies on the poetic trope of lively heels identifying Scottish dancing. Inveroran is only a few miles from Dalmally Inn, where Thornton saw the 'Glen Orgue kick' some 39 years earlier. Step dancing was likely still in fashion in this part of Argyll in the 1820s, even in 'naked' feet.

This same passage by Burns was also used to describe dancing at an inn near Arrochar in 1817 in *Letters from Scotland: by an English commercial traveller*, an anonymous English writer:

> we quickened our pace, but were completely drenched in the rain before we reached Arrochar—an inn, once the seat of a powerful chief. So few have been the changes of property in the Highlands, that their inhabitants feel a lively regret in the circumstance of a house, which was once the honoured residence of a chieftain, being degraded into a public inn. For my part I felt no regret at a change which enabled us to command comforts to which circumstances had given a more than ordinary value. As the rain still continued, we determined to remain here all night. In the course of the evening a party arrived, among which were some ladies whom F. knew, and to whom he introduced us. The Scotish ladies have a good deal of the characteristic prudence of their country, which makes them reserved in mixed society, but when in the company of their intimate friends, their *naivete* and grace is charming. We had not been long together when someone expressed a regret that we had no music for a dance. It was proposed to send for a performer on the bagpipes, which of all the instruments in the world produces the most execrable sounds,

122 *A few more flings and shuffles*

when, as good luck would have it, an itinerant fidler was heard torturing his cat gut in the kitchen. S. soon obtained his instrument, and produced such animating sounds, that we started up by a simultaneous movement, and

Hornpipes. jigs. strathspeys and reels
Pat life and mettle in our heels.

By the bye these lines of Burns will show you that Scotish dancing is not exactly on 'the light fantastic toe.' But what it wants in grace is compensated by the heartfelt gaiety which it expresses. I certainly shall not soon forget our evening's amusement.

When the ladies retired, the gentlemen paid their respects most heartily to the national drink, and I was induced to join them in their libations of whisky, on the assurance that *there was not a headache in a hogshead of it.*[64]

Again, footwork made an impression on the observer, whomever he was. The writer used Burns's lines to contrast with the 'light fantastic toe' quotation from John Milton's *L'Allegro*, identifying a difference between English styling, emphasising grace, and Scottish styling, emphasising gaiety. This account places another dance description in Argyllshire, as Arrochar is 32 miles south of Inveroran/Bridge of Orchy, with Dalmally between the two villages. Inveroran Hotel, which dates to about 1708, is still a functioning inn in Glen Orchy.

T B. Dance Book, 1826, and Lowe brothers, 1831

A notebook with the words 'Dance Book' proudly emblazoned on its title page, and inscribed 'T B. 1826' offers another glimpse of some dances associated with the Scottish dancing traditions. The majority of the dances in the book reflect professional dancing of the time. Many of the directions for the dances seem notated in a kind of shorthand, giving only cues for step combinations. Some descriptions are accompanied by drawings depicting pathways dancers would have taken across a stage and in relation to each other. These arrangements were for dancers ranging in number from the *Pas Seul* to up to 12 dancers. Spellings in the manuscript conform neither to current French nor Gaelic orthography; the terms will be presented as they appear in the original.[65]

Two dances classified as Shauntreuse occur early in the manuscript, and are arranged for six to eight dancers. The first of these, an 'Irish Shauntreuse,' includes terms such as 'Heel & Toe aside & shuffles,' 'Jettè & Glissade for do: with L.F. & two shuffles,' 'Two Jettès forward, toe-beat & two hops,' 'Two toe-beats & two hops,' 'Beat behind & before, and heel & toe aside,' and 'Eschappez 2 passes behind & before forw^d 3 times & shuffles.'[66] A drawing indicating dancers' pathways shows that these steps did travel; the majority of the steps travelled in straight or angled pathways, though for a few of the steps moved in sweeping arcs. Often the dancers would retrace pathways just danced.

The dance labelled as a Scotch Shauntreuse features similar terminology: 'Eschappez hop & beat behind & before,' 'Eschappez & toe beat etc.,' 'Eschappez aside toe beat,' 'Toe beat & 2 Jettès forw^d,' '2 Eschappez & two toe beats etc.,' 'Heel & toe,' 'Toe beat & 2 hops round,' and 'Toe beat & two cuts to cross the foot.'[67] The diagram of dancers' pathways shows that the 'Heel & toe' step travelled in a straight line in one direction for the first half, and then retraced that pathway back to the starting point. This kind of lateral travel is seen in the side-heel-and-toe step in the twentieth-century Highland *Seann Triubhas*, and in the 'National' dance, Highland Laddie. It is also common in Cape Breton strathspey steps.

There are other references to 'Scotch Steps' in the manuscript. One is in a dance titled *Pas Quatre*/dance for four. This dance features a majority of circular pathways, with the Scotch steps being exceptions. The fourth of ten steps described is labelled the 'New Scotch step' and the diagram shows dancers moving in straight pathways toward one another in a 'quick movement,' and then giving 'Hands across back with LH.' The step following this is captioned 'Sissons and Scotch Steps' showing a side-to-side motion again retracing its pathway. The worded description puts this as involving 'Single sissons before & behind, 2 single steps all behind, single sissons & shuffles.'[68] The use of the word *sissone* resonates with Peacock's description of the lematrást as a series of *sissones*.

The 'English Hornpipe' occurring much later in the manuscript uses the term 'Highland fling' as shorthand for one of its steps. Other evocative terms showing up in the lists of Hornpipe steps include 'Double shuffle forward,' 'Toe & heel,' 'Rocking step round,' 'Shuffles round,' 'Toe beats crossing,' 'Heel rattles,' 'Heel round,' and 'Heel rattles round.'[69]

The manuscript is especially of interest because it is in the Lowe family collection at the Alexander Turnbull Library in New Zealand. This collection of manuscripts comes from the family of Scottish dancing masters who published dance guides, such as the 1831 *Lowes' Ball-Conductor and Assembly Guide*. Joseph Lowe, Sr., served as the dancing master for Queen Victoria and the Royal family at Balmoral. His journal, written 26 years later than the T B. manuscript, shares an anecdote that is telling about the evolution taking place in Scottish dance fashions in the middle of the nineteenth century. He writes:

> the carpet in the Dining Room was rolled back, and the whole party went through everything that was done the day before at Abergeldie with the addition of the Reel of Tulloch in which Her Majesty took a part and danced in the most spirited style. Her Majesty then said that she would like to show me some more Steps that she had learned before and asked my opinion of them. I told Her Majesty that they were truly Scotch Steps but in my opinion too rough for Ladies and more adapted for Men. Her Majesty said she was of the same opinion and that she thought my Steps much more elegant and the best for Ladies she had ever seen.[70]

124 *A few more flings and shuffles*

This vignette gives us a delightful glimpse of a dance master in action, teaching Victoria to be even more Victorian! Lowe agrees that the 'rough' steps are 'Scotch,' then teaches what he and his pupil deem are more appropriate, 'elegant,' and presumably still Scotch enough to be included in the Reel of Tulloch. The Lowe brothers, named Joseph, Robert, J.S. [James], and John, in their 1831 *Ball-Conductor and Assembly Guide*, remarked disparagingly, as noted earlier in Chapter 5, on the practice of gentlemen 'capering, rattling, and shuffling their feet in the rudest manner' on the dance floors of the day.[71] While the authors clearly disapproved of the practice, their comment reveals that it was common to hear rattling at social dances. Later in his career, in 1857, Joseph Lowe proudly advertised that 'it has been his aim for many years to smooth down and assimilate as much as possible the dancing of our Reels and Strathspeys to the style of the present day.'[72] The Lowe brothers were influential in smoothing and softening Scottish dancing through the nineteenth century.

While it is not yet known how *The Extraordinary Dance Book T B. 1826* came to be in the possession of the Lowe family, the different versions of Shauntreuses and Hornpipes show that these dances were regarded more as types or genres of dance than as one dance with a discrete set of steps. It is not known with certainty what T B. stands for. We discovered documentation of a performance of one of the lesser-known Hornpipes in *The Extraordinary Dance Book T B.* in the *Edinburgh Dramatic Review*. Miss Mary Eyre, billed as a 'pupil of Mrs Wm. Barrymore,' performed Madame Milanie's Hornpipe at the Theatre-Royal Edinburgh in 1822.[73] The dance preceding Milanie's Hornpipe in the manuscript is titled 'Mrs. B's Waltz,'[74] and this makes us wonder if 'B' could stand for Barrymore.

Regardless of its original owner, the *Dance Book T B.* shares valuable information about these dances, and, in some cases, provides accompanying music. A Shauntreuse is depicted as a type of dance that could be Irish or Scottish, and one that can be arranged for varied numbers of performers. This manuscript helps connect the Scottish High Dance legacies to theatrical practices.

James Logan, London, 1831

Antiquarian James Logan's writings depicting various practices and customs of Scottish Gaelic culture were famously recorded in his two-volume collection *The Scottish Gael*, published in 1831. In it, Logan's stated focus was on the 'Gaelic Manners,' which 'the singular habits of the aboriginal Celts [...] most tenaciously retained.'[75] He refers to Gaels' musical abilities often, and observes that:

> Dancing, among the Gael, does not depend on the presence of musical instruments. They reel and set to their own vocal music, or to the songs of those who are near; people, whose hearts are light and responsive to their native melodies, will find their limbs move in consonance to its music, however produced.[76]

Aberdeen-born James Logan (1797–1872) was the son of a merchant and educated at Aberdeen grammar school and Marischal College. With the support of Lord Aberdeen, he moved to London, studied at the Royal Academy of the Arts, worked as a journalist, and was employed by the Highland Society of London. Material for *The Scottish Gael*, or *Celtic Manners* was collected on walking tours he conducted through the Scottish Highlands and Islands in the 1820s where he collected Gaelic antiquities. His work shares important information in respect to the Highland customs observed and described, but other aspects, such as the historical material, are now regarded as obsolete.[77]

Logan followed the fashion of the era by including classical philosophical references to support the propriety of certain practices. Also, Logan's writing is imbued with a tone of national romanticism, evident when referring to the Gaels as 'aboriginal Celts.' The supporting quotation he chose below particularly reflects percussive dancing:

> The cultivation and practice of poetry and music are chief amusements of the Gael, and connected with both is DANCING. If the Scots excel in the former, they certainly of all nations are preeminent in partiality to the latter. Their passion for this pleasing and healthy exercise is indeed so strong, that it seems part of their nature. The art of dancing, which a person without a musical ear can never attain, is a harmonious adaptation of the bodily powers to time and measure, accompanied with grace, ease, expression, position, &.c.; yet the Scots have been said to be 'entirely without grace' in their dances. Their agility may surprise, without pleasing, those who do not understand the national system, but that a person should be able to execute the most intricate and complex steps with the utmost ease, keeping the justest time, without 'a particle of grace,' is surely impossible. Grace, in dancing, is described as 'fitness of parts and good attitude,' and that the Highlanders possess these necessary qualifications cannot be denied; indeed, their aptitude for music is not more striking than their fondness for the national reel.
>
> Dancing has been practised by almost every people; it formed, in fact, part of the religious ceremonies of almost all nations, and the gods are not only said to have been pleased, but were themselves emulous in the dance. Pindar represents Silenus as 'Strenuous in the dance to beat/ Tuneful measures with his feet.'[78]

Logan seems to be defending the style of Scottish dancing in contrast to dancing styles of London, where the book was originally published. He seems to be refuting Topham's assertion that the Scots dancing was 'entirely void of grace' and arguing for audiences to view the dancing with the values the Gaels themselves hold: timing and intricacy of pattern. Logan draws a quotation from Francis Peacock on page 339, and then goes on to reiterate Peacock's list of steps, only adding a short elaboration:

126 *A few more flings and shuffles*

All these, and many more are combined in one dance, and the association depends on the taste of the party. That called the back step, in which the feet are each alternately slipped behind, and reach the ground on, or close to, the spot occupied by the one just removed, is of difficult acquirement, and severely exerts the muscles of the calfs of the legs. So much dexterity can some persons display in this, that they will go through the setting time of the music without moving beyond a space marked by the circumference of their bonnet.[79]

The 'back step with a hop' may not, to a contemporary dancer, connote a percussive nature, depending on idiom and context. However, the 'Shetland back step' is an example where this motif is percussive, emphasising the back foot hitting the floor with a loud accent. Other accompanying movements often combined with a backstep, such as digging or beating your feet into the ground three times after two backsteps are common percussive elements used.

The borrowed phrase 'tuneful measures of the feet' and the assertion that steps always vary from occasion to occasion show that characteristics highlighted by Colonel Thornton and Francis Peacock in the early part of the nineteenth century were still in practice in 1831.

Logan also made much of shows of skill and improvisational abilities celebrated in vernacular-style Step dancing among the Gaels:

I have seen two brothers of the name of Grant, who were good violin players, exhibit feats of great agility. Part of their performance consisted of dancing the Highland fling, in that style called the Marquis of Huntley's, Strathspeys over a rope, and Gilli-Callum over a fiddle bow; and one of them danced a Strathspey, played the fiddle, played bass on the bagpipe, smoked, spoke Gaelic, and explained it in question and answer at the same time![80]

The 1841 Scottish census lists a Donald Grant, born in 1776, from Urquhart in Moray, as a Teacher of Dancing and Musician. Was he possibly one of the Grant brothers Logan observed?

La Sylphide, 1836, and August Bournonville, Denmark (1805–1879)

August Bournonville was the 'grand old man of Danish Ballet.'[81] He was born and raised in Copenhagen, son of a prominent Ballet dancer, and trained in Ballet from an early age. In 1824, he studied extensively with Auguste Vestris in Paris, and passed his *Paris Opéra* examinations in 1826. Bournonville travelled as a soloist to various cities through Europe, including London, before returning to Copenhagen for a lengthy and productive career as a soloist, principal choreographer, and eventually director of the Royal Danish Ballet.

A few more flings and shuffles 127

Bournonville's *La Sylphide* was not the first production of a ballet featuring dancers depicting fairies dancing high on the tips of their toes—an earlier version was a ballet with the same title that wildly popularised the already emerging trend of dancing *en pointe*, and catapulted Marie Taglioni to stardom in 1832. *La Sylphide* is set in the Scottish Highlands, and the plot follows a young bridegroom who becomes captivated by a fairy, and subsequently leaves his own wedding to chase after the fairy. After being dissatisfied with the overall effect of Filippo Taglioni's Paris production, Bournonville decided to mount a version of his own, in which he himself played the leading man, James.

Bournonville writes, 'I made several changes in the plan.' Among other things, 'I gave the ballet a national color [Scottish] which is not to be found in the Parisian version.'[82] Indeed, dance critic Walter Terry's feeling about Bournonville's presentation of national dances is that 'August was profoundly concerned with the customs, the characteristics, the feelings of a people. Today it might be said that he was not content with exotic surfaces but, as far as the Ballet idiom of the day permitted, was concerned with reasonably accurate ethnic reporting.'[83] Another dance critic, Deborah Jowitt, describes realism as an integral aspect of the genre of Romantic Ballet, without which the supernatural themes would have no resonance. 'Even in supernatural ballets, they prided themselves on the detail of their crowd scenes, the verisimilitude with which they evoked a Highland revel or a Naples dockside or a village festival.'[84] Bournonville's goal would be to present a Highland wedding and dance realistically.

Percussive dance is a prominent feature of the 'Wedding festivities' scene in Act 1. While the fairies wear *pointe* shoes to enhance their ethereal nature, and James wears ballet slippers to allow him to dance virtuosic *batterie*, the Wedding party folk, including the bride, wear hard shoes. Stamping and stylised shuffling are pronounced features of the dance, which also includes other motifs enduring in Highland dance today, such as Tulloch-type turns, Highland Second arm position, and the Highland Sailor's Hornpipe arms and front cuts. An excerpt from the Royal Danish Ballet's 1988 production is available on YouTube.[85] Bournonville's choreography has been maintained fastidiously by the Royal Danish Ballet since the ballet was created in 1836. The percussive nature of this dance can be seen as reflecting how Bournonville, an astute observer and practitioner of dance, typified Scottish dancing.

Words used for dancing in this chapter

Distilling terminology and words used by these authors in the earlier part of nineteenth century to describe dancing creates the following composite:

> Footing it; cross passes, kicking steps, hop backsteps; shuffles, heel-and-toe steps, pounding and thumping noises; each foot kept that wonderful

128   *A few more flings and shuffles*

time, feet stamping, fingers snapping; the clattering noise produced; thumped through telling every step, the addition of a few side kicks to finish [...] the lads brogue it so heartily; three flegs with the feet, and two stamps with the heel alternately; [...] the noise the feet make seems to speak [...] beetling it, they are next taught to fleup through the side-step; beating accurate time all the while to the music; Put life and mettle in their heels; beat behind & before, and heel & toe aside [...] capering, rattling, and shuffling their feet; tuneful measures of the feet.

Dancing in Scotland is in for a big shift at this particular point in history. Even though Scottish dances were fashionable in London early on in the nineteenth century, after Victoria's ascension in 1837, and coronation in 1838, as Victoria gravitates to Scotland, dancing traditions come to be associated with the aristocracy and the military. Dancers will be further encouraged to leave percussive steps at home as processes of refining and gentrifying Scottish dance practices intensify.

Notes

1. Wilson 1811: 194. Wilson's prices for classes were costly. The Shantruse cost £4 4/- (four guineas) to learn in 1811. Today that would be equivalent to £341.47, roughly equivalent to €390 in the Eurozone or $422 in the United States. The website https://www.in2013dollars.com/ was used to calculate these equivalencies. [Accessed 25 April 2020].
2. Smout 1990: 484.
3. Smout 1986: 2.
4. Smout 1990: 485.
5. Devine 2011: 97–99.
6. Campbell 1804: 264–265.
7. Fraser 1911. See also Aberdeen Council Register, 17 January, and 14 February 1747.
8. Russell 2014: 129.
9. Peacock was trained by Desnoyer, (possibly Denoyer, dancer and choreographer (d. 1788), who danced at London Theatres such as Drury Lane, and was dancing master to the Prince of Wales (Highfill *et al.*, Vol. 4, 1975: 332), Glover (Leach Glover, d. 1763), was an *entr'acte* dancer, like Desnoyer, and actor on the London stages in the beginning of the eighteenth century and later, after 1741. Later, he was dancing master to the Princesses Amelia and Carolina (*ibid*, Vol. 6, 1975: 335)), and Lally (another *entr'acte* dancer at Drury Lane) (Milhous 2003: 489).
10. Nicol, *The Reel* 254, 2005: 11.
11. Jaffray 1835: 146.
12. Peacock 1805: 18.
13. Peacock 1805: 86.
14. Peacock 1805: 88–89.
15. Peacock 1805: 91–98.
16. MacLeoid 1969: 19–20. The quotation reads: *"N uair a bhiodh an luadh réidh, dhean-adh iad réiteach air an t-seòmar, is shìneadh iad ri na dannsaichean Gàidhealach le cuide-achadh-ciùil o na fidhlearean a bhiodh 's a' chuideachd. Bha ainmean Gàidhlig aca 's an là us air son a h-uile ceum is tionndadh a bhiodh 's an dannsa, gu h-àraidh 's an dannsa-clis, 's an dannsa-deise, 's an ruidhil. So agaibh cuid diubh:—ceum-siùbhla, ceum-coisiche, leum-trasd, siabadh-trasd, aiseag-trasd, ceum-baideanach, fosgladh, cuartag, ceum-cùil, gearradh-àrd,*

gearradh-dùbailte, seatadh, agus bruichcath. Cha robh gluasad-cuirpe air a cheadachadh 's an dannsa-clis, (no, gradcharach), ach, o bhun a chnàmha-droma do bhonnaibh nan cas. Bha na làmhan rag ri gach taobh de 'n dannsair. Bhiodh stri is farpuis eatorra ach có a b' fheàrr cuideachd. Chuala mi iomradh air 'Farpais nan Seachd Coinnlean' far am biodh seachd coinnlean air an ùrlar, troigh eatorra 's iad laiste. Bha e mar earraig air an dannsair, lasair-bhuaic nan seachd coinnlean a chur às, té an deidh té, le breab a dhà chois.'

17. Patricia Ballantyne includes some pages of Peacock's book at the University of Aberdeen's James 'Scott' Skinner website: https://www.abdn.ac.uk/scottskinner/peacock.shtml.

18. Francis Peacock's book is available online in its entirety at the Library of Congress's American Ballroom Companion website: http://hdl.loc.gov/loc.music/musdi.133. The proceeds from the sales went to the then newly built 'Lunatic Hospital' to which, with other charities, he left over £1000 sterling in his will (Aberdeen City Archives). He was, according to his obituary, said to have been 'a useful citizen and a good man' (Elphinstone Manuscript 1998).

19. Melin 2012a.

20. Flett 1979.

21. Tubridy 1998; Foley 2012 and 2013.

22. Peacock 1805: 92–93; Dwelly 1988: 233.

23. This step was first taught to J.F. and T.M. Flett by their teachers George D. Taylor and Jack McConachie, and was widely known in the Highlands, Orkney and Shetland (Flett 1985: 124, 211–212), Cape Breton (Rhodes 1985: 284), and in France (Guillard 1989: 32).

24. Guillard 1989: 25–26.

25. Topham 1776: 265 in Guillard 1989: 25.

26. Rhodes 1985: 282.

27. Guillard 1989: 25–26.

28. Cramb 1953: 6; Emmerson 1972: 162; and Peacock, F. 1762.

29. Emmerson 1972: 154.

30. Peacock 1805: 85–86.

31. Peacock 1805: 98.

32. Grant 1911: 13.

33. Grant 1911: 41.

34. Grant 1911: 45.

35. Grant 1911: 213.

36. Grant 1911: 218.

37. Stapleton 2014: 84.

38. Stapleton 2014: 84.

39. Wake 1909: 47–48.

40. Wake 1909: 277.

41. Wake 1909: 267.

42. Campbell, 1815: 35–36 quoted in Dickson 2006: 18.

43. Flett 1956b: 350.

44. Emmerson 1972: 244.

45. From the playbill archive at the National Library of Scotland: https://digital.nls.uk/playbills/bigpic/?pic=74417695.

46. Theatre-Royal Edinburgh, playbill for 4 June 1821.

47. For more about this and other styles of Hornpipes presented in Edinburgh, see Joan Flett's writing about Hornpipes at: http://chrisbrady.itgo.com/dance/stepdance/hornpipe_conference.htm.

48. *Edinburgh Dramatic Review* 1825: 864. 'In the Third Act of the Opera, Mr. J Stanley will dance THE HORNPIPE IN FETTERS.'

49. *Edinburgh Dramatic Review* 1822: 132–133.

50. *Edinburgh Dramatic Review* 1823: 23.

130 *A few more flings and shuffles*

51. *Edinburgh Dramatic Review* 1825: 48.
52. Email correspondence with the author 4 March 2015. Will Lamb further quotes Roderick Cannon: 'an anonymous printed collection in two volumes, *Celtic Melodies,* [1823, 1830], National Library Glen 399(1,2). Keith and I have put some effort into trying to identify the compiler, so far without success. For reasons that I can't just now remember we've suspected it comes from Islay, and we have wondered about a certain Alexander MacKay, who published a collection of reels etc. arranged for piano, ca 1822, NLS Glen 344.'
53. MacTaggart 1824: 263.
54. Emmerson 1972: 157.
55. Emmerson 1972: 158.
56. Emmerson 1972: 158.
57. *The Edinburgh Magazine,* 1824: 385–397. The critical Edinburgh article can be found on link: http://books.google.ie/books?id=Xls3AQAAMAAJ&pg=RA1-PA385&d-q=john+mactaggart+1824+Gallovidian&hl=en&sa=X&ei=Q3e5U62QFc_H7Ab-3pYGQDg&redir_esc=y#v=onepage&q=john%20mactaggart%201824%20 Gallovidian&f=false [Accessed 6 July 2014].
58. Cunningham 1825: https://ia600306.us.archive.org/7/items/songsofscotlanda-01cunn/songsofscotlanda01cunn.pdf [Accessed 30 May 2017].
59. Cunningham 1825: 149.
60. Cunningham 1825: 149–150.
61. Cunningham 1825: 151–152.
62. Cunningham 1825: 117–118.
63. Hazeltine Carter 1829: 299.
64. Anonymous 1817: 136–187.
65. T B—Dance Book: http://natlib.govt.nz/records/23231219 [Accessed 2 June 2017].
66. Aldrich *et al.* 2000: 72.
67. Aldrich *et al.* 2000: 74.
68. Aldrich *et al.* 2000: 76.
69. Aldrich *et al.* 2000: 100–107.
70. Thomas 1992: 27.
71. Lowe 1831: 162.
72. Thomas 1992: 10.
73. *Edinburgh Dramatic Review* 1822: 104.
74. Aldrich *et al.* 2000: 119.
75. Logan 1831: title page.
76. Logan 1831: 440.
77. D.S. Thomson, *Oxford Dictionary of National Biography,* online ed.
78. Logan 1831: 437.
79. Logan 1831: 440.
80. Logan 1831: 440.
81. Terry, 1979: front matter.
82. Terry 1979: 41–42.
83. Terry 1979: 86.
84. Jowitt 2010: 162.
85. The 1988 Royal Danish Ballet production of La Sylphide is posted on YouTube at: https://www.youtube.com/watch?v=TLs3kpe7G0I [Accessed 20 June 2019].

8 Aberdeenshire to the Hebrides
Nineteenth-century
accounts, 1840–1899

Highlandism, balmorality, and tartanism—influencing factors on Scottish dance practices

On 28 June 1838, Victoria was crowned Queen of the United Kingdom, and in 1840, she married Prince Albert. When Victoria and Albert developed their deep affection for the Highlands of Scotland, and built Balmoral castle in Aberdeenshire for themselves and their family in the 1850s, certain Scottish cultural signifiers became highly fashionable. Growing influences that impacted the evolution of dance traditions in Scotland were the ideologies of highlandism, tartanism, and balmorality:

> It was mainly in the first half of the nineteenth century that 'Highlandism' became an integral but manufactured part of Scottish identity. Tartan, bagpipes, kilts and the bens and glens of the Highland landscape were the instantly recognizable symbols of Scottishness in the Victorian era. In essence, Scotland, through an extraordinary alchemy, was transformed into a 'Highland' country[1] [...] The tartan and kilt of the Highlands had been appropriated even before 1830 as the national dress. But its adaptation was given further impetus by the heroic and well-publicized deeds of the kilted regiments in the Empire, by the growing number of Caledonian societies [...] and, not least, by Queen Victoria's love affair with the Highlands. The monarch built a residence at Balmoral on Deeside and, from 1848, spent every autumn there on holiday [...] The fact that Victoria showed such fascination with the Highlands and was sometimes even heard to proclaim herself a Jacobite at heart was bound to have a major effect. Highlandism had now been given wholehearted royal approval and tartan recognized as the badge of Scottish identity.[2]

On the growing number of Highland Gatherings and Piping competitions, where dancing was featured, tartanism had a major impact on the aesthetic development on dancing in Scotland.

The nineteenth century saw the demise of the Minuet and Cotillion, although Country Dances remained popular throughout the century.

132 *Aberdeenshire to the Hebrides*

Romantic Ballet continued to develop through the middle of the century, setting a fashion for white dresses worn for dance performances. Codes of etiquette and refined, smooth movement styling became associated with high-class standing. Some dancing masters, including the Lowe family, J.F. Wallace, and David Anderson, to name but a few, published little ballroom guides, which provided dance instructions and ballroom etiquette, and helped spread the new dance forms around the country. Dancing masters William Adamson, David Anderson, and John Reid taught treepling and other percussive dance steps for both country and solo dances.[3] The century also saw a shift towards Reels being prominently featured as a competition dance at the emerging Highland Games and at piping competitions. Our first reference from 1840 describes one of these.

Catherine Sinclair, Blair Atholl, before 1840

The Scottish novelist and writer of children's literature Catherine Sinclair was born in Edinburgh in 1800 and died in 1864. She was the daughter of Sir John Sinclair, famed for his *Statistical Accounts* and an active member on the Committee of the Edinburgh Highland Society. Her book *Shetland and the Shetlanders or The Northern Circuit*, published in 1840, describes an earlier Brig o' Tilt Meeting in Blair Atholl. The event must have been something of a novelty to her, as she wrote,

> All that feet can do, these Highlanders did, and more than I ever saw any feet attempt before, but we all looked on in solemn silence, as if watching an execution ... Nothing ever looked more like insanity than the reels at last. Four stout Highlanders, in full dress, raised on a wet slippery wooden platform, dancing in the open air, under a torrent of rain, cracking their fingers to imitate castanets, shuffling, capering, cutting, whirling round, and uttering the sudden yell, customary here, during a very animated dance, to encourage the piper.[4]

The dance here seems to be the Reel of Tulloch, and her remarks on the snapping of fingers and heuchs bring life to the picture of the Games dancing style of that date. Catherine Sinclair also alludes to the Sword Dance, *Gille Chaluim*, performed over sticks, in a separate passage given as an endnote.[5]

Frederick Hill, Aberdeenshire, 1841

A notebook titled *Frederick Hill's Book of Quadrilles & Country dance &c &c, March 22nd, 1841* provides many written descriptions of solo High Dances. Of the fourteen High Dances in this notebook, five employ trebling as well as motifs enduring in today's Highland Games dancing. Those five dances are College Hornpipe, Flowers of Edinburgh, Trumpet Hornpipe, King of Sweden, and Earl of Erroll, all in 4/4 time. Two dances, Dusty Miller, and

Wilt Thou Go to the Barricks [Berwick] Johnnie are triple-time Hornpipes written in 3/2 time, sometimes reflected as 6/4 time. Other notated dances closer in character to today's Highland Games dancing are Highland Laddie, Shantruish, Blue Bonnets, Scotch Measure, the Irish Jig, and two arrangements of the Marquis of Huntly's Highland Fling by Huat and Taylor. Some of the 'National' dances competed at Highland Games today in fact come directly from interpretations of this manuscript.

Former RSCDS archivist and president the late Dr Alastair MacFadyen (1936–2015), together with Anita Mackenzie and Alan Macpherson, published a reproduction of the manuscript with notes in 2009. Frederick Hill was born in Hammersmith, Middlesex, England in 1815. He appears to have lived in Clatt, near Alford in Aberdeenshire in the 1841 Scottish Census where he was listed as a tailor. He died in Alford in 1903. Hill studied with several local mid-nineteenth century northeast dancing masters active at that time. Their names, [John] Allan (born *c.* 1809), Huat (possibly William Howat of Turriff, born *c.* 1816; however, contemporary newspaper articles mention a Huat as well), [Adam] Myren (various spellings, born *c.* 1782 in Mortlach), and [James] Taylor (born *c.* 1800 in Banff), are given as sources for many of the dances.[6] There was also a dancing master by the name of John Taylor, born in Fochabers, Elgin about 1812 according to the 1851 Scottish Census. Both Taylors seem to have been active in the same area at the same time period, and either could have been the one to whom Hill attributed one of his versions of the Marquis of Huntly's Highland Fling.

Hill's manuscript was kept as a personal notebook and he used terminology no longer in use today. We cannot know with absolute certainty what was meant by many of the terms he used such as Shallie or Bound Four. However, Shallie appears to be related to the Baroque dance term Sallie, a *pas échappé*, or what modern Highland dance terminology calls a spread and Peacock gave as *fosgladh*. Likewise, Bound is a Baroque dance term referring to a spring from one foot to the other, as described by John Weaver in his book *Orchesography or, the Art of Dancing*, a translation of Raoul Feuillet's work with the same title from 1706. Records show that John Weaver himself performed in a dance interlude titled the 'Dance of the Bonny Highlanders' at Drury Lane in London in 1700.[7] This series of springs may be related to Peacock's seby-trast step, and the motif known as balance in Highland dancing today.

Hill's unconventional spelling of names and words may reflect fluidity in English orthography of the time, or could indicate that he misheard or misunderstood local pronunciation of certain words. There is a case where Hill explicitly points out that the movements in question were audible. In the directions for a social dance titled the Dashing White Serjeant [spelling as in original], we find the following instruction: 'Beat time Slow 1, 2. 3, 4. Quick, '-, |,\, i, n, u, c.'[8]

Dances in the Hill manuscript, as it is commonly referred to in Scottish dance literature, have been interpreted in varying ways regarding phrasing, time signatures, and with greater or lesser emphasis on the percussive nature

134 *Aberdeenshire to the Hebrides*

of the movements.[9] In the 1950s, the Hill notebook's solo dances were interpreted as soft-shoe dances in a Ballet-informed style, aesthetics valued in Scottish dance circles at that time. Mrs Isobel 'Tibbie' Cramb, interpreted three of the dances, the Earl of Erroll, the King of Sweden, and the Scotch Measure, for publication by the RSCDS in 1953, and more recently in 2009. Cramb's interpretations of the dances do not follow the Hill manuscript to the letter and were influenced by 'Miss Flora Cruickshank.'[10] Mrs Flora Buchan[11] (*neé* Cruickshank) descended from a line of northeast dancing masters. Both her grandfather, John Cruickshank of Fyvie (born *c.* 1781), and father, George Cruickshank (born *c.* 1838), had been based in Peterhead. Flora Buchan assisted and advised in the interpretation of the Hill manuscript dances, and also passed on other dances, such as Flora MacDonald's Fancy and The Graces to Mrs Cramb. Buchan, then in her 80s, insisted that the soft and elegant style of dancing her father had instilled in her should be applied. This styling has since been a hallmark of what is termed 'Ladies' Step Dancing' by the RSCDS, and was initially applied to what is now labelled 'Scottish National Dancing' appearing in syllabi of various dance teachers' organisations affiliated with the RSOBHD.[12]

In the 2009 RSCDS publication *The St Andrews Collection of Step Dances,* Ron Nedderman wrote about the philosophy behind Cramb's aesthetics for these dances:

> Within the field of Step Dancing, as in all other aspects of human endeavour, it is futile to believe that there was once a Golden Age of uniform perfection. Inevitably the selection and style of the dances, as well the dress and the footwear, differed from district to district, teacher to teacher and time to time. What Miss Cruickshank's family tradition and the Hill manuscript have given us is the style of dancing in Aberdeenshire in the early years of the nineteenth century. Miss Cruickshank's insistence on the soft balletic style is all the more convincing, since that was a period during which grace and elegance were much prized. Moreover, this style of dancing has merit in its own right and its continuation is a just tribute to the pioneering work of Mrs. Cramb, to the assistance she received from Miss Cruickshank and to Dr. Milligan's encouragement.[13]

Nedderman also speculated regarding footwear worn in the late eighteenth and early nineteenth centuries:

> Except in the large towns, tuition was in the hands of dancing masters who toured the district, giving private tuition to the young ladies of the great houses, and on the same visit, public classes in a hastily swept corner of the barn. A dance, now lost, was entitled 'Pas Seul for Miss Burnett of Leys.' Miss Burnett was the daughter of a wealthy landowner [...] She doubtless performed her eponymous dance to entertain her father's dinner guests, dancing on the drawing room carpet wearing her prettiest

frock and soft indoor shoes...Her contemporaries in the barn danced in whatever they could afford. It is noteworthy that Hunt's engraving (1825) of the dance class at Robert Owen's School at New Lanark shows some girls wearing ballet shoes and some barefoot (Figure 8.1).[14]

There are differences in the ways medal testing organisations (*i.e.* BATD, SDTA, and UKA) describe and teach these dances today. A conversation in the mid-1980s with the late Robert 'Bobby' Watson, a twentieth-century Aberdeen dancing master, revealed that when Mrs Cramb taught these dances at workshops and was asked about certain details, she responded that some movements were open to interpretation, opening the door to differing versions of the dances.[15] It is only natural for dance teachers to alter dances, as they adapt to different levels of learners or other contextual circumstances, or make improvements that they prefer. Dancing masters taught different styles in different areas, different styles to different genders, and different levels of difficulty depending on payment.[16] Some interviewees in Angus during a 1998–2002 Traditional Dance Development project[17] indicated that local dancing masters, for example, Dancie Reid and Dancie Kydd, taught girls softer styled dancing while boys were sometimes made to wear wooden soles attached to their dancing shoes to make more sound when dancing Hornpipes.[18] Clog and Hornpipe dances were part of many dancing master repertoires and were widespread generally around 1900. Best shoes, boots, or clogs were worn, and dancers of both genders danced them though they were less popular among the girls.[19]

Figure 8.1 Mr Robert Owen's Institution, New Lanark, 1825. *Quadrille Dancing*
Source: Image used with permission by the New Lanark Trust.

136   *Aberdeenshire to the Hebrides*

Another difference in interpretation lies not in *what* some of Hill's terminology meant, nor *how* percussively one favoured these dances to be performed but regards the *timing* of two steps—'single' and 'double treble'—in relation to the music. These two Treble steps are named as such in the Hill manuscript, single indicating a movement occupying one bar of music and double meaning occupying two bars of music. They occur in the Earl of Erroll, the King of Sweden, the College and Trumpet Hornpipes, and the Flowers of Edinburgh.

In soft-shoe versions of the first two dances performed by RSCDS, BATD, SDTA, and UKA dancers today, the movement starts with the first beat of the bar of the accompanying music. This means that the supporting foot is not always in contact with the ground on the dominant beats of the music. This may be why the step performed in this timing is not accented, and employs a very balanced weight distribution between both feet. A letter from Mrs Cramb to Tom Flett reiterates that to her, the 'double trebling' [another term for 'tripling'], was a well-known step and 'by no means obsolete' after he had asked her about its rhythm.[20] She defended her publication by asserting that 'expressions' such as 'treble' or 'shallie' 'are not exact terms of art and their use varies both in time and place. The Earl of Erroll is written down exactly as taught to me by Miss Cruickshank.' Cramb cautioned that one 'must be wary of accepting the written word as sacred when common sense, a knowledge of dancing and music and the experience of a long line of sincere teachers of dancing make a variation the only possible interpretation.' Regarding shoes, she added 'I have always mentioned in demonstrating and discussing these dances that I felt that they were probably danced in hard-soled shoes,' but 'I see no reason why they [the dances included in the book *Four Step Dances,* 1953] should not be performed in our present day shoes' [*i.e.* soft ghillie dancing pumps].

In comparison, hard-shoe interpretations of these dances exhibit anacrusis, following the timing of Hornpipe dance traditions in Irish and English Step dancing, and aligning with the pickup notes of the musical phrase preceding the downbeat of the first bar of music. Notations of hard-shoe dances from West and East Scotland by the Fletts and Rhodes (1979, 1996), Chris Metherell (1982), and Colin Robertson (1982) consistently begin on the anacrusis in this way. As a result, the flow of movements aligns with the flow of the musical phrases. Starting treble movements with the anacrusis means that the supporting foot becomes a natural timekeeper of the main downbeats in the music, as illustrated by the examples below.

These two interpretations may reflect varied timing preferences. Hard-shoe motifs that start with anacrusis are more common in various Step dancing traditions from the nineteenth century onwards. The evolution of the soft-shoe version may have been influenced by fewer men and boys taking dance classes in some areas in the late nineteenth and early twentieth centuries, encouraging adaptation of the dances into softer, more balletic versions to suit the teaching of young girls.

The two 3/2 hornpipes in the manuscript have also been interpreted in soft-shoe Highland style. Dusty Miller appeared as a 6/4 National dance

Single Treble counting for Earl of Erroll

Hop brush | **step** shuf-fle step **step**, Hop brush | **step** shuf-fle step **step**
L   R | R   L   L   L   R   R   L | L   R   R   R   L

Soft shoe 2/4:	**1**	an	&	a	**2**	an	&	**3**	an	&	a	**4**	an	&	
Hard shoe 2/4:	**&**	a	**1**	an	&	a	**2**	**&**	a	**3**	an	&	a	**4**	
Hard shoe 4/4	**8**	&	**1**	&	**2**	&	**3**	**4**	&	**5**	&	**6**	&	**7**	

Double Treble counting for Earl of Erroll

Hop brush | **step** shuf-fle step **step** step **step** shuf-fle step **step**
L   R | R   L   L   L   R   L   R   L   L   L   R

Soft shoe 2/4:	**1**	an	&	a	**2**	an	&	a	**3**	an	&	a	**4**

Hop brush | step shuf-fle step step step step step step shuf-fle step step

Hard shoe 2/4:	**&**	a	**1**	an	&	a	**2**	an	&	a	**3**	an	&	a	**4**
Hard shoe 4/4	**8**	&	**1**	&	**2**	&	**3**	**&**	**4**	&	**5**	&	**6**	&	**7**

Notes:
Brush = a 'brush in' or 'catch in.
Shuffle = is a 'catch out' followed by a 'catch in.'
Bold counts and terms are signifying weight bearing or supporting foot movements and counts.
| = indicates change of weight bearing or supporting foot from one side to the other.
& = is most commonly written as 'and' in most printed Scottish dance descriptions.

Figure 8.2 Single and double treble counting exampled in 2/4 and 4/4 time

in Scottish dance manuals in the 1960s. Dusty Miller includes flinging movements, which have been interpreted as a movement motif popularly called shedding, a core movement in the Highland Fling.

The other 3/2 dance in the manuscript has notation resembling that of Dusty Miller. Its title is Wilt Thou Go to the Barricks, Johnnie, which might more accurately be titled 'Go to Berwick, Johnny,' a well-known 3/2 Borders hornpipe tune and song. This dance, however, has undergone a remarkable transformation to twentieth-century Highland Dancing style with its name changed to 'Wilt Thou Go to the Barracks, Johnnie?.' In the early 1950s, both Isobel Cramb and Bobby Watson worked on interpreting the manuscript notes. According to a conversation with Watson in 1989, his version was set to the 6/8 pipe tune 'Cock O' the North.' After hearing a local pipe band performing in Duthie Park, Aberdeen, he had been inspired to devise the third step and performed it in an alternative double-time syncopated rhythm (performing four movements rather than two in the first four bars of the step) to mimic the bass drum rhythm. When Bobby Watson taught the dance in 6/8 time the last two steps (seven and eight) were always given at a quicker tempo.[21] Since the 1950s the suggested time signature for Highland dance competitions and medal test examinations has been changed to 2/4 timing. Today 'Barracks Johnnie' is often performed to pipe marches, such as the 'Braes O' Mar,' and sometimes danced to 4/4 marches or 4/4 slow strathspeys.

138   *Aberdeenshire to the Hebrides*

At some point since the 1950s, a story developed and spread that the dance was once used as a recruiting dance by the Scottish regiment the Gordon Highlanders in Aberdeen. An enquiry to the Gordon Highlanders and all Scottish regiments in the mid-1980s asking whether this dance, or any other Highland dance, was ever used for recruitment revealed no evidence of this practice.[22] It seems that Hill's writing Berwick as 'Barricks' and the subsequent misinterpretation of that word as Barracks have led to an assumed connection with the local Highland regiment. This presumed Army connection may be why the 2/4 March time is suggested today.

Even when written descriptions are not available, interpretation of orally transmitted material and observations can vary, and be swayed by an agenda or preferences of a notator or researcher. This is a fairly common occurrence in oral transmission. However, a dance that has been reconstructed this significantly, and to unrelated music, cannot truthfully be called a traditional dance.

The step timing of Will Ye Go to Berwick Johnny would have reflected the rhythms of that 3/2 tune closely, an effect lost when the dance is set to alternate tunes in 6/8 or 2/4. Both Dusty Miller and Will Ye Go to Berwick Johnny can, performed in 3/2 hornpipe tempo, be interpreted equally well as two fairly straightforward percussive Step dances.

Dance competition, Glasgow, 1841

The *Belfast Chronicle* of 2 August 1841 reports on a 'Competition of Pipers at Glasgow.' The article describes the all-male competitors' performances on the pipes and the dancing during the four-to-five-hour-long competition in a Glasgow theatre:

> To those only accustomed to the city ball-room, the dancing of the Highlandmen must have appeared not only vigorous, but a desperate effort. There was here none of the easy sliding motions of modern art, but the rapid spring, the lofty cutting, the genuine treble-shuffle, the sledge-hammer-like beating of the heel and toe upon the boards, the cracking of the thumbs, jerking of the elbows, and the wild whoop with which they accompanied each other in the foursome-reel, or change in the music. During the short period of their dancing exhibition, the Celts must have endured more real bodily labour than falls to the lot of most folk, for a week, and in verity they did not spare the floor.—The characteristic sword and dirk dances were splendid, and executed with a fearlessness and nicety of footing which must have required years of practice to bring to perfection. In fact, we hold it to be as difficult as performing a minuet on a chimney top, and we have no doubt that Angus M'Kay, the piper, is as clever in his peculiar line as Mademoiselle Taglioni is in pirouetting on her great toe, and certainly he does harder work for infinitely less pay[…]Altogether the exhibition was a realization—calling to life again, as it were, of the peculiar characteristics of an ancient people which are

fast passing away[…]At the close of the competition, the judges retired to decide on the award of the prizes, and during their absence several of the competitors danced hornpipes and Highland reels.

First prize for dancing, after much deliberation, went to Angus M'Kay, late piper to W.F. Campbell, Esq of Islay; second was awarded to Duncan Campbell, a piper from Foss, Perthshire; and third went to Peter Comrie of Comrie who also won a special first prize for 'Dancing Strathspeys.' Considering the nature of the description of the Reel dancing, it was not just a visual spectacle but also an audible one due to the treble shuffles and beating of toes and heels. With the time and place in mind it is most likely that dancers, who were also pipers, wore hard-soled shoes.

Worth noting is the comparison between celebrated Swedish/Italian ballerina Marie Taglioni (1804–1884) of the Romantic Ballet era, the same ballerina mentioned in the first production of *La Sylphide*, who is said to be one of the first ballerinas to truly dance *en pointe*, and the dancing of piper Angus MacKay. It gives an indication of emerging comparison and admiration for, and between, the Romantic-era Ballet aesthetic ideals and those of the Highland dance aesthetics of that time.

Playbills, Inverness, 1842

Regional theatres in Scotland hosted repertoire similar to shows presented across the United Kingdom, including popular plays, with music and dancing between acts. Dramatisations of the works of Sir Walter Scott retained particularly strong popularity in Scotland. Isaac Pocock's adaptation of *Rob Roy* was, according to Alasdair Cameron, 'remembered as the play which saved the Theatre Royal Edinburgh and turned it, under the management of Mrs Henry Siddons and her brother, W H Murray, himself a practised adaptor of Scott, into the foremost theatre in Scotland.'[23] Dances seen on the stage would have influenced dancing masters and local dance practices. In the nineteenth century, there were Theatre-Royal patent theatres in Edinburgh, Glasgow, Greenock, Paisley, Dumfries, Ayr, Kilmarnock, Coatbridge, Perth, Arbroath, Kirkaldy, Dundee, and Inverness as well as performance spaces and venues in towns such as Airdrie, Dunfermline, Falkirk, Motherwell, and Stirling.[24]

Playbills from Inverness from Thursday, 7 July 1842 and Tuesday, 16 August 1842 list Clog dances that appeared along with comic songs as *entr'actes* between dramatisations of Oliver Twist, Tam O' Shanter, London Assurance, and Les Noyades.[25]

John Nicholson, Galloway, Southern Scotland, 1843

John Nicholson (1777–1866) was a publisher, antiquarian, and local historian from Kirkcudbright who wrote *Historical and Traditional Tales in Prose and Verse connected with the South of Scotland* with his

140 *Aberdeenshire to the Hebrides*

great object [...being] to contribute to the illustration of Galloway in those particulars which are generally over looked, or but slightly treated of in history—to exhibit our ancestors, not on days of state parade or on fields of strife, but in the privacy of their homes and their various social relations.[26]

The collection contains local historical stories, traditional folklore and poetry of Dumfries and Galloway. On pages 401–414, a description of 'A Country Kirn' describes a rollicking, clattering evening of dance:

[I]t was about nine o'clock when my companion and I set out for the barn. The dancing was already begun. The barn smelled strongly of whisky toddy; mirth beamed in every eye, and joy and hilarity prevailed throughout.— In a corner, behind a large oaken table, sat the goodman, filling the mirth-inspiring beverage from a jolly looking punch bowl into wine glasses, to be distributed amongst the company by a half-grown lad, who served him in the capacity of herd. So soon as he saw me, he beckoned me to come towards him, and placing me on his left hand, presented me with a glass of punch, and drank to myself and family, which compliment I returned, wishing him luck and prosperity in his agricultural concerns.[27] [...]

While these hearty blades were thus sacrificing to the rosy god, and drowning their cares in the howl, the dance was kept up with great spirit and gaiety by the lads and lasses, and every Jockey had his Jenny, who was his partner in the dance, and the object of his care and attention throughout the evening.[28] [...]

The young farmer danced several reels with the lasses, and was so particular in his attentions to Miss Mary, that several began to think his coming that night was not altogether accidental. [...] The dancing was now left off for half an hour, until the company had partaken of a cold collation; after which the punch was again set a circulating, and, to give the fiddler a rest, we had some excellent songs.[29] [...]

After a few more songs, the younger part of the company betook themselves to dancing with ten times more spirit than before.—Ceremony was now laid aside, and nothing was to be heard but the sound of the fiddle, and the clattering of iron-shod shoes on the barn floor. The goodman himself, who had by this time forgot both his cares and his years, sprung up, and making one of his best bows to the dairymaid, prepared for a reel, amidst loud and long continued cheering.—The tune struck up, and away flew the carle, cocking his little old knee before him, and beating one, two, three, and a hop. He set to Nell, and Nell set to him; and Nell took hold of her skirt on each side, with her finger and thumb, and she skipped first to the one side of him, and then to the other, accompanying each hop with a fascinating inclination of the head; the goodman, on the other hand, his skipping days being over, contented himself with raising his hands towards his shoulders, snapping his fingers, and lifting his feet like a maid in a washing pail. The tune changed—*whough*, cried the goodman, and off he ran, keeping his left hand before him, amidst the reiterated acclamations of every one present, and to the amazement of some half a score of little urchins playing at 'hide and seek' in the other end of the barn, who stood gaping with wonder to see 'the master' footing it so merrily with the byre-woman. The principal dancers of the evening were a young joiner and blacksmith, who took the lead in all the dances, directed the fiddler, and were scarcely ever off the floor.—They kicked, capered, and wheeled—did the treble shuffle, and the double treble; and, by holding out longest, were looked upon as the best dancers in the house. But the kirn was drawing to a close; the effects of the whisky were becoming gradually more conspicuous—wives began to use their eloquence in persuading their husbands to go home—the fiddler waxed muddy, and was often heard scraping behind the fiddle bridge.[30]

One thing to note about this passage is its close proximity in time to Frederick Hill's manuscript. While Hill's notes have been interpreted and taught in soft-shoe styles over the course of the twentieth century, this passage describes the 'treble shuffle' and 'double treble' as part of the 'clattering' by people in 'iron-shod shoes.' The *Elgin Courant* newspaper reported that T. Taylor held his 'school ball' similarly 'in a large barn belonging to Mr J. Hardie, Barnhill, which was neatly decorated with evergreens and comfortably fitted up by him for the occasion' on Thursday, 22 March 1849. Hill's notebook also mentions a dancing master with the last name Taylor. The *Courant* report dates six years after Nicolson's description was published, and eight years after Hill dated his notebook.

Carl Gustav Carus, Breadalbane, 1844

Frederick Augustus II, King of Saxony, made an informal visit to England and Scotland in 1844. The King's personal physician Carl Gustav Carus accompanied him and kept a journal of the trip, which was published under the title *The King of Saxony's Journey through England and Scotland* in 1846. In this journal, an evening of dinner and entertainment enjoyed at the house of Breadalbane is described, where the Sword Dance was performed. Carus made it clear that he did not care for the bagpipes by writing 'everything was admirable except the music of the Scotch piper, who [...] filled the dining-room with his nasal thrilling tones,' and that he preferred the after-dinner entertainment featuring the piano playing of the celebrated 'Scotch musician Miller.' However, Carus was to endure more piping, as the piper was brought forward another time, for the 'exhibition of a national dance, and the drone was an indispensable accompaniment to the exhibition.'[31] Carus continued his description:

> The company moved into another room, and several men immediately entered, dressed in full Highland costume. The piper commenced his enlivening strains, and a young man in Scottish garb first appeared with

142 *Aberdeenshire to the Hebrides*

two naked swords. He laid them crosswise on the floor, and with a particular jerking motion of his legs and arms, began to dance to the music of the bag-pipes. With a certain rhythm, he stamped with both feet on the ground, quicker and quicker, trod now on this side and now on that, of the naked sword blades, without ever touching them—threw up his arms in the air, and one while assumed the attitude of an attacking, and at another of a defending warrior. At length, he seized the swords again—swung them over his head, and disappeared [...]

Next appeared two, and then four Highlanders, who performed a dance of similar character and significance as the former, but without weapons. At the moments of their liveliest movement, they continually uttered a sort of quick, lively, exclamatory song, which was succeeded by fresh vehemence in dancing, stamping of the feet, throwing about the arms, and advancing and retreating. I found it impossible to avoid recalling to my mind the drawings and dances among the New Zealanders and other savages, which I had often seen. One must be inspired with a complete interest in all the national peculiarities of Scotland, to be able to follow those movements and bursts of music and shouts with attention.[32]

Many elements of Highland dance as seen today are discernible in this description, such as full Highland garb, two swords, dancing over and around the swords without touching them, and the four Highlanders dancing together. In contrast, today's Sword Dances and Highland Reels generally avoid making sounds and the techniques implemented align more with shapes of Ballet than with the intimidating stamping, slapping, and shouting of the Maori Haka[33] brought to Carus's mind. The dancers may be shouting *port a beul* lyrics along with the pipes in the 'moments of their liveliest movement.' A version of the Sword Dance still performed by Victorian Scottish Union dancers in Australia is highly animated, and incorporates the dancer removing his or her bonnet and waving it during the quicker, final step. A bold, aggressive, martial styling of Highland dance was more prominent in 1844. C.N. McIntyre North's 1880 description of a Sword Dance also stamped in time to the tune '*Gillie Calluin*,' perhaps connected to this emphatic performance style, will be included later.

Johann Georg Kohl, Killin, 1848

Another international traveller to Scotland remarked on the dancing seen there. Johann Georg Kohl published narratives of travels to many countries, including Russia, Poland, the United States, Canada, and Ireland. He recounted his travels across Scotland, and while near Killin, in Perthshire, now known as Stirling, observed a Highland Reel.

As I never had the opportunity of witnessing a 'reel' in Scotland, and had now a man before me who might be replied upon in the matter, I asked him what might be the peculiarity of the Scottish reel, as a dance. But, alas!

I could arrive at nothing very satisfactory through my friend on the subject. The 'reel,' in English, is properly a winch, or kind of spinning-wheel; and 'to reel,' signifies to turn or wheel about. Should this have anything to do with the name of the dance, it would awaken no particular partiality for the art, or gracefulness of the dance. According to the definitions of my fiddler, I saw nothing very artificial about it. The reel, he said, is danced by four persons, two lads and two lasses, 'who keep constantly tacht to the tune, and make their manoeuvres.' 'Farther than this,' he said, 'there is nothing particular in a Scotch reel.' I asked him in what these manoeuvres consisted. 'Firstly, as I have already said, in keeping tacht, and then they go through the figure of an echt,' (an eight.) I asked him again, what he meant by going through the figure of an eight? He answered, 'to go through the figure of an echt is all the same as saying, "to go through the reel,"' And then he made the figure ∞ in the sand on the road. In order, in their movements, that the dancers may always be *tacht* with the music, and that they may be constantly keeping in the figure of *echt*, each returns always exactly to his own place. And this, then, is the peculiar reel. I believe, after this description, my readers will have a tolerably correct notion of the rude way in which the Highlanders dance this dance.[34]

A footnote Kohl made to this description avers 'now that I have seen several Scottish reels, I can confirm all this.'

Some of the words used in this description are not standard and likely reflect dialectic pronunciation as interpreted through a German-speaker's ears. Aberdeenshire Scottish fiddler Paul Anderson suggests the following understanding of the word *tacht*:

> sounds like the fiddler was fairly broad spoken and the German has given his best effort at transcribing what was said. Echt is eight and I'd almost guarantee that tacht is tight; 'the dancers must be tight with the music.' Depends on the district as what sounds like tacht in one area might be ticht in another. It's Clachnaben north of the Cairn o Mount and Clochnaben to the South.[35]

R.R. McIan, London, 1848

Born in Scotland in 1803, Robert Ranald McIan was an actor in Bristol and Bath before devoting himself to painting in London, where he died in Hampstead in 1863. He is best known for his romanticised depictions of Scottish clansmen in battle and domestic settings, such as in *Gille Calum*, shown in Figure 8.3. His paintings supported the romantic revival of interest in a Highlandist version of Gaeldom very much led by Queen Victoria, to whom his 1845 book *The Clans of the Scottish Highlands* was dedicated. McIan's (1848) *Highlanders at Home* details Highland folkways, an increasingly popular subject at that time. In fact, James Logan, author of *The Scottish Gael*

Figure 8.3 Gille Calum by R.R. McIan, 1848

Source: Image in public domain. The woman in the left of the picture plays a jaw harp to accompany the dancing. The tromb or trump (also known as mouth harp or jaw/jew's harp) and port-a-beul (mouth music) may not be popularly associated with Scottish dances today, but it commonly provided accompaniment for Step dances.

just 15 years prior to this publication, provided descriptive letterpress for McIan's book. Along with descriptions of hunting, farming, and distilling practices, McIan described dancing and its connected martial exercises. He explained Scottish dancing generally thus:

> The effect of Scottish dancing is very much heightened by the picturesque costume, as well as the manner of using the arms by the men, and knacking the finger and thumb, with an occasional shout of exhilaration in unison with the notes, which we think peculiar to Scotland. The steps and passes are varied, and in many cases elegant, generally requiring great agility to be well performed.[36]

McIan qualified this description with a comment resonating with this investigation: 'In variety, they are a contrast to those of Ireland.'[37] The snapping of fingers again is a prominent characteristic, and in the painting illustrating the section, snapping of fingers by both the dancer and an onlooker is evident.

Charles St John, Scourie, 1849

A brief mention of dancing is mentioned as an aside in one of the writings by naturalist Charles St John, who was from England but lived in Scotland between the 1830s and 1850s. St John wrote a number of books about Scotland's flora and fauna. In his 1849 *A Tour in Sutherlandshire*, he recounts a noisy evening at the Scourie inn where he was staying:

> The inn at Scowrie, kept by a man of a most un-Highland name, viz., 'Tough,' is excellent, and most cleanly and comfortable did we find it, and the people full of civility. Unluckily there were two shiploads of emigrants on the point of leaving a harbour near Scowrie, and their friends were wishing them a good voyage in many a bumper of whisky, with the usual accompaniment of bagpipes and reels; so that what with their songs, their music, and the beating of their feet, as they danced under the inspiration both of whisky and pipes, there was a tolerable noise kept up till daylight. But mountain travelling and a feeling that it was impossible and unjust to be angry with the poor fellows enabled me soon to sleep as comfortably as if all had been still.[38]

Of particular interest to this study is that the people leaving Scotland are taking a form of dance with them that is notably percussive. Left out of this account is the potato blight affecting the Highlands at that time, a possible reason for the emigration depicted.

Balmoral Castle Ball, Aberdeenshire, 1850

A report on the Braemar Gathering in the *Banffshire Journal and General Advertiser* in September 1850 includes a description of dancing:

> As usual, a splendid ball came off in the hall of the Castle in the evening. It was attended by a considerable proportion of the noble and gentle visitors of the day, who returned, in the evening from Corriemulzie, Mar Lodge and Invercauld House; and the slippers of the fair dames and gallant swains of Braemar had several hours of vigorous shuffling and thumping on the ancient floor of the hall. Dancing only ceased at a late hour in the morning.[39]

One may question whether the vigorous shuffling and thumping referred to percussive footwork or to a general din of the assembled company. The floor is referred to as 'ancient,' which indicates that dancing took place in the old castle, before Queen Victoria bought the estate and commissioned the building of the new castle, finished in 1856.

Ewen MacLachlan, South Uist and Isle of Barra, 1840s–1870s

Precious few facts are known about the life of Ewen MacLachlan (1799–1879), a dancing master of South Uist and Barra. He taught a number of solo dances from the 1840s to the 1870s, and so he began teaching about

146   *Aberdeenshire to the Hebrides*

the same time the Hill Manuscript was written. MacLachlan's repertoire of solo dances was handed down by oral, aural, and kinaesthetic transmission modes and his legacy has been passed on in these same ways. Some of the dances from his repertoire that incorporate percussive footwork are: the First of August, Scotch Measure, Miss Forbes, Over the Water, Highland Laddie, and Aberdonian Lassie. The heel-toe beat step featured in the last dance has been described in various ways. Flett and Rhodes describe it as:

and   *Place R heel about 6 inches to the right of L instep*
a   *Rock the RF to place the ball of the foot on the ground, transferring weight to it. The heel should be kept low off the ground*
1   *Close LF to 5th Rear Position flat*

The beats with heel and ball should be accented, but the strong beat is with the back foot on the count '1.'[40] The late Barra native and dance teacher Fearchar MacNeil demonstrated the 'heel toe' movement in a more sliding 'catch out, catch in' fashion, making the three individual movements flow into each other and not be perceived as separate units.[41]

First of August is a set solo Step dance including trebles as recurring motifs. Other dances of MacLachlan's repertoire reflect an amalgamation of percussive Step dancing movements with Victorian dancing-master aesthetics, including light, elevated movements. Published versions of these dances, besides the Fletts' and Rhodes's 1996 notations, downplayed the percussive nature of the dances. Edinburgh dance teacher D.G. MacLennan observed a number of the dances performed at the Askernish Highland Games in South Uist by Archie MacPherson and Donald *Roidean* MacDonald in the mid-1920s. MacLennan subsequently published them in altered and rearranged fashions in 1950, which he admitted in correspondence with Tom Flett.[42]

Another Highland dancer, Jack McConachie, from Carron in Speyside, learnt a number of these dances from John MacLeod of Iochdar, South Uist in 1949. McConachie's notes, which differ from MacLennan's in many places, were subsequently published after McConachie's death in 1972.[43] In McConachie's descriptions, new movements have been added, such as: *Entrechats*, jumps from two feet in third or fifth position with aerial movements of straight legs beating around each other before landing on two feet again; 'High cuts,' a series of springs from foot to foot with the gesture leg touching the back of the supporting leg's calf; and 'Leaps,' which in Highland dance terminology refers to jumps from the balls of both feet, followed by aerial stretching of both legs and feet out to the sides, and then landing on the balls of both feet on bent legs and forced arches. These movements may possibly have been added to appeal to Highland and Scottish Country dance communities of the second half of the twentieth century or may have been embellishments that suited McConachie's own dancing style. Terminology such as *bourrée* and *pas de Basque*, elevated gestures of the feet such as *jeté, ronde de jambe*, and *coupé*, and inclusion of Highland dance arm positions indicate the influence of Ballet vocabulary adopted by Highland and Country Dance teachers. McConachie played an active part in dance standardisation efforts, eventually affiliating himself with the Imperial Society of Teachers of Dancing based in London.

It is unknown whether MacLachlan had names for motifs, or if he taught using any English or completely through the medium of Gaelic. In 1989, Fearchar MacNeil indicated that there were no names for motifs in use. Dancers learnt by copying movements of the teacher or other dancers performing the steps. In Fearchar's opinion, there were no arm movements used in these dances. Ewen MacLachlan himself had unusual arms, described variously as having hands 'almost at shoulder level' to 'deformed.'[44] MacLachlan's irregular arms produced no impediment to his ability to teach these dances, further reflecting that arm movements were not important within the dance traditions of the Hebrides. Informants that the Fletts and Rhodes met in the 1950s did, however, include some Highland–dancing-style arm movements.

John Francis Campbell of Islay, Isle of Barra, 1859

The late Joan F. Flett suggested the possibility that it was dancing master Ewen MacLachlan mentioned in J.F. Campbell of Islay's journal of 1859. John Francis Campbell (1821–1885), a renowned collector of folk tales, author, and scholar, noted, 'There is a dancing master without arms who is now in Barra and who has hundreds of Sgeulachd [stories…] One of his best steps is to leap up and extinguish a lamp with his heel without spilling a drop of the oil.' This was the feat known as *Smàladh na Coinnle*—smooring the candle.[45] One dances around a candle placed on the floor, keeping feet close to or passing over the flame without extinguishing it, as shown in Figure 8.4. At the end, the dancer jumps up over the candle and clicks the toes or heels together to snuff the candle without toppling it.

The late Canon Angus MacQueen, formerly a priest in South Uist, once described *Bean Iain Ic Sheumais*/wife of John, James's son, former housekeeper to the priest in Bornish. She clearly remembered MacLachlan putting out candles with his big toe: *cur às nan coinnlean le òrdaig*. This happened in the priest's barn where the dancing classes happened. He would stand on tiptoe and swinging round completely he would snuff the candles with the wind caused by the speed of the gyration.[46] Another story depicting MacLachlan dancing *Smàladh na Coinnle*, as told to Calum MacLean, the collector of Gaelic stories and related lore, this time from the Barra tradition, told by the 'Coddy,' or Iain MacPherson, from Northbay:

> The Coddy heard from Calum MacMillan about the *Dannsair Ciotach* and how he had been at a wedding feast in Ormaclete in South Uist and had danced at it. This man was so good at dancing that he managed to snuff out candles with his feet seven times in a row. The dancers in

South Uist and Barra were taught dancing by this man. He was going to become a priest but had to give this up because of his injured hand.[47]

This dancing feat was also known in Nova Scotia and Cape Breton Island amongst settlers from the Highlands and Islands.

Figure 8.4 A member of the Scottish dance company *Dannsa*: Step dancer Sandra Robertson performing the *Smàladh na Coinnle* at Crear, Argyll

Source: Photo © M. Melin, 2004.

Highland Gathering, Castle Grant, Speyside, 1864

An article with the heading 'A Pedestrian Tour to the Highlands' by 'Gentleman Free-and-easy' appeared on the front page of the weekly paper *The Hamilton Advertiser* on 28 May 1864.[48] The anonymous writer described a Highland gathering apparently at Castle Grant in Speyside. The dancing there was illustrated as follows, in a humorous vein and perhaps from an outsider's perspective, as details not included below suggest Airdrie as the writer's home:

[...] But the dancing: the reel and strathspey! 'Muse of the many twinkling feet! Whose charms are now extended up from legs to arms, terpischore!' Here were thy true worshippers. The dancing was executed with extraordinary agility, and in capital time, though the deportment was deficient, the dancers holding a constant communication between their eyes and their toes, and being generally at a loss how and where to dispose of their hands and arms. It must be remembered, however, they had no side pockets.

'They reel't, they set, they cross'd, they clockit,' and they danced the reel again and again as nimbly as ever, when ordinary people would have been forced to cry, 'hold! enough.' We naturally suppose we saw it danced to perfection, for were we not in the heart of the Strathspey country, while Tullochgorum itself, which has become a household word for every Scotchman, from the reel of the same name, was but five miles to the south-west. 'O! Tullochgorum's my delight,' sing we. [...]

[...] one with Scottish heart and Scottish taste, who can fully appreciate her simple, native-born music and music's twin sister, dancing. Preacher of muscular Christianity: right glad would we be to 'shake a fit' with you in the ecstatic mazes of the bounding reel. Tullochgorum! thou speak'st of the times that are gone. Thy name recalls many pleasant reminiscences of weddings, 'kirns,' Highland gatherings, and 'sprees' innumerable, which cheered the hearts of our Scotch forefathers. Tullochgorum! in thy giddy mazes one forgets all care, all sorrow, all trouble, all toil, as surely as a bath in the waters of Lethe. Two sturdy Highland blades, and two strapping Highland lasses, for the 'foursome reel;' a row of New Monkland farmers, and a row of their buxom wives for 'The Duke o' Perth.' A barn floor, easy boots, a ranting fiddle, or a roaring bagpipe, and then the fun! 'Treeple,' double-shuffle, 'paddybas,' the cleek, the wheel, the stamp, the 'hough,' and at it 'just like linky.' Then you see— no, you *feel*—that the spirit of Scotchmen is in the sight, and that you are in a land of 'honest men and bonnie lasses.' [...]

A smile on every face, and a sparkle in every eye, you see that every heart is in the dance, that for once a kindred soul is thinking the same thoughts, and delighting in what you delight in, while her foot (may we not say her heart!) beats in unison with your own. Happiness! thousands have worshipped and are daily worshipping at thy shrine. Happiness! for which in

150   *Aberdeenshire to the Hebrides*

this way, or her way, every 'created intelligence' makes it the daily concern of his, or her life, to attain. [...] For a few short minutes at least with thee, lighting up their faces, and stirring up their spirits, these dancers are equal to peer or prince Happy then they are, because they feel enjoyment themselves, but twice happy because the other natures are partakers of the same. Thrice happy we think them to be because they have the *summum bonum* of this life, that's something which are gold and silver cannot give, but which they, too often, alas, too often take away—good health, sound limbs, sound constitutions, strong appetites, and can get up at five in the morning, though they may go *reeling* home at two. But our modern spark, with his sighing 'ladye love' hanging on his arm, retire 'for an airing,' when the reel is announced, for twould be to him no laughing matter if, by giving his legs an *extra* stretch, he found he had disjointed them, or even kicked them away. We will 'bide a wee yet,' and to the soul-subduing, soul-inspiring airs of auld Scotia—'As lang as we have breath to draw, We'll dance till we be like to fa' The reel o' Tullochgorum.'

The writer had a good eye for detail, and uses lines from Lord Byron's poem 'The Waltz,' Robert Burns's poem 'Tam O' Shanter,' and Rev John Skinner's lyrics sung to the tune of the Reel of Tullochgorum well to illustrate his points. He made good use of terminology describing the dancing. The beating of feet, treepling, and double shuffle all relate movements heard by this observer when the 'barn floor' connected with the 'easy boots.' This gentleman also observed that there were no standardised movements for arms in the Foursome Reel. Today, Tullochgorum is categorised as a strathspey, while the Reel of Tulloch and Foursome Reel are classified as reels. These terms are not delineated or separated in this passage. To put this article in perspective on a global historical timeline, the articles in adjacent columns describe, in graphic detail, the grim fighting in Virginia during the American Civil War and memories of the Crimean war.

The lyrics for the Reel of Tullochgorum have been analysed by Anne McKee Stapleton regarding their political perspective. She suggests that the tune typifies and characterises the Strathspey structure. Stapleton asserts that in dancing to Tullochgorum, 'steps and movements also echo or accent key words and ideas in the song while the tune literally propels the dancer.'[49] Tullochgorum's lyrics for verses 1 and 2 read:

Tullochgorum[50] by Rev John Skinner (1721–1807). Published in 1776.

[1] Come gie's a sang, Montgomery cried,
And lay your disputes all aside,
What signifies't for folks to chide
For what's been done before them?
Let Whig and Tory all agree.
Whig and Tory, Whig and Tory,
Let Whig and Tory all agree
To drop their whig-mig-morum;

Let Whig and Tory all agree,
To spend the night with mirth and glee,
And cheerfu' sing alang wi' me,
The reel of Tullochgorum.
[2] O' Tullochgorum's my delight,
It gars us a' in ane unite,
And ony sumph that keeps up spite,
In conscience I abhor him.
For blyth and cheery we's be a,'
Blithe and cheery, blithe and cheery,
Blithe and cheery we's be a,'
And mak' a happy quorum.
For blythe and cheery we's be a,'
As lang as we hae breath to draw,
And dance, till we be like to fa,'
The reel of Tullochgorum.

Stapleton's analysis points out a strong reliance on pickup notes in this particular strathspey, explaining:

> Although the printed poem appears to have nine lines of iambic tetrameter […] circumscribing three lines of a trochaic refrain or chorus […], the music and words printed […] illustrate that the first word of the 'iambic' lines actually falls on a pickup note of the previous measure.[51]

Notation for Tuloch Gorm from Angus MacKay's (1857) *Tutor for the Highland Bagpipe* in the Appendix includes pickup notes. Perceptions of when music and movement motifs begin and end are not universal, however. Anacrusis, a parallel dancing structure of lighter movements leading to or setting up a strong downbeat, is viewed differently by different practices, sometimes being eliminated altogether, sometimes present but viewed instead as a step's ending. The Earl of Erroll interpretations examined earlier provide an example of different opinions about placing a sequence of movements to music.

Lochaber poem, 1868

In the *Inverness Courier* newspaper on Thursday, 3 September 1868, appears a poem written in the month of August in Lochaber by Dr Norman MacLeod titled 'Dance, My Children.' It appears in several other newspapers in England around the same time.

Dance, my children! Lads and lasses!
Cut and shuffle, toes and heels!
Piper, roar from every chanter
Hurricanes of Highland reels!

Make the old barn shake with laughter,
Beat its flooring like a drum,
Batter it with Tullochgorum,
Till the storm without is dumb!
Sweep in circles like a whirlwind,
Flit across like meteors glancing,
Crack your fingers, shout in gladness,
Think of nothing but of dancing!
Thus a grey-haired father speaketh,
As he claps his hands and cheers;
Yet his heart is quietly dreaming,
And his eyes are dimmed with tears.
Well he knows this world of sorrow,
Well he knows this world of sin,
Well he knows the race before them,
What's to lose, and what's to win!
But he hears a far-off music
Guiding all the stately spheres—
In his father heart it echoes,
So he claps his hands and cheers.

The lines indicating the floor is being beaten like a drum and that the dancers 'batter' to the strathspey Tullochgorum strongly suggest that the dancers are Step dancing during the Reels. Later commentary in the *Aberdeen Free Press* on 24 January 1885 by the then-late Dr MacLeod, titled 'The Dancing Controversy' declares that the contents of the poem 'are in striking contrast with the views propounded by some of our social reformers of the present day, and cannot fail to be read with interest.' Dr MacLeod may have been Rev Norman MacLeod, who was born in Campbelltown in 1812 and died in Glasgow in 1872, and was a clergyman and author.

The Feeing Fair, Falkirk, 1869

On the second page of the *Falkirk Herald* on the ninth of December 1869, the poet, songwriter, and storyteller Robert Buchanan (1835–1875) described the scene of the Falkirk Feeing Fair. It is not quite clear whether his colourful reminiscences describe a recent fair or events of 20 to 30 years earlier.

Buchanan's Scots language brings this story to life, but the language chosen to depict blackface minstrelsy is offensive, repugnant to us. The similarity of dancing in Falkirk to staged percussive dances is important to our study, however. While Master Juba, considered by some to be a father of Tap dancing, did tour England and Scotland in the late 1840s with Pell's Ethiopian Minstrels,[52] minstrel shows typically featured white performers with burnt cork smudged on their faces. Master Juba's performances created a sensation and we wonder how his popularity may have influenced dancing and dancing masters' repertoires afterward.

Aberdeenshire to the Hebrides   153

Among Buchanan's observations are the following lines, describing what 'Jock,' heading down Rabert's Wynd, encounters:

> the gaed wi' a daud to the Folly, whaur a hunner mair o' their kind were cutting, shuffling, and treepling wi' their feet, and hooching, shouting, and harrooing wi' their mooths wi' sic stentorian ability that the Bulls o' Bashan, had they heard them, wad hae thocht shame in the middle o' a fine spring day—the din, the crood, the stoor making the place like a perfect pandemonium. [...] Through the reel they sprang, wheeled and set to partners, and aye ere they reel'd again and hale o' them brocht doon their tackety shoon wi' sic a tremendous bang on the flair that the maisic was fairly drooned. A fig for yer niggers and their break-doon staps—a' the troups in the warld combined could'na produce sic a concussion—it wad be like snapping a percussion cap beside a park o' artillery. [...]
>
> As the shades of evening begin to fa,' every dancing-room, as weel's the 'Folly,' is crammed to suffocation wi' the dancing daft. [...] The dancing is kept up wi' undiminished ardour till far in the morning—in fact, till 'The sun through the winnocks is blinking,' being diversified in a fecht noo and again merely to gae a kin' o' zest to the enjoyment. Six o'clock bell rings, and the maist o' the boddies are steering their way homeward [...].[53]

This description highlights the din of the dancers' feet and their hoochs as they dance, which are loud enough to drown out the music. Dancers wear hard-soled 'tackety' shoes or boots for the Reels. A picture of wild, energetic, and loud dancing through the day and night emerges. The writer uses 'cutting,' 'shuffling,' 'treepling,' and 'breakdown steps' to describe the percussive, noisemaking steps of the dancers' feet. These same terms were used by both David Anderson and Dancie John Reid. The quotation about the sun seems derived from a poem depicting a homely kindly Grannie titled 'Oor Toon 'En' by Tom M'Ewan.

Mr Fettes, Brechin, Angus, 1871

The *Stonehaven Journal* ran a short news item on Thursday 23 March 1871 reporting on a dancing event in Brechin:

> Dancing Assembly—Mr Fettes' dancing classes at Brechin were brought to a close for the season on Friday evening by a grand dress ball in the City Hall. There were upwards of 70 pupils, and a large number of their parents and friends were present. The first part was for pupils exclusively, and the manner in which the various high dances and step dances were gone through reflected great credit on Mr Fettes as a teacher. From the fact that this is the twentieth season of these classes and considering the popularity which they have gained, it is needless for us to particularise. There was an efficient quadrille band in attendance, and altogether the ball was a great success.

154   *Aberdeenshire to the Hebrides*

It is a pity that no more details can be gleaned as to the nature of the 'high' and 'step' dances so enjoyed in this short newspaper account of dancing classes. John F. Fettes was about 42 years old in 1871; the Scottish Census of that year gives his birth date as *circa* 1829 in Auchinblae, Kincardineshire. His occupation was listed as Professor of Dancing, and he was living in the district of Fetteresso (later Dunnottar) in the town of Stonehaven, Kincardineshire, at that time. In 1881, he was listed as a dancing master, with a wife, Ann, and six children. He was again listed as a Teacher of Dancing and Music in 1891. In 1901, aged 72, still listed as a dancing master and Musician, he was living alone in Newbigging, near Inveresk in Midlothian. By that time, he would have been teaching dancing for more than 50 years.

Charles Niven McIntyre North, London, 1880

Leabhar Comunn nam Fior Ghaël,[54] or *Book of the Club of True Highlanders*, includes a very clear set of instructions for the Sword Dance in his book detailing Gaelic folkways. Its author, Charles Niven McIntyre North, who was born in London in 1838 and died in Tonbridge, Kent, in 1899, was an architect, surveyor, and author based in London. He had a strong connection to one of the oldest and most famous aristocratic families in Scotland, the Elphinstone family; the current Lord and Lady Elphinstone are cousins to Queen Elizabeth II. McIntyre North built himself a house in the style of a Scottish castle called *Caisteal Tuath*/North Castle in Brockley Park, Lewisham, and lived there until the mid-1890s.[55]

McIntyre North attributed the version of the Sword Dance he described to A. McBain, who learned it from 'Sandy McIntyre of Perth. (Who taught Sandy we know not.)' This Sword Dance, depicted in Figure 8.5, employs a different rhythm than the imperfect half-beat rhythm seen in today's competitive style; this version aligns with the melodic rhythm, with movements happening in conjunction with the notes, so that the footsteps change as the notes change. Also significant in this version is the inclusion of shuffles. McIntyre North describes:

> We generally, for a setting step to the second figure, use a shuffle step of three beats, which takes up the time of a quarter of the bar: thus, from the first position bring the heel of the right foot over the left instep, beating the ground with the ball of the right foot; (two) then advance the right foot to the right front, beating the ground as before; (three) bring the right foot in a line with, and about one inch from, the ball of the left foot, beating the ground; repeat in the same manner with the left.[56]

These details of an early Sword Dance show that at one point in time a version existed with footwork closely following the melody of *Gille Chaluim*, generating sounds that exactly mimicked the stress and timing of the tune in its step pattern.

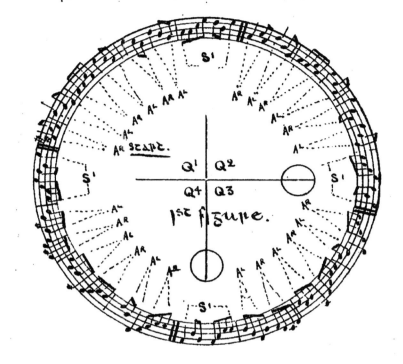

Figure 8.5 Sword Dance diagram, McIntyre-North, 1880

Source: Image in public domain.

The fourth step of this Sword Dance makes use of an inverted toe position, where a dancer's leg is rotated inward to affect a striking shape in the ankle and foot. Inverted positions are often used in percussive dancing to give visual variety. Inverted positions had been more regular features of Highland dancing before standardisation; some inverted positions endure in the Sailor's Hornpipe and in the *UKA Highland, National, and Hebridean Book*'s instructions for Hielan' Laddie and Over the Water to Charlie.

George Roberts, 1886, and Harry Mackay, 1895

The earliest Scottish newspaper account where the term Step dancing is used announces George Roberts 'Step dancing' at a Dundee Music Hall event in

156   *Aberdeenshire to the Hebrides*

the *Dundee Courier* on 2 March 1886. Almost 10 years later, a 'Social Meeting' news brief in the *Brechin Advertiser* on 29 March 1895 reported simply that 'Master Harry Mackay' performed 'Step dancing' during the evening's proceedings. Step dancing as a label for a dancer showing a sequence of steps seems to emerge in the late 1800s.

David Anderson, Dundee, 1897

From about 1886 until about 1902, Dundee dancing master David Anderson (1852–1907) published many editions of his popular ballroom guides, printed in thousands of copies, as *Anderson's Ball-Room and Solo Dance Guide, with full tuition in the art of dancing without the use of French terms. Dundee.* The 1897 edition contains a section with descriptions on how to perform 'trebles' and 'flatters' on pages 129–131.

The information about how to perform 'Trebles' is provided in David Anderson's (1897) *Ball-Room and Solo Dance Guide*:

> A *catch in* is hold up right foot in front, same time hop one on left foot, bring right in with a beat, then bring right down behind, which counts three with the hop. The reverse with left foot.
>
> SINGLE BACK TREBLE.
>
> Beat out, beat in, with right.
> Hop one on left and bring right down behind.
> Then beat out, beat in, with left.
> Hop one on right and bring left down behind.
> Repeat from beginning.
> Single Back Treble counts 4.
>
> SINGLE TREBLE
>
> Hop one on left.
> Catch in with right and put right down behind, then beat out, beat in, with left.
> Bring left down in front, beat behind with right.
> Then hop one on right.
> Catch in with left and put left behind, then beat out, beat in, with right.
> Bring right down in front, beat behind with left.
> Repeat from beginning.
> Single Treble counts 7.[57]

Note the use of particular terminology such as 'catch' and 'treble' but also the use 'hop,' 'bring left [or right] down,' 'beat out,' and 'beat in.' He notes that there are seven counts in the 'single treble' but does not say whether the movement starts on the anacrusis or on the downbeat. As described previously in the Hill manuscript section, the way to time these movements so that the supporting footsteps on the downbeat would be to start with the hop and catch as anacrusis, or pickup beats. This was no doubt made clear in his classes but is now left for readers to interpret and reconstruct in conjunction with suitable music for the movements.

Anderson's description of the double treble and a 'Finish' goes:

DOUBLE TREBLE

Hop one on left.
Catch in with right and put right behind, then beat out, beat in, with left.
Bring left down in front and beat behind with right, then beat out, beat in, with left.
Put left behind and beat in front with right then beat out, beat in, with left.
Bring left down in front and beat behind with right.
Then hop one on right
Catch in with left and put left behind, then beat out, beat in, with right.
Bring right down in front and beat behind with left, then beat out, beat in, with right.
Put right behind and beat in front with left then beat out, beat in, with right.
Bring right down in front and beat behind with left.
Repeat from beginning.
Double Treble counts 15.

FINISH OF TREBLES

Beat out, beat in, with right.
Hop one on left.
Bring right down behind, beat in front with left, and bring right up in first position.
Reverse, beat out, beat in, with left.
Hop one on right.
Bring left down behind, beat in front with right, and bring left up in first position.
Finish of Trebles counts 6.[58]

A motif called the 'double flatter' is outlined on the next page, and given as:

DOUBLE FLATTER.

Spring on left.
Beat out, beat in, with right.
Hop one on left.

158 *Aberdeenshire to the Hebrides*

> Beat out, beat in, with right.
> Change with a spring on right, then beat out, beat in, with left.
> Hop one on right.
> Beat out, beat in, with left.
> Change with a spring on left.
> Repeat from the beginning.[59]

This is probably the earliest printed motif notation of explicitly percussive footwork as practised in Scotland. 'Trebling' is not described in detail in print again until the Fletts' book appears in 1964; however, another unpublished description was included in Angus-based fiddler and dancing teacher Dancie John Reid of Newtyle's personal handwritten notebook from 1935. Dancie Reid was primarily a pupil of Dancie James Neill of Forfar, but he did take classes from David Anderson as well[60] because his notebook indicates this. No hints are provided in Anderson's guides regarding which dances 'trebles' and 'flatters' should be used in, apart from these motifs appearing in his versions of the Sailor's Hornpipe and Irish Jig. Were 'trebles' and 'flatters' only for solo dancing? Or, did Anderson teach them for use in Country Dances such as Petronella, practices the Fletts described as common in areas such as East Lothian, Roxburghshire, West Berwickshire, and Fife around the same time?[61] Anderson's clear descriptions of these 'treble' and 'flatter' movements confirm that percussive steps formed part of this Dundee dancing master's repertoire in the late nineteenth century, and from thence extended into an Angus dancing master's repertoire into the late 1930s and early 1940s.

Clog dancing world championships, late 1800s

Scotsmen, including a man by the name of Joe Lowe, competed in the wooden Clog dancing World Championships at Princess Theatre in Leeds in 1880.[62] In 1898, at another World Championships held at the People's Empire, Bow, London, two Scotsmen, J. M'Pike and Glaswegian James Burns, were among the winners, with Burns winning the final and the prize of £20.[63] The level of Clog dancing in Scotland at the end of the nineteenth century clearly was high. Clog dancing remained popular in both England and Scotland up until at least the beginning of the Second World War.

From footing and heel beats to treble and flatter

Extracting terminology and words used by various authors throughout the middle and late nineteenth century to describe dancing creates the following chronological word mosaic:

> Cracking their fingers to imitate castanets, shuffling, capering, cutting; catch in, single and double treble; the genuine treble-shuffle, the

sledge-hammer-like beating of the heel and toe upon the boards, the cracking of the thumbs; the sound of the fiddle, and the clattering of iron-shod shoes on the barn floor [...] They kicked, capered, and wheeled—did the treble shuffle, and the double treble; stamping of the feet; the dancer jumps up over the candle and clicks the toes or heels together to snuff the candle without toppling it; a barn floor, easy boots, a ranting fiddle, or a roaring bagpipe, and then the fun! Treeple, double-shuffle, paddybas, the cleek, the wheel, the stamp, the heuch; Beat its flooring like a drum, Batter it with Tullochgorum; through the reel they sprang, wheeled and set to partners, and aye ere they reel'd again and hale o' them brocht doon their tackety shoon wi' sic a tremendous bang on the flair that the maisic was fairly droned; beating the ground; trebles and flatter

Places where this dancing occurred were assembly rooms, barns, castles, and stages. Footwear ranged from slippers, to bare feet, to iron-shod tackety boots. Dancing had a wide geographical reach, from the Highlands and Islands to central and southern Scotland. While some dancing masters worked to assimilate and smooth out Scottish dance styles for ballroom events, a multiplicity of dance styles would present some choice regarding individual physical expression. A more influential wave of standardisation, where dancers were encouraged to look and move as alike as possible, was to come in the twentieth century.

Notes

1. Devine 2011: 152.
2. Devine 2011: 170.
3. Flett 1996; Anderson 1897; Reid 1935.
4. Sinclair 1840: 342–343.
5. Catherine Sinclair, *Shetland and the Shetlanders or The Northern Circuit* 1840, pages 341–342: At Blair Atholl—'Highland dancing displays incomparable execution, and requires a rapidity of movement which the eye can scarcely follow. One of the performances would have amused you much, on account of the extreme precision and neatness which it required, being quite in the hair-breadth style. Two walking sticks are laid on the ground in a horizontal cross, within the four angles of which a dancer undertakes to perform with matchless rapidity a series of the most intricate steps, but the instant his foot accidentally touches one of the sticks, he is obliged to stop. Formerly two sharp swords supplied the place of those inoffensive poles, and they so effectually disabled a performer, after the slightest *faux pas*, from continuing to exhibit, that he might as well have executed his hornpipe among red-hot ploughshares. The dance gets quicker and quicker, the music more rapid, and the steps more intricate every instant, while the competitor passes with ceaseless activity over the prostrate sticks, springing so lightly across, that his feet seem only pointing at the ground, without ever resting on it. All that feet can do, these Highlanders did, and more than I ever saw any feet attempt before, but we all looked on in solemn silence, as if witnessing an execution.'
6. MacFadyen and MacPherson 2009: 2–3.

160 *Aberdeenshire to the Hebrides*

7. Emmerson 1972: 127.
8. MacFadyen and MacPherson 2009: 26.
9. Some interpretations to note are by Cramb (RSCDS) 1953; BATD 2019; Brisbane Scottish Dancing Festival Committee 1976; Robertson 1982; SDTA 1991; SOHDA; UKAPTD 2019.
10. Cramb 1994: 23–24.
11. According to what Ena Thomson of Aberdeen, teacher of famed Highland dancer Mary Aitken said in a letter to the paper (*Aberdeen Press and Journal*, October 18, 1948: 2, col 6), Miss Cruickshank had her father's notebook which was dated 1820 and which included a description of the Earl of Erroll.
12. These are: British Association of Teachers of Dance (BATD), Scottish Dance Teachers Alliance (SDTA), Imperial Society of Teachers of Dancing (ISTD), and United Kingdom Alliance of Professional Teachers of Dancing (UKAPTD).
13. RSCDS 2009: ii.
14. RSCDS 2009: iv.
15. Melin 2006.
16. Flett 1985.
17. A Scottish Traditions of Dance Trust and Angus Council funded project backed by the Scottish Arts Council 1998–2002.
18. Melin 2006.
19. Flett 1996: 42.
20. Flett Collection, 12 January 1954.
21. Melin 2006.
22. Melin 2006.
23. Cameron: http://special.lib.gla.ac.uk/collections/sta/articles/national_drama/index.html [Accessed 14 January, 2019].
24. From a list of Britain's Provincial Theatres: http://www.arthurlloyd.co.uk/BritainsProvincialTheatres.htm [Accessed 14 January 2019].
25. Playbills are made available for viewing at https://www.ambaile.org.uk/. [Accessed 14 January 2019].
26. Nicholson 1843: iii.
27. Nicholson 1843: 405–406.
28. Nicholson 1843: 407.
29. Nicholson 1843: 410.
30. Nicholson 1843: 413–414.
31. Carus 1846: 320.
32. Carus 1846: 320–321.
33. Haka as movement system: http://www.maoritelevision.com/news/regional/new-year-new-focus-raukura-te-arawa-secondary-school-haka-regionals [Accessed 14 January 2019].
34. Kohl 1849: 175.
35. Anderson, 2017. Conversation with Mats Melin.
36. McIan 1848: 236–237.
37. McIan 1848: 237.
38. St. John 1884 [1849]: 25.
39. *Banffshire Journal and General Advertiser*, Tuesday 17 September 1850.
40. Flett manuscript collection.
41. Melin 2019a.
42. Flett 1996: 64.
43. Other publications of Hebridean dances are by Metherell 1982, *Còmhlan Dannsa nan Eileanach* 1995, and UKAPTD 1990.
44. Flett 1996: 17.

45. *Smàladh na Coinnle*—smooring the candle. *The Concise Scots Dictionary* (1987: 637) says that *smooring* (the fire); a ritual damping down of the domestic fire at night, once common in Highland Catholic districts. Dwelly's *Illustrated Gaelic to English Dictionary* (1988: 867), adds—*smàladh,—aidh*, Snuffing, act of snuffing a candle. *smàladaireachd*, Act of candle-snuffing. *cnap-smàlaidh*, a gathering coal, to keep the fire alive overnight.
46. Personal correspondence 8 April 1992, with Canon Angus MacQueen, Bornish, South Uist.
47. http://carmichaelwatson.blogspot.co.uk/2009/11/ewen-maclachlan-dance-master-catechist_27.html [Accessed 12 February 2014].
48. *Hamilton Advertiser*, 28 May 1864, front page, col 4.
49. Stapleton 2014: 50.
50. Walker 1883. *The Life and Times, The Rev John Skinner of Linshart, Longside, author of 'Tullochgorum,' etc*. London: W. Skeffington & Son.
51. Stapleton 2014: 51.
52. Seibert 2015: 84.
53. 'The Cock o' the Steeple to the Bairns o' Falkirk,' *Falkirk Herald*, 1869. The text also appears in Robert Buchanan's *Poems, Songs, and Other Writings* (1901).
54. In modern Gaelic orthography this title would be spelled *Leabhar Comunn nam Fìor Ghaidheal*.
55. http://www.charles-north.com/html/biography_.html [Accessed 30 December 2016].
56. McIntyre North 1880: 43.
57. Anderson 1897: 129.
58. Anderson 1897: 130.
59. Anderson 1897: 131.
60. Flett 1985: 18.
61. Flett 1985: 260–266.
62. http://insteprt.co.uk/world-clog-dance-championship-leeds-1880/ [Accessed 20 February 2019].
63. https://insteprt.co.uk/world-clog-dance-championship-bow-london-1898/ [Accessed 2 March 2019].

9 Breakdown

Twentieth-century accounts

The impact of war and social change on dance practices

The twentieth century saw a complex maze of social, industrial, political, and economic changes. World Wars I and II caused upheaval and devastation for most people in Scotland. The huge numbers of male casualties in the First World War resulted in a loss of cultural tradition bearers of all kinds. Storytellers, singers, musicians, and dancers never came back or were changed by injury, physical and/or mental, as individuals. At least a thousand piper casualties, 500 killed in combat, were recorded during the First World War alone.[1] Young dancer William McKimmie, a soldier in the Sixth Gordon Highlanders regiment, and son of dancing master J.E. McKimmie of Portsoy, was killed in action in France in 1915.[2] McKimmie was just one of many losses, sadly. This had a profound impact on dance traditions.

One result was that more women started dancing together through the Women's Rural Institute. Other women began teaching dance, and were now more accepted in doing so. The male-dominated era of the dancing master was over. Dance tuition and schools became the domain of women. In Highland dancing, the period of the inter-war years saw the shift from a male-dominated world of teachers and competitors at Highland Games to one hugely influenced by female teachers. Kim Whitta's thesis on Highland dancing in New Zealand presents the point of view that the emerging standardisation process, of the RSOBHD in particular, served to remove the 'unifying element of drama' embedded in Highland dance in Scotland, and further, that an 'emasculation' took place, in 'the loss of its early practitioners for whom the Highland Solo Dances were composed and whose spirit permeates the Reels—the male dancer.'[3]

The Scottish Country Dance Society was in its embryonic stages, set up by two women in 1923. Two male dancing masters, Dancie Reid of Newtyle and D.G. MacLennan of Edinburgh, saw the end of an era out. The Scottish Country Dance Society garnered patronage in 1947, and was granted a Royal designation in 1951. In Scotland, two Highland dance organisations were formed: the SOHDA in 1947; the SOBHD in 1950. Scottish dance examination bodies such as the BATD, ISTD, SDTA, and UKA offered medal tests following progressive syllabi, which came to form regular and regulated learning processes for Highland dancers. Competitions increased in number and Highland dancing became a global sport, spreading first to the former British Empire colonies and later beyond. Likewise, Scottish Country dancing spread via the RSCDS to most corners of the world. The RSCDS started out with a relatively small number of Country dances in repertoire. Since the 1950s, the idea of devising new and often more complex dances has become a worldwide hobby and now well over ten thousand Scottish Country dances are available in books and online.

The Reeling dance form endures, with a fairly limited repertoire of mainly Country dances engaged in by a relatively small subset of Scottish society. The Ballroom repertoire of dances introduced by nineteenth-century dancing masters, plus some Country dances, lives on under the label of Old-Time dancing or Tea dancing. A particular segment of these dances, sometimes performed in a faster, more boisterous manner, becomes referred to as Ceilidh dancing, a term from the 1970s. The dancing of Quadrilles declined as a mainstay of social dancing from the 1950s onwards and has almost disappeared apart from some pockets of enthusiasts in Shetland, South Uist, and Angus. A relatively recent introduction has been Step dancing, introduced by teachers from Cape Breton Island who have taught numerous workshops since the early 1990s. A small grassroots subset of Step dancers exists around Scotland today.[4]

While early-century written accounts more appropriately relate to the end of the nineteenth century, percussive dance memories and observations persist all the way through the century.

Unidentified Step dancer and piper, Campbeltown, Argyll, 1900

The photograph of a man Step dancing in Scotland in Figure 9.1 shows him dancing to a piper at a fair in Campbeltown, Argyll, around the year 1900. The photograph belongs to the McGrory Collection.

The heels on the heavy shoes or boots can be seen clearly from this perspective, behind the dancer. His weight is forward on the balls of the feet, while his head inclines downward slightly. All eyes, of the audience members and of the piper, are fixed on the dancer's feet. Was he improvising? Was he dancing one of the hornpipes popular at the time?

James Scott Skinner, Aberdeenshire, 1905

The People's Ball Room Guide, edited in 1905 by fiddle virtuoso and dancing master J. Scott Skinner (1843–1927), quotes Dr Norman MacLeod's poem 'Dance, My Children,' shared in the previous chapter, to illustrate the essence, the vigour and life, of Scottish dances. This ballroom guide, claims Skinner, 'teaches how to dance and how to behave in the ball room.' His

Figure 9.1 Dancing to the piper at a fair in Campbeltown, Argyll *c.* 1900 (SLA 58.35.26)
Source: Image used with kind permission by the MacGrory Collection, Live Argyll Libraries.

remarks on the percussive action of snapping are of particular interest. He writes, 'There is a danger now of over-refinement. Let us keep the native vigour of the Reel, with the crack of the thumbs, and even the "hooch," if these accompaniments are not made too obtrusive.'[5]

James's father, William Skinner of Arbeadie, near Banchory (*c.* 1801–1845), also had been a dance teacher. Scott Skinner's style of dancing may have been heavily influenced by that of Professor William Scott of Stoneywood, near Aberdeen, with whom he took classes in the early 1860s.

Frederick Rea, South Uist, 1906

Catholic Englishman Frederick Rea's memoirs of his time as a schoolteacher in South Uist are found in his book *A School in South Uist; Reminiscences of a Hebridean Schoolmaster, 1890–1913*.[6] Rea remarked that the Reel was the only social dance in use by the islanders. His memoirs vividly describe a dance in the school at Garrynamonie in about 1906. The evening started off with Donald the Piper playing airs as dancers filled the benches around the sides of the room. Suddenly, the piper played a wailing tune, a signal to start off the dancing. At this, the young men arose to form the dancing sets, and beckoned partners to join them. When all the dancers were partnered, Donald the Piper launched into playing Reels:

> At once more than a hundred pairs of feet shod in heavy boots were thudding on the floor in some step of the reel, but all in time: all faces devoid of a smile, serious as though dancing was a business, the men looking upwards, and the girls with downwards eyes. The rhythm of the tune changed with an increase in time. With a loud yell the men now danced together in pairs – they whirled and sprang in a mad dance till, when they were pouring with perspiration, Donald slowed down his tune; it died away and the dancers were glad to rest – Donald knew his work! […] All were absorbed in the pleasure of dancing in a large room with a good floor, and to the music of Donald's playing; and, when he shortly recommenced, the floor was soon filled and another reel was danced. Hour after hour was passed and reel followed reel almost without pause till I wondered that they were not exhausted, especially the piper; but they danced on, apparently as fresh as ever. I fancy they had danced fourteen or fifteen reels on end when I approached Donald and put my hand on his shoulder. He stopped playing and I asked him to tell them in Gaelic that there would be an interval for refreshments […] In half an hour the piper began to 'tune up' and the dancers returned, keen to resume […] The dance went on into early morning, reel succeeding reel as though there were no other dance, and I strongly suspected this to be the only dance they knew.[7]

No doubt Rea was more familiar with current fashionable Ballroom dances, such as the Polka, Waltz, and the Quadrille of his native England. His observations are not as derogative as some earlier English authors tended to be. His accounts show great interest in his island community, even though he doesn't seem to have learnt Gaelic, predominantly spoken in South Uist at that time.

Rea specified that Donald *Bàn* MacDonald from Daliburgh taught a Highland dance class.[8] This piper was *Dòmhnall Bàn* or Donald *Roidein* MacDonald (1864–1945) from Daliburgh, South Uist, a renowned piper who danced 'Hebridean' dances at the Askernish Games from 1923 onwards. *Roidein* was also known as a Step dance piper and often competed in both piping and dancing at the Uist Games. He knew Scotch Blue Bonnets, First of August, Flowers of Edinburgh, Highland Laddie, Miss Forbes, Over the Water to Charlie, Scotchmakers, and *Tulloch Gorm*.[9]

Frederick Rea's account depicts a community in transition, where Reels were still in practice. But, as pointed out in a foreword to Rea's memoirs written by his pupil Kate MacPhee, outside influences were present. MacPhee stated that, by the early 1900s, a dance teacher from Perth taught a weekly Country dance class and brought her own violinist. Other vital connections between piping, Gaelic song, and dance in the South Uist community, and changes to them, are discussed in Joshua Dickson's (2006) book *When Piping Was Strong*. Both Dickson and Rea outline many mainland influences that

166　*Twentieth-century accounts*

ousted the older percussive and improvised dance traditions in favour of smoother, more structured traditions of mainland Scotland. In the 1980s and 1990s, this process was still ongoing, with mainland dance and music teachers continuing to visit the Hebridean islands to hold workshops and classes.[10] Rea's description illustrates the prominence of the Reel as a social dance, the noise of the dancers' feet, and that men dance together, expressed by Topham over a hundred years earlier.

Traveller dancing in Galloway in the late 1800s and early 1900s, A. McCormick, Dumfries, 1907

The 2007 edition of Andrew McCormick's 1906/1907 book *The Tinkler-Gypsies* shares observations of the history and culture of a Travellers' community in southwest Scotland in the late nineteenth and early twentieth centuries. Dancing is mentioned as occurring in the Galloway camp:

> A Cumberland Tinkler and a Carlisle lad who were travelling in company as clog dancers next favoured the company with a break-down. One of the two played a mouth harmonium as they danced, and better playing or dancing one could not wish for. This merely served to whet the appetite of William, the King of the Marshall gang, and he speedily formed a square for a reel. He and his consort were partners and soon amidst much 'hooching' and yells of laughter, they were cleeking and swinging and footing gaily the jolliest reel imaginable. Sometimes it was the mouth harmonium that served as an accompaniment, but King William had a distinct preference for singing out at double quick time the chorus of the "Tinkler's Waddin"—
>
> 'Dirrim day doo a day,
> Dirrim doo a da dee O,
> Dirrim day doo a day,
> Hurrah for the Tinkler's waddin' O.'
>
> At the close of the reel I left the breathless dancers to go to resume my interview with old Grannie Stewart ... (1907).[11]

The Travellers described in this book come from all over Scotland and England. In the same chapter, Travellers from Argyllshire and Perthshire, such as Grannie Stewart, Carlisle, and Cumberland intermingle and share languages, including cant and Gaelic, and lore. Clog dancing appears just as normal as the cleekit (linking arms and swinging) in the Reel. A blind minstrel with a harp appears near Newton-Stewart in another segment:

> As I drew near to them, the female caused him to raise his harp and he began to play the well-known air, 'Kenmure's on an' awa,' Willie.' It was

a calm evening in the month of April, and the melodious sound of the harp soon brought a crowd of peasants from the neighbouring hamlet of Machermore, and the fields of Kirroughtree, which, with a fiddle played by one of the younger branches of the minstrel's family, formed a band that called into action the dancing powers not only of the other children, but likewise of several of the spectators.[12]

Even though percussive dance elements are mentioned, also of interest are the wandering Travelling musicians, and how both the harp and fiddle provide dance music. Singing, dancing, and the playing of the fiddle and harp were strongly favoured in this Travelling community.

Dance exhibitions, Aberdeen, 1907 and 1909

Newspaper reports from Aberdeen frequently refer to 'Step-dancing' activities in the early twentieth century. In 1907, Miss Bella Hardy and Master George Hendry '[...] gave an excellent exhibition of Highland and Step-dancing which was greatly enjoyed, the youthful couple appearing eight times during the evening.'[13] This report distinguishes between Highland and Step dancing but we do not know how.

Gondoliers Dancing Academy, led by Mr and Mrs Donald, performed an exhibition of dances in the Reception Rooms, North Silver Street, Aberdeen—'The children went through the various quadrilles, reels, etc., and gave exhibitions of the latest dances, the Boston two-step, esparano, universal two-step, valeta, imperial waltz; while the pupils of the step-dancing classes performed the Irish Jig, Highland fling, sword dance, eightsome reel etc.'[14] Step dancing is differentiated from social dancing in this case. Another report making this distinction in Lanarkshire refers to Motherwell dance classes featuring Mr James D. Muir's Quadrille Dance every Saturday, while Miss J Muir offers classes in 'Step-dancing.'[15]

Bride's reel, Orkney, 1913

In the Viking Club's *Old-Lore Miscellany of Orkney, Shetland, Caithness and Sutherland. Vol 6*, we find this description of dancing celebrating a wedding:

All the dances were reels—none of your modern polkas, schottisches, quadrilles, etc.—there were the foursome or two couple reel, the six-some or three couple reel, and the eightsome or four couple reel. Those were the days when dancing was engaged in with a vigour and an abandon which could be considered rude in the ballroom of the present day. The men, with perspiration streaming down their faces, threw off both coat and waistcoat and 'tripped it' in their 'sark sleeves,' while the women tucked up their wide skirts, or spread them out on either side, as they assumed a variety of pose and airs worthy of a professional exponent of

168   *Twentieth-century accounts*

the skirt dance. When the music changed from slow to quick time, not a step nor a beat was missed, but in heavy walking shoes they 'toed it and heeled it' with perfect precision. The measure was accented by a loud tap of the iron shod heels and a snap of the fingers; what a storm of sound arose; the men waving hands and arms and shouting like people 'all possessed,' made the rafters ring with many a 'Heeuch' and 'Yeeuch,' in which the women did not disdain to join.[16]

The fiddler signalled the end of the Bride's Reel by playing a screeching sound indicating the ladies should give kisses to partners their partners as payment for the pleasure of the dance. More kisses on the dance floor were shared when the occasion ended with the 'Bobadybouster,' or Bob-at-the-Bolster, a dance where partners accumulate, dance together, then, one by one, leave the floor, and end the party. The dancing described seems to have taken place rather earlier than 1913, and the writer reflects that this kind of dancing was no longer fashionable at the time of writing.

An Comunn Gàidhealach, Inverness, 1913

A lesson for Gaelic learners in the '*Mios deireannach a' Gheamhraidh*'/last month of winter 1913 edition of the *Deo-Gréine*, the magazine of the Gaelic Society, presents a situation for learning terms about New Year's celebrations. A young man asks his grandfather about New Year's feasts and customs of older times. The grandfather goes on to describe the dancing: ''S bochd nach fhaca tu do shenair air an ùrlar 'nuair a bha e òg; 's e *a bhragadh a chruadhan*.'[17] The first part of the phrase can be translated as 'it's too bad you never saw your grandfather on the floor.' The italic words, employing idiomatic use of a word for hooves, were translated in the publication as 'his heels would rattle the floor,' in other words, clarifies the editor, '*he* was the boy who could dance.'[18] Later in the passage the dance the grandfather shows off is the *Seann Triubhas*, while the boy and his sweetheart follow by dancing the *Gille Chaluim*.

Scottish dances, silent film, *ca.* 1915

A silent film clip[19] hosted by the National Library of Scotland shows a dancer presenting a *Seann Triubhas*, Highland Fling, and Sword Dance at a time predating technique promoted by D.G. MacLennan. The film itself is not dated; an estimate of 1915 has been suggested by the National Library of Scotland. The dancer is a woman, accompanied by two pipers who stand on both sides of her while they play. One of the pipers appears to be George Douglas Taylor, originally from Aberdeen, who became well known as a dancing teacher, publishing directions in *Some Traditional Scottish Dances* under the auspices of London's Imperial Society of Teachers of Dancing in 1929. Taylor also, notably, taught piping to members of the Dagenham Girls Pipe Band. If the estimate of the date of the film given is correct, this footage would likely have been taken before Taylor was wounded through the heart by shrapnel at the Battle of Loos.[20]

The dancer, currently unidentified, wears shoes, which, though difficult to see clearly, appear to be of the soft-soled Highland dancing pumps type; however, the shoes also sport buckles, keeping in the tradition of heavier shoes worn for dancing before 1900. A step she dances in the *Seann Triubhas*, the first dance shown, though not labelled as such in the film, features double heel beats, a motif which no longer survives in the dance as taught by any governing bodies of Highland dance, so far as we are aware. This motif still occurs in the 'Irish Jig' and in the non-competitive Over the Water to Charlie. The *Seann Triubhas* quick time steps and the Highland Fling in the film also exhibit a much faster tempo than is customary for Highland dancing today.

One of two quick-time *Seann Triubhas* steps at the end of the dance, after the dancer claps her hands twice, is similar to a step described in MacLennan's book,[21] published about 35 years later, featuring an inverted toe position at the beginning of a toe-heel-toe-heel step, which she follows with spring points, not the rocking movements suggested by MacLennan. While this quick-time step is not included among the *Seann Triubhas* steps in Taylor's book, his Highland Laddie description does employ an inverted toe position.[22]

Arm movements the silent film dancer uses correspond closely to seven arm positions outlined in Douglas Taylor's book. They include some positions no longer recognised, with arms curving to the front and sides of the body at the level of the breastbone.[23] His sixth position shows the arms held down together straight in front of the body, fingers interlaced, a position still used in the Sailors' Hornpipe. When arms are held up or out to the sides, Taylor specifies that fingers should be grouped so that both the middle and ring fingers touch the thumb for hand placement.

While Taylor's book is often described as reflecting the wave of refinement occurring in Highland dancing in the twentieth century, his presence in this film helps us look at the material reflected in his book more closely and critically, and may reflect traditions closer to earlier practices than has been considered. The costume the silent film dancer wears bears closer resemblance to the kilt skirt and argyle hose suggested as suitable by MacLennan's later book than the outfit modelled in the line drawings of a girl dancing in Taylor's book. It is not clear if the footage was filmed in Scotland; it takes place in front of a painted backdrop showing a castle, water, and a mountain. Since Taylor was based in or near London, having taught in Bushey,[24] there is a possibility it could have been filmed there.

Motherwell, 1919–1921

Percussive dancing seems to have been particularly popular in Motherwell, and we have found a number of newspaper accounts about Step dancing classes. Don MacMillan offered 'Highland and Step-Dancing Classes' in Orange Hall, Milton Street.[25] Mr Nelson's Select Dancing offered 'Highland

170   *Twentieth-century accounts*

and Step-Dancing' with Champion Highland dancer Miss Peggy Struthers assisting.[26] H. Biggins at Shepherd's Hall, Craigneuk, advertised his 'Step Dancing Academy,' where 'Clog, Wooden-shoe, Schottische, Big Boots, Top-Boots, Sand, Waltz Time, and International' were offered. Biggins encouraged that 'Anyone desiring to take up same can now be enrolled [...] Pupils already on stage.[27]

In 1921, an advertisement by two dancing teachers starting classes reads:

> STEP-DANCING.
> J.P. SHELLEY and W.T. M'GUIGAN
> are commencing Classes for all kinds of Step-Dancing,
> Including Buck, Schottische, Clog, Top Boot,
> Sand Dance, Waltz, Irish Jig, Sailor's Hornpipe, etc.
> Intending pupils call between the hours 6 to
> 7 p.m., or write J.P. SHELLEY, 25b
> QUARRYHALL Street, Motherwell.
> Terms moderate.[28]

This list of popular percussive and novelty dances in North Lanark emphasises showy performance-oriented pieces. Only two of these dances have continued in the Highland Dance repertoire in Scotland: the 'Irish' Jig and the Sailor's Hornpipe, The New Zealand Academy continues to include Clogs and Waltzes as well.

South Uist and Barra Highland Gathering, 1923–1931

Dances with percussive footwork, such as First of August and Over the Water, feature in an *Oban Times* report from the 1923 South Uist and Barra Highland Gathering held at Askernish in South Uist:

> ### South Uist and Barra Highland Gathering
> This well-known piping, dancing and athletic gathering was held on the machair at Askernish, South Uist, on 17th July. The attendance was good under the circumstances. [...] A novel feature was a competitive exhibition of old Highland dances which are remembered in South Uist and Barra, but which are almost forgotten in other parts of the Highlands. There were two competitors. Mr Archibald MacPherson, Iochdar, South Uist, who is over 75 years of age, and Mr Donald MacDonald, Daliburgh. This event was much appreciated by the judges and spectators, and will be suitably developed at future gatherings.
> [Among the] Results:
>
> Old Highland Dances (prizes presented by the Royal Celtic Society)—
> 'The First of August,'—Archibald MacPherson, Iochdar, £2, Donald MacDonald, Daliburgh.

Figure 9.2 Hebridean dancing at South Uist Games, 1920s

Source: Image used with kind permission by Edinburgh Central Library and www.ambaile.org.uk.

'Over the Water to Charlie,'—Donald MacDonald, £2, Archibald MacPherson.
'Scotch Blue Bonnets Over the Border,'—Donald MacDonald, £2, Archibald MacPherson.[29]

The exact date of the photograph in Figure 9.2 is unknown. In 1924, we read in the *Oban Times*:

South Uist and Barra Highland Gathering
REVIVAL OF ANCIENT CELTIC DANCING

The annual Highland Gathering organised by the South Uist and Barra Sports Committee was held on the Machair at Askernish, South Uist, on Tuesday, 29th July. The weather was perfect and the games were thoroughly enjoyed by the large concourse of spectators.

The signs given last year of a great improvement in the local gathering were more than realised, and the results reflect great credit on the Committee in charge. A unique feature of the programme was the dancing of old Highland dances still remembered in South Uist and Barra, but not now practised elsewhere in the Highlands. Special prizes were offered by the Royal Celtic Society for competitions in these dances and for the teachers of learners who made meritorious performances. The teachers' prizes were won by Mr Arch. MacPherson, Iochdar, who is now 76 years of age, and Mr Donald MacDonald, Daliburgh, who is over 60 years of age. They also won a prize each in the competitions, and the third prize was awarded to Miss Annie Walker, Daliburgh. In order to encourage the learning of these dances Mr William Donald, Glasgow, had offered a prize of two guineas to the best dancer of these dances under the age of 30 years and a second prize of one guinea. Similar prizes were also offered to the teachers of these prize-winners. The learners' prizes were won by Mr Louis MacEachen, Iochdar, and Miss Annie Walker, Daliburgh, whose teachers were respectively Mr Arch. MacPherson and Mr Donald MacDonald.

These dances were first taught in Uist over eighty years ago by Mr Ewen MacLachlan, a native of Moidart, and seem to indicate some of the dances which were in common use a century ago from which the reels were evolved and which were danced by solo dancers when parties could not be got together to do them. A quartette of four dancers from Daliburgh—Miss Annie Walker, Miss Bella MacDonald, Miss Sarah MacDonald, and Miss Harriet MacDonald—gave an exhibition of two old dances called 'Miss Forbes' and 'The Scotchmakers.'[30] This so pleased the gathering that Captain Cattanach, Lochmaddy, and Captain Ranald Carswell, North Berwick, rewarded their efforts by special prizes.

The old Highland dances are undoubtedly of great interest and it is understood that endeavour will be made to send a team of dancers to exhibit them on the mainland.[31]

These were the Games from which D.G. MacLennan took his knowledge of the 'Hebridean' dances he published in 1950, albeit in a slightly altered form, as mentioned in the information about Ewen MacLachlan. As can be seen from these prize lists, not many individuals were left that knew these dances in the 1920s. Many of these prize winners were documented as informants in the Fletts' research about dances from the Hebrides detailed in *Traditional Step-dancing in Scotland*. The full list of prize winners is featured in Mats Melin's 2019 book *Hebridean Step Dancing*.[32]

Dancie John Reid, Newtyle, 1935

John Reid was born in Alyth, Angus in 1869. He succeeded James Neill as the 'Dancie,' short for dance master, of the Angus and Perthshire area. He taught from about 1890 until his death in Kirriemuir in 1942. Mr Reid was principally a pupil of Dancie James Neill of Forfar, but also took classes from David Anderson in Dundee. He may, according to a letter from D.G. MacLennan to Hugh Foss in 1955, have taken classes from John McNeill Snr. of Edinburgh (1831–1891); it is likely he also picked up McNeill's steps by watching him at dance competitions.[33] Mr Reid made his headquarters in Newtyle, from whence he travelled through his territory. His notebook titled 'Solo Dances,' written in 1935 in Newtyle, describes two percussive 'Hornpipe' dances and the Irish Jig. Trebling is described, as shown in Figure 9.3, and included in

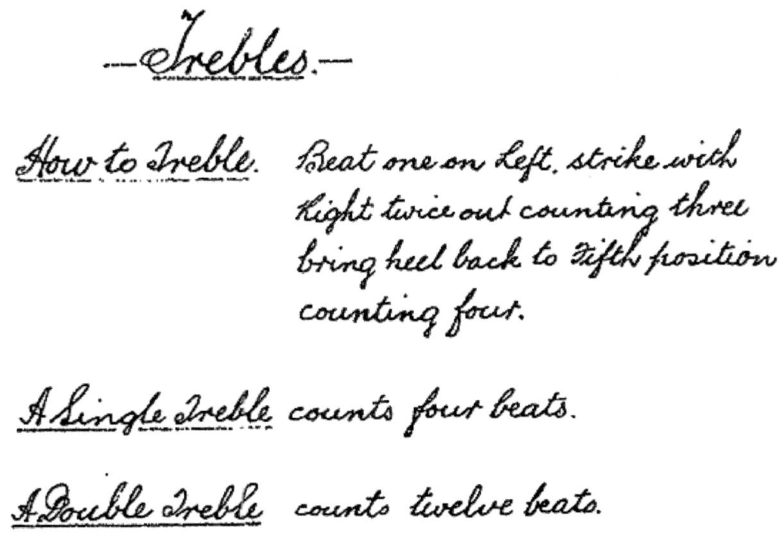

—Trebles.—

How to Treble. Beat one on Left. strike with Right twice out counting three bring heel back to Fifth position counting four.

A Single Treble counts four beats.

A Double Treble counts twelve beats.

Figure 9.3 Extract from Dancie Reid's notebook. Example of treble description

Source: Melin personal archive.

two dances Reid refers to as Hornpipes: the Flowers of Edinburgh, and Jacky Tar Hornpipe. He gives 12 steps for the Jacky Tar Hornpipe, 11 steps for the Flowers of Edinburgh Hornpipe, and 11 steps for the Irish Jig. Reid's version of the Flowers of Edinburgh is very similar to the Hill manuscript description.

Reid also uses the term 'Breakdown,' a term often used to describe a recurring motif in percussive dance. The notebook describes that 'A Breakdown is done by hopping on the Left come down on the Right toe behind, hop on the Left and bring forward the Right.'[34] Reid also used the terms 'catch,' and 'treble,' which feature in the Reid's step description in Figure 9.4.

Jack McConachie, Glasgow, 1949

Jack McConachie (1906–1966) was a Scottish Highland and Country dancer from near Carron in Speyside who moved to London in 1936. He was a successful Highland dance competitor and later taught several forms of dancing in London. He is known for his various publications in Scottish Highland, Hebridean, and Scottish Country dancing. In 1949, he met John MacLeod, from Iochdar in South Uist, in Glasgow and learnt several dances handed down from Ewen MacLachlan via Ewen's pupil Archibald MacPherson. McConachie used some early-1950s standardising terminology for most of his descriptions, published and unpublished, as well as some he preferred, including Ballet terminology such as *ronde de jambe*. Regarding percussive dance motifs, McConachie described shuffles, treble shuffles, tap-close-beat and, though not giving them the same names, he described movement sequences

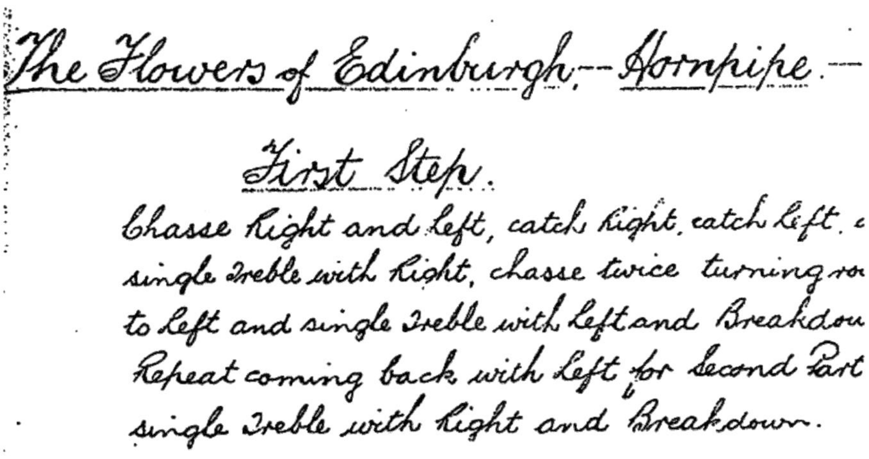

174   *Twentieth-century accounts*

The Flowers of Edinburgh.-- Hornpipe.--

First Step.

Chasse Right and Left, catch Right, catch Left, a
single treble with Right, chasse twice turning rou
to Left and single treble with Left and Breakdou
Repeat coming back with Left for Second Part
single Treble with Right and Breakdown.

Figure 9.4 Extract from Dancie Reid's notebook. Description of the first step of the Flowers of Edinburgh

Source: Melin personal archive.

in his version of the First of August that match the motifs the Fletts, Rhodes, Reid, and Anderson all referred to as single trebles and double trebles.[35]

It is unlikely McConachie picked up any of the terminology he used from MacLeod; he seems to have applied his own terminology, from an *etic* point of view, to movements he learned. He probably modified movements to align with his accustomed repertoire of Highland dance motifs, as the 'treble shuffles,' 'leaps,' and 'high cuts' he described were not included in the Hebridean repertoire of any other sources. Adding these motifs may have made these dances more acceptable to Highland dancing students, by incorporating more ambitious technical demands. McConachie was known for rearranging and modifying dances; as an example, he took David Anderson's version of Highland Laddie, set it to a popular jig, and renamed the dance with the tune's name, Bonnie Dundee.

Donald G. MacLennan, Edinburgh, 1950

Edinburgh dancing master D.G. MacLennan's book *Highland and Traditional Scottish Dances* uses terminology such as shuffles, single and double 'tripples,' and 'stamps.'[36] His descriptions of the modern-day Highland dance motif hop-brush-beat-beat includes onomatopoeic words such as 'skiff' (a brushing movement), and 'double beat' to describe sliding and beating across the floor.[37] The rest of his descriptions are dotted with Ballet terms and other Scottish dance terminology becoming standardised at that time.

MacLennan included inverted foot positions in his dance descriptions. One occurred in the first quick-time step of the *Seann Triubhas*: 'Hop Left and do turned-in right toe, and heel turned-out in second position.'[38] He included another inverted position in his Highland Laddie steps: 'very quickly beat right toe turned in at second position, and beat Left where it is.' In the years since standardisation, inverted positions have been removed from competitive Highland dances, and occur but sparingly in some National Dances. In his 1952 *Highland Dances of Scotland* textbook, William Cameron advises 'In all "Highland" dances ALWAYS keep the thighs, knees, and toes well turned to the side, NEVER dance NO TIME pigeon-toed fashion.'[39] While inverted positions were included in McIntyre North's Sword Dance and Highland Fling,[40] and MacLennan's *Seann Triubhas* steps, they are no longer seen in these dances and seem to have gone out of fashion around the same time the RSOBHD was taking shape. Inverted positions may have provided greater variety in earlier versions of dances and steps that didn't employ arm positions.

In the Fletts' unpublished archive there are letters in which MacLennan admitted that he altered dances he had observed in South Uist in the mid-1920s to 'improve' them.[41] In a letter from Edinburgh dated 27th October 1952, MacLennan tells Tom Flett that 'often a teacher would hear of or see a dance, and not being taught it would try to compose (or 'cook-up') a version of his own.' On the 4th of April 1953, MacLennan described how he 'arranged introductory and finishing steps' to what he called a 'mime' dance of 'no great steps,' *Cailleach an Dùdain* (The Old Woman of the Milldust), and continued:

> sometimes a dancer or teacher would know very little about a dance but would 'fake' bits; perhaps alter the original, so you may find different versions [...] many have copied [steps and dances] from my own arrangements of [Highland Laddie] and Hebridean [dances] which I found too easy and repetitive. An instance! —My brother [William] had been teaching in America one winter, and arrived back just a few days before a big Highland Gathering where 'H. Laddie' was on the programme, for first time: he happened to be last to dance (or nearly last), and looked on when others danced; then went on, and made up the dance—gaining 1st prize and the plaudits of all competitors! [...] In fact, all the difficult steps in S.T. [Seann Triubhas] are my arrangement (Flett Archive, unpublished).[42]

Most informative of all regarding MacLennan's perception of his own artistic license to improve is his response to the question of whether he would be willing to teach Tom Flett the Flowers of Edinburgh and Over the Hills and Far Away exactly as 'old Archie' [MacPherson] taught them to MacLennan in South Uist in the mid-1920s. MacLennan wrote:

> Not worth learning: too much a copy of the others, and only 3 or 4 steps. I <u>finished</u> all those in my book.

176 *Twentieth-century accounts*

MacLennan was no exception to a norm among dancers and dance teachers altering dance material, sometimes tailored to reflect strengths or avoid weaknesses within certain dancers' capabilities. In some ways, these changes and innovations can also be seen as part of a dance form that promoted improvisation and personal choices in its earlier days. After all, evolution is part of how a 'tradition' is kept alive; it is reshaped and kept in constant change. However, continuing to attribute a dance directly to a source after changing material seems disingenuous and reflects a lack of respect for the original.

Percussive footwork motifs used in social dances

Social dances in Scotland involve beating and clapping in time to music. Reelers often clap before turning partners or corners. A few RSCDS dances, such as Prince of Orange, Hooper's Jig, and Princess Royal, involve stamping and clapping. A Ceilidh dance named Square Dance incorporates stepping towards a partner, clapping right hands with that partner three times, stepping back to the side and stamping three times, then repeated clapping left hands.[43] Percussive variants of the Highland Schottische are popular in the Highland and Islands, with dancers' beating sounds accenting rhythms and growing louder as the swing of the music surges. Up in northwest Sutherland a variant of schottische type couple dance The Baden Powell involves vigorous foot tapping movements and finger snapping. More details about this dance appear in Chapter 11.

An instance of a softer percussive motif occurs in a dance titled Call to the Piper. We have written documentation of this dance from the teaching of John Armstrong, a well-known teacher from London, England, who had been a member of Jack McConachie's dance team. Armstrong taught Scottish dances in 1952 for the Country Dance Society of America session of Pinewoods Camp, near Plymouth, Massachusetts in the United States. One of those dances was Call to the Piper, a dance in a couples-round-the-room format that came to be notated by Frank Kaltman, who attended Pinewoods Camp that year. Couples begin the dance in Allemande hold. Kaltman's instructions for the steps at the beginning of the dance read:

> Measures 1–2: Beginning right, take four walking steps in line of direction. This is a very proud walk, foot brushing floor slightly with each step.
> Measures 3–4: Beginning right, brush foot forward lightly (ct. 1), back across left foot (ct. 2), forward (ct. 1), and step in place (ct. 2).[44]

This sequence then repeats on the left side. Jeanetta McColl, a dancer and teacher originally from London living in the Boston area since the 1960s, who danced this many times, remembers the sequence differently, with the brushing happening first in sequence and the walking second.

The brushing movement of the gesture leg in this motif is the same action used in the kick step, but here occurs without a hopping motion of the supporting leg. This type of movement swiping the floor has been described earlier by D.G. MacLennan as a 'skiff,' and by Dancie Reid as a 'catch.' These brushing movements can also be seen as being similar to the Highland Fling motif going around the leg, though this version is distinctly gently percussive and occurs in a parallel leg position. It also can be seen as a slow-time shuffle crossing over the standing leg. This particular motif sits nicely between Scottish hard-shoe and soft-shoe styles, revealing a bit of common ground between them.

The second half of the dance consists of rotating around one's partner with four low *pas des Basques* (measures 9–12), followed by taking right hands and dancing *pas de Basque* right and then left (measures 13–14), and concludes with walking four steps in the line of direction, turning the lady under to resume Allemande hold (measures 15–16), ready to begin again. Jeanetta McColl remembers hearing the dance called 'Call of the Pipes.' Her father, Alexander C. McColl, was a piper and dance teacher originally from Glasgow. Alexander McColl played pipes for Jack McConachie's London-area dance classes and often played for a medley of dances consisting of a 2/4 or 4/4 march Gay Gordons, a 6/8 Call of the Pipes, then a Highland Schottische. While the *Dance a While* book gives the time signature as '2/4,' Frank Kaltman's notes outline that 'in the absence of the specific tune, they selected the tune "Ab Schenken" as a desirable one.'[45] *Ap Shenkin* is a Welsh title of a 6/8 tune also known as the Tempest, indicating that Armstrong did teach the dance in 6/8 time.[46]

There are other versions of dances also known by similar names, such as 'Call o' the Pipes.' One that is similar in form but employs a heel and toe beating motif instead of brushing is described at the Canadian Olde Tyme Square Dance Callers' Association website. The dance is described there, taken from *Alex Mulligan's Collection of Square Dance Calls* as follows:

> *Call of the Pipes*
>
> Position—Lady on gent's right; each with arm around the other at the waist
>
> Heel (gents left, ladies right) and toe (same foot) — 4 beats
>
> Walk forward four steps & on fourth step U-turn putting lady on gent's left
>
> Heel-Toe, Walk forward four steps and on the fourth step face partner.
>
> Balance to partner, left and right, lady putting hands over head:
>
> Turn together once around on four two-steps. C.W.[47]

Lillian Beckwith, Isle of Skye, 1959

Lillian Beckwith wrote a series of semiautobiographical books based on her experiences living in the Isle of Skye and Soay. In one of them, *The Hills is*

Lonely, a dance is described where the men wear tackety boots. The dance is advertised by a sign including a request for ladies to bring soap flakes as part of the cost of admission:

> 'Why the soap flakes?' I asked.
> 'To make the floor slippery,' he explained; 'though I'm thinkin' it's whole bars of soap they'll need for fillin' up the holes where the rats have eaten through.'
> I wondered why they did not use french chalk.
> 'French chalk?' he echoed. 'I don't sell that. What like of stuff would that be?'
> I enlightened him regarding the properties of french chalk but he was not impressed. Soap flakes, he maintained, were the best thing in the world for sticking to the men's tackety boots. 'Makes them lighter about the feet,' he added. It was my turn to be supercilious.
> The prospect of a dance where one's partners were likely to be wearing tackety boots was not inviting to me, but it acted as no deterrent to the rest of the village.[48]

The barn floor where the dance takes place:

> [...] could not by any stretch of the imagination be called a dance floor, but I daresay it was good enough for tackety boots. [... T]he dancers leaped and stamped their way through innumerable schottisches and reels, their shrill 'yeeps' and screams outrivalling the frantic efforts of the belligerent instrumentalists who, with carefully averted eyes, played with the single-mindedness of two greyhounds chasing a hare and with much the same result; the fiddle invariably reaching the winning post two or three bars ahead of his antagonist.[49]

While the description does seek to garner a few laughs, sometimes at the expense of the characters in the scene, it reflects that some dances in rural areas in the mid-twentieth century retained a spirit and ambience similar to the 'Country Kirn' and the Falkirk Feeing Fair depictions in the nineteenth century.

The Fletts' and Rhodes's research 1950s–1960s

There are many references in the Fletts' and Rhodes's research to Step dancing of a percussive nature. Their description of treepling in East Lothian, Roxburghshire, and West Berwickshire in various Country Dances such as Petronella, Flowers of Edinburgh, and Jacky Tar may be the only documentation of this form.[50] Treepling seems to have been in use until at least 1914. The Fletts' descriptions of the First of August, Scotch Measure, and Aberdonian Lassie feature percussive shuffles and trebles.[51] The East Fife Clog Hornpipe, Fife Liverpool Hornpipe, and Wigtownshire Liverpool Hornpipe all appear in a chapter about Clog dances in their book *Traditional Step-dancing in Scotland*. All are described in detail with background information on context and sources. Clog and Step dances of a percussive nature were quite commonplace until the early 1900s, according to their informants.

Since the Fletts and Rhodes published their findings, little, if any, mention of percussive Step dancing has been mentioned in relation to Scottish dancing since. Forms of Step dance were common to most parts of the Scottish mainland and Islands, but since the 1920s, the primary focus in dance-related material published has been about the soft-shoe aesthetics promoted by Scottish Country and Highland dancing organisations. Mid-twentieth-century interpretations of dance manuscripts were coloured by these aesthetics, and have influenced a popular perception of traditional Scottish dance as a smooth, Ballet-influenced style of dance. This perception persists in Scotland and internationally.

Thomas Flett's (1923–1976) obituary written by Frank Rhodes in 1976 makes it clear that Scottish and English dancing were Tom's real-life passions. He was as meticulous in his research methods as he was in learning steps and dancing. He balanced this with family life and with a career as professor of pure mathematics at the University of Sheffield.[52] His late wife Joan was an active partner in this research and she arranged its publication after Tom passed away. All of the Fletts' manuscripts, archived in digitised formats, will be available on Instep Research Team's website www.instep.co.uk in PDF format.

Joan Henderson, Outer Hebrides, 1980s

Scottish dance scholar and educator Joan Henderson conducted research in the Hebrides in the mid-1970s and 1980s. She looked at social dancing in the Isle of Lewis, South Uist, and Barra, and compared the dancing of these different island communities. Her work *The Traditional Dances of the Outer Hebrides* was published in 1995.[53] She noted various Hebridean solo dances of the time that included percussive foot movements. She also analysed a number of social dances, including the Scotch Reel (pictured in Figure 9.5) and the Highland Schottische, and compared different versions. Uist and Barra versions of the Highland Schottische included audible foot tapping.

Colin Robertson, London, 1982

In 1982, Colin Robertson, teacher of Highland and Step dance in London, published a booklet titled *Hard Shoe Step Dancing in Scotland and The Flowers of Edinburgh*. This publication outlines observations and research on hard-shoe Step dancing in Scotland and shares an interpretation of the solo Step dance the Flowers of Edinburgh. He also outlines that he believes certain step motifs, such as hop-brush-beat-beat, shuffles, and double beats, come from an earlier practice of hard-shoe dancing.

Figure 9.5 Members of Drumalban Dance company performing a Scotch Reel, at a Scottish Traditions of Dance Trust conference, Stirling, 2003

Source: Photo © M. Melin.

Robertson brought attention to the earlier common practice of wearing of hard-soled shoes for the classic Highland dances and pointed out:

> Reference to the older form of footwear can be traced through 'The Highland Fling.' A forerunner of this dance is 'The Marquis of Huntly's Highland Fling' (Hill MS.) and within it is the origin of the Sixth Step of today's 'Highland Fling,' known as the 'Crossover Step.' An earlier name for the same Step was the 'Cross the buckle Step,' referring to the buckle worn at the front of the dancer's shoes. Photographs, drawings and paintings of these shoes being worn can be seen in many early publications and are a clear indication of the shoes worn by men and women for Highland and Step dancing before the 'Ghillie.'[54]

Robertson's publication also outlines the hard-shoe dancing tradition featuring single and double treble movements usually set to Scotch measure and hornpipe tune styles. He listed the Earl of Erroll, the First of August, the King of Sweden, and the East Fife Hornpipe as some examples.

Janet T. MacLachlan, Canada, 1990s–2003

The late Canadian Highland dance teacher Janet [Jenny] T. MacLachlan (1928–2003) from Ontario wrote four self-published booklets in the 1990s giving directions for solo and group dances. Dances she described that are notably percussive are: The Fisherwife, A Hornpype from New Zealand, The White Cockade (directions are very similar to the Hill manuscript notations Flowers of Edinburgh), Over the Water to Charlie, the First of August, and three versions of the Flowers of Edinburgh. She did not state the sources for all her published dances, but her descriptions are a valuable resource. In conversation and letter correspondence with Mats Melin in the 1990s, MacLachlan expressed her conviction that what has survived in evolved forms in Cape Breton, Prince Edward Island, New Brunswick, and Newfoundland as percussive Step dance was related to an older form of dancing from Scotland.

John G. Gibson, Cape Breton, 1998–present

Scottish-born, Cape-Breton-Island-resident John G. Gibson has written two books on Gaelic bagpiping: the 1998 *Traditional Gaelic Bagpiping, 1745–1945*; the 2005 *Old and New World Highland Bagpiping*. Most recently, he researched Step dancing and published *Gaelic Cape Breton Step-Dancing: An Historical and Ethnographic Perspective* in 2017. He does not describe or analyse steps or motifs but he traces the people who danced, played pipes and fiddle, and sang at countless ceilidhs and events through time. His work is invaluable to anyone searching for information about Scots Gaelic music and dancing.

Patricia Ballantyne, Aberdeen, c. 2000–present

Pat Ballantyne has researched Cape Breton Step dancing and the dance repertoire of Aberdeenshire dancing masters.[55] Her writing often focuses on the relationship between music and dance and different types of community interactions existing around social dancing. She is also looking at how Scots are developing their own Step dancing tradition based on the Cape Breton steps taught in Scotland in the 1990s, largely by comparing the differences between dance contexts and styles of musical accompaniment present in the two locations. She has published a number of papers on the subject and in 2019 released the book *Scottish Dance Beyond 1805: Reaction and Regulation*.

Mats Melin, research across Scotland and Cape Breton Island, 1985–present

Mats Melin has carried out extensive research into Step dancing in Scotland and relevant findings are detailed later in this book (see Chapter 11). He has analysed aspects of Scottish and Cape Breton Step dancing since 1985 with various outputs, including books and articles since 1997.

182   *Twentieth-century accounts*

Researchers looking at Scottish or diasporic Gaelic and Scottish dance forms and emerging scholars

It is worth mentioning here that there is a small number of scholars who write about Scottish dance and often interact with percussive aspects of the dancing. Heather Sparling, professor at Cape Breton University, Canada, is a primarily Gaelic and Disaster song scholar, who also has also a deep interest in dance and recently researched the Scotch Four and Cape Breton Square Sets. Celticist and independent scholar Michael S. Newton has written a number of articles on primarily Gaelic aspects of Scottish dance. Gaelic song scholar and Step dancer Màiri Britton (2016) has done recent research in Scottish and Gaelic Step dance. Virtuoso dancer Nic Gareiss recently conducted research into and explored the art of treepling through a First Footing Dance Residency, supported by the Traditional Dance Forum of Scotland (2018–2019).

Summing up the percussive terms of the twentieth century

Words taken from accounts in this chapter are:

> crack of the thumbs; the 'hooch;' feet shod in heavy boots were thudding on the floor [...] all in time; breakdown; swinging and footing gaily the jolliest reel imaginable; a bhragadh a chruadhan/his heels would rattle the floor; Buck, Schottische, Clog, Top Boot, Sand Dance, Waltz, Irish Jig, and Sailors' Hornpipe; tapping; Cross the buckle Step, shuffles, treble shuffles, tap-close-beat, single and double 'tripples,' stamp, skiff, double beat, brush, treepling.

Words indicating the feet making sounds on the floor remain an important component of Scottish dancing.

Notes

1. Stewart 2000: 63. The following website gives some information about military pipers: http://www.historic-uk.com/HistoryUK/HistoryofScotland/Scottish-Piper-War-Heroes/ [Accessed 20 February 2020].
2. ancestry.co.uk records.
3. Whitta 1982: 107.
4. Melin 2005 and 2013b.
5. Scott Skinner 1905: 16.
6. Rea 1964, 1997. Reproduced with permission of The Licensor through PLSclear.
7. Rea 1964, 1997: 133–134. Reproduced with permission of The Licensor through PLSclear.
8. Rea 1964, 1997: vi, 149–150. Reproduced with permission of The Licensor through PLSclear.
9. Melin 2019a.

Twentieth-century accounts 183

10. Melin 2006.
11. McCormick 1907: 183.
12. McCormick 1907: 222–223.
13. *Aberdeen Press and Journal*, Wednesday 4 December 1907.
14. *Aberdeen Press and Journal*, Monday 11 January 1909.
15. *Motherwell Times*, Friday 12 March 1909.
16. Johnston 1913: 176–177.
17. Comunn Gaidhealach 1913: 58.
18. Comunn Gaidhealach 1913: 58.
19. National Library of Scotland: http://movingimage.nls.uk/film/8199 [Accessed 20 April 2019].
20. Haynes 1957: 23.
21. MacLennan 1950: 51.
22. Taylor 1935 [1929]: 32–33.
23. Taylor 1935 [1929]: 11–15.
24. Haynes 1957: 24.
25. *Motherwell Times*, Friday 26 September 1919.
26. *Motherwell Times*, Friday 15 August 1919.
27. *Motherwell Times*, Friday 26 September 1919.
28. *Motherwell Times*, Friday 9 September 1921.
29. *Oban Times*, 4 August 1923.
30. Mrs J.F. Flett believes that 'Scotchmakers' is the same as 'Scotch Measure.' Letter to M. Melin 9 February 1991.
31. *Oban Times*, 9 August 1924.
32. Melin 2019a: 93–96.
33. Donald Collection,' Edinburgh City Library; Copy of a Letter from D.G. MacLennan to Mr Hugh R. Foss, 5 August 1955.
34. Melin forthcoming: 26.
35. McConachie 1972: 33–40.
36. MacLennan 1950: 63
37. MacLennan 1950: 62.
38. MacLennan 1950: 51.
39. Cameron 1951: 32.
40. McIntyre North 1880: 84.
41. Melin 2013a.
42. Flett Archive. www.insteprt.co.uk.
43. Ewart 1996: 61–62.
44. Harris *et al.* 1968 [1950]: 188.
45. Harris *et al.* 1968 [1950]: 188.
46. Pinewoods Camp; 1952 Binder Archives.
47. Canadian Olde Tyme Square Dance Callers' Association website. http://sca .uwaterloo.ca/cotsdca/1CoupleDances.html [Accessed 13 October 2017].
48. Beckwith 1959: 143.
49. Beckwith 1959: 152–153.
50. Flett 1985: 260–266
51. Flett 1996.
52. See Rhodes's obituary of Thomas Muirhead Flett: http://www.jstor.org/ stable/4522005 [Accessed 5 February 2009].
53. Henderson 1995.
54. Robertson 1982: 1.
55. Ballantyne 2016.

10 *An t-Seann Dùthaich*
Dancing in the Scottish diaspora

The search for information about Scottish dance legacies must not ignore the thousands of Scots who emigrated to far-flung places such as Canada, the United States, Australia, and New Zealand. They brought language and cultural customs, including dancing, to their new homelands. Close adherence to expressions of ethnic identity helped emigrants feel connected to their homeland. In Cape Breton Gaelic, for instance, Scotland is referred to as *an t-Seann Dùthaich,* the old country, as opposed to the more formal or distant national appellation of *Alba.* Different aspects of dancing traditions from Scotland have been perpetuated globally. These vary, due to how strong the cohesion to cultural expression was in different areas, and at what point in the evolution of dance practices the dancing migrated abroad.

As John G. Gibson has suggested, the Scottish dance tradition was always stratified.[1] Parallel practices coexist alongside each other. Differing aspects of legacies endure in the diaspora. Percussive traditions that emigrated along with Scots, removed from the constrictions of European class structures, were able to thrive in places far removed from the influence of Ballet and London's fashions. There was no longer pressure to conform to upper-class expectations of gentility. From a Step dancing point of view, Atlantic Canada provides plenty of links to Scottish percussive dancing, still practised in mainland Nova Scotia, Cape Breton Island, Prince Edward Island, and Newfoundland.

Cape Breton Island, Canada

Percussive dancing is the style of dancing predominantly practised in Scots-Gaelic-speaking communities in Cape Breton Island and eastern Nova Scotia. The Gaelic song trope of praise regarding the beauty of dancing on a smooth wooden floor, *air ùrlar réidh,* may have encouraged the practice of percussive dancing in this geographical area where trees were plentiful. Settlers built wooden houses with wood floors in Canada; back in the old country, walls built from stone and dirt floors were more customary. Figure 10.1 depicts dancing inside a farmstead in Washabuck, Cape Breton.

An often-quoted account of early settlements in Cape Breton is found in John MacDougall's *History of Inverness County,* giving details about the

Figure 10.1 Sunday afternoon ceilidh[20] at the MacLean farmstead in Washabuck in the late 1940s or early 1950s. Johnny 'Red' Rory MacLean (aka Johnny Washabuck) is Step dancing to the fiddle playing of his cousin Michael Anthony MacLean. The man sitting in the background is Michael Dan MacLean (Mickey 'Red' Rory), Johnny's brother. The man sitting in the foreground is Angus MacDonald, a relation by marriage and his wife Florence. The house is Johnny MacLean's childhood home on the original homestead of the settlers from Barra. Johnny's father, Red Rory/Ruaraidh Dearg ic Domnull, is in the portrait on the wall as a young man. He was also a great dancer. He kept his dance slippers under his chair and pulled them out as soon as Johnny came home. Johnny was also a noted fiddler

Source: Pencil drawing by Finn Harper (2015), based on a photo by John MacLean, is used with kind permission.

pioneers of one of the four counties of Cape Breton, located on the western side of the island. MacDougall's accounts show that the old forms of Scottish dancing played a significant role in the social life of these Scottish communities. One reference to early Scottish dancers in Cape Breton regards the MacMillans (The Dancers) of Inverness County:

> Allan MacMillan was born in Lochaber, Scotland, About the year 1817 he came to America, landing at Pictou and spending his first winter in the new world with relatives at the Gulf shore of Antigonish. In 1820, he came to Rear Little Judique in the county of Inverness where he took 200 acres of land. [...] He was a celebrated dancer, and after coming to this country, kept a dancing class in both the settlements of Judique and Creignish. He had four of a family, namely John, Donald, Ann and Sarah.[2]

186   *Dancing in the Scottish diaspora*

MacDougall also mentions Angus *Bàn* MacDougall who came to West Lake, Inverness County, from Moidart, Scotland, in 1812 and whose son, Angus, was 'a superior dancer.'[3] Lauchlin MacDougall emigrated from Moidart in the late eighteenth century and, after first staying in Antigonish, crossed to Inverness County in 1808. There he settled three of his grown-up sons, Alexander, Duncan, and Archibald, side-by-side on the last 600 acres at Broad Cove Banks, and the last one, Hugh, a little further north in Dunvegan. Duncan had a son, John, 'a great man of industry and good judgement, a famous dancer, and withal a kind and genial host.'[4]

Cape Breton songwriter and cultural researcher Allister MacGillivray has uncovered other early performers and dance teachers. One was Alexander Gillis/*Mac Iain ic Alasdair*, who arrived from Morar in 1826 and settled in South West Margaree. His great-granddaughter, Margaret Gillis, explained, 'He had been a dance instructor in Scotland and continued to be one here.'[5] Dancing was handed down from generation to generation, and Margaret herself is an excellent exponent of her family's dancing legacy. Archie Kennedy, father of Ranald Kennedy (1870–1958) of Broad Cove Chapel, was a famed Step dance teacher and was taught by his own father, John Kennedy, who emigrated from Canna in 1790 and began dancing classes in Broad Cove not long after.[6] Certain families are still known and famed for their dancing skills. The Beatons of Mabou Coal Mines are a good example of a family of famous Step dancers and fiddlers descending from Mary MacDonald Beaton/*Mairi Aonghuis Thullaich* (1795–1880).[7]

Most of the dances recorded in Cape Breton by Frank Rhodes in Cape Breton in 1957 involved percussive footwork. Rhodes's observations about their Scottish lineage show his conviction about the dances' roots:

> The dances taken from Scotland to Cape Breton Island in the early nineteenth century seem to have been four-handed and eight-handed Reels with stepping, and some solo dances. There were also a few dance-games. [...] The various forms of the Reels are related to Highland and Hebridean forms of these dances. The stepping used in Cape Breton Island often involved a continuous marking of the rhythm which toe and heel beats. In some ways it resembled the 'treepling' which survived in East Lothian, Roxburghshire, and West Berwickshire within living memory [...]. The style certainly goes back in Scotland to the beginning of the nineteenth century.[8] [...]
>
> In 1957, the Cape Breton step-dances looked very different from Highland Games dancing. However, one can see from the instructions for the dances how they are related to the solo dances collected in Scotland at that time. The overall impression is of a common collection of dance movements which had come to be danced very low on the ground in Cape Breton and much higher on the toes in Scotland. [...] The Cape Breton solo dances (with the exception of the Sword Dance) all involved fast beating steps.[9]

The structured solo dances that Rhodes was told had been taught were the Fling, the Swords, *Seann Triubhas,* Flowers of Edinburgh, Jacky Tar, Duke of Fife, The Girl I Left Behind Me, Tullochgorm, Irish Washerwoman, and Princess Royal, all ten dances originally having twelve steps.[10] Each of these dances was set to a tune, often reflected by the title.

Titles for the dances are predominantly in English despite having been taught in what were at the time Gaelic-speaking areas. This usage of English tune titles may indicate that these dances had mainland Scottish connections. Families preserving these traditions in Nova Scotia hailed from Lochaber, Moidart, Morar, Barra, and Canna, with an immigration period spanning between 1790 and 1830.[11] One of the dances, The Flowers of Edinburgh, was given a Gaelic title: *Dannsa nan Flurs*; however, *Flurs* is a Gaelicised English word displaying the English plural form as opposed to the Gaelic plural form *flùraichean*. This word '*flurs*' may reflect a pronunciation of the title sometimes rendered as 'Flooers o' Edinburgh.' The spelling of the word '*nan*' Frank Rhodes recorded does not follow contemporary Gaelic language rules, where the word should be '*nam*' to accommodate the initial 'f' consonant.

Most of these dances had a structure consisting of travelling in a circular pathway during the A part of the melody using six *chassé* type of movements with a beating finishing refrain, then dancing on the spot to the B part of the melody with a percussive stepping sequence preceding the reiterated refrain. Steps were uniform in structure although the order of the B-part steps was sometimes altered. When Rhodes observed these dances in 1957, they were each danced to their accompanying tunes played in an ABAB fashion, where each part was eight-bars long:

> [the Reel] is always danced singly, that is, the parts are never doubled. Steps are danced to eight bars, then the dancers glide round in a circle to the next 8 bars, when they resume their steps, performing as a rule the reverse of the former step [...] It is the custom in many
>
> places to divide the reel into two portions, the first portion consisting of simple, graceful movements, wholly devoid of trebling, the second portion consisting almost solely of the most difficult trebling steps.[12]

The Cape Breton solo dances seem to have been taught mainly during the 1800s but some continued into the early 1900s. Certain families kept these solo dances alive, passing them from father to son, and sometimes daughter. Step dances were occasionally taught in school situations; Clare MacDonald Currie remembered a Sailor's Hornpipe, an Irish Washerwoman jig, and the Liverpool Hornpipe being taught in New Waterford at St. Agnes School by Christena Mac Donald for performance in concerts. Clare's sister, the noted pianist Mary Jessie MacDonald, learned them in school.[13] Four solo dances have been notated by Rhodes.[14] One of these dances, the Flowers of Edinburgh, seems to have been particularly popular. Margaret Gillis, from

188 *Dancing in the Scottish diaspora*

South West Margaree, is one of the very few living Cape Bretoners who have 'gone through' the Flowers of Edinburgh. When interviewed by Allister MacGillivray in 1987, she said:

> I think *The Flowers of Edinburgh* was one of the dances in Scotland, and you'd have *The Jacky Tar* and all the hornpipes that were danced individually. There was form to it, a format. *The Seann Triubhas* was a different dance than the one that they do in Highland dancing today with piping. That wasn't *The Seann Triubhas* our early settlers had at all! Our old *Seann Triubhas* had eight steps, and you didn't go around in a reel. You see, each dance had a method to it with different steps. It would be like singing a song where you would have to know every verse and do them in order. For instance, with *The Flowers* you start with the first step, but then the pattern for ending of each step is the same. There's a continuity, you know. It follows a pattern where each step is a little different but the ending is the same. So, with our *Seann Triubhas* you had a 'shuffle' at the end of each step. *The Flowers*, of course, was always danced to the tune *The Flowers of Edinburgh,* and there were twelve steps, each one being done twice [note that this means an AABB music pattern]. It didn't necessarily get more complicated as it went on, though [...] Besides *The Flowers*, my father did a quite a few other solo dances like *The Jacky Tar* and *Princess Royal*. Plus my father and my aunt would do a *Seann Triubhas* and had lovely steps for the strathspey—a lot of strathspey steps. Then they had reel steps and they had the different steps for the hornpipes. They also danced a solo jig which is just a change in your tempo.[15]

As with any dance form, dancing in Cape Breton has evolved and changed over time. The following remarks by Margaret MacEachern Dunn, about Margaret and Helen Gillis and their aunt Sadie Gillis MacEachern, illustrate this change:

> I recall seeing a Mrs MacEachern from Maple Brook dancing. She was formerly a Gillis from Margaree, and her grandfather, Alexander Gillis, was one of the people who originally brought the step dancing here from Scotland. He was called a 'dancing master.' The dancing taught then wasn't exactly what we have now. This Mrs MacEachern used to do a dance that they called *The Flowers of Edinburgh*, and I was told that it had some thirty steps to it.[16]

Rhodes's detailed descriptions of these dances do not share what terminology the Gillises used to describe or categorise the movements. We rely on terminology applied by Rhodes, which includes 'walks or chassés with extra beats' 'heel,' and 'toe beats,' 'single' and 'double' beats of the ball of the foot, 'single' and 'double shuffles, 'and 'triples' to understand the movements.[17]

Dancing in the Scottish diaspora 189

John G. Gibson includes many references about dancing in his two books on Gaelic piping in Cape Breton and Scotland.[18] His piping books do not detail how people danced, but they do show that the dancing was widespread. His 2017 book on *Gaelic Cape Breton Step-Dancing* provides more background details on many of the sources referred to in this publication.

Canadian ethnomusicologist Heather Sparling has researched the Gaelic song tradition extensively. In the case of *puirt a beul*/mouth music practices in Cape Breton, she has analysed the connection between song and movement rhythms:

> To start, the overall rhythm of a dance performance varies as each dancer improvises a combination of steps. Even the same dancer is likely to dance differently to the same tune on two different occasions. Sometimes the dancer's steps reinforce the melody's rhythm, and other times they fill in eighth and sixteenth notes that are not a part of it. Second, although many dance steps produce eighth-note rhythms, the percussive timbres vary depending on the way the step is executed. In other words, steps produce different sounds depending on whether they involve, for example, hopping, shuffling, tapping, or stepping. Third, the visual element of the step is not easily notatable. I suspect this is particularly important when a step involves a rhythmic movement that does not actually produce a sound: there is a visual and motor rhythm, but not necessarily a sonic one. At the same time, silent rhythms are seen and felt in relation to the music's rhythm; both visual/motor and audible rhythms are interrelated and cannot be understood as independent of one another.[19]

Recent years have seen a growth of interest in Cape Breton music and dancing, and in the last five years, many video clips of Step dancing, current and historical, have been posted on YouTube, Vimeo and on social media sites such as Facebook.

1970s Newfoundland, Canada— Scottish Gaelic connections

Scottish folklorist Margaret Bennett paints a lively and warm picture of the life and traditions of Codroy Valley, Newfoundland, in her 1989 book *The Last Stronghold*. The book focuses on the MacArthur family, whom we follow over the course of a year, and outlines Scottish Gaelic traditions surviving in Newfoundland. The following citations centre around music, dancing, and the ceilidh. The events described took place in the early 1970s:

> Various instruments were thought more suitable for certain purposes. The bagpipes were regarded as the best instrument for an old-fashioned eight-hand reel and for 'set' (square) dancing. The accordion, while good for these old dances, was especially well liked for old-fashioned waltzes. The fiddle, also suitable for any kind of dance performance in those days,

190 *Dancing in the Scottish diaspora*

however, was the favourite instrument of the step-dancers, as its volume did not overwhelm and drown out the percussion effects of feet on the wooden floors [...]

Step dancing, which people from other parts of the island often say is performed in 'different style' in the Valley to what they usually see, has always been extremely popular at a ceilidh. [At the time of writing, 1989, there had been very little research on the history of dance, and it was not][21] unusual for Scottish visitors to the Codroy Valley or Cape Breton to assume that this step dancing has been 'invented in North America.' This conclusion does not follow, however, as the old style of step dancing which exists in the New World is something much older than the Highland Dancing popularised in Scotland and standardised by the Scottish Official Board of Highland Dancing and Military Regiments, who taught it during more recent years. At any rate, the testimony of the Scots in the Codroy Valley and in Cape Breton bears witness to the continuity of this old form of dancing said to have been brought over to the New World, where it survived after its disappearance from Scotland [...]

At any ceilidh the step dancers would generally listen to a tune or two on the fiddle before getting out on the floor. Usually two or four people got out in the middle of the floor, and with the rest of the company sitting or standing around the edges of the room ready to watch every move, the dance would begin. Facing one another, the step dancers would start off with one of their least spectacular steps. As the music got livelier to the encouraging shouts of '*Suas e! Suas e a bhodaich!*' the dancers would not only dance more quickly to keep up with the music, but would also progress to the most complicated steps they knew. This phrase, '*Suas e! Suas a bhodaich!*' still heard in the Valley even though it is now almost entirely English-speaking, is addressed to the fiddler. Used when the fiddler is being encouraged to step up the tempo of his music, the phrase translates literally as 'Up with it! Up with it, old man!' its equivalent in other areas of Newfoundland would be 'Heave it outa ye, ol' man!' [...]

While the dancers might start off doing the same step, each danced the sequence of steps of his own choice, trying all the while to out-do the other dancers, not only in style and complexity but also in stamina. Throughout the dancing there would be shouts of encouragement and praise to the dancers and to the fiddler, who could always play as long as any dancer could last out on the floor. The entire show of step dancing would come to an end after all but one dancer, usually the best one, would sit down out of fatigue, thus voluntarily eliminating themselves from the display. The dancer who was left would dance one or two solo steps and then, like the others before him, would sink into a chair laughing. Simultaneously, the fiddler would draw the last few strokes of the bow over the strings and everyone would applaud, praising the dancers with comments like, 'Well, by golly, he's good,' or sometimes clapping him on the back saying, 'Well done, yourself.' [...]

Instrumental music was not, however the only accompaniment for dancing. As Allan MacArthur said, 'Some of the step-dancing tunes they used to be in Gaelic.' Just as in the Highland and Islands of Scotland, these tunes in Gaelic, *puirt-a-beul* or 'mouth-music' as they were generally called, were very popular in the Valley and were referred to as *puirt luath* by the Gaelic speakers. Since this type of singing required exceptional breath control in order to sing long enough for a step dancer, there were never more than a few people in the Valley at the one time who had mastered this art. Consequently, during the joint performance of mouth-music and step dancing, the audience at the ceilidh were doubly excited, watching the feet of the dancer and listening to the accuracy of the singer who, if he took a breath in the wrong place or for a split second too long, might loose the beat and spoil the entire effect.[22]

Bennett makes the point that, although the dancing in Newfoundland doesn't resemble dancing popular in Scotland in the twentieth century, it does not follow that the dancing didn't originate there. An example of evolution within a dance after the period of emigration can be observed in the *Seann Triubhas*. Cape Bretoner Margaret Gillis said that the modern *Seann Triubhas* is not the same as the dance she learned from her father. She particularly notes the modern first step, danced in a circular pathway. Elsewhere we have corroboration that the circular first step is a newer innovation in this dance. D.G. MacLennan asserted that it was invented by himself, modelled after his brother's 'Franco-Scottish dance, "Parazotti"' in the late 1800s, and that before that time, 'no other dancer ever copied it' and 'the first step was always "pas de basque" from side to side,'[23] which endures as an alternate first step in today's competitive *Seann Triubhas*. Margaret Gillis's version of the *Seann Triubhas* begins with double toe beats, a motif similar to *pas de Basque*, danced side to side, reflecting the older version.[24] This example provides one instance of a dance preserved in an earlier, historical form outside the country of its origin.

New Zealand and Australia

So far, little research into Scottish percussive dancing migrating into vernacular use in New Zealand and Australian settlement communities has been undertaken. Heather Clark's current research is a welcome addition, forming a base of knowledge about Australian Clog and Step dance.[25] There are some historical snippets revealing that this type of dance existed within Scottish emigrant communities and culture ways.

The first reference does not plainly identify percussive dance but describes the Gaelic speaking settlers of Waipu on the North Island of New Zealand, who arrived from west coast Sutherland via Cape Breton island in 1854. Even with the strict morality of their Presbyterian faith, music and dance continued among the settlers. Specific details about what they danced for social

192   *Dancing in the Scottish diaspora*

dances were not recorded. Given the time of emigration from Sutherland in Scotland to Cape Breton between 1810 and 1830, and various references documented by Gibson in relation to the piping, Step dancing, and Scotch Four reel dancing in the Presbyterian areas of Cape Breton Island, there is a strong likelihood that Step dancing was at the heart of the Waipu settlers' dancing.[26] It was only when the Waipu Caledonian Games were established in 1871 that wearing Highland dress for Highland dances such as the Highland Fling, Sword Dance, *Seann Triubhas*, and the Highland Reel became important to the settlers.[27]

Early records regarding music and dance are scant, but Gordon MacDonald[28] described a wedding where piping featured prominently in the festivities, and where the ceilidh was an 'institution in early Waipu':

> The 'ceileidh', or corroboree, shifted from house to house according to circumstances. The evening was generally spent in reciting the news of the district or the contents of letters and any newspapers received from abroad. Excepting Maoris they had no neighbours, but the language barrier effectually shut them off from Maori intercourse. Music, songs, story-telling, and dancing were the common means of whiling the time away[29] [...] The public games are held on New Year's Day, and attract large bodies of competitors and people from the surrounding districts. Tartan, pipers, and athletic youths make a gallant show, while the language of Eden [Gaelic] is universal. [...] Many a stiff back and bent leg itches to join in the Scottish Reel and shout 'hooch hooch' as in the days of old.[30]

Maureen Molloy found that in 1881, the *Auckland Weekly News* reported on a debate focusing on dancing and other forms of entertainment in Waipu:

> The writer of 'The North' series heard all about dancing during his four-day sojourn in the town:
>
>> [...] it was gently insinuated to me, by one who professes to know, that although the hall is not really a dancing hall, nor built for that purpose, yet that the young Nova Scotians go in for dancing most enthusiastically, and in it take supreme delight: while the old people hold up their hands in pious horror at the folly and wickedness of the young folk, the minister, of course, not at all sympathising with the dancers. The truth is that he has been preaching against it, but without avail (AWN, 1881: Feb 5).

Dances are a major part of the folklore of Waipu. Before the hall was built young people danced on the bridges [just as in Scotland and in Cape Breton]. Dances commonly lasted until dawn because the roads were too bad to be travelled on after dark. When there was no musician the dancers whistled or sang to provide themselves with music. Young women were often forbidden to attend dances and, abetted by their brothers and

Dancing in the Scottish diaspora 193

male cousins, crept out the windows after their parents were asleep to dance the night away, taking care to return home in order to complete their morning chores before their parents woke.[31]

Further research may unearth whether fiddlers or pipers played for these dances and what dances were done.

More glimpses of dancing emerge through newspaper reports on competitions at the Highland, or Caledonian Games in the second half of the nineteenth century. Good examples are found in New Zealand Highland dancer Shiobhan O'Donnell's (1998) dissertation *Dancing at the Auld Cale: A history of highland dancing in Dunedin, New Zealand between 1863 and 1900*. Dances that appear regularly in newspaper reports from 1863 onwards are the Highland Reel, Highland Fling, Sword Dance, and *Seann Triubhas*. The Sailor's Hornpipe appears in 1865 and the Irish Jig in 1866 and they subsequently become consistent features. The Reel o' Tulloch also makes regular appearances. It should be noted that the Irish Jig at the Caledonian Games was distinctly referred to as hailing from Ireland and, to this day, New Zealand Highland Dancing includes a style of Irish dancing in its dancing syllabus called Irish National dancing. The *New Zealand Academy of Highland and National Dancing, Syllabus of Technique for Irish Step Dancing, Stage two* states:

> The early 19th century saw a revival of national tradition and gave rise to the founding of many dancing schools such as those of Limerick, Kerry and Cork [...] The polishing of steps and elaboration of footwork followed [...] unfortunately, the dancing masters were not interested in the people's dances of the remote countryside and in imposing their more polished style on the peasants, many of the occupational gestures were eliminated with the result that the dancing lost much of its spontaneity [...] The constant interchange of population between Ireland and Scotland, the characteristics acquired from both nations from regiments during the time of war and visiting sailors, has led to interchange of tunes and steps [...] introduced to New Zealand by the early settlers and members of religious orders from Ireland [...].[32]

Surviving today within the competitive structure of New Zealand Academy Highland Dancing is a whole section of Irish hard-shoe dances: Single- and Double-time Jigs, the Irish Hornpipe, and the Irish Reel, a group dance for four. All these dances are performed in a costume particular to the New Zealand Academy and incorporate standardised arm actions. These New Zealand Irish Jigs and Hornpipes only slightly resemble the footwork of what is considered 'traditional' or 'old style' Step dancing in Ireland today, and also bear only faint resemblance to the 'Irish' Jig danced within the RSOBHD competitive framework. This unique style of Irish dance is singularly placed within the New Zealand Academy dance syllabus. A characteristic distinguishing these dances is that they are performed at fairly slow speeds, allowing more time for intricate beating and battering patterns of

194   *Dancing in the Scottish diaspora*

the feet. A 1994 letter from Jeanie Paton, then secretary of the New Zealand Academy, emphasised this difference:

> Our Irish dancing is not like the traditional Irish dancing, nor is it like the Irish Jig Single time performed in Scotland. Those of us who are in the older age group think our Irish dancing is a sort of missing link. Our dancing was mostly taught by the nuns that came out in the early 1800s. We also had a few older men who came out from Scotland and Ireland who were only Irish dancers. The Double Irish Jig which was taught to me in the mid-1920's was called the Kerry Jig and I have never changed it. The same with my Irish Hornpipe. Neither of these dances have any resemblance to the traditional Irish dancing. However, many of the movements can be seen in the Cape Breton dancers on the tape which you sent me. The Irish Reel which has four dancers also came from the early immigrants.

The Hornpipe is a version of a British theatrical Sailor's Hornpipe similar to the one competed in Scotland, but with more animated content and a greater selection of steps and movements of feet and arms. Versions of the Sailor's Hornpipe as danced in New Zealand since the 1940s have been notated in 1989 by the New Zealand Academy and around 1990 by the late Janet T. MacLachlan of Ontario.

O'Donnell's research[33] shows that in 1867 the Clog Hornpipe made an appearance at the games. A Hornpipe category was held that year in which three dancers competed. Two chose to dance the Sailor's Hornpipe and were placed first and second respectively. The third, unplaced, competitor danced a Clog Hornpipe. There is no detailed description of this dance. This was not the only instance a Clog dance was performed; a 'Clog Dance' also appeared in the 1884 Dunedin Caledonian Games in an open section where the dancers chose what dance to perform.[34] Unfortunately, these Clog dances never became regular features of competition. The 1867 Hornpipe category was the only dance category in which Mr Palmer, the gentleman who performed the Clog Hornpipe, danced. There are no reports of him competing in subsequent years, perhaps explaining why the Clog Hornpipe as a dance was only ever mentioned once. The Clog dancing tradition, however, has not disappeared entirely from New Zealand Highland Dancing competitions. There are two descendants performed by Highland dancers around New Zealand to this day. One Clog dance included in the medal test syllabus of the New Zealand Academy of Highland and National dancing is the Melbourne Clog. In their *Medal Tests, Junior Gold and Gold Star syllabus* we are told that:

> The Melbourne Clog is one of the popular step dances from the clog dancing group…It has been a popular concert and festival dance and is performed to its own music, 'The Melbourne Clog.'[35]

The late dancing teacher and adjudicator Mrs Orma Smith of Timaru learned the Melbourne Clog in 1933 from Ruby Ford. Mrs Smith said that this 'type of clog dance was performed mostly in the South Island of New Zealand at Competition Festivals before World War II.'[36] The Melbourne Clog was always performed to piano accompaniment whilst the Waltz Clog was danced to the pipes. Accompaniment on the more portable bagpipes made it easier for the Waltz Clog to be danced at National Dancing Competitions, which may be why the Waltz Clog remained popular. The Waltz Clog is still performed by Highland dancers, although not danced within as strict a technique or covered by the Piping and Dancing Association of New Zealand rules. It is frequently performed by girls, although boys learn it too. Both Clog Dances are performed in leather-soled shoes similar to those used for New Zealand Irish dancing.[37]

Very little evidence exists about what music accompanied the dances, but O'Donnell gleaned a few bits of information from newspaper articles:

> [The dancers] also had opportunities to vary their dancing repertoire and perform different and new dances. For example, in the 1885 newspaper report, the reporter stated that 'Mr. D. Steward Burt is to dance the hornpipe 'Drops of Brandy' during today's programme' [Otago Daily Times, 3 January 1885]. The tune today known as Drops of Brandy has a time signature of 9/8. [...] What the presence of the 'Drops of Brandy' tune indicates, is that the Jacky Tar style of Hornpipe, of which the Sailor's Hornpipe is an example, was not the only type of Hornpipe being performed. [...] The 'Drops of Brandy' example seems to have been for demonstration rather than competition, as the results of the Sailor's Hornpipe section do not mention Mr Steward Burt dancing.[38]

Information about percussive dance in the Scottish diaspora in Australia is an area that could use further investigation, particularly as to its vernacular practices. There are some similarities in content between the syllabus of the New Zealand Academy and the syllabi of the Victorian Scottish Union, established in 1906, and the Highland and National Dancers' Association of Victoria.

The Victorian Scottish Union has a Sailor's Hornpipe with about 40 steps, an Irish Jig in double jig time, an Irish Reel, a Shillelagh Jig in single jig time, and a combination Irish Jig and Reel. The Sailors' Hornpipe is danced in soft shoes while the Irish dances are done in leather-soled shoes with a small heel. All dances have percussive movements named shuffles, triples, grinds performed with toes and heels, stamps, clicks, beats, slaps, hits, and side runs.[39] The Irish dances are considered as having come from Ireland while the Hornpipe is seen as having come through the British stage dance tradition.[40]

Guidelines of the Highland and National Dancers' Association of Victoria for 1982 give only brief outlines for a dancing syllabus, listing only dances and step names and including some hints on general execution of their aesthetic preferences. Their Sailors' Hornpipe lists 32 step names; the Irish Jig is

196 *Dancing in the Scottish diaspora*

a hard-shoe dance with 21 steps listed; a 'Home Style Irish Jig' or Shillelagh Jig lists four steps with an indication that expression, styled handwork, and dress movement should be 'used in accordance with feet work.' There is also a 17-step Irish Reel. There is no indication of origin given for any of these dances. Terminology in step motifs indicating percussive effects appears in their syllabus, including shuffle, triple, drum, beat, click, toe-and-heel, run, and double-heel-down.[41]

The current research by Australian dance historian and researcher Heather Clark may in time shed more light on the extent of vernacular percussive dance in Australia.[42] Did other vernacular Scottish styles survive in Africa, South America, or Asia? Forms of Highland Dancing have thrived in some of these places. Their stories have yet to be uncovered and told.

Appalachia and beyond

Future research into other parts of the Scottish diaspora may uncover more related material. Dance traditions in other parts of Canada and the United States may be able to trace specific connections to Scotland. For instance, musician and dancer Susie Petrov remembers seeing Tap legend Jimmy Slyde make a statement that 'this dance comes [...] from the Celtic countries' before performing a 'low and smooth' dance to diddling.[43] Both Tap dancing and Appalachian Clogging share varied and mixed influences that, over time, have informed what is seen in the styles today. There is, for these dance genres, no single point of origin. Research has yet to shed light on specific connections between steps, dances, and origins.

American old-time musician, flatfoot dancer, square dance caller, and dance historian Phil Jamison in his book *Hoedowns, Reels, and Frolics: Roots and Branches of Southern Appalachian Dance* explains that the Step dancing form found in the Appalachian region of the United States

> [...] did not develop in isolation, nor does it come from a single source, but like the Southern square dances, it is a hybrid mix of northern European, West African, and Native American dance traditions that developed in the New World. As early as the mid-1600s, black and whites danced together [...] and since that time, generations of dancers have shared dance steps and styles scross racial and ethnic lines to create this uniquely American form of step dancing. [...] These dances have roots in the step dances of the British Isles, but they also incorporate elements adopted from the sub-Saharan African dance tradition. [...] Traces of the earlier dance traditions from which these step dances evolved, however, can still be seen in the characteristic movements, common footwork, and general style of dancers in Appalachia today.[44]

Jamison further points out that while Appalachian Step dancers may share certain steps, there is no prescribed footwork; some perform memorised

Dancing in the Scottish diaspora   197

sequences of steps, others, 'doing their own thing,' are more improvisational and freeform in their movements.[45] This very much ties in with the overall feel of the recollections presented in this volume from Scotland. There is a range of performance modes from the prescribed to the improvised vernacular. Jamison continues, that 'depending on one's personality, age, and stamina, the steps may be energetic, loud, and percussive, or smooth, subtle, and relaxed. Generally, though, the feet stay close to the floor, and the footwork consists of a variety of rhythmic movements involving the toe, the heel, or the entire foot.'[46] A dancer should, as one may say, dance the tune with your feet.

The characteristics outlined above have also been investigated by American dance scholar Susan Eike Spalding in her 2014 book *Appalachian Dance* and by jazz historian Marshall Stearns in his 1994 *Jazz Dance: The Story of American Vernacular Dance*. Both emphasise the multiple influences informing American dance forms and their conglomerate natures. Jamison also writes in detail about regional Appalachian practices of Threesome and Foursome Scotch and Irish Reels. The dancing of setting steps in Reels is described as 'rhythmic footwork.'[47]

Notes

1. Gibson 1998, 2005.
2. MacDougall 1922: 259.
3. MacDougall 1922: 521.
4. MacDougall 1922: 328–330.
5. MacGillivray 1988: 60. Text from MacGillivray's book is used by kind permission.
6. MacGillivray 1988: 79.
7. MacGillivray 1988: 24.
8. Rhodes in Flett 1996: 187.
9. Rhodes in Flett 1996: 194.
10. Rhodes in Flett 1996: 189.
11. Rhodes in Flett 1985, 1996.
12. O'Keeffe and O'Brien 1914 [1902]: 106.
13. MacGillivray 1988: 48.
14. Fletts 1996: 194–211.
15. MacGillivray 1988: 60–61.
16. MacGillivray 1988: 53.
17. Flett 1996: 195–197.
18. Gibson 1998, 2005.
19. Sparling 2005: 288–289.
20. *Ceilidh* is a Gaelic word meaning 'visit.' Traditionally, a ceilidh was an informal social visit, typically occurring in the evenings, that could involve any number of people. Hosts and visitors alike would share news, stories, songs, music, dance, food, and so on.
21. Dr Margaret Bennett suggested this insertion 4 May 2020.
22. Bennett 1989: 76–80; used by kind permission.
23. MacLennan 1950: 27.
24. Flett 1997: 201.
25. Clarke 2018: Social dance and early Australian settlement: An historical examination of the role of social dance for convicts and the 'lower orders' in the period between 1788 and 1840 | QUT ePrints [Accessed November 1 2018].

198   *Dancing in the Scottish diaspora*

26. Gibson 1998, 2005
27. Molloy 1991; MacDonald 1928; Pearce 1976.
28. MacDonald 1928: 104–105.
29. MacDonald 1928: 107.
30. MacDonald 1928: 153.
31. Molloy 1991: 61.
32. New Zealand Academy Syllabus 1989: 3–4.
33. O'Donnell 1998: 37–39.
34. *Otago Daily Times*, 3 January 1874.
35. New Zealand Academy Syllabus 1988: 3.
36. Smith 1990.
37. In the typed documents, it is stated that one version of the Waltz Clog was choreographed by Orma Smith for her junior pupils in around 1955 and another for her senior pupils in 1956 to meet the demands of the Highland and National Dancing Competitions.
38. O'Donnell 1998: 39–40.
39. Victorian Scottish Union, *The Theory of the Irish Jig* n.d.
40. Victorian Scottish Union 1974, n.d.
41. Highland and National Dancers' Association of Victoria, 1982.
42. See website: http://www.colonialdance.com.au/ [Accessed 20 February 2020].
43. Petrov 2017.
44. Jamison 2015: 130.
45. Jamison 2015: 130.
46. Jamison 2015: 130.
47. Jamison 2015: 24–28.

11 First-hand Step dance encounters and recollections in Scotland from the 1980s to 2016 collected by Mats Melin

Isle of Barra, 1989–1990

As part of my ongoing dance research in the Highland and Islands of Scotland, I encountered many recollections of percussive Step dancing. In 1990, I visited *Fearchar*/Farquhar Mac Neil (*Fearchar Eoin Fhearchar*, 1909–1997) in his home in Upper Brevig, Castlebay, Isle of Barra, pictured in Figure 11.1. As well as being a storyteller, Fearchar was a living link to the old island dance tradition. The discussion took place in his living room and, in a mix of English and Gaelic, Fearchar told me of his dancing memories as a young boy and his thoughts on percussive Step dancing. He also showed me a good number of steps from local solo dances. Even though he had to support himself on the back of an armchair, he was light on his feet for his age. Some steps were percussive in nature. He whistled the tunes as he danced the steps. There was no formality about MacNeil's dancing. Fearchar was adamant that these dances be danced close to the floor, with light force and low elevation. A lot of Fearchar's footwork was lightly percussive in nature and the rhythm of the steps could be clearly worked out by just listening to him dancing in Castlebay in 1990.[1] Fearchar himself was convinced that the style of Step dancing found in Cape Breton Island, Canada, today was similar to what he saw the older Barra generation dance when he was a child.[2] Similar recollections were published in an interview with Fearchar for the Canadian magazine *The Clansman* in 1993:

> There was an old woman, a cripple and her sister who used to come to our house very often. And one time I called in on them to find out how she was, you know, while I was passing. "Oh dance for us, dance for us," they said—I was then dancing on the q-t [quern-top], however, I did dance. (Then) the fit one, she got up and she said, "this is how I danced when I was young." And of course there was an *earthen* floor and she had a long skirt on and I could see the toes peeping out underneath the bottom of the skirt. I said to myself, she must have seen tap dancing or something somewhere. But I did admire the way, the rhythm of it. You couldn't hear anything but seeing the toes peeping out. Well, a year or

Figure 11.1 Fearchar MacNeil, Isle of Barra, 1990
Source: Photo © M. Melin.

two later I was in another house, maybe three or four miles away and something the same happened. It happened on three different occasions and different people. But it was this tapping thing, and the moment I saw Mary Janet [MacDonald] dancing,[3] I knew that was what they were doing. Farquhar does not remember any hand movement and says he is almost positive their hands were kept by their sides.[4]

Cape Breton Step dancer and teacher Mary Janet MacDonald recollects her meeting with Fearchar when teaching Step dance at the Barra *Fèis*, a Gaelic music, song, and dance festival, in July 1983:

I was like a fish out of water and had hardly even flown before so I was really out of my element when I got there. I was given the schedule for my classes and then went ahead and began teaching. I would meet up with fellow tutors at breaks and lunch and conversations took place just to familiarize myself with what everyone was doing—it was my introduction to clarsach, shinty, and Hebridean dancing. So, Farquhar was there and was asking me questions and that was about it. He could be found in the kitchen with the two local highland dance teachers [...] holding the back of the chairs and showing them the steps and telling them how to teach the next class. He must have gone with them for a while and then he'd come to my class, sit in the back, and watch [...] silently. I was a little worried, didn't know how to take that. Then BBC were there— questioning me about this 'step dancing' and for the first time in my life I felt I had to defend its [Step dancing's] roots—knowing that it came from Scotland – but not really equipped with stats that they [BBC] wanted to hear. I was quite sad about the feelings I was having, but then later in the week, dear Farquhar took me aside and said—'I've no doubt in my mind but that this is a dance that we had here in Scotland, and it is bringing back memories of me as a young lad watching my grandmother on the pier, and lifting her skirts a bit and doing this dancing with her feet.'[5]

Gaelic singer and clarsach player Maggie MacInnes from Barra shared a story with that her mother, renowned Gaelic singer Flora MacNeil, remembered regarding Step dancing:

When my mother, Flora MacNeil went out to Cape Breton in the 70's she was told by all the step dancers and musicians she met that their dancing had come over from Scotland. When she came back here [Isle of Barra] and mentioned this to a few people who she thought might know about it, she received a generally dismissive attitude, which made reference to it being more likely to have come from Ireland. It was not until she spoke to her mother, Annie Gillies who was born in Barra in 1889 that she was told otherwise. My [MacInnes'] Granny, speaking in Gaelic, apparently said something along the lines of 'Of course I remember the step dancing. My mother was good at it but her sister, my aunt Fionnghuala was better.' Granny had not step danced herself, but the earlier generation clearly did. She went on to describe the dancing as close-to-the-floor dancing and the more sound you made, the better.[6]

Fearchar Mac Neil corroborates this story in a letter to Mary Janet MacDonald, and adds that Flora's grandmother and auntie would be of an age of Fearchar's own granny, thus born around the 1860s.[7] The Barra connection does not stop there. In an email in October 2010, folklorist Dr Margaret Bennett told me how she interviewed *Ciorstaigh*/Christina Docherty, living in Torcroy near Kingussie about Step dancing for a 1994 Scottish Television programme

202   *Step dance encounters and recollections*

about Margaret's research called 'Time Quines.' Ciorstaigh learnt her Step dancing from her mother, from Barra. According to Bennett, Ciorstaigh said:

> [...] that she did this dance at home though it wasn't encouraged as she was 'sent to Highland dancing lessons' and was doing well [...] but still the memories and the steps stayed with her – or at least as few.[8]

While visiting the Isle of Barra in 2002 to teach social and Step dancing, I met Mairi MacLean in Eoligary, Northbay, who recalled a similar story. Mairi had travelled to Cape Breton to visit relatives sometime in the 1970s. When returning home, Mairi told her grandfather about the Step dancing she had seen, asking why she had not seen it in Barra, as it was claimed 'over there' to be from the Islands. Her grandfather got up from his chair in the front room and said, 'was anything like this?' Supporting himself on the mantle-piece, he did some Step dancing. Mairi said it was very similar to what she had seen in Cape Breton. When she asked her grandfather why he had never shown her this before, his reply was along the lines that his dancing was old fashioned, and that her generation had the Schottisches and Barn Dances, and so he had therefore not shared it. Not only did they do Step dancing at home but also at crossroads and on bridges, around 1900, her grandfather recalled.[9]

These three recollections all place Step dancing primarily in the home context in Barra within living memory, while in the public context, more modern forms of dance were encouraged. Perhaps the steps stayed at home because their practitioners were afraid of being ridiculed?

Fife, 1990s

Margaret Bennett mentions another woman who could Step dance, whom Bennett met in the course of her own research:

> a former Highland dance champion [...] she discovered that her own mother, brought up in the Stirling area, and by then in her seventies, had a repertoire of step-dances which she had never demonstrated until she saw a film of step-dancing in Canada. Till then, the older lady had thought her daughter who 'had been trained to dance properly' might ridicule her.[10]

This was Highland dance teacher Gillin Anderson, from Larbert, who further described to Maggie Moore how her mother, Mary McHarg, 'leapt out of her chair on seeing Cape Breton step dancing on television, and proceeded to step away beautifully in exactly the same manner.'[11]

Fellow Step dancer and researcher Maggie Moore detailed more encounters like this in a 1994 paper where she mentioned some of her own discoveries:

> It can equally well be seen in Scotland where there are families, which have been famous for generations for their piping, or their singing or

indeed their dancing. One such family is that of Anna Bain, from Leslie in Fife. She is the eighth generation of dance teachers in her family and her mother, Sheila McKay remembers being taught step dancing by her own mother in the 1920's. I met Sheila and Anna earlier this year, and when Sheila saw me performing Cape Breton step dancing, her immediate reaction was: *I can do that. That's the same as I learnt when I was young*, and to my delight she proceeded to dance some of the steps that I had been doing myself [...] Ann Johnston who comes to my dance class in Birnam was told by her grandmother in Dunkeld that her father, Hugh MacDonald, was a wonderful step dancer and teacher. A friend's granny in [Isle of] Lewis described how, when she was young, they used to meet and step dance on a particular bridge near Callanish.[12]

At a Step dancing seminar I organised in Dingwall Town Hall in April 1997,[13] I, and fellow attendees, had the pleasure of meeting Sheila McKay, in the photo of Figure 11.2. Sheila McKay was born in Fife and learnt her Step dancing at the age of five or six years old from her mother. At the time of the seminar, she was 77. Sheila claimed she was the seventh generation of teachers in her family. She stated her steps hailed back to the mid-eighteenth century, and that they were her grandfather's steps. The family came originally from the Durness area in Sutherland—'Mackay country' or *Duthaich MhicAoidh*. Her grandparents taught their children everything: music, song, dance, and 'even the pipes.' The family moved south, and no family or relations remained north in Sutherland, according to Sheila. Her mother in turn came out of a family of 17, all of whom

Figure 11.2 Anna Bain, Sheila McKay, Maggie Moore, and Sandra Robertson. Photo taken at Step Dancing Seminar, Dingwall, 1997. Sheila McKay shared her memories of Step dancing at this event

Source: Photo © M. Melin.

204 *Step dance encounters and recollections*

were involved with music and dance. Sheila's parents seem to have had their own travelling concert party in which the children performed. When someone at the seminar queried as to why Step dancing had more or less vanished, she did not quite address the question, but said she had not even passed on her Step dancing style to her daughter, Anna Bain, who was the director of the UKA[14] Scottish Branch at the time, and had never thought about it until she saw Maggie Moore Step dancing. Sheila said she felt the Step dancing died out because nobody was interested any longer. She also said she used to dance an old Clog Hornpipe, do Tap dancing, Ballet, and a Sand Dance (a soft-shoe shuffle on a sprinkle of sand on the floor). As a young girl, she was made to dance on stilts, dance a jig on full point at the age of six, and do acrobatics, like Tap dancing hanging upside down. Presumably this could have formed part of a variety act. She established the McKay School of Dancing in Glenrothes, Fife in 1930 and became a very well-respected figure within the Scottish Highland dancing community.[15]

Sheila showed the seminar attendees several steps, done sitting as she was recovering from a leg break. The steps were very percussive in nature with lots of triplets, and shuffles with the toe touching the ground before the heel. When Maggie Moore demonstrated the Basic Hop step as danced in Cape Breton, she said she used that as a progressive movement. Sadly, I was never able to meet with her again before she passed away to further interview her on these matters.

Easter Ross, the secret Highlands seminar, Alness, November 1998

On 2nd November 1998, I was asked to give a presentation at a seminar titled *The Secret Highlands: Traditions of Scotland's Far North* in the village of Alness, north of Inverness, and organised by the Highland Council. One of the presenters was Timothy Neat, the well-known historian, broadcaster, photographer, and writer on the Scottish travelling communities. Other presenters and workshop leaders were Scottish Traveller tradition bearers Essie Stewart and Alec John Williamson, and folklorist, singer, and storyteller Sarah Grey. Neat's 1976 film, *The Summer Walkers* was shown. Many Travellers were in attendance on this day of exploration of the life and lore of the Travelling People. My short presentation on my then-current findings regarding Step dancing and other dance traditions in Sutherland concluded with me being asked to demonstrate a few steps to the audience. No sooner had I taken to the floor when at least five or six audience members got up and joined me. I was quite surprised. They were all Travellers and they improvised freely using percussive footwork closely resembling some of the *Sean nós* dancing I was to see many years later in Connemara. I do recall that each dancer had individual footwork vocabulary and that steps were very much one with the music. They danced slightly leaning forward and used a combination of toe-and-heel movements and shuffles of the toe-toe variant. Some hop-backsteps were also in use. They did not always keep their arms still by the sides but raised them to the sides as *Sean nós* dancers often do, and/or raised one or the other in front of the torso in time with the music. Further details would be misleading to give as I did not make any detailed notes at the time and I only have these memories now.

I do regret I did not, at the time, interact with the dancers more afterwards to find out more about their dancing. This was the only crowd in Scotland that I ever performed for that got up and spontaneously joined in.

Sutherland, Isle of Lewis, and beyond, 1990s

Recollections of Step dancing at the crossroads and memories of dancing on bridges as mentioned by Moore have also been shared with me by people in several places round Scotland. When I taught social and Step dancing in Siabost/Shawbost and Barbhas on the west side of Isle of Lewis during the late 1990s, several attendees at the classes, being 60–80 years of age, shared their memories over breaks in the sessions. Seeing Step dancing triggered memories of something similar danced both at home and on bridges and at crossroads. A similar recollection was told to me regarding Step dancing at the crossroads in Rogart, Sutherland. The crossroads intersection makes, by design, a natural meeting point, but did it function in the same way as a bridge did? Were they landmarks for meeting or did they provide good dancing surfaces? Many were stone but others were wooden. Both would provide good acoustic effects if danced upon.

However, nobody could show me exactly how the dancing was done. My style of dancing simply reminded informants of something they recalled seeing back in time. When I taught Step dancing at a youth music and dance festival, *Fèis Latharna*, in Oban in April 2002, piping instructor and one-time pipe major of Glasgow City Police Pipe Band Ronnie Laurie told me that my Step dancing reminded him of his grandfather's Step dancing in Oban. I never got any further details in what specific way that was so.

While visiting Farr High School in Sutherland in May 1996, the Gaelic language teacher at the time, Donald 'Donnie' MacKay, originally from the Hebridean island of Bernera, told me of a Step dance recollection shared with him by the last teacher of Torrisdale School, Sutherland. The teacher had told Donnie that when she was young (*c.* 1915–1920) they Step danced at house parties in Torrisdale. They would sit around the walls of the house and would get and Step dance, and sometimes if there was a gathering in the room, they would take turns, 'just getting up and step dancing on the spot.'[16] This former teacher also told Donnie MacKay that the stepping always began before the music so that the timing and tempo was set and that both pipes and fiddle provided the music.

While working as Traditional Dance Development officer for Sutherland from 1996 to 1998, I came across reference of a man renovating a house in the Black Isle in Ross-shire. He said they had been puzzled to find a floor stone with strange scratch marks on it next to the fireplace. Eventually they queried an old man in the village about it, who simply said, 'that it was the step dancing stone, it was always danced on.'[17]

While working in Durness and Tongue on the north coast of Sutherland, I learned the local version of the couple dance The Baden Powell, which I later described in my 1997 booklet *A Sutherland Dance*. There is a motif in this dance that involved hopping on one foot and tapping the other quite firmly on the floor, creating a hop-tap, hop-tap rhythm of the feet that can only be described as percussive. Indeed, local dancers told me at the time, which was 1996–1997, that in years gone past, when musicians played the tune 'Inverness Gathering' in particular, the older generation of male dancers put extra effort in to their footwork, creating lively lift and sound in the dance.

The late Highland fiddler Farquhar MacRae from Roshven in Moidart recalled to Liz Doherty 'two brothers by the name of Gillis who would be invited up to step dance during the intervals at dances. This continued until the 1960s when the brothers would have been over 70 years of age.'[18] Musician and music researcher Dr William Lamb informs me that one of the brothers, Lachlan Gillies, was recorded by the School of Scottish Studies in Edinburgh in the 1950s. He was a Gaelic-speaking fiddler from Arisaig who knew a number of strathspeys and reels. What impressed Lamb about his playing, when he came across his tapes serendipitously, was how much closer his style seemed to the Cape Breton style than most Scottish players. This opinion was also shared by renowned West Highland fiddler Angus Grant Sr when Lamb played these music clips for him. Grant wondered that 'Gillies was from a Catholic area, and perhaps the Catholics had preserved an older style of playing the fiddle?' Lachlan Gillies was also a renowned judge of Highland dancing.[19]

Orkney and Shetland, 1990s

A faint glimpse of Step dancing in Orkney has materialised from a find in Kirkwall Library. In the Viking Club's book series *Old Lore Miscellany of Orkney, Shetland, Caithness, and Sutherland, Volume 1*, I discovered that 'the late Morrison Snody danced an old Orkney step dance, which he called *Clumpie*, and which has died with him.'[20] What distinguished this dance and in what way it was percussive, as the heavy 'clumpy' title suggests, we may never know for certain.

Craig Mishler describes a connection to Orkney and influence on the dancing style of the Red River Jig of the Gwich'in Athapaskan Indians and other tribal groups in northeast Alaska, the Yukon, and the Northwest Territories in his 1993 book *The Crooked Stovepipe*. He refers to the Fletts' research and outlines both the couple and solo dance versions of the Red River Jig of the Gwich'in.[21] He discusses shuffles, heel and toe beats, and stamps in detail and describes the shouts of encouragement at competition similar to that described by Bennett of the Step dancing in Codroy Valley in Newfoundland.

The Red River Jig is also very popular among the Turtle Mountain band of Ojibway and Métis in North Dakota [...] where it is understood to be a unique combination of aboriginal Indian dance steps and Scottish jig steps, but where only one male or female dancer at a time takes the floor as a caller sounds out each individual's name.[22]

The Canadian Métis dance tradition has its origins in the mix of First Nations, French, English, Scottish, and Orcadian people from whom the Métis Nation was born. This style of fast jigging, generally performed to reel-time music, has similarities to dance in Quebec and Maritime Canada today and also to some elements of British Step dancing.[23] Anne Lederman's (2015) article *Jigging: A Summary of Research in Western Manitoba, 1988* provides well-detailed descriptions of steps, dress code, competitions, and development of the dance style. She points to Orkney connections as being an influential part in the mix of this style of jigging, labelled from the French word for Step dancing, *giguer*, as performed by Aboriginal dancers, thus including both Métis and First Nations, 'whose communities and culture are inseparably interwoven in southern Manitoba.'[24] The style of this fast-paced dance is a mix of both percussive elements and lighter movements, and '[...] the value placed on quietness and brushing the floor, even in modern–day competition and performance, may point to some Aboriginal influence, although further comparative work would have to be done to establish that definitively.'[25] The influences on and evolution of the Métis dance style is an ongoing process.

In the summer of 1995, I met John Harald Johnson in Lerwick, Shetland, and he recalled fishermen Step dancing from when he was young. John Harald indicated they must have known the steps well, as, often, they were drunk, but they danced on top of tables in the local bars without falling off. Whether the fishermen were local or visiting he could not remember for certain, but indicated he thought it was a mix of both and that some fishermen were from Canada. Certainly, some of the Shetland Reel steps (Figure 11.3 shows a Shetland Reel being danced) in use are percussive, in particular, the scruffle step, still danced by some. The scruffle is somewhat similar to a Cape Breton 'jig shuffle' but done quickly in Reel time. Also, the Shetland backsteps mentioned elsewhere are performed in percussive manner with loud stamps, or digs, integrated in the footwork.

Angus and Aberdeenshire, 1990s–2000s

During my time as a Traditional Dance Development officer for the Angus District from 1998 to 2001 on behalf of the Scottish Traditions of Dance Trust (STDT), I found much evidence that local dancing masters in Angus, Fife, southern Aberdeenshire and eastern Perthshire had percussive Step dances in their repertoires.

For example, 'mouthie'/mouthorgan/harmonica player and diddler Jock Gordon of Kinaldie, Angus, who was 79 at that time, showed me some jig

Figure 11.3 Shetland Folkdance in 1995 dancing a four-couple Shetland Reel. Here they are backstepping and scruffling

Source: Photo © M. Melin.

shuffle steps when I interviewed him in November 1998. He called this the Jacky Tar step: shuffle right twice and shuffle left twice; he used to use it locally in Country dances. He invited me into his kitchen, where he started playing the 'mouthie' and began his shuffles. He was in his socks, so the sounds were soft, but there was a definite step on the left foot and a toe-toe shuffle with the right foot twice on each foot, with the back, supporting, foot being the time-keeper on the dominant count of the music (1 and a, 2 and a …). He only showed me this step once at one of our meetings but seemed to indicate it was quite common.

During my time living in Angus between 1998 and 2005, several sources also shared memories of local dancing masters, including Dancie Neill, Dancie Kydd, and Dancie Reid, all teaching percussive footwork separate from the motifs in the Sailor's Hornpipe and the Irish Jig character dances. Some sources recalled having to strap small pieces of wood to the soles of their shoes so as to make louder sounds while dancing.

My Angus project assistant from 2000 to 2002, Mrs Marion Robson, from Laurencekirk, Aberdeenshire, recalled her father Step dancing. In an email, Marion shared that *Dallum's Fancy Footwork* was the name a friend of her father's gave to his solo dance steps. Marion's father was Gordon McIntosh, who lived at Dalbrack Farm, Tarfside, in Glenesk, Angus. Gordon was born in 1920, and grew up in the Lumphanan area, later moving to Glenesk in 1957, at the age of 37. Gordon got his steps from his father Robert McIntosh, who lived at Tillyorn Farm, Lumphanan, in Aberdeenshire. Robert grew up in the Kildrummy area of Aberdeenshire and his father, William McIntosh, was a heavy athlete and dancer who performed at local Highland Games. William won medals for his dancing. The dance steps, 'which my father and grandfather danced, were practically the same' as those illustrated in a video folklorist Margaret Bennett showed at the STDT.[26] Marion Robson wrote:

> My mother was present at the STDT Conference and it was she who said that [Frank MacArthur's] dancing was just the same as that which her father-in-law used to do, but it was not called step dancing, just dancing. It used to be my Grandfather's party piece at weddings, home-entertainment and social occasions. Mother does not remember anyone other than her father-in-law or my father dancing such steps. My mother is 81; she grew up in Torphins and Lumphanan areas of Aberdeenshire.[27]

Again, this indicates that Step dancing was actively passed on from generation to generation within family networks, rather than through formal teaching contexts.

In 2016, north-east fiddler Paul Anderson revealed that local singer Danny Cooper could recall seeing his grandfather Step dancing. Paul's great grandfather John Cromar, who was born on the Muir of Gellan near Tarland in the Howe o' Cromar, also Step danced, according to Paul's grandmother. John Cromar moved to the farm of Midclune on the banks of the Feugh in Finzean when he married Julia Beattie. It was here that Paul's 93-year-old grandmother was born and brought up. She recalls he could not keep his feet still when the music started, and he would get up and his feet would 'go like the clappers.' Paul said, 'my great grandfather was the only person my granny remembers step dancing.' Furthermore, adds Paul, everyone did Country dancing in the days when his grandfather was courting. The men, most of whom were agricultural farm workers, wore white gloves so that their rough hands did not damage the women's dresses. They would also wear dancing pumps to a dance rather than the 'tackety beets,' which would be their daily work wear. Like so many other men, John Cromar would walk or cycle up to a dozen miles to a dance, every weekend, and then cycle the same distance back home and that was after a hard day's work and with an early rise to sort the horses at 5:00 am. Perhaps, this change of shoes worn for the dancing may have contributed to a decline in Step dancing as part of social occasions and social dancing?

A question that follows these types of recollections is: How many more examples like this could researchers, like myself, Margaret Bennett, Maggie Moore, and others, have found round Scotland in the last decade of the twentieth and early twenty-first centuries if a systematic research project had been set up at the time? What these short snippets of information show us, however, is how widespread Step dancing was in Scotland and that the memories, even though now are few and far between, still remain.

Notes

1. Melin 2006.
2. Personal correspondence between Fearchar Mac Neil and Mary Janet MacDonald, Leanish, Isle of Barra, 18 June 1985, Melin personal archives, Limerick.
3. Mary Janet MacDonald visited and taught Cape Breton Step dancing in Barra at the local Barra *Fèis* in July 1983.
4. MacEachen 1993: 7.
5. MacDonald 2005 p.c.
6. MacInnes, email to author, 15 April 2005.
7. MacDonald 2005 p.c.
8. Bennett 2010.
9. Melin 2006, conversation with Mairi MacLean, Northbay, Isle of Barra, 1 February 2002.
10. Bennett 1994.
11. Moore 1995: 18.
12. Moore 1995: 18–21.
13. *Step-Dancing Seminar & Workshop*. The seminar was inspired by Fiona Hay, Dancer in Residence, and arranged by Mats Melin for the Highland Council with the support of the Scottish Arts Council, Dingwall Town Hall, 5–6 April 1997.
14. United Kingdom Alliance of Professional Teachers' of Dancing (UKAPTD).
15. Melin 2006.
16. Melin 2006.
17. Melin 2006. Information provided by dancer and choreographer Frank McConnell, Conon Bridge.
18. Doherty 2006: 105.
19. Lamb 2014.
20. Johnston and Johnston 1908: 247.
21. Mishler 1993: 63–72.
22. Mishler 1993: 68.
23. One of the many good online clips of Red River Jig is this one: https://www .youtube.com/watch?v=-sQa6uGnxKQ [Accessed 20 February 2020].
24. Lederman 2015: 54.
25. Lederman 2015: 58.
26. Scottish Traditions of Dance Trust Conference at the Tolbooth, Stirling 2003. Bennett's video was of Frank MacArthur from Codroy Valley, Newfoundland, Step dancing in his kitchen. See Bennett's book *The Last Stronghold* for more information on the Gaelic customs and traditions of the MacArthur family (Bennett 1989).
27. Robson 2010.

12 Weaving the steps to the music

This chapter's analysis of percussive dance vocabulary used to describe existing dance forms that also appeared in notations from the nineteenth century helps fill in some detail to the broader sketches of percussive dancing in Scotland drawn in the previous chapters. Names applied to Highland dancing motifs indicate roots in percussive dancing. Connotations within these words' meanings are considered, while the structures of the words themselves are suggested as communicating rhythms for the performance of dance motifs.

Onomatopoeia within surviving soft-shoe Highland dance terminology

The 1843 *Dictionary of Science, Literature and Art* edited by W.T. Brande defines onomatopoeia as '… a word expressing by its sound the thing represented.' The modern-day *Merriam-Webster Dictionary* puts this idea as 'the naming of a thing or action by a vocal imitation of the sound associated with it.' Highland dancing terminology includes the words shuffle, brush, and beat as names for foundational movements. These words can be seen as relics of an earlier percussive dance tradition. The sounds and syllables intrinsic to their pronunciations reflect sounds made by dancing feet. These words, which teachers continue to use to communicate dance motifs to dancers, contain important information about the rhythmic execution and styling of the movements.

Although soft-soled dancing pumps are required in competitions today, 100 years ago this was not the case, as presented in Chapter 3. Figure 12.1 provides an example: an illustration in Donald R. MacKenzie's 1910 book shows a male dancer wearing heeled hard-soled shoes in the Highland Fling and in the Sword Dance.[1] As Highland dance is practiced today in soft-soled 'ghillies,' the sounds that these moves make are relatively softer, yet they are still audible. When Highland dancers don hard-soled shoes for competition, still in practice today for the 'Irish' Jig and for the 'Irish' Reel, Hornpipe, and Single and Double Jigs in the New Zealand Highland dance repertoire, some of the motifs are heard more distinctly because the hard shoes help amplify the sounds.

Figure 12.1 Hard shoes with heels are shown in this illustration of doing the backstep in the Highland Fling taken from D.R. MacKenzie's *National Dances of Scotland* ([1910], 1939 reprint edition), page 34

Source: Image in public domain.

Teachers' pronunciations and accents of these words shift slightly, because subtle changes in rhythm are necessary for different dances and time signatures. The embedded rhythms and qualities within these terms themselves may provide information about historical practices. We are going to explore these words' meanings more deeply in this chapter. All etymological information about the following terms comes from the *Oxford English Dictionary*. Because tactile imagery is also an important element in sharing the expressive shadings of dance movements, some connotations of the words are also included. The key terms we look at are: shuffle, treble, flatter, brush, beat, fling, and backstep.

Shuffle

The word shuffle with its two syllables reflects two connected motions of the gesture foot, called the 'working foot' in current Highland notation. A shuffle can be comprised of one inward and then one outward swipe of the floor, as in the *Seann Triubhas*, Highland Reel, the break motif in Flora MacDonald's Fancy, and the Hebridean versions of Highland Laddie, Over the Water to Charlie, Miss Forbes, and *Tulloch Gorm*. Alternately, it can consist of one outward and then one inward swipe, such as in the Sailor's Hornpipe, the Earl of Erroll, and the diagonal travel step of Flora MacDonald's Fancy. The fricative 'sh' and 'ff' sounds reflect the sweeping noises the foot makes as it glides across the dancing surface. The centralised, untensed vowels in each

Weaving the steps to the music   213

syllable reflect a balance of light, quick effort in the step; the foot swipes a small area of the ground in one direction, and then quickly retraces its path in the opposite direction.

This word sometimes changes accent and timing as needed to fit a rhythmic variation in a dance. For instance, the way a teacher articulates the word for the move as danced in the Sailor's Hornpipe has even timing and accent [shuf-ful] because it is danced on an even duple. Usually this kind of shuffle is not initiated on a downbeat. The 'shuffle' motif in the *Seann Triubhas*, however, is danced with a quicker, snapped rhythm, and the first movement of the move does occur on the downbeat. This accent is reflected in the way the word is spoken [**shuf**-ful] with an accent on the first syllable and a swallowed, shortened vowel on the second.

Whether a dancer is wearing soft- or hard-soled shoes, the foot creates sounds while doing this motion. The word seems to have a Germanic origin. Connotations of the word include dragging of the feet, a tricky exchange, and moving an object or objects from one place to another. The fact that shuffles are so prominent a motif in Highland dancing make it very likely that a percussive dance tradition is at the root of this dance form, even if it has been styled to a softer form.

Treble, treeple, triple, and flatter

Similarly, to shuffle, the word treble indicates outward and inward swipes of the foot described above, generally with louder sound making indicated. In Irish dance, for example, the words treble, shuffle, rally/raleigh, and batter are used interchangeably, all meaning the same type of sound-producing movements of the feet. It should be noted that this usage of the term treble is distinctly different from the longer movement motif of the same name occurring in Scottish solo dances, including the Earl of Erroll, the First of August, and the Flowers of Edinburgh. Those dances use the term treble to refer, lexically, to the three movements and sounds made between the stronger beats of the supporting foot.

The terms treeple or triple are other versions of this label signifying three sounds made by one foot in a treble movement motif. The triple and treble motifs are described in Figure 12.2. It may be of interest to note that *The Concise Scots Dictionary*[2] tells us that treeple, to treble/triple, in northeast Scotland, means to play a tune in triple time or dance to it, *e.g.* waltz; or to beat time with the foot to a dance tune.

The Scottish word flatter seems to display affinities with the words treble, shuffle, and batter, and is another two-syllable percussive dance term displaying consonance with the 'f,' 't,' and 'r' sounds popping up throughout these evocative words. In their books, the Fletts use the word 'flatter' to indicate a very quick shuffle immediately following a hop, as in the triplet motif found in Irish and Cape Breton Step dance styles. A hop-shuffle motif, though not commonly referred to as a flatter, is used in the Scottish 'Irish' Jig and in the Sailor's Hornpipe.

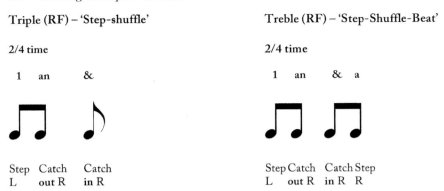

Figure 12.2 Illustration shows difference between a triple and a treble. The initial *step* in the triple can be either a *hop* or a *spring*

Brush

A brush is a movement of the gesture/working foot that slides along the dancing surface without taking weight. In Scottish dance, this occurs to the front of the body, either through 4th position (directly front) or 4th intermediate position (diagonally front) and can be made in an outward or inward manner. The plosive 'b' reflects a stronger attack that is especially evident when the brush originates near the body and moves outward from a definite point of contact with the floor in 1st, 3rd, or 5th position. The alveolar tap of the 'r' and the fricative sibilant 'sh' reflect the swiping sound the foot makes as it goes and the short vowel reflects the quick, light touch required to sweep the floor steadily with the foot.

The origin suggested for this word is the French word *brosser*. The word evokes images of moving a brush across a surface, quickly avoiding something, rushing past another person, or sweeping. This action can be seen as instrumental use of the body; the foot can sweep objects or dust across the floor by virtue of the quality of the movement.

Beat

Beat is an instance when a foot takes weight in order to make a sound on the dancing surface in time with musical accompaniment. The word reflects the motion and resulting sound with its plosive beginning and ending, and the tense 'e' in the middle reflects the precision with which the move must be performed. Beat is assigned a Germanic origin; however, the French word *battement* indicates another sort of beat also seen in Highland dance, a quick motion of an aerial foot towards the other leg, such as an *entrechat*, or a highcut. Connotations of the word beat reach from the heartbeat to the beat of a drum, from a steady rhythm underlying musical phrases to a hit or strike.

A common combination that recurs as a motif in Highland dancing is hop-brush-beat-beat, which combines some of the terms we have just examined. It is similar to the treble illustrated above, but we'll outline the differences here: a treble starts with a strong step, followed by the other foot dancing a shuffle and then a beat taking weight; the hop-brush-beat-beat begins with a strong first hop followed by the other foot making just one brush in towards the supporting leg, then taking weight and beating, followed by a closing beat of the original supporting foot. Good timing of a hop is kept by the landing of the foot on a dancing surface, and in Highland dancing, occurs in time with a downbeat in accompanying music. The hop movement itself is comprised of several parts: a spring into the air from the dancing surface with a strong channelling of energy to create an upward surge; a short amount of time in the air; and an ending with that same foot landing and supporting the weight of the dancer on the dancing surface. The landing, which makes sound, is the part that keeps time in this motif, and a strong downward thrust on the floor helps achieve accurate timing. The sound made by the hop is the strongest in the sequence, as a full-weight landing after a moment of elevation, while the three following beats are lighter: the brush is made by the non-weight-bearing leg, then the beats are weight-changing steps from foot to foot. In New Zealand, the hop-brush-beat-beat motif is known by the name 'shar,' which we speculate likely comes from the Gaelic word *sèarr*, meaning the verb to cut. Many New Zealand settlers were Gaelic speakers. The word cut is of unclear origin, and may be Old English.

The motif hop-point-(tap)-beat-beat described by Jack McConachie in his *Hebridean Solo Dances* booklet is similar to hop-brush-beat-beat but done with slightly less elevation. The second count consists of a point or tap of the working foot on the floor in an open position forward. Thus, this version can create stronger sound in its execution. This motif has seen a number of vernacular variations, which can be compared in the different traditions of Over the Water to Charlie.[3] Here is the late Barra teacher Fearchar MacNeil's version of point-close-beat: hop or spring on to LF (and); point RF in 4th Intermediate Position (1); Low, lilted spring on to RF in 5th Position (and); place LF in 3rd Rear Position (2). It must be performed with ease and a hop-sink body action.[4] Slightly different was South Uist native John MacLeod's version of the motif as notated by the Fletts in 1953 and here called 'hop 1, 2, 3' and is described as: 'hop on LF and lift RF up as far as it will go in 4th Intermediate Position [1] and bring it in. When it touches the ground, beat with it [and]; then beat with RF in 5th Position [a]; and beat LF in 5th Rear Position [2], taking RF off to next position.'

Flap, a movement in the Scottish 'Irish' Jig, is attributed an onomatopoeic origin outright, with connections to Dutch and German words for slapping or applauding. The word flap as used by percussive dance teachers today usually takes on an extra schwa sound between the 'f' and the 'l' to reflect the two parts of the movement. A foot swipes the floor with the instep for the first part of the move, then beats sharply, taking weight, to finish the

216 *Weaving the steps to the music*

motif. The spoken patter that reflects these two actions is pronounced with an accent on the second syllable [fuh-**lap**].

Fling

The name for one of the most iconic dances in the Highland repertoire, the 'Fling,' evokes a quality of movement no longer valued by dancers and teachers today: a loose, uncontrolled swinging motion. We know that the movement had historically been performed in a looser, swingier manner from various descriptions and video footage. David Anderson's (1897) *Ballroom and Solo Dance Guide* describes the first, namesake step of this dance, as 'spread' and then 'swing three.'[5] A film listed in Chapter 9 shows a dancer performing in this looser style.[6] The word fling begins with a fricative 'f' but then is elongated from a liquid 'l' to the nasal 'ng,' suggesting a longer, flexible movement. There are motifs in the Cape Breton Step dancing tradition that combine elements of the flinging or swinging motion described above with brushing or tapping of the gesture, or working, foot on the floor in forward, backward, and sideways directions.

The *Oxford English Dictionary* attributes an onomatopoeic derivation for the term fleg, meaning a random strike or kick, and connects it to the word fling. Fleg was the term MacTaggart used to describe the 'Peter a Dick's Peatstack' combination in 1824. The term kick is used frequently in the Cape Breton Step dance repertoire of movement motifs to denote an outward brush or strike of the heel or toe of the gesture leg on the dancing surface. The Cape Breton Fling step incorporates kicks.[7] A Gaelic term in use is *dannsa breabaidh*/kicking dance as mentioned earlier. Cape Breton dancers and teachers such as Mary Janet MacDonald, Jean MacNeil, Harvey Beaton, and Mary MacGillivray use this term to denote this particular movement. In the early nineteenth century, Colonel Thornton saw the Glen Orchy kick as the 'true' cultural expression of Scottish dance.

Heel-and-toe, or its reverse, toe-and-heel, is another idea that recurs in Highland dancing that describes an intricate change of a foot's point of contact with the dancing surface. It occurs as a light movement requiring rhythmic precision to keep appropriate timing. In the *Seann Triubhas*, the side-travelling heel-and-toe movements are placed on the floor to time with the upbeats, a practice also found in Cape Breton Step dancing. In the Highland Fling, the toe-and-heel occurs on the downbeats, in simultaneous timing of the landing of the hopping supporting foot. The First of August, known as a percussive dance in the Scottish tradition, also reflects this kind of timing. The quick-time *Seann Triubhas* steps involving toe-and-heel and heel-and-toe moves also exhibit this simultaneous timing; quick-time *Seann Triubhas* steps used today were originally Highland Fling steps, even though D.G. MacLennan wrote that the quick-time of the *Seann Triubhas* should have 'nothing to do with the Highland Fling, and a different tune ought not to be played for this part.'[8]

Other earlier dance terms that are suggestive of rhythmic, percussive sounds due to the very evidence of the sounds of which they are comprised are slips, slaps, stamps, skiffs, and scuffs. From Shetland and Orkney, we also find the evocative words clumpie and scruffle.

Backstep

The two syllables in the term backstep can align with rhythmic sounds created by the hop and step sequence at the heart of this motif. The word back refers to the working, or gesture, foot, being brought to the back of the standing leg during the hop. When the foot is placed down to take weight, it steps behind the other. The patter 'back, step' aligns with the hop-step sequence, which is comprised of two eighth notes or beats, with the second beat, the step, usually occurring on the down beat. This phrase becomes accented [back-**step**] to denote the stronger beat resulting with the spring. This motif is also known as a backstep with a hop, a Shetland backstep, a *retiré* skip in Highland dancing, and as *ceum cùl dùbailte* by dance teachers in the Isle of Barra in the 1990s.

In competitive Highland dance, the motif has evolved to omit the hop and Highland backsteps now consist of springs on the spot keeping the working leg on the supporting leg as it travels up the front of the shin and down the back of the calf. This Highland movement is executed in one spring, and the resulting bodily shape after the leg switch is held briefly. However, *retiré* skips also survive in the National dance repertoire in Blue Bonnets Over the Border and the Irish Jig. The Sailor's Hornpipe motif of shuffle over the buckle contains this motif with a shuffle preceding the backstep combination of a hop and a step.

Cape Breton Step dancing also inserts a shuffle, toe-toe or heel-toe, before the hop. It is one of the fundamental movements in this style of Step dancing. A description of one backstep motif, in 4/4 reel time, would be a step on left foot (count 'one'), a shuffle with the right foot (counts 'an &'), and a hop on left foot (count 'a').

The backstep can be, in all its forms described: a series of sharp springs from foot to foot; a series of hop-steps; or a series of shuffle-hop-steps; a core movement used to transfer movement energy from one foot to the other. This transfer of weight from foot to foot with a controlled upwards motion in between steps requires strong anti-gravity exertion.

Language rhythms and dance rhythm

It may be significant that very little dance terminology has roots in the Gaelic language, even though a percussive dance tradition has been practiced widely in Gaelic-speaking areas of Cape Breton. Today most of the teaching of the Scottish and Cape Breton repertoire of steps occurs in the English language. Gaelic language is emphasised in this tradition in the practicing and presenting

218   *Weaving the steps to the music*

steps to *puirt a beul*/mouth music tunes sung in Gaelic. It is not known if there has been Gaelic terminology for dancers, but a few words seem to indicate the sounds of the moves. One such word is *breab*/kick. Gaelicised English of the same idea, *cig*/kick, is used in the following passage:

> *Chi mi thall an dannsa 's Griogar ann*
> *'S ann 's an Sgoil-Dannsa fhuair e na Cigichean*
> (Yonder I see the dance, and Gregor there/it's in the Dancing School
>   he got the Kicks)[9]

The word *sèarr*, mentioned earlier, refers to the hop-brush-beat-beat motif in the New Zealand Highland dancing community. The word is spelled 'shar' in the New Zealand Academy syllabus and is used rhythmically in teaching the movement.

Qualities of dancing valued in both Gaelic and English references are neatness and lightness in Step dancing. On the face of it, this may be seen as being at odds with percussive, sound-generating footwork, but on the contrary, it is a common aspiration for Step dancers. Competitive Highland dancers constantly work to keep step placement neat, and strive for high elevation in dancing. We have heard 'neat' and 'light' used to refer to these qualities in Irish *Sean nós* and old style Step dancing, in Clog and Step dancing in England, and frequently in Cape Breton Step dancing. The Gaelic word *grinn*/neat/clean/elegant is used in Scottish Gaelic, ultimately associating lightness and neatness with beauty. An example of the use of '*grinn*' and also the word '*sgiobalta*' (agile, neat, tidy) would be the line from a *port a beul* reel well suited for dancing—'*Grinn donn sgiobalta mo ghiobag air an ùrlar*'/Neatly-formed, brown-haired, agile, my neat one of the dance floor).[10] Today, cues of 'being light on one's feet' or 'dancing as light as a feather' are commonly given in the Cape Breton community to reflect the value of neatness and lightness in dancing.

A few points regarding differences in language pulses and linguistic influence on dancing are worth mentioning here. In Cape Breton, there is an ongoing discussion of whether or not a Gaelic sound, or flavour, called '*blas*' in Gaelic, is a defining factor in the local vernacular fiddle style. Until the early decades of the twentieth century, learning tunes through the medium of Gaelic *puirt a beul* or *canntaireachd* was regarded as a key transmission method in the informal settings of the home and ceilidh house among Cape Breton Gaels, as it would have originated in Gaelic-speaking areas in Scotland.[11] Two of the main ideas in this area of research are: (1) the difference in language rhythm between Gaelic and English; and (2) that the rhythm of the predominantly dance-orientated tunes played is directly tied to Gaelic songs associated with the tunes. According to some people, there is a certain rhythmic characteristic embedded in the Gaelic language. Along this way of thinking, this is particularly expressed through *puirt a beul*, and the prominence of transmission of tunes via *puirt a beul* has been noted in Cape Breton music.[12]

Opinions on this topic are polarised. Some claim that, by extension, Gaelic Cape Breton music and song cannot be fully understood or reproduced without an ability to speak Gaelic. Others take a different point of view, stating that the music has absorbed this Gaelic rhythm and can thus be picked up through the music alone by anyone with a good musical ear as the music has retained the core of the 'dirt'[13] or 'flavour.'[14] A third way of looking at it would be that change is inevitable in a living tradition, Gaelic or not, due to continual modifications made by those performing the music.

Following the above arguments, one may ask if a Gaelic-language environment, in contrast to an English-language environment, has had different influences on how rhythm is aurally transmitted or understood. Can a rhythm be heard differently if sung or spoken in one language as opposed to another, or if played on an instrument? A distinction can be made here between rhythm and pulse. Etymologically the word rhythm comes from the Greek word *rhuthmos*, which is related to *rhein*/to flow. The English definition is given by the *Oxford Online Dictionary* of English as 'a strong, regular repeated pattern of movement or sound,' which can be described as a dynamic flow of accent, subdivision of beats, and elongation of sounds. It can be regular but also irregular depending on context. Pulse is more like a heartbeat underlying it all, a base from whence we get a sense of feeling and timing. This concept ties in with Michael Newton's point that

> The Gaelic language has a number of features which complicate the relationship between melody and words but which make a close correspondence all the more powerful and integral to the native speaker. Unlike English, the lengths of vowels are important in Gaelic: they can be short or long (according to the amount of time that they are held) and their lengths are phonemically significant. [...] This vowel system, along with regular initial-syllable stress and other features, causes speech utterances to conform to particular rhythmic patterns which are usually observed when the song is sung. It is the long notes (long vowel and diphthongs) which receive melodic ornamentation.[15]

Sutherland-based Gaelic scholar and piper Alasdair MacMhaoirn suggested in a conversation that 'by singing the tune [in Gaelic] the pulses have to come out right because the language steers the timing and this in turn gives the tune its feeling or, as is often said, puts the song in it.'[16]

However, the issue of how movement or dance informs music and song genres, or if language rhythm or pulse impacts Step dance, had not been addressed before Mats's research on Cape Breton Step dance.[17] If the demise of the Gaelic language has not caused significant change to the fiddle style in Cape Breton Island, as Elizabeth Doherty has suggested, can the same be said of the dance rhythms related to the musical style? If the links between Gaelic tunes and *puirt a beul* are still marginally maintained, even though the lexicon is not understood by a majority of dancers, would not step rhythms also carry an inherently understood function, existing independently of the Gaelic language? Have dance rhythms changed along with a decline of Gaelic flavour within musical accompaniment in Scotland in the same time period?

220 *Weaving the steps to the music*

Jen suggests that the vernacular Step dancing in Cape Breton is 'Gaelicised,' framed by understanding through a Gaelic-language rhythmic filter, due to the fact that the anacrusis providing transitional flow, described in Chapter 8, in percussive Step dance styles[18] is present, but is perceived as coming at the *end* of the motif. Cape Breton steps are taught as starting on the first strong beat, which is how Scottish Gaelic is accented. Steps align with the first beat of a bar of music. This theory is an area for further investigation. The steps in the solo *Dannsa nam Flurs*/Flowers of Edinburgh[19] start with anacrusis. It's possible there were different, mixed cultural origins of these solo dances in the Gillis family repertoire. Rhodes's (1996) notations of the steps for the Fling and *Seann Triubhas* start on the downbeat by taking full weight on a foot. Over the Hills and Far Away and *Dannsa nam Flurs* have shuffle preceding the downbeat in some steps, displaying anacrusis. Steps 5 and 6 of the *Dannsa nam Flurs* display a remarkable similarity to the first and sixth steps that Frederick Hill wrote out in English for the Flowers of Edinburgh in his notebook, which may suggest that the dance reached across Scots, English, and Gaelic cultural areas.

Time signature and anacrusis

Many references omit mention of what time signature of music accompanied the dancing that was observed. However, music collections of the eighteenth and nineteenth centuries reflect a trend in dance music shifting away from uneven, asymmetric time signatures such as 3/2, 6/4, 9/8, and towards even and symmetric time signatures such as 2/4, 4/4, and 6/8. For example, Bremner's 1761 second edition of *Scots Reels and Country Dances* includes both 3/2 and 9/8 tunes for dances. It has been suggested that there are differences in the ways dances make meaning depending on whether they occur in uneven meters or in even time signatures. In her 2013 book *The Dancing Goddesses*, Elizabeth Wayland Barber suggests that motifs that fit triple time signatures stand out as special, in contrast to symmetrical, pedestrian gaits that keep duple 2/4 or 4/4 time, such as walking or marching. Barber highlights instances of uneven metres in many dance forms in Eastern and Western Europe and illustrates that they are seen as special.

Ballad, or song dances displaying uneven meters where participants join together in circles or lines are still seen today in the Faeroese *kvad* dance, and in different forms of *kan ha diskan*/call and response song dancing from Brittany. Another dance making use of a triple time meter is the 3/4 Waltz popular throughout Europe in the late eighteenth and nineteenth centuries. Barber suggests, among other things, that these uneven movement patterns signal 'that the occasion and people [involved] are special, not ordinary,'[20] and that it helps focus the minds and embodied knowledge of the dancers on the task of moving together as a group, or, as a solo dancer, on the triple meter. This sort of dancing with asymmetrical weight-bearing patterns, according to Barber, helps solidify individual and community cohesion by creating special moments that are set apart from the ordinary rhythms of daily life.

Weaving the steps to the music 221

This idea may resonate in the practice of Step dancing in triple meter time, as in the Quebecois *gigue* Brandy, also known as *Grande Gigue Simple*, danced in 3/2 time featuring different types of shuffle motifs which do start on the anacrusis.[21] Similar motifs appear in some 3/4 English Waltz Clog routines, and perhaps these motifs from uneven metered dancing shifted and came to be arranged for common duple times of 2/4 or 4/4 when they became more popular and predominant. A question that arose in the interpretation of the trebles in the Earl of Erroll in Chapter 8 was whether the catch motif should start on the anacrusis, called pickup notes in music, or on the downbeat. If a treble motif, as an example, starts on the anacrusis in 2/4, 4/4 or 6/8 time, the feel, or cohesion, of this motif sits in *contrast* to the main, even pulse of the music, thus making the movements, and the feeling of them, special, in the sense that they stand out. They can stand apart visually, aurally, and kinaesthetically, and embellish, as opposed to mirror, the main rhythm of the music. Starting movements on the anacrusis generally set up that the downbeats of the music will align with the weight-bearing movements of hops, steps, or springs in the dance. Sometimes a desired effect is achieved by emphasising off-beat syncopation, but aligning weight-bearing movements with downbeats is a solid way of dancing right in steady time with music. Syncopation can be seen as a kind of embodied harmony between the ordinary and the unusual. The lighter beats of the pickup notes serve as a transition, or more gradual flow of accent, into a steadier cadence of changes in weight bearing in the ongoing step.

Starting on the anacrusis, and having an off-beat emphasis, brings to mind the Rant step associated with northern England, southern Scotland, and the province of Quebec. Scholarly analysis of the Rant step by Quebecois Step dancer and researcher Pierre Chartrand questions its origin and how this particular step became popular in Quebec.[22] In the British Isles, the Rant step is commonly associated with north English longwise Set dances such as the Morpeth Rant, danced on both sides of the current border. Versions of Rant steps that Chartrand found[23] appear within the current Irish *Sean nós* dancing tradition. This is an area still being investigated.

Dance step segmentation

There seems to be no analysis available to date on how and why steps of different genres are performed in a particular way. One current common practice for Scottish dances is that steps are danced in reel, jig, or hornpipe time for the duration of eight bars on the right side and then repeated contra on the left foot. The 16 bars thus complete one full step. To use musical terms, this would be a symmetrical binary form, with the A and B parts being of roughly equal length, each part being repeated in AABB format. AABB would then signify two steps with a repeat each. In contrast, vernacular forms incorporate a variety of differing step lengths and segmentations. Dancing occurs as a sequence of movements comprised of a mix of shorter and longer motif phrases. Each performance is unique in terms of length and choice of steps. Some segments are two bars long, while others are four or eight bars long. Some set Step

222 *Weaving the steps to the music*

dances exhibit combinations of three-bar phrases and are asymmetrical in that a dancer does not exactly repeat a motif danced on one side on the other side.

As a balance of movement content and symmetry between right and left sides is not always valued in vernacular genres as discussed above, it may be that certain Step dance legacies have borrowed ideals from theatrical dancing, including the binary musical form that gained popularity during the Baroque period where the emerging choreographic aesthetic emphasised a symmetrical balance between right and left sides. Around the middle of the eighteenth century, Western art music evolved to favour the Sonata form, while traditional music practices retained a binary form of two or more related parts which are each repeated. Having an equal practice of skills on both the right and left sides may have been a preference of dancing masters, encouraging bodily symmetry. It could reflect a wider view, where symmetry and balance guided overarching artistic metaphors suggesting stability and equanimity. Dance historian Jennifer Nevile tells us that

> Dance is an art form that is concerned with the manipulation, controlling, and ordering of space. Dance creates patterns in space: patterns which form and reform and trace out shapes in the air and on the ground. Therefore, throughout the fifteenth, sixteenth, and seventeenth centuries dance shared a common heritage with other artistic practices that were also concerned with the manipulation and ordering of patterns in space, especially garden design and architecture. Throughout the fifteenth to seventeenth centuries these arts shared similar design principles: order and proportion, geometrical forms and figures, and symmetry. In garden design and architecture human skill and knowledge transformed the matter of nature into an artificial human order, but this was still an order that reflected the numerical order of cosmos. [...] Dance moved into the realm of an art when music was played and the dancers adjusted their steps to fit the music.[24]

Balance and symmetry were core components of a broader symbolism favoured by the élite for well over three centuries. Possibly these values have endured and been passed down through these dances, even though not every formal Step dance structure follows this objective to the letter.

There is a convention in many of these solo dances of starting on the right foot. Exceptions exist but a majority of Step dances commence with the right side as the gesture leg. Beginning a dance on the right side may relate to superstitions. Barber points out that in circle dances, one can travel either to the left, known as clockwise or sunwise, or to the right, known as counter-clockwise or anticlockwise. For some cultures, the clockwise, or sunwise, direction was 'perceived by the farming tradition as health-giving, good' but for some, movement to the left, 'which according to the Bible, is the evil side,' was avoided.[25] Perceptions of direction may well have influenced starting dances with the right side of the body when prejudices discouraging left-handedness were more prevalent.

Frequently, Scottish solo dances share names with specific tunes such as the Flowers of Edinburgh, Highland Laddie, or Blue Bonnets that dances fit well to and that have binary AABB repeat patterns. Tunes associated with particular set solo dances are often tunes derived from songs or *puirt a beul* dominated by verse-and-chorus form, as in the strathspey *An Gille Crùbach anns a' Ghleann*/Miss Drummond of Perth, used for the Scotch Reel. Other factors may have shaped the repeat patterns in these dances today. See the Appendix for examples of music in different time signatures; most of the examples share titles with dances.

In the case of Scottish dancing, the Reel is the earliest and most commonly danced social dance recorded, surviving to this day as a competitive and performance dance. In modern Highland dance competitions, it manifests as the Highland Reel or Strathspey and Highland Reel, sometimes with the Reel of Tulloch attached to it. It is danced by Reelers at annual Balls and house parties in Scotland,[26] and a form is danced in Cape Breton, referred to as the Scotch Four. The common denominator linking all forms of Reels is a binary form: one eight-bar part of the tune is used for the Reel section consisting of travelling in a figure of eight or a circle while dancers swap partners; the other part of the tune is dedicated to steps danced on the spot facing a partner or opposite.[27]

Music for these Reels includes strathspey tunes where each musical part length is four bars: playing AA provides enough music for the travelling section; playing BB equals the time needed for the setting section. In reel time, the music functions similarly: if a reel is a 'short reel,' playing AABB creates 16 bars of music; if it is a 'long reel,' then playing AB equals 16 bars of dancing. Short reels fit vernacular extemporary Step dancing and older Reels. Specific long reels played in AABB format for 32 bars of music have become associated with choreographies bearing the same name as an associated tune, where an AA or BB played covers a whole step danced off the right foot and then repeated on the left foot for a 16-bar segment.

To illustrate this concept, we can look at the two eight-bar dancing sections of the Scotch Reel, which keep the same spatial travelling and setting structure in strathspey or reel time. Each part, travelling or stepping on the spot, covers eight bars of music. This dancing structure can be synchronised to either short or long reels. This repeat pattern can also be likened to a song with the travelling figure, such as a circle or figure of eight, serving as the chorus, and the stepping on the spot, which keeps changing, as the verses.

In 1957, Frank Rhodes described the Fling, *Seann Triubhas*, Over the Hills and Far Away, and The Flowers of Edinburgh/*Dannsa nam Flurs* surviving in Cape Breton Island as *all* having a solo Reel travelled in a circular pathway danced by the dancer to eight bars of an A part of the tune and percussive stepping on the spot for eight bars of the B part of the tune. Each eight-bar phrase of the step finishes with a two-bar break of percussive footwork on bars seven and eight. Two of the four dances observed featured series of

224   *Weaving the steps to the music*

triples, also known as trebles. Thus, steps coinciding with the B musical part were danced only off the right foot.[28]

However, in 2007, Margaret Gillis revealed that when she had performed The Flowers of Edinburgh as a duet with her late sister, the circular A–part Reel *was* danced both to the right and to the left, and the B–part steps were repeated: eight bars off the right foot then eight bars off the left foot. Thus, the dance as remembered 50 years later occurred in 16-bar AABB segments. This pattern results in a dance twice as long as the material given 50 years earlier. Was this a result of evolution due to a perception that the dance looked better when the sisters danced together in performance that the steps mirrored each other, or had the fashion of playing the tune changed locally? Or, had Rhodes not understood or absorbed deeper resonances in local practice—that a step might be shown and shared from the right side as a means of transmission, with an unspoken assumption that the step would be repeated on the left? Frank Rhodes gave the accompanying musical sequence as an ABAB repetition while Margaret Gillis in 2007 gave it as an AABBAABB repetition. Miss Gillis did not note that the structure had changed over time.

The repertoire of Scottish solo Step dances in jig or reel time has survived primarily as six–step length dances, with those six steps chosen from a larger catalogue of steps connected to that specific tune or song. Having six steps results in a dance length of 96 bars of music per dance, with each step being 16 bars long, meaning, played AABB. Steps are danced to eight bars of music on the right foot and then that dance motif is repeated on the left side to a repeat of the same eight bars of music. Many of the dances share names with the tunes they are danced to, as do 'Flowers of Edinburgh,' or 'Over the Water to Charlie,' but not all follow this rule. Exceptions are The First of August and Aberdonian Lassie. Internal segmentation of these dances varies, but one–bar, two–bar, and four–bar breaks are common at the end of each eight-bar side. These breaks can be compared to refrains, where a characteristic pattern repeats to indicate the end of a section.

A limited amount of evidence regarding this structure exists in early sources. Usually only dance names are listed in playbills or reported from concerts or Finishing Ball programmes. Steps performed by John Durang on the American stage in the 1790s have been listed.[29] In 1855, his son, dancer Charles Durang, provided a list of 22 names of steps John Durang danced for a 'Sailor Hornpipe Old Style' arrangement. Durang's list ends with a note that 'each step takes up one strain of the tune' without specifying whether each tune part repeated. However, in 1858, a similar step list was published by Boston dancing master Elias Howe, set to the tune 'Durang's Hornpipe,' with an added instruction after each step to 'repeat first change,' indicating a repeat pattern. Though it does not specify that repetition should occur on the opposite foot, this seems likely for a strenuous dance. Dundee dancing master David Anderson's *Ballroom Guide* of 1897 contains descriptions for the *Seann Triubhas*, Sailor's Hornpipe, and the Irish Jig. Each step is 16 bars long, commencing with 8 bars starting with the right followed by 8 bars on the left. This pattern shows up in most Scottish solo dances, both hard- and soft-shoe style, from this point in time onwards in respect to jig, hornpipe, and reel time dances.

In Frederick Hill's 1841 notebook, most of the solo dances exhibit this repeat pattern of eight bars danced on the right and then repeated on the left, corresponding to four bars in 4/4 strathspey time and in 3/2 horn-pipe time. Some Highland Fling and Tulloch Gorm steps are examples of this. Dances in 3/2 or 6/4 such as Dusty Miller and Wilt Thou Go to the Barricks Johnnie also repeat this pattern of four bars danced on each side alternated, as does the soft-shoe solo dance the 'Scottish Lilt' in 9/8 time. A similar structure is found in a Highland Fling from late-nineteenth-century Edinburgh dancing master John McNeill the patterns of the steps repeat evenly on right and left sides. Comparison between historical manuscripts shows that the convention of starting dances on the right side was not pro-moted by *all* dancing masters, however. Frederick Hill detailed an exception that dancing master Taylor's version of the Marquis of Huntly's Highland Fling 'Begins with the left.'[30]

A Highland Fling arrangement in Dancie John Reid's 1930s notebook titled John MacNeill's Highland Fling contains a number of steps that do not repeat symmetrically. These steps have a repeating structure of a two-bar motif starting on the right foot, repeated on the left foot, repeated on the right foot, and a two-bar finishing motif. This structure also occurs in cur-rent Reel setting steps in Highland dancing.[31]

Dance and step structures have been analysed by Hugh Thurston, who identified two overarching structures for the set step solo dances in the Scottish tradition, such as Over the Water to Charlie, Highland Laddie, Wilt Thou Go to the Barricks Johnnie, and Blue Bonnets. The first structure divides the step in two identical halves: A on the right foot for eight bars and A on the left foot for eight bars, as outlined above. The second structure exhibits a doubling up of this, but with each segment being shorter, *e.g.* four repetitions of a four-bar phrase fitting in to a 16-bar AA music part; or four repeats of a two-bar motif or phrase fitting in to one eight-bar A music part. Thurston points out that some dances, such as The First of August, have a circular starting step of a full circle danced clockwise over 16 bars, for two repetitions of the A part of the tune, rather than an eight-bar circle one way and then repeated the other. For Thurston, this variation does not undercut the overall logic of the structure: 'even in these steps the foot movements themselves obey the general rule.'[32] He finally remarks that this is quite an obvious kind of symmetry to find in a step and that in Gaelic it is known as '*ris is leis*' ('with and against').[33]

The First of August has a regular structure: a two-bar motif; a two-bar half break motif; a repeat of the two-bar motif used at the start of the step; and a two-bar finishing motif or break. The step is then repeated contra

226 *Weaving the steps to the music*

to align with an AA tune repetition. The northeast version of Flowers of Edinburgh in the 1841 Hill manuscript has a structure of: a two-bar motif on the right foot; the same two-bar motif on the left foot; and then a four-bar closing break; all then repeated contra on the other side to a repeated AA tune accompaniment.

See Table 12.1 below for examples of repeat patterns of step segmentations for a number of solo dances. Table 12.2 gives a list of step lengths and repeat patterns in solo dances of a percussive nature.

Table 12.1 Some examples of common dance and music structural segmentations

Examples of segmentations

Reel, Jig, or Hornpipe time
A and **B** parts of tune = 8 bars each   **A** and **B** parts repeated = 8 bars each
Step on RF   Step on LF

Exception (variation of the first step for the First of August)
Full circle danced through both **A** musical parts; step pattern follows 8-bar RF then 8-bar
 LF rule

Strathspey time
A and **B** parts of tune = 4 bars   **A** and **B** part repeated = 4 bars
Step on RF   Step on LF

Typical segmentation, or repeat pattern of motifs in a 'step'
Reel, Jig, or Hornpipe time
A and **B** parts of tune = 8 bars each, each repeated

2-bar motif RF   2-bar motif LF   2-bar motif RF   2-bar Finish motif (Break)
or
2-bar motif RF   2-bar motif LF   1-bar motif RF   1-bar motif LF   2-bar Finish motif
                                                                        (Break)

or
4-bar motif RF   4-bar motif LF

Strathspey time
A and **B** parts of tune = 4 bars, each repeated

1-bar motif RF   1-bar motif LF   1-bar motif RF   1-bar Finish motif (Break)
or
2-bar motif RF   2-bar motif LF

Dannsa nam Flurs repeat pattern ABAB
A part = 8 bars
Six chassés RF, LF (6 bars), 2-bar Finish motif (Break) RF

B part = 8 bars
2-bar motif RF   2-bar motif LF   2-bar motif RF   2-bar Finish motif (Break) RF

First of August repeat pattern AABB
A and **B** parts of tune = 8 bars each, repeated on the other side

2-bar motif RF   **2**-bar half break motif LF   **2**-bar motif RF   **2**-bar Finish motif (Break)
                                                                                RF

Weaving the steps to the music 227

Table 12.1 (Continued)

Hill Manuscript Flowers of Edinburgh repeat pattern AABB
A and **B** parts of tune = 8 bars each, repeated on the other side

2-bar motif RF   2-bar motif LF   4-bar Finish motif (Break) RF
or
1-bar motif RF   1-bar motif LF   2-bar motif   4-bar Finish motif (Break) RF
or
1-bar motif RF   1-bar motif LF   1-bar motif RF   1-bar motif LF   4-bar Finish motif
                                                                                (Break) RF

Motifs are roughly equivalent to words in language systems. A motif is the 'Smallest significant form-unit having meaning for the dancers and the dance system. Put together through repetition, variation, or grouping to form.' Kaeppler in 'Dance Structures' 2007: 54.

Table 12.2 Some common structures of a selection of named percussive dances

Dance name (tune title given when different)	Time signature	Step length	Melody repeat pattern	Tune length
1841—College Hornpipe	4/4	8+8	AABB	A8 B8
1841—Dusty Miller	3/2 or 6/4	4+4	AABB	A4 B4
1841—Earl of Erroll	4/4	8+8	AABB	A8 B8
1841—King of Sweden	4/4	8+8	AABB	A8 B8
1841—Irish Jig: Tune not specified	6/8	8+8	AABB	A8 B8
1841—Flowers of Edinburgh	4/4	8+8	AABB	A8 B8
1841—Shantruish★; Tune assumed to be 'Whistle O'er the Lave o't'	4/4	4+4	AB	A8 B8
1841—Wilt thou go to the Barricks Johnnie Tune: 'Go to Berwick Johnny'	3/2	4+4	AAB	A4A4 B8
1841—Trumpet Hornpipe	4/4	8+8	AABB	A8 B8
1850s—First of August; Tune: 'White Cockade'	4/4	8+8	AABB	A8 B8
1850s—Over the Water to Charlie	6/8	8+8	AABB	A8 B8
1850s—Highland Laddie/*Mac Iain Ghasda*	4/4	8+8	AABB	A8 B8
1850s—Aberdonian Lassie; Tune: 'Quaker's Wife'	6/8	8+8	AAAA BB	A4 B8
1850s—Scotchmakers; Tune: 'Dornoch Links'	2/4	8+8	AABB	A8 B8
1850s—Scots Blue Bonnets	6/8	8+8	AABB	A8 B8
1850s—Tulloch Gorm	4/4	8+8	AAB	A4 B8
1957—Fling (Cape Breton); Tune: 'Stirling Castle'	4/4	8+8	AB	A8 B8
1957—*Seann Triubhas*★★ (Cape Breton); Tune: 'Whistle O'er the Lave o't'	4/4	8+8	AB	A8 B8
1957—Over the Hills and Far Away (Cape Breton)	2/4	8+8	AB	A8 B8
Flowers of Edinburgh/*Dannsa nam Flurs* (Cape Breton)	4/4	8+8	AB	A8 B8

★   Note that dance repeat pattern is AABB.

★★   Note that structures of steps are not all uniform.

228   *Weaving the steps to the music*

Notes

1. These images are accessible at the University of Aberdeen J. Scott Skinner website: https://www.abdn.ac.uk/scottskinner/collectiondisplay.php?Record_Type= DRM SD
2. *The Concise Scots Dictionary* 1987: 735.
3. A good resource for comparing versions of this Step dance is a list available on Ian Brockbank's website: http://www.scottishdance.net/highland/dances/OerTheWater ToCharlie.html [Accessed 7 August 2017].
4. Melin 2019a.
5. Anderson 1897: 138.
6. See this silent film, *Scottish Dances*, hosted by the National Library of Scotland and featuring inaudible piping by dance master G. Douglas Taylor, at: http://movingimage.nls.uk/film/8199 [Accessed 20 April 2019].
7. Rhodes 1996: 198.
8. MacLennan 1950: 23.
9. This citation of Gaelic poetry comes from an article by Michael Newton (2000) at: http://www.electricscotland.com/history/literat/gaelictrad.htm [Accessed 18 February 2016].
10. Dòmhnallach 2012: 142.
11. For a discussion of oral/aural learning through the medium of Gaelic, see Dembling 2005; Dickson 2006; Doherty 2006; Dunn 1991; Gibson 1998, 2005; Graham 2006; Kennedy 2002; MacInnes 1997; Shaw 1992–1993; Sparling 2000, 2003, 2005.
12. Doherty 2006: 177; Kennedy 2002: 194–195, 205–207; Sparling 2000: 225–226, 2014; Shaw 1992–1993: 44.
13. The term 'dirt' is used among Cape Breton musicians to indicate an older, grittier, quality to the music. Certain grace notes, phrasings, bowings, and accents that characterises a particular sound.
14. Doherty 1996: 176, 307; Garrison 1985: 234–235; Kennedy 2002: 207; Sparling 2000: 259.
15. Newton 2009: 249.
16. MacMhaoirn 2014.
17. Melin 2015.
18. Movement on the anacrusis is used in most Irish step dance forms but rarely in *Sean nós* dancing. In English Clog and Step dances, there is a varied mix of the use of anacrusis and on-the-first-downbeat motifs, often within the same routine. Further research could perhaps reveal any linguistic, musical, and regional ties to this movement usage.
19. In Scotland, the Flowers of Edinburgh is today translated to Gaelic as *Lusan Dhun Èideann*. The Cape Breton name suggests it to be a 'Gaelicised' English title.
20. Barber 2014: 323.
21. Chartrand 1991.
22. Chartrand 2009. http://www.mnemo.qc.ca/spip/bulletin-mnemo/article/la-gigue-quebecoise-dans-la-marge [Accessed 29 September 2015].
23. Pierre Chartrand demonstrates a number of Rant/Reel/Polka steps in this clip: https://vimeo.com/140683424 [Accessed 19 December 2016].
24. Nevile 2008: 295–296.
25. Barber 2014: 361.
26. The term 'Reelers' refers to a group of people with a particular style of dancing Scottish Country dances and round-the-room couple dances. It is a genre for which research is lacking, and which exists outside any formal associations or affiliations. Dancers often come from Scottish Regiments, or from well-to-do upper middle class, farming, or landowning backgrounds, but the activity is not exclusive to

these groups. What distinguishes Reelers' dances is a limited repertoire of Country dances, including, for example, Hamilton House, Duke of Perth, Reel of the 51st Division, Eightsome Reel, and Highland Reel, consistently performed at functions and balls. It also refers to a particular style of dance steps used at these events for setting and turning partners and other figures. Some elements of this style may well be vestiges of nineteenth and early twentieth century dancing master practices.

27. See Flett 1985, 1972, 1973 for detailed descriptions of these Reels.
28. Rhodes 1985, 1996.
29. Emmerson 1972: 216–218.
30. MacFadyen and MacPherson 2011: 71–73.
31. Melin forthcoming book on Dancie Reid and his dances.
32. Thurston 1984: 76.
33. Thurston 1984: 76.

13 Echoes and reflections

In this compilation of references to Scottish percussive dancing, we have pulled together accounts portraying the Step dancing spread out in such varied forms across Scotland. Through these references, we can envision their intricate footwork. We can almost hear the dancers treepling in time together to the strains of 'Petronella,' spinning across the set and back. We can sense the pulse created by partygoers snapping in time to driving dance music, on the dance floor and off. Dancers once admonished from heuching on the dance floor are heard once again. Beats from all the soles that have been silenced over the course of two centuries echo through these writings, as well as in traditions maintained far from home.

In-depth step instructions in Hill's 1841 notebook, Anderson's *Ballroom Guides* of the late nineteenth century, Reid's (1935) notebook, and the Fletts' and Rhodes's book spell out practices out most clearly. Every one of these sources includes the treble motif, the treeple used in Country dances. The detailed notations written by the Fletts and Rhodes enable us to reconstruct the dances and experience them for ourselves. They help us to connect contemporary Scottish dance forms to earlier forms of percussive Step dancing in Scotland.[1]

Scepticism

Mats travelled extensively round Scotland from the mid–1990s to early 2000s as a professional dance teacher, researcher, and performer. Most of the people he met shared that they perceived the Cape Breton and even Hebridean styles of Step dancing as having Irish origins. Mats has gone on to discuss this theory with Irish dance colleagues at the Irish World Academy of Music and Dance at the University of Limerick and other academics and dancers. These discussions have revealed that although these styles look similar to an untrained eye, Scottish movement motifs have a different rhythmic relationship to the music than Irish ones have. The timing of the steps and the way dancers hold their centres of gravity differ substantially between these dancing styles.

Jen's 2004 performance of Cape Breton steps at the Irish Connections festival in Canton, Massachusetts, with dancer Abbie MacQuarrie brought a curious query of 'What is that?' from Irish Step dancer and teacher Michael Boyle. Irish dancers quickly identify that Hebridean and Cape Breton Step dance forms are *not* Irish, whereas observers from outside the Irish dance discipline are quick to point out a perceived affinity.

A result of organised promotion of Scottish dance in a light and balletic style has been that Scottish percussive dance legacies have vanished. The widespread use of percussive dance has been so effectively erased from the Scottish consciousness, or 'gesturescape,'[2] that when Cape Breton Step dancing was introduced at workshops in the 1990s,[3] many questioned that percussive dance ever existed in Scotland. Similar questions were asked in writings by Cape Bretoner Sheldon MacInnes who questioned the Scottish roots of the Cape Breton style because, to him, Cape Breton dancing practices had more in common with Irish dancing than they had with Scottish Highland or Scottish Country dancing.[4]

In the early 1990s, when a then-commonly labelled 'revival' of Step dancing was taking place in Scotland, a few newspaper articles in the *West Highland Free Press* (WHFP) discussed whether this was a new imported dance style or whether an older Scottish style was being revived.[5] The first article, 'Step-dancing makes its return journey across the Atlantic,'[6] discussed that Cape Breton Step dancing was taught by Harvey Beaton at *Sabhal Mòr Ostaig*, the Gaelic College, in the Isle of Skye that summer. Dancer and Gaelic culture activist James MacDonald Reid wrote a response in WHFP:

> Over 30 years ago I returned to Scotland as a young boy from a small community in Canada (not Cape Breton) [Glengarry, Ontario] with Gaelic as my first language and a broad vocabulary of traditional dances, including step dance. During the 1960s, I performed step dances in many ceilidhs and concerts throughout Scotland. Although the general public opinion held that this style of dance was entirely Canadian or 'Irish Dancing', many old people told me that they remembered seeing dancing just as I did as being customary in small, private occasions, and quite a few people could actually perform step dance themselves [...] Step dancing did not die out in Scotland; it simply didn't make it into the spotlight because of its relatively private and un-theatrical nature.[7]

The following week, Dr Michael Kennedy, who at the time was working at the School of Scottish Studies in Edinburgh, replied to WHFP:

> James MacDonald Reid claims that step dancing has not died out in Scotland [...] The fact that there has been so much decline and cultural interference in the Highlands makes it difficult to determine with any confidence whether what has been observed represents the vestigial elements of a highly attenuated tradition or remnants of dance forms

232 *Echoes and reflections*

imposed from outside the Gàidhealtachd. What Cape Breton dancing represents is a healthy community tradition—what has been found in the Highlands are memories of something, which are not altogether clear. [...] Step dancing in Canada is widespread and after 200 years of evolution and cross-cultural contact it is extremely difficult, if not impossible, to prove that any of the styles are peculiarly Scottish, particularly since there is no living tradition in Scotland with which to compare.[8]

Both individuals highlight processes of change and transition in Scottish and Canadian dance traditions and the difficulty of tracing the remnants of the Scottish Step dance tradition. A mindset doubting Scottish forms of Step dance was an undercurrent. A few months later, Scottish folklorist Dr Margaret Bennett wrote an article in WHFP referring to these articles that illustrated various changes in Scottish dance traditions. Bennett focused particularly on the institutionalisation of Scottish Country and Highland dance and how aesthetic preferences within these styles changed the nation-wide perception of dancing. She added, having outlined her interviews with Ciorstaigh Docherty and Mary McHarg mentioned in Chapter 11:

It is easy to understand why individuals such as these [Docherty and McHarg] have kept silent about their ability; forever since they went to school they have been shown how to dance 'correctly'. And, having mastered the RSCDS dances, both women channelled their childhood energy and love of dance into Highland Dance, which also has all the acceptability and status lacking in the steps they had learned at home.[9]

This last statement highlights a core problem facing researchers of the home-grown percussive dance legacies in Scotland. If people felt that the Step dancing they knew at home was not fashionable enough to be passed on, and feared being ridiculed for dancing in a 'rougher' or, to use a Cape Breton term, 'dirtier' way, then that helps explain why Step dancing has receded in Scotland. The newer, promoted ways of dancing made Step dancing seem obsolete to the people who knew the older, traditional ways.

That outsiders' opinions take precedence in judging what is correct and what should be valued may be linked to the national Scots' crisis of confidence outlined in 2004 by Carol Craig, a factor that resonated throughout discussions regarding the Scottish Referendum on Independence in September 2014. Craig argues, 'there are various reasons why the Scots' relationship with England undermined, and continues to undermine, Scottish self-esteem and confidence.'[10] Craig continues that

it is mistaken to believe that the Union and the relationship with England is the sole cause of Scotland's feelings of inferiority. Indeed, rather than seeing Scotland as a country with an inferiority complex it is better to see Scotland as suffering from *complex inferiority*. In other words, the reasons for the Scots' lack of confidence are many and varied. [...] I have shown how much of the Scottish belief system is designed to encourage individuals to know their place and so is more likely to undermine than to build confidence.[11]

Perhaps this complex inferiority contributed to Step dancing being given up in deference to modern styles.

Another aspect effecting changes, highlighted throughout this book, has been the influence of individual dancing masters. In Scotland, structured dance teaching began in the seventeenth century, spread to all social levels of society, and came to dominate dance learning from the late eighteenth century onwards.[12] Even in the remotest parts of the Scottish Highlands, Islands, and Orkney and Shetland, itinerant dancing masters appeared, generally having come from the south, and brought outside aesthetic standards and ideals.[13] This was the beginning of a shift away from dance transmission primarily in a home environment towards classes in public places. This transmission mode moved slowly away from individual expression, and towards discrete solo dance choreographies even while dancing masters taught unique versions of well-known solo and social dances. Dancing traditions began to emphasise masters' choreographic ideas, as opposed to communal invention and evolution, and migrated from processes of dancing to dances as products.

Scottish dance traditions were turning toward codification. Ballroom guides and dance manuals were widely disseminated. The twentieth century saw the end of the dancing master's era and the rise of dancing schools and governing organisations. The RSCDS and RSOBHD publish written guidelines that continue to be edited and refined, with new editions of textbooks proclaiming evolving preferences regarding motifs, body positions, timing, and dress code. Examination and adjudication rules are issued on a regular basis, today including online web guides. Success within these forms is judged by how closely dancing conforms to written descriptions. While organisations' guidelines exist primarily for members, these ideas, proclaiming what constitutes correct dancing, have had a much wider global reach. Today, these rules have come to form international perceptions of what Highland and Scottish social dancing look like.

This is not to say that other forms of Scottish dancing do not exist outside these organisational domains. They do; however, other forms do not receive the same press and have not garnered a similar impact on a global mindset. Local variants of social and Country dances quickly disappear as their exponents age if a younger generation lacks repeated exposure to them.

The vital connection to an understanding of playing music for dancing is thinning as music and dance come to be treated as separate entities. Both music and dance have written notation forms influencing transmission. Ear learning still occurs, but to a lesser extent than it used to. In the process, skills involved in and strengthened by 'just picking it up,' or learning through 'osmosis,' have been greatly reduced. Awareness of one's body in space,

234   *Echoes and reflections*

balance, and what the movements feel like are of essential importance to all dancers. These processes of embodiment can be ignored when visuals and text-based rules are overemphasised.[14]

As Scottish dance has developed into a hobby, weekend, leisure, or competitive activity in specialised environments, intermittent exposure to dancing has, in some cases, shifted participants away from a depth of practice building on years of slow learning within a community setting and from attending regular classes with dancing masters. Dances, packaged sets of steps or formations, become prioritised, and are seen as results attendees can take back home. This model may inadvertently emphasise the quantity of dances known at the expense of deeper nuances relating to qualities embodied in dancing.[15]

All of these factors have contributed to the erosion of the historically indigenous percussive Step dancing practices of Scotland.

Current legacies in Scotland

In this book, we have highlighted the legacies of many individuals who influenced percussive Step dance forms in Scotland over the centuries. The story does not stop there, however. Some legacies have morphed into other dance forms, some have disappeared, while others have been reinterpreted in recent decades.

The dancing of Hebridean dance master Ewen MacLachlan did not die with him in 1879. It was embodied and performed by his pupils, who in turn passed it on. Archibald MacPherson, Donald '*Roidein*' MacDonald, John MacLeod, Fearchar MacNeil, and many more, shared their knowledge with the Fletts, Frank Rhodes, D.G. MacLennan, and Jack McConachie, as described earlier. Different notations and teaching have resulted in varied interpretations of these dances today.

In the case of one dance, The First of August, Ewen MacLachlan's legacy was transmitted directly to MacPherson and MacDonald, who passed the dance on to John MacLeod, who shared it with Tom Flett, who taught it to Chris Metherell of Newcastle, who taught it to Mats Melin. The version published by Jack McConachie was taught by Ron Wallace to Robert McOwen, who shared it with Jen Schoonover. These versions have motifs in common yet reflect wide stylistic differences. Mats has made a point of observing dancing in South Uist and Barra, and, combined with stylistic parameters he learned from Chris Metherell, has amalgamated all this information in his individualised version and sometimes adapt the material to fit recorded music tracks that require new segmentations to be choreographed and used. Jen teaches the version she learned, incorporating pointed feet and split leaps, to competitive Highland students to provide variety and a fun challenge. In turn, we both teach this dance to share these embodied legacies of Ewen MacLachlan in our own ways. All these ways can be seen as being correct in and of themselves. A dance is only alive during an act of it being performed by a human being, who makes choices and becomes an embodied interpretation of the material.[16]

In the early 1990s, a relatively small number of Scottish dancers and musicians 'discovered' Cape Breton Step dancing. Since that time, there has been a subsequent emergence of a style of Step dancing within Scotland responding to Scottish music aesthetics and relying on distinct preferences as distinct from the Cape Breton tradition. Based on Mats's research and personal participation in, and observation of, the Scottish vernacular dance community of the time, approximately 20–30 Scots became interested in Cape Breton Step dance. These individuals visited Cape Breton and other North American venues where Cape Breton Step dancing was featured, and attended summer school workshops in Scotland where Cape Breton Step dancing came to be taught. Historical links were explored and cultural links between Cape Breton and the Scottish Highlands were advocated. This Step dance genre was represented to others as an older form of Scottish dancing.[17] Similarly, some individuals suggested that the Cape Breton fiddling and piping styles are older forms of Scottish music.[18] Some Cape Bretoners were also invested in the belief that they had maintained a 'pure' form of traditional Scottish music and dance.[19] Although scholarship has demonstrated the unsurprising fact that Cape Breton fiddling and Step dancing have evolved and developed in their own distinctive ways since first coming to the island with Scottish settlers, this was often largely ignored or downplayed by the Scottish interest group.[20]

Many of those involved in Step dancing in the early and mid-1990s often incongruously referred to the 'discovery' of Cape Breton's percussive Step dancing as a revival of a 'lost' Scottish dance form. It is important to note, however, that, at that time, the little research there was regarding percussive Step dancing in Scotland was based on fragmented and scattered memories. The current Cape Breton genre of Step dance came to be assumed to be the form identified in these memories. Those who engaged with this form of percussive Step dancing sometimes saw it as a dance form signifying Scottishness or Gaeldom.

To our knowledge, no vernacular Step dancing form as remembered in Scotland has actually been revived. Rather, it is clear that the core material of Step dancing currently practised in Scotland is drawn from Cape Breton dance practices. Evidence for this can be tracked in naming conventions. Steps were attributed to Cape Breton sources, such as 'Donald Beaton's step,' or 'a Jean MacNeil step.' In recent years, some of these same steps have become attributed to their Scottish teachers' names, with the original Cape Breton link reduced or forgotten all together. One must, nonetheless, remember that with certain Cape Breton steps, including 'Donald Beaton's step,' there is an embedded connection to Scotland given its transmission from a settler from the Highlands. Furthermore, through that step, his descendants maintain a connection to his repertoire of steps, but have added to and modified them in an embodied, ongoing legacy. The Cape Breton way of naming steps after

236   *Echoes and reflections*

particular people is like an intricate web of traditional sourcing acknowledging origins but allowing for change.

An essence recognised in Step dancing from Cape Breton in the early 1990s was a quality of 'dirt' and a surging referred to as 'swing' or 'drive,' terms also used in relation to Cape Breton music. Many Scots felt the Scottish dancing of the time lacked these qualities, a result of having become refined and restrained by associations and governing bodies.[21] This quality of 'dirt' was a rawer, less institutionalised practice, often also perceived as more 'authentic.'

In the early 1990s, the influential Scottish fiddler Alasdair Fraser and piper Hamish Moore promoted and became important points of access to Cape Breton-style music and Step dancing in Scotland. They both arranged to bring Cape Breton musicians and dancers to teach at traditional music and dance summer programs in Scotland. While the timing of Fraser's and Moore's interest is significant, traditional Cape Breton musicians and dancers had ongoing communication with the 'old country,' touring Scotland in the 1960s and 1970s, and having recordings broadcast in the UK by the BBC.[22] Jonathan Dembling suggests that the failure of the 1979 referendum on home rule and the following 18 years of Conservative rule from Westminster led to increased nationalistic attitudes toward cultural expression, and more self-conscious shaping of the arts and culture in Scotland. In the period leading up to devolution and the opening of the Scottish Parliament in 1999, 'a great deal of thinking and discussion about what it means to be Scottish in the twenty-first century' ensued.[23]

Fiddler Alasdair Fraser made it clear that his personal journey of discovery of Cape Breton music and dance was set in a wider context of seeking Scottish identity. Alasdair describes growing up in a Scotland where his mother tongue, Scots, was discouraged, and where, in his opinion, cultural self-esteem—his own and the country's—was low. Alasdair felt disillusioned by what he saw as a lack of interest in the 'roots' of Scottish music and dance. In the Highlands, he said, the 1970s traditional music scene was unhealthy with only a handful of indigenous fiddlers around, such as Angus Grant Sr and Farquhar MacRae. Against this backdrop, Alasdair Fraser travelled to Cape Breton in 1981 and 'found the fluency in the culture of Cape Breton that [he] wanted in [his] own culture.'[24]

From the outset, many of the budding Step dancers in Scotland aligned themselves and their dancing with Gaelic traditions in both Cape Breton and the Scottish Highlands. The fact that the two main summer schools where Cape Breton Step dancing was taught, *Sabhal Mòr Ostaig* in the Isle of Skye and *Ceòlas* in South Uist, are situated in the *Gàidhealtachd*, and that both featured Gaelic language and song content prominently in their programming, strengthened this connection. Furthermore, the Gaelic youth music movement, *Fèisean nan Gàidheal*,[25] adopted Step dancing as one of their class options from the early 1990s. Of course, not all Scottish Step dancers attached Gaelic connections to their dancing. The historical Gaelic framework was not central for those who were more interested in Step dancing for its percussive nature alone, or simply as a fun hobby and good form of exercise.[26]

Some facts are available that reflect the impact individuals who taught Step dancing in Scotland have had since the 1990s. Step dancing was recognised by the now defunct Scottish Traditions of Dance Trust and continues to be recognised by the Traditional Dance Forum of Scotland as a style of its own. It was taught at the Royal Academy of Music and Drama, now the Royal Conservatoire of Music in Glasgow, for at least a 10-year period, up until about 2015. Step dancing continues being taught at the *Ceòlas* and *Sabhal Mòr Ostaig* annually and at other weekend and short courses around Scotland. *Fèisean nan Gàidheal* has promoted it, but not all their festivals include it. Relatively few individuals taught regular classes over the years and fewer still ventured in to teach at primary and secondary levels. A few local Step dance groups were set up, but were located far apart from one another across the country.

Over a 12-year period in the late 1990s and early 2000s, Mats taught Step dancing in over 375 primary and secondary schools around Scotland, often giving 10 or more classes to the same schools and to multiple class groups. What impact this had, apart from some level of awareness among the participants, is difficult to determine. Mats knows of only three or four dancers that he taught during that period who continued Step dancing. How many people know, at any level, how to Step dance in Scotland today? Perhaps a future study will reveal these facts and figures.

Among the Step dancing that has continued, however, the motifs and movement practices taught by Cape Breton Step dance teachers since 1992 have morphed and changed as they have been embodied and shared. A new style of Step dancing is developing in Scotland today, one in which individual dancers emphasise percussive qualities of motifs and steps modified and made up themselves. This is, as Pat Ballantyne remarked,[27] in subtle but fundamental contrast to aesthetic core values cherished in Cape Breton today.[28] Regarding Step dancing in Scotland in 2012, Cape Breton Step dancer and pianist Mac Morin reflected, 'They don't make up steps the way we do.'[29] Dancers in Scotland today creating their own percussive Step dance legacies, making up their own 'True Glen Orchy kicks!'

Since about 2010, Scottish Step dancers, such as Màiri Britton, Sophie Stephenson, and Jayne MacLeod, have become a new wave of indigenous Scottish Step dancers. Others, such as Kae Sakurai, add their influence to the genre, too. New steps have been created in Scotland that are not in use in Cape Breton, and so these can be regarded as Scottish, if place of origin is important. Step dancing in Scotland is developing naturally along its own path, due to contextual and musical influences that are different from those in Cape Breton, and is forming its own aesthetic characteristics. This form of Step dancing is slowly developing into an integral part of the current Scottish traditional dance scene.[30] One current certainty is, that with the expanding practice of recording almost anything on video, Step dancing of today, in all its forms, will be recorded somewhere for posterity.

Notes

1. Flett 1985, 1996; Rhodes 1985, 1996.
2. Melin 2012a, 2017.
3. Melin 2005.
4. MacInnes 1994: www.siliconglen.com/celtfaq/3_2.html [Accessed 25 June 2012], 1996 and 1997.
5. Melin 2005.
6. Murray 1994.
7. MacDonald-Reid 1994.
8. Kennedy 1994.
9. Bennett 1994.
10. Craig 2004: 240.
11. Craig 2004: 240.
12. Emmerson 1972; Flett 1985.
13. Flett and Flett 1985, 1996.
14. Melin 2012a.
15. These issues are explored in depth in Melin 2013b, 2013c.
16. See Melin 2005.
17. Moore 1995; Sparling 2011.
18. Dembling 2005; Shears 2008; Sparling 2011.
19. Sparling 2011.
20. Dembling 2005; Sparling 2011; Doherty 2006; Melin 2012a.
21. Melin 2005.
22. Doherty 2006.
23. Dembling 2005: 183.
24. Melin 2005: 30.
25. *Fèisean nan Gàidheal* was established in 1991 as the independent umbrella association of the fèis movement. 'Fèis' is 'festival' in Gaelic (the plural is 'fèisean'), and the fèis movement was designed to provide an alternative to competition in which children could learn traditional Gaelic-centred expressive forms (including music, dance, and song). According to the *Fèisean nan Gàidheal* website, approximately 13,000 young people participate in *Fèisean nan Gàidheal*-supported activities See: http://www.feisean.org/en/information/index.php [Accessed 10 March 2013].
26. Melin 2013b: 41–43, 44–45.
27. ICTM 44th World Conference at the University of Limerick, 15 July 2017.
28. See also Melin 2012a, 2015.
29. Melin 2013b: 35.
30. See Melin 2013b.

Appendix—Tune examples as given in the text

Minuet

Figure A.1 Minuet example: 'Minuet' from James Oswald's 1745 *Caledonian Pocket Companion*: 3/4 time with 8-bar A part and 16-bar B part

Go to Berwick Johnnie
O Irioghuill ort, irioghaill ort Anna

Figure A.2 Earlier triple-time hornpipe (sometimes seen notated as 3/2, 9/8, or 6/4): 'Go to Berwick, Johnnie' from Angus MacKay's 1857 *Tutor for the Highland Bagpipe*: 9/8 time with 4-bar A and B parts. Embellishments have been omitted

Figure A.3 Strathspey example: '*Gille Crubach anns a' Ghleann*/Miss Drummond of Perth' from Angus MacKay's 1857 *Tutor for the Highland Bagpipe*: 4/4 time with 4-bar A and B parts. Embellishments have been omitted

Figure A.4 Strathspey example: '*Tuloch Gorm*/Tulloch Gorum' from Angus MacKay's 1857 *Tutor for the Highland Bagpipe*: 4/4 time with 4-bar A part and 8-bar B part. Embellishments have been omitted

Appendix 241

'S truadh nach bu leis &c.
Oer the Hills and Far Awa

Figure A.5 Reel example: *'S truadh nach bu leis &c.*/Oer the Hills and Far Awa' from Angus MacKay's 1857 *Tutor for the Highland Bagpipe*: 2/4 time with 8-bar A and B parts. Embellishments have been omitted

College Hornpipe

Figure A.6 Hornpipe example: 'College Hornpipe' from James Stewart Robertson's 1884 *Athole Collection*: 4/4 time with 8-bar A and B parts

Over the Water to Charlie
Null air an Uisge gu Tearlach

Figure A.7 Jig example: 'Over the Water to Charlie/*Null air an Uisge gu Tearlach*' from Angus MacKay's 1857 *Tutor for the Highland Bagpipe*: 6/8 time with 8-bar A and B parts. Embellishments have been omitted

The Flowers of Edinburgh

Figure A.8 Scottish measure example: 'Flowers of Edinburgh' from James Stewart Robertson's 1884 *Athole Collection*: 4/4 time with 8-bar A and B parts

Appendix sources: Angus MacKay's 1857 *Tutor for the Highland Bagpipe* (Melin Personal Archive); James Oswald's 1745 *Caledonian Pocket Companion* (https://archive.org/details/caledonianpocket01rugg/page/n43/mode/2up [Accessed May 2 2020]); James Stewart Robertson's 1884 *Athole Collection* (https://tunearch.org/wiki/).

Bibliography

Manuscript and Archives Collections

British Library Newspaper Archive. https://www.bl.uk/collection-guides/british-newspaper-archive

Flett, T.M. and J.F. *Tom and Joan Flett's Archive*. Online access at www.insteprt.co.uk

Irish Traditional Music Archive. Francis O'Neill Collection, Dublin.

Live Argyll, Bibliographic and Local Studies. *MacGrory Collection*, Live Argyll Libraries, Dunoon, Scotland.

Melin, Mats. *Mats Melin Personal Dance Archive Collection*. Privately held, Limerick, Ireland.

Robertson, Colin. *Colin Robertson Personal Dance Archive Collection*. Privately held, USA.

Royal Scottish Country Dance Society. RSCDS Archive. Edinburgh, Scotland.

General

Alburger, Mary Anne. (1983). *Scottish Fiddlers and Their Music*. London: Victor Gollancz Ltd.

Aldrich, Elizabeth, S.N. Hammond, and A. Russell, Ed. (2000). *The Extraordinary Dance Book T B. 1826: an Anonymous Manuscript in Facsimile*. Dance and Music Series No. 11. Stuyvesant, NY: Pendragon Press.

Anderson, David. (1897). *David Anderson's Ballroom Guide and Solo Dance Guide*. Dundee: W.P. Saunders.

Anderson, Paul. (2016). Email correspondence with Mats Melin. Tarland, Scotland. 14 June.

———. (2017). Email correspondence with Mats Melin. Tarland, Scotland. 4 June.

Anklewicz, Mike. (2012). Extending the Tradition: KlezKanada, Klezmer Tradition and Hybridity. MUSICultures, 39, 2.

Anonymous. (1817). *Letters from Scotland: by an English Commercial Traveller*. Edinburgh: Archibald Constable and Co.

Anonymous. (1823). *Celtic Melodies, being a Collection of Original slow highland airs, pipe-reels and cainntearachd*. Never before published. Selected and arranged by a Highlander. Published for the Editor by Robert Purdie, Edinburgh. [In the National Library of Scotland Glen 399(1,2)]

Astier, Régine. (2004). Académie Royale de Danse. In *International Encyclopedia of Dance*. Ed. S.J. Cohen. Vol. 1. Oxford: Oxford University Press.

Au, Susan. (1997). *Ballet and Modern Dance*. London: Thames and Hudson.

244   *Bibliography*

Bakka, Egil. (2001). The Polka before and after the Polka. *Yearbook for Traditional Music,* *33,* 37–47.

Ballantyne, Patricia H. (2016). *Regulation and Reaction: The Development of Scottish Traditional Dance with Particular Reference to Aberdeenshire, from 1805 to the Present Day.* PhD Thesis, Aberdeen, Scotland: University of Aberdeen.

———. (2019). *Scottish Dance Beyond 1805. Reaction and Regulation.* Routledge Studies in Ethnomusicology. London and New York: Routledge.

Barber, Elizabeth J.W. (2014). *The Dancing Goddesses: Folklore, Archaeology, and the Origins of European Dance.* New York: W.W. Norton and Company.

Beck-Friis, Regina, M. Blomkvist, and B. Nordenfelt. (1998). *Dansnöjen Genom Tiden— Barocken.* Vol. 1. Lund: Historiska Media.

Beckwith, Lillian. (1959). *The Hills Is Lonely.* London: Hutchinson and Company, Ltd.

Bennett, Margaret. (1989). *The Last Stronghold. The Scottish Gaelic Traditions of Newfoundland.* St. John's, Newfoundland: Breakwater Books.

———. (1994) 'Step-dancing: Why we must learn from past mistakes,' *West Highland Free Press,* 14 October.

———. (2010). Email correspondence with Mats Melin. Glasgow, Scotland. 8 October.

Biskop, Gunnel. (2015). *Menuetten—Älsklingsdansen. Om meuetten i Norden—särskilt i Finlands svenskbygder—under trehundrafemtio år.* Helsingfors, Finland: Finlands Svenska Folkdansring RF.

Brainard, Ingrid. (2004). Renaissance Dance Technique. In *International Encyclopedia of Dance.* Ed. S.J. Cohen. Vol. 5. Oxford: Oxford University Press.

Brande, William T. (1843). *Dictionary of Science, Literature and Art.* New York: Harper and Brothers.

Brereton, Charlotte. (1990 [1742]). To A—-A M—A Tra—S. An Epistle from Scotland. In *Eighteenth Century Women Poets: An Anthology.* Ed. R. Lonsdale. Oxford: Oxford University Press.

Brisbane Scottish Dancing Festival Committee. (1976). *A Collection of Lesser Known Highland Dances.* 1st ed. Brisbane.

British Association of Teachers of Dancing. (2019). *The Scottish National Dances.* Glasgow: BATD.

Britton, Màiri. (2016). *Bùird is brògan:* Material culture and the percussive qualities of traditional Scottish stepdance. Unpublished paper. Edinburgh, Scotland: University of Edinburgh.

Buchanan, Robert. (1901). *Poems, Songs, and Other Writings.* Falkirk: F. Johnston.

Buckland, Theresa Jill. (2011). *Society Dancing: Fashionable Bodies in England, 1870–1920.* London: Palgrave MacMillan.

Burchill, Kenneth. (1938). *Step Dancing.* 3rd ed. London: Sir Isaac Pitman and Sons.

Burns, Robert and J. Currie. (1806). *The Works of Robert Burns: With an Account of His Life, and a Criticism on His Writings. To Which Are Prefixed, Some Observations on the Character and Condition of the Scottish Peasantry.* 5th ed. London: T. Cadell and W. Davies.

Burt, Edward. (1876 [1754]). *Burt's Letters from the North of Scotland. (Facsimile of London Edition of 1754 Pertaining to 1726.).* Vol. 2. Edinburgh: Paterson.

Byron, Lord [George Gordon]. (1898). *The Complete Works of Lord Byron.* Ed. E.H. Coleridge. London: John Murray.

Cameron, Alasdair. Scott, Rob Roy and the National Drama. University of Glasgow Library. http://special.lib.gla.ac.uk/collections/sta/articles/national_drama/index.html

Cameron, William. (1951). *Highland Dances of Scotland.* Aberdeen: Aberdeen Journals, Ltd.

Bibliography   245

Campbell, Alexander. (1804). *The Grampians Desolate*. Edinburgh: John Moir.

Campbell, Alexander. (1815). *A slight sketch of a journey made through parts of the Highlands and Hebrides; undertaken to collect material for Albyn's Anthology, by the Editor; in Autumn, 181. [La. III. 577].* ([La. III. 577], [La. III. 577]). Special Collections, University of Edinburgh Library.

Campbell Family. (2013). *Fonn—the Campbells of Greepe: Music and a Sense of Place in a Gaelic Family Song Tradition*. Stornoway: Acair Ltd.

Canadian Olde Tyme Square Dance Callers' Association. Couple Dances. http://sca.uwaterloo.ca/cotsdca/1CoupleDances.html

Carleton, William. (1852). *Traits and Stories of the Irish Peasantry*. New Edition. London: Routledge.

Carter, Nathaniel Hazeltine. (1827 and 1829). *Letters from Europe, Comprising the Journal of a Tour Through Ireland, England, Scotland, France, Italy, and Switzerland in the Years 1825, '26, and '27*. New York: G. and C. and H. Carvill.

Carus, Carl Gustav. (1846). *The King of Saxony's Journey Through England and Scotland in the Year 1844*. London: Chapman and Hall.

Census for Scotland. (1891). Ancestry.co.uk online database.

Chambers, Robert. (1829). *The Scottish Songs*. Vol. 2. Edinburgh: William Tait.

Chartrand, Pierre. (1991). *La Gigue Québécoise [Quebec Step-Dancing Tutor and History]*. Quebec: l'Association Québécoise des Loisirs Folkloriques.

———. (2009). La gigue québécoise dans la marge de celle des Îles britanniques. http://www.mnemo.qc.ca/spip/bulletin-mnemo/article/la-gigue-quebecoise-dans-la-marge

Comhlan Dannsa nan Eileanach. (1995) *Hebridean Dances/Dannsa nan Eileanach*. Stornoway: Acair.

Comunn Gaidhealach. (1913). *An Deo-Gréine, the Monthly Magazine of An Comunn Gaidhlealach*. Vol. 8, October 1912 to September 1913. Glasgow: An Comunn Gaidlealach.

Concise Scots Dictionary. (1987). Aberdeen: Aberdeen University Press.

Craig, Carol. (2004). *The Scots' Crisis of Confidence*, Edinburgh: Big Thinking.

Cramb, Isobel. (1953). *Four Step Dances: Three Solo Dances Based on the Hill Manuscript, Aberdeen, 1841, and One from Miss Cruickshank of Peterhead*, London: Paterson's Publications Ltd.

———. (1994). *Step Dancing in Scotland's Dance: A Review of the 1994 Conference on the Diversity of the Scottish Traditions of Dance—25/26 October, Albert Hall, Stirling*. Edinburgh: Scottish Arts Council.

Creighton, Helen and Calum MacLeod, Ed. (1979 [1964]). *Gaelic Songs in Nova Scotia*. Ottawa: National Museums of Canada.

Cullinane, John P. (1987). *Aspects of the History of Irish Dancing*. Cork: Privately Published.

———. (1990). *Further Aspects of The History of Irish Dancing (in Ireland, England, New Zealand, North America, and Australia)*. Cork: Privately Published.

Cunningham, Allan. (1825). *The Songs of Scotland, Ancient and Modern*. Vol 2. London: John Taylor.

Dalyell, Sir John Graham. (1849). *Musical Memoirs of Scotland with Historical Annotations and Numerous Illustrative Plates*. Edinburgh: Thomas G. Stevenson.

Daye, Anne. (1997). *The First Refinement—The Scottish Connection*. Salisbury: Dolmetsch Historical Dance Society.

Delaney, Frank. (1994). *A Walk to the Western Isles after Boswell and Johnson*. London: Harper Collins Publishers.

Dembling, Jonathan. (2005). You Play It As You Would Sing It: Cape Breton Scottishness and the Means of Cultural Production. In *Transatlantic Scots*. Ed. C.R. Ray. Tuscaloosa: University of Alabama Press.

246   *Bibliography*

Devine, Thomas M. (2011). *To the Ends of the Earth. Scotland's Global Diaspora 1750–2010.* London: Allen Lane.

Dickson, Joshua. (2006). *When Piping Was Strong. Tradition, Change and the Bagpipe in South Uist.* Edinburgh: John Donald Publishers.

Doherty, Elizabeth A. (2006). Bringing It All Back Home? Issues Surrounding Cape Breton Fiddle Music in Scotland. In *Play It Like It Is: Fiddle and Dance Studies from Around the North Atlantic.* Ed. I. Russell and M.A. Alburger. Aberdeen, Scotland: Elphinstone Institute, University of Aberdeen.

Dòmhnallach, Goiridh. (2010). Personal correspondence with Mats Melin. Cape Breton, Canada.

Dòmhnallach, Rob. (2012). *An Cùrsa Gàidhlig. Gaelic 521 Course Notes.* An Gearran: Àrd-Sgoil Chòirneil MacIlleghlas.

Dunn, Charles W. (1991). *Highland Settler. A Portrait of the Scottish Gael in Cape Breton and Eastern Nova.* Vreck Cove, Cape Breton, Canada: Breton Books.

Dwelly, Edward. (1988 [1911]). *The Illustrated Gaelic-English Dictionary.* Glasgow: Gairm.

Elphinstone Institute Manuscript. (1998). *Francis Peacock Information.* Personal fax communication with Mats Melin. Aberdeen 12 August 1998. Melin Personal Archive. Limerick.

Emmerson, George S. (1970). The Hornpipe. *Folk Music Journal,* 2(1), 12–34.

———. (1972). *A Social History of Scottish Dance: Ane Celestial Recreatioun.* Montreal and London: McGill-Queen's University Press.

———. (1988). *Rantin 'Pipe and Tremblin' String. History of Scottish Dance Music* (1971. 2nd Revised ed. 1988): Galt House, Canada.

———. (1995). *A Handbook of Traditional Scottish Dance.* Oakville, Ontario: Galt House.

Ewart, David and May Ewart. (1996). *Scottish Ceilidh Dancing.* Edinburgh: Mainstream Publishing.

Faujas de Saint-Fond, Barthélemy. (1799). *Travels in England, Scotland and the Hebrides, undertaken for the purpose of examining the state of The Arts, The Sciences, Natural History and Manners in Great Britain.* London.

Feintuch, Burt. (1993). Musical Revival as Musical Transformation. In *Transforming Tradition: Folk Music Revivals Examined.* Ed. Neil V. Rosenberg. Urbana: University of Illinois Press.

Fergusson, Donald A. (1977). *Beyond the Hebrides/Fad Air Falbh As Innse Gall.* Halifax, NS, Canada: Lawson Graphics Atlantic Ltd.

Fergusson, Robert. (1785). *Poems on Various Subjects.* 3rd ed. Edinburgh: T. Ruddiman and Co.

Flett, Joan. F. (1993). *The Hornpipe in Scotland.* Paper presented at the Conference "The Hornpipe" The National Early Music Association, Sutton House, Homerton, London.

Flett, Joan F. and Tom M. Flett. (1956a). Dramatic Jigs in Scotland. *Folk-Lore, LXVII* (67), 84–96.

———. (1956b). Some Early Highland Dancing Competitions. *Aberdeen University Review 36,* 345–358.

———. (1972). The History of the Scottish Reel as a Dance Form I. *Scottish Studies,* 16(2), 91–119.

———. (1973). The History of the Scottish Reel as a Dance Form II. *Scottish Studies,* 17(2), 91–109.

———. (1979). *Traditional Step-Dancing in Lakeland.* London: English Folk Dance and Song Society.

Bibliography   247

———. (1985 [1964]). *Traditional Dancing in Scotland.* Appendix: Dancing in Cape Breton Island, Nova Scotia. F. Rhodes. London: Routledge and Kegan Paul.

———. (1996). *Traditional Step-Dancing in Scotland.* Appendix: Step-dancing in Cape Breton Island, Nova Scotia. F. Rhodes. Edinburgh: Scottish Cultural Press.

Foley, Catherine E. (2001). Perceptions of Irish Step Dance: National, Global, and Local. *Dance Research Journal, 33*(1), 34–45.

———. (2007). The Creative Process Within Irish Traditional Step Dance. In *Dance Structures. Perspectives on the Analysis of Human Movement.* Ed. A.L. Kaeppler and E.I. Dunin. Budapest: Akadémiai Kiadó.

———. (2008). Percussive Relations: An Exploration of Percussive Dance at *Tráth na gCos* 2002. In *Close to the Floor. Irish Dance from the Boreen to Broadway.* Ed. Mick Moloney, J'aime Morrison, and Colin Quigley. Madison: Macater Press.

———. (2011). The Irish Céilí: A Site for Constructing, Experiencing, and Negotiating a Sense of Community and Identity. *Dance Research, the Journal of the Society for Dance Research, 29*(1), 43–60.

———. (2012). *Irish Traditional Step Dancing in North Kerry: A Contextual and Structural Analysis.* North Kerry Literary Trust.

———. (2013). *Step Dancing in Ireland, Ashgate Popular and Folk Music Series.* London: Ashgate.

Forbes, Robert. (1897). *The Lyon in Mourning.* Edinburgh: T & A Constable.

Fraser, George Milne. (1911). *Aberdeen Street Names. Their History, Meaning, and Personal Associations.* Aberdeen: William Smith.

Gallini, Giovanni-Andrea. (1772). *A Treatise on the Art of Dancing.* By Giovanni Andrea Gallini; London. Printed for the author and sold by R. Dodsley [etc.].

Garnett, Thomas. (1811). *Observations on a Tour Through the Highlands and Part of the Western Islands of Scotland.* London: John Stockdale, Piccadilly.

Garrison, Virginia H. (1985). *Traditional and non-traditional teaching and learning practices in folk music: An ethnographic field study of Cape Breton fiddling.* Madison: University of Wisconsin.

Gibson, John G. (1998). *Traditional Gaelic Bagpiping, 1745–1945.* Montreal: McGill-Queen's University Press.

———. (2005). *Old and New World Highland Bagpiping.* Edinburgh: Birlinn Ltd.

———. (2017). *Gaelic Cape Breton Step-Dancing. An Historical and Ethnographic Perspective.* Montreal: McGill-Queen's University Press.

Glassie, Henry. (2003). Tradition. In *Eight Words for the Study of Expressive Culture.* Ed. B. Feintuch. Urbana and Chicago: University of Illinois Press.

Graham, Glenn. (2006). *The Cape Breton Fiddle. Making and Maintaining Tradition.* Sydney, NS, Canada: Cape Breton University Press.

Grant, Elizabeth. (1911). *Memoirs of a Highland Lady: the Autobiography of Elizabeth Grant of Rothiemurchus Afterwards Mrs. Smith of Baltiboys 1797–1830.* Ed. Lady Strachey. London: John Murray, Albemarle Street.

Grattan Flood, William H. (1927 [1906]). *A History of Irish Music.* Dublin: Browne and Nolan.

Green, Sarah. (1824). *Scotch Novel Reading; or Modern Quackery. A Novel Really Founded on Facts. By a Cockney.* Vol. 2. London: A.K. Newman and Co.

Guillard, Yves, R. Lange, and Centre for Dance Studies. (1989). Early Scottish Reel Setting Steps and the Influence of the French Quadrille. *Dance Studies, 13,* 7–113.

Hall, James. (1807). *Travels in Scotland, by an Unusual Route.* London: J. Johnson.

Hardie, Alastair J. (2005). *The Caledonian Companion/The Fiddler's Companion: A Collection of Scottish Fiddle Music and Guide to Its Performance.* Revised edition. Edinburgh: Hardie Press.

248   *Bibliography*

Harris, Jane A., Anne Pittman, and Marlys S. Waller. Ed. (1968 [1950]). *Dance A While: A Handbook of Folk, Square, and Social Dance*. 4th ed. Minneapolis: Burgess Publishing Company.

Haynes, A.H. (1957). *The Dagenham Girl Pipers*. London: Faber and Faber.

Henderson, Joan. (1995). The Traditional Dances of the Outer Hebrides. In *Dance Studies Vol. 19*. Ed. R. Lange. Jersey: Centre for Dance Studies.

Highfill, P.H., P.K.A. Burnim, and E.A. Langhans, Ed. (1975). *A Biographical Dictionary of Actors, Volume 4, Corye to Dynion: Actresses, Musicians, Dancers, Managers, and Other Stage Personnel in London, 1660–1800*. Carbondale and Edwardsville: Southern Illinois University Press.

Highland and National Dancers' Association of Victoria, Inc. (1982). *Copied sheets on Positions, Handwork, Highland Fling steps, Shean Truis, Strathspey and Reel and Reel of Tulloch, Clansman Sword Dance, Sword Dance, Irish Reel, Sailors' Hornpipe, Irish Jig, Home Style Irish Jig (Shillelagh)*. Victoria: Australia.

Hilton, Wendy. (2004). French Court Dance. In *International Encyclopedia of Dance*. Ed. S.J. Cohen. Vol. 1. Oxford: Oxford University Press.

———. (2004). Minuet. In *International Encyclopedia of Dance*. Ed. S.J. Cohen. Vol. 1. Oxford: Oxford University Press.

Hobsbawm, Eric. (1984). Introduction: Inventing Traditions. In Eric Hobsbawm and Terence Ranger (Eds.), *The Invention of Tradition*. Cambridge: Cambridge University Press.

Hume, David. (1891). *The Imperial History of England: From the Earliest Records to the Present Time; Comprising the Entire Work of David Hume, Copiously Supplemented and Annotated; and the Later History of the British Empire, Derived from the Most Authentic Sources; With Summaries of Events on the Continent, Illustrating the Course of Contemporaneous Continental History, Brought Down to the Present Time by William Cook Stafford and Henry W Boulton*. London: Ward, Lock and Company.

Hunter, James. (2010). *The Making of the Crofting Community*. Edinburgh: Birlinn Ltd.

Instep Research Team. World Clog Championship, Bow, London, 1898. https://insteprt.co.uk/world-clog-dance-championship-bow-london-1898/

Jaffray, Alexander. (1835). Recollections of Kingswells from 1755–1800 *The Miscellany of the Third Spalding Club. Vol. 1, Issue 4*. Aberdeen: Spalding Club.

Jamison, Phil. (2015). *Hoedowns, Reels and Frolics. Roots and Branches of Southern Appalachian Dance*. Urbana, Chicago, and Springfield: University of Illinois Press.

Johnson, Samuel and James Boswell. (1985). *A Journal to the Western Islands of Scotland and the Journal of a Tour to the Hebrides. 1773 and 1786*. London: Penguin Books.

Johnston, Alfred W. and Amy Johnston, Ed. (1908). *Old-Lore Miscellany of Orkney, Shetland, Caithness, and Sutherland. Vol 1*. London: The Viking Club.

———. (1913). *Old-Lore Miscellany of Orkney, Shetland, Caithness, and Sutherland. Vol 6*. London: The Viking Club.

Johnstone, Christian Isobel. (2003 [1815]). *Clan-Albin*. Glasgow: Association for Scottish Literary Studies.

Jowitt, Deborah. (2010) In Pursuit of the Sylph, Ballet in the Romantic Period. In *The Routledge Dance Studies Reader*. Ed. Alexandra Carter and Janet O'Shea. Chapter 20. London/New York: Routledge.

Kaeppler, Adrienne L. (2007). Method and Theory in Analyzing Dance Structure with an Analysis of Tongan Dance. In Ed. Adrienne Kaeppler and Elsie Ivancich Dunin. *Dance Structures: Perspective on the Analysis of Human Movement*. Budapest: Akadémiai Kiadó.

Bibliography 249

Kennedy, Michael. (1994). Stepdancing in Scotland. *West Highland Free Press*. 19 August 1994.

———. (2002). *Gaelic Nova Scotia: An Economic, Cultural and Social Impact Study*. Halifax, Nova Scotia, Canada: Nova Scotia Museum.

Knox, John. (1787). *A Tour through the Highlands of Scotland and the Hebride Isles, in 1786*. London.

Kohl, Johann Georg. (1849). *Travels in Scotland. Translated from the German*. London: J. and D.A. Darling.

Laban, Rudolf. (1963). *Modern Educational Dance*. London: MacDonald and Evans.

Lamb, William. (2014). Email correspondence with the Mats Melin. Edinburgh, Scotland, 20 November.

Lederman, Anne. (2015). Jigging: A Summary of Research in Western Manitoba, 1988. *Canadian Folk Music*, *49*(2/3), 54–61.

Lloyd, Arthur Estate. Britain's Provincial Theatres. http://www.arthurlloyd.co.uk/BritainsProvincialTheatres.htm

Logan, James. (1831). *The Scottish Gael*. Vol. 1. London: Smith, Elder, and Co.

Lowe. David. (1991). Extracts of a letter from David Lowe to Dr MacFadyen. Crieff, Scotland 5 April. Melin personal archive, Limerick, Ireland.

Lowe, Messrs. (1831). *Lowes' Ball-Conductor and Assembly Guide*. Edinburgh: Messrs Lowe.

MacArthur, Kelly. (2012). Personal correspondence with Mats Melin. Sydney, Cape Breton, Canada.

Mac-Dhughaill, Iain. (1860). *Dain Agus Orain*. Glasgow: Mac-na-Ceardadh.

MacDonald, Gordon. (1928). *The Highlanders of Waipu or Echoes of 1745. A Scottish Odyssey*. Dunedin: Coulls, Somerville, Wilkie.

MacDonald, Keith Norman (2012 [1901]). *Puirt-à-Beul: the Vocal Dance Music of the Gaels*. Ed. William Lamb. Isle of Skye: Taigh na Teud.

MacDonald, Mary-Janet. (2005). *Farquhar Macneil and the Barra Fèis 1983*. Email correspondence with Mats Melin, Port Hood, Cape Breton, 18 April.

MacDonald-Reid, James. (1994). Stepdancing did not die out in Scotland. *West Highland Free Press*. 12 August 1994.

MacDougall, John L. (1922). *History of Inverness County, Nova Scotia*. Strathlorne, NS: Canada.

MacEachen, Frances. (1993). Memories of the Barra Women Step Dancing. *The Clansman*, December/January issue, 7.

MacFadyen, Alastair and Adams, Florence H. (1983). *Dance With Your Soul: a Biography of Jean Callander Milligan by Alastair MacFadyen and Florence H. Adams*. Edinburgh: RSCDS.

MacFadyen, Alastair and A. MacPherson, Ed. (2009). *Frederick Hill's Book of Quadrilles & Country Dances Etc Etc, March 22nd, 1841: A Reproduction of the Original Manuscript*. Stirling, Scotland: Hill Manuscript Group: MacFadyen, Mackenzie, and Macpherson.

MacGillivray, Allister. (1988). *A Cape Breton Ceilidh*. Cape Breton: Sea-Cape Music Ltd.

MacIlleDhuibh, Ragnal. (1993). Highland leather, Highland shoes. *The Quern-Dust Calendar, West Highland Free Press*, 10 December.

MacInnes, Maggie. (2005). Flora MacNeil's recollection of step dancing. Email correspondence with Mats Melin, Glasgow. 15 April.

MacInnes, Sheldon. (1994). *Cape Breton Step-dance: an Irish or Scottish Tradition*. Paper presented at the 1994 Cork Cape Breton Festival. www.siliconglen.com/celtfaq/3_2.html

———. (1996). Stepdancing: Gach taobh dhe'n Uisge ('Both Sides of the water'). In *The Centre of the World at the Edge of a Continent*. Ed. C. Corbin and J. A. Rolls. Sydney, NS: University College of Cape Breton Press.

250   Bibliography

————. (1997). *A Journey in Celtic Music—Cape Breton Style*. Sydney, NS: University College of Cape Breton Press.

MacKay, Angus. (1857). *The Tutor for the Highland Bagpipe. With a Selection of Marches, Quicksteps, Strathspeys, Reels and Jigs. Amount to One Hundred Tunes by William McKay in 1841. 1843 Corrected and Improved by Angus MacKay. Piper to her Majesty.* 3rd ed. Edinburgh: Alex. Glen Bagpipe Maker.

Mackay, John G. and Norman Macleod. (1924). *The Romantic Story of the Highland Garb and the Tartan.* Stirling: Eneas MacKay.

MacKenzie, Donald R. (1910). *The National Dances of Scotland.* Glasgow: MacLaren.

MacLachlan, Janet T. (*c.* 1990). *Book 1 of a Highland Dancer's Notebook.* Stratford, Ontario: MacLachlan.

————. (*c.* 1991). *Book 2 of a Highland Dancer's Notebook.* Stratford, Ontario: MacLachlan.

————. (1992). *Book 3 of a Highland Dancer's Notebook.* Stratford, Ontario: MacLachlan.

————. (1994). *Book 4 of a Highland Dancer's Notebook.* Stratford, Ontario: MacLachlan.

MacLagan, Robert C. (1901). *The Games and Diversions of Argyllshire.* London: Folklore Society.

MacLennan, Donald G. (1925). *Highland Dancing. Guide to Judges, Competitors, and Teachers as approved at a Conference held in Edinburgh, 2nd April 1925.* Edinburgh.

————. (1950). *Highland and Traditional Scottish Dances.* Edinburgh: W.T. McDougall.

————. (1952). *Highland and Traditional Scottish Dances.* 2nd Ed. Edinburgh: T&A Constable Ltd.

MacLennan, Malcolm. (1979 [1925]). *Gaelic Dictionary. Gaelic-English English-Gaelic.* Aberdeen/Stornoway: Aberdeen University Press/Acair.

Macleod, Norman (1868). Dance, My Children. *Inverness Courier,* Thursday 3 September. British Library Newspaper Archive.

MacLeoid, Calum Iain M. (1969). *Sgialachdan a Albainn Nuaidh.* Glaschu: Gairm.

McColl, Jeanetta. (2016). Interview with Jennifer Schoonover, Framingham, Massachusetts, 14 October.

McConachie, Jack (Posthumous). (1972). *Hebridean Solo Dances.* Ed. Peter White. London: Caber Feidh Publications.

McCormick, Andrew. (1907). *The Tinkler-Gypsies.* Dumfries: J. Maxwell and Sons.

McGill, John. (1752). Manuscript. https://archive.rscds.org/index.php/mcgill-manuscript

McIan, Robert R. (1848). *Highlanders at Home.* London, Ackermann and Co.

McIntyre North, Charles N. (1880). *Leabhar Comunn nam Fior Ghaël/Book of the Club of True Highlanders.* London.

McKay, Ian. (1992). Tartanism Triumphant: The Construction of Scottishness in Nova Scotia 1933-1954. *ACADIENSIS, XXI*(2), 5–47.

MacMhaoirn, Alasdair. (2014). Personal correspondence with Mats Melin. Rogart, Sutherland, Scotland.

MacNeill, Seumas. (1995). Editorial. *The Piping Times,* 16–17 January.

MacTaggart, John. (1824). *The Scottish Gallovidian Encyclopedia.* Glasgow: Wardlaw and Cunningham.

Magri, Gennaro, I.E. Berry, and A. Fox. (1988). *Theoretical and Practical Treatise on Dancing:* London: Dance Books.

Martin, Martin. (1713). *A Description of the Western Islands of Scotland. Circa 1695.* 2nd ed. London: Andrew Bell.

Melin, Mats. (1997). *A Sutherland Dance, Compiled by Mats Melin.* Golspie: The Highland Council in association with the Scottish Arts Council. The Northern Times Ltd.

————. (2005). *"Putting the Dirt Back In"—Investigating Step Dancing in Scotland.* Unpublished MA thesis, University of Limerick, Ireland.

Bibliography 251

———. (2006). Unpublished research notes on observations on dance in Scotland 1985–2006. Melin personal archive. Limerick, Ireland.

———. (2012a). *Exploring the Percussive Routes and Shared Commonalities in Cape Breton Step Dancing*. Unpublished PhD thesis, University of Limerick, Ireland.

———. (2012b). Gendered Movements in Cape Breton Step Dancing, in *Proceedings of the 26th Symposium of the ICTM Study Group on Ethnochoreology 2010*. In *Dance, Gender, and Meanings: Contemporizing Traditional Dance*, Ed. E.I. Dunin, D. Stavelova, D. Gremlicova, and Z. Vejvoda. Trest, Czech Republic: Academy of Performing Arts in Prague; Institute of Ethnology of the Academy of Sciences, v.v.i. of the Czech Republic, Prague.

———. (2013a). Unpublished research notes on observations on dance in Cape Breton, Scotland and Ireland 2006–2013. Melin personal archive, Limerick, Ireland.

———. (2013b). Step Dancing in Cape Breton and Scotland: Contrasting Contexts and Creative Processes. *MUSICultures. Special Issue: Atlantic Roots and Routes*. Ed. Heather Sparling, Kati Szego, and Frances Wilkinson, 40(1), 35–56.

———. (2013c). Visual Learning in the 21st Century: Cape Breton Step Dance on the Small Screen and as a Learning Tool in the Dance Class. *Canadian Folk Music*, 46(4), 1–6.

———. (2015). *One With the Music: Cape Breton Step Dancing Tradition and Transmission*. Sydney, Canada: Cape Breton University Press.

———. (2017). Images, Voices, and Reflections on Cape Breton Step Dance Style. *Canadian Folk Music*, 49(2/3), 19–25.

———. (2018). *A Story to Every Dance. The Role of Lore in Enhancing the Scottish Solo Dance Tradition*. Limerick: Lorg Press.

———. (2019a). *Hebridean Step Dancing: The Legacy of Nineteenth-Century Dancing Master Ewen MacLachlan. Tales, Histories, and Descriptions of Ten Solo Dances from South Uist and Barra*. Limerick: Lorg Press.

———. (2019b). A Favourite Scotch Measure: the Relationship Between a Group of Scottish Solo Dances and the Tune 'The Flowers of Edinburgh. In *Òn gCos Go Cluas— From Dancing to Listening*. Ed. Liz Doherty and Vallely, Fintan, Vol. 5. Aberdeen: Elphinstone Institute, University of Aberdeen.

———. (forthcoming 2021). *Dancie John Reid of Newtyle: Notes on His Life as a Dancing Master, Including Extracts of Several Solo Dances from His Repertoire*. Limerick: Lorg Press.

Melish, John. (1812). *Travels in the United States of America, in the Years 1806 & 1807, and 1809, 1810, & 1811: Including an Account of Passages Betwixt America and Britain, and Travels Through Various Parts of Great Britain, Ireland, and Upper Canada; Illustrated by Eight Maps*. Philadelphia, US: author, and for sale.

Merriam Webster Dictionary. https://www.merriam-webster.com/

Mhàrtainn, Cairistìona. (2000). *Tog Fonn 2: Òrain Is Puirt Dannsaidh Leabhar 2*. An t-Eilean Sgitheanach: Taigh na Teud.

Milhous, Judith. (2003). The Economics of Theatrical Dance in Eighteenth-Century London. *Theatre Journal*, 55(3), 481–508.

Milligan, Jean C. (1982). *Won't You Join the Dance?* London: Paterson.

Milligan, Jean C., and Donald G. MacLennan. (1950). *Dances of Scotland*. London: Max Parrish.

Mishler, Craig. (1993). *The Crooked Stovepipe. Athapaskan Fiddle Music and Square Dancing in Northeast Alaska and Northwest Canada*. Urbana and Chicago: University of Illinois Press.

Molloy, Maureen. (1991). *Those Who Speak to the Heart. The Nova Scotian Scots at Waipu 1854–1920*. Palmerston North, New Zealand: Dunmore Press Ltd.

Moore, Margaret. (1995). Scottish Step Dancing, Scotland's Dances. In *A Review of the 1994 Conference on the Diversity of the Scottish Traditions of Dance—25–26 October*. Albert Hall, Stirling: Scottish Arts Council.

252   Bibliography

Morer, Thomas, (1702). *A Short Account of Scotland*. London: Thomas Newborough.

Morrison, Cecily. (2003). Culture at the Core: Invented Traditions and Imagined Communities. Part 1: Identity Formation. *International Review of Scottish Studies, 28*, 3–21.

———. (2004). Culture at the Core: Invented Traditions and Imagined Communities. Part 2: Community Formation. *International Review of Scottish Studies, 29*, 49–71.

Morrison, Fiona (2015). *The Development of Oban as a Tourist Resort 1770–1901*. PhD thesis, Poole, England: Bournemouth University.

Murray, Linda. (1994). Stepdancing makes its return journey across the Atlantic. *West Highland Free Press*. 5 August 1994.

Nevile, Jennifer. (2008). *Dance, Spectacle, and the Body Politick 1250–1750*. Bloomington and Indianapolis: Indiana University Press.

New Zealand Academy of Highland and National Dancing, Inc. (1989). *Syllabus of Technique for the Sailor's Hornpipe Exam. Stage 1. 1989.*

———. (1989). *Syllabus of Technique for the Sailor's Hornpipe Exam. Stage 2. 1989.*

———. (1989). *Syllabus of Technique for Irish Step Dancing Examination. Stage 2.*

Newton, Michael S. (2000). An Introduction to the Gaelic Musical Tradition. Electric Scotland: http://www.electricscotland.com/history/literat/GAELICTRAD.HTM [Accessed 4 April 2020].

———. (2009). *Warriors of the Word: the World of the Scottish Highlanders*. Edinburgh: Birlinn.

———. (2013). 'Dannsair Air ùrlar-déile thu': Gaelic Evidence About Dance from the Mid-17th to Late-18th Century Highlands. *International Review of Scottish Studies, 38*, 49–78.

———. (2015). *Keeping it Reel: The Origins of the Reel in a Scottish Gaelic Context*. Unpublished paper, Available on Academia.edu: https://www.academia.edu/12364911/Keeping_it_Reel_The_Origins_of_the_Reel_in_a_Scottish_Gaelic_Context

———. (2019). *The Earliest Gaelic Dances*. https://www.academia.edu/7061946/The_Earliest_Gaelic_Dances [Accessed 29 April 2020].

Ni Bhriain, Orfhlaith. (2006). *The Institutionalisation of Competitive Irish Step Dance*. Paper presented at the Dance Research Forum Ireland—First International Conference, Limerick, Ireland: University of Limerick.

———. (2008). *The Terminology of Irish Dance*. Madison: Macater Press.

———. (2010). *An Examination of the Creative Processes in Competitive Irish Step Dance*. PhD thesis, University of Limerick, Limerick.

Nicholson, John. (1843). *Historical and Traditional Tales in Prose and Verse: Connected with the South of Scotland. Original and Select*. Kirkcudbright: John Nicholson.

Nicol, Wilson. (2005). Francis Peacock—Aberdeen Dancing Master c.1723–1807. *The Reel, No 254*. London Branch of the RSCDS.

O'Donnell, Shiobhan. A. (1998). *Dancing at the Auld Cale. A History of Highland Dancing in Dunedin between 1863 and 1900*. BA Honours in History thesis, University of Otago, Dunedin, New Zealand.

O'Keeffe, J.G., and Art. O'Brien. (1914 [1902]). *A Handbook of Irish Dances*. 2nd ed. Dublin: M.H. Gill & Son Ltd.

Oswald, James. (1745). *The Caledonian Pocket Companion Containing Fifty of the Most Favourite Scotch Tunes Several of Them With Variations, All Set for the German Flute*. London: J. Simpson.

Oxford Dictionary of English. https://www.oxfordreference.com

Paton, Jeanie. (1994). Letter correspondence with Mats Melin, Christchurch, New Zealand, 2 August.

Peacock, Francis. (1762). *Fifty Favourite Scotch Airs. For a Violin, German Flute, and Violoncello. With a Thorough Bass for the Harpsichord, etc.* Aberdeen: Francis Peacock.

———. (1805). *Sketches Relative to the History and Theory, but More Especially to the Practice and Art of Dancing … Intended as Hints to the Young Teachers of the Art of Dancing. By Francis Peacock …* Aberdeen: J. Chalmers & Co.

Pearce, Gilbert L. (1976). *The Scots in New Zealand.* Auckland: Collins.

Pennant, Thomas. (2000 [1771]). *A Tour in Scotland 1769.* Edinburgh: Birlinn Limited.

Petrov, Susanne. (2017). Conversation with Jen Schoonover, Watertown, Massachusetts. 27 February.

Pforsich, Janis (2004). Hornpipe. In *The International Encyclopedia of Dance.* Ed. Selma Jeanne Cohen and the Dance Perspectives Foundation. Oxford: Oxford University Press.

Pike, Kenneth. (1954). *Language in Relation to a Unified Theory of the Structures of Human Behavior.* Glendale, California: Summer Institute of Linguistics.

Pinewoods Camp. 1952 archives, Plymouth, Massachusetts.

Porter, James. (1998). *Folklore of Northern Scotland: Five Discourses on Cultural Representataion.* Oxford: Taylor and Francis.

Quigley, Colin. (2008). Step Dancing in Canada: From Shared Vernacular to Regional Styles. In *Close to the Floor—Irish Dance From the Boreen to Broadway.* Ed. Mick Moloney, J'aime Morrison, and Colin Quigley. Madison: Macater Press.

Ramsay, Allan. (1794 [1724]). *The Tea-Table Miscellany: A Collection of Choice Songs, Scots and English.* Dublin: Brett Smith.

Rea, Frederick G. (1964). In *A School in South Uist. Reminiscences of a Hebridean Schoolmaster, 1890–1913.* Chapter 9. Ed. John Lorne Campbell. London: Routledge and Kegan Paul.

———. (1997). In *A School in South Uist. Reminiscences of a Hebridean Schoolmaster, 1890–1913.* 2nd ed. Ed. John Lorne Campbell. Edinburgh: Birlinn Limited.

Reid, John. (1935). 'Solo Dances/John Reid, Newtyle.' Melin personal archives, Limerick, Ireland.

Rhodes, Frank. (1976). Thomas Muirhead Flett 1923–1976. *Folk Music Journal, 3*(2), 186–187.

———. (1985 [1964]). Dancing in Cape Breton Island, Nova Scotia. In *Traditional Dancing in Scotland.* J.F. Flett and T.M. Flett. London: Routledge and Kegan Paul.

———. (1996). Step Dancing in Cape Breton Island, Nova Scotia. In *Traditional Step Dancing in Scotland.* J.F. Flett and T.M. Flett. Edinburgh: Scottish Cultural Press.

Rinehart, Adam Paul. (2017). French Society Abroad: The Popularization of French Dance Throughout Europe, 1600–1750. *Musical Offerings, 8* (2), Article 3.

Robertson, Colin. (1982). *Hard Shoe Step Dancing in Scotland and The Flowers of Edinburgh.* Reading: Scottish National Dance Company.

Robertson, James Stewart (1884). *The Athole Collection of the Dance Music of Scotland.* Edinburgh: Maclachlan and Stewart.

Robson, Marion. (2010). *Dallum's Fancy Footwork.* Email correspondence with Mats Melin, Laurencekirk, Scotland, 13 September.

Rogers, Ellis. (2002). *Five Basic Quadrilles. Three French and Two Scottish Quadrilles of the Early 19th Century.* Orpington: Ellis Rogers.

———. (200   8 [2003]). *The Quadrille.* 4th ed. Orpington: C. and E. Rogers.

Ross, Alexander. (1778). *Helenore, or the Fortunate Shepherdess.* 2nd ed. Aberdeen: J. Chalmers.

Ross, Alexander. (1974 [1895]). *Scottish Home Industries. A Reprint of an Account Written by Provost Alexander Ross of Inverness in 1895.* Glasgow: Molendinar Press.

254 *Bibliography*

Royal Scottish Country Dance Society. (2009). *The St Andrews Collection of Step Dances.* Vol 1. Edinburgh: RSCDS.

———. (2009). *Scottish Country Dancer Magazine.* Edinburgh: RSCDS.

———. (2010). *The St Andrews Collection of Step Dances.* Vol 2. Edinburgh: RSCDS.

Royal Scottish Official Board of Highland Dancing. (2018). *Highland Dancing. Textbook of the RSOBHD.* 8th ed. Glasgow: Lindsay Publications.

Russell, Colin. (2014). *Who Made the Scottish Enlightenment?* Bloomington, IN: Xlibris Corporation.

Scott Skinner, James. (1905). *The People's Ball-Room Guide.* Dundee and London: John Leng and Co., Ltd.

Scottish Dance Teachers' Alliance. (1991). *The Scottish National Dances.* 8th ed. Glasgow: SDTA.

Scottish Official Highland Dancing Association. (1995). *The Technical Committee of the SOHDA: Leaflets on Highland and National Solo Dances—The Earl of Erroll.* Edinburgh: SOHDA.

Seibert, Brian. (2015). *What the Eye Hears: a History of Tap Dancing.* New York: Farrar, Straus, and Giroux.

Self, Susan. (2002). Scottish Dance: Towards a Typological-Historical Approach. *Studi Celtic—Italian Celtic Studies Journal, 1,* 205–236.

Sharp, Cecil. (1911). *The Morris Book IV.* London: Novello.

Shaw, John. (1992/1993). Language, Music and Local Aesthetics. Views from Gaeldom and Beyond. *Scottish Language, edited by J. Derrick McClure, Association for Scottish Literary Studies, 11/12,* 37–61.

Shears, Barry. (2008). *Dance to the Piper.* Halifax: Nimbus Publishing.

Sinclair, Archibald/Mac-na-ceàrdadh, Gilleasbuig. (1879). *The Gaelic Songster. An t-Oranaiche; no co-thional taghte do Òrain Ùr agus shean a' chuid mhòr dhiubh nach robh riamh roimhe ann an clò.* Glasgow: Archibald Sinclair.

Sinclair, Catherine. (1840). *Shetland and the Shetlanders, or the Northern Circuit.* New York: Appleton and Company.

Sklar, Deidre. (2008). Remembering Kinesthesia: An Inquiry into Embodied Cultural Knowledge. In *Migrations of Gesture.* Ed. C. Noland and S.A. Ness. Minneapolis: University of Minnesota Press.

Smith, Orma. (1990). Typescript of descriptions for the Waltz Clog and Melbourne Clog. Melin personal archive, Limerick, Ireland.

Smout, Thomas C. (1986). *A Century of the Scottish People 1830–1950.* London: Fontana Press.

———. (1990). *A History of the Scottish People 1560–1830.* London: Fontana Press.

Smythe, W. (1830). *A Pocket Companion Containing the Directions for the Performance of Quadrilles, Scotch, English, Irish, French and Spanish Country Dances, Reels, etc.* 2nd ed. Edinburgh: J. Glass.

Spalding, Susan Eike. (2014). *Appalachian Dance: Creativity and Continuity in Six Communities.* Urbana: University of Illinois Press.

Spalding, Susan Eike, and Woodside, Jane Harris (Eds.). (1995). *Communities in Motion. Dance, Community, and Tradition in America's Southeast and Beyond.* Westport: Greenwood Press.

Sparling, Heather L. (2000). *Puirt-A-Beul: An Ethnographic Study of Mouth Music in Cape Breton.* (Master of Arts), York, Toronto.

———. (2003). 'Music is Language and Language is Music': Language Attitudes and Musical Choices in Cape Breton, Nova Scotia. *Ethnologies, 25*(2), 145–171.

———. (2005). *Song Genres, Cultural Capital and Social Distinctions in Gaelic Cape Breton*. PhD thesis, York University, Toronto.

———. (2011). Cape Breton Island: Living in the Past? Gaelic Language, Song, and Competition. In *Island Songs: A Global Repertoire*. Ed. G. Baldacchino. Lanham and Toronto: Scarecrow Press.

———. (2014). *Reeling Roosters and Dancing Ducks: Celtic Mouth Music*. Sydney, NS: Cape Breton University Press.

———. (2015). History of the Scotch Four: A Social Step Dance in Cape Breton. *Canadian Folk Music 49* (2/3) (Summer/Fall).

———. (2018). Squaring Off: The Forgotten Caller in Cape Breton Square Dancing. *Yearbook for Traditional Music*, 50, 165–186.

St. John, Charles. (1884 [1849]). *A Tour in Sutherlandshire: With Extracts from the Field-Books of a Sportsman and Naturalist*. Vol. 1. Edinburgh: David Douglas.

Stapleton, Anne McKee. (2014). *Pointed Encounters: Dance in Post-Culloden Scottish Literature*. Amsterdam: Rodopi.

Stearns, Marshall and Jean Stearns. (1994 [1968]). *Jazz Dance: The Story of American Vernacular Dance*. New York: Da Capo Press.

Stenhouse, William. Ed. (1839 [*c.* 1820]). Museum Illustrations. In *The Scots Musical Museum*. Eds. James Johnson and David Laing. Edinburgh: William Blackwood and Sons.

Stewart, Charles. (*c.* 1798–1801). *A Collection of Strathspeys, Reels, Giggs, etc.* Edinburgh.

Stewart, Tim. (2000). 'The Pipes Play on.' Canadian Pipers at War, 1914–1918. An Inspired Tradition. *Canadian Military History*, 9(4), 57–64.

Sutton, Julia. (2004). Canary. In *International Encyclopedia of Dance*. Ed. S.J. Cohen. Vol. 2. Oxford: Oxford University Press.

Taylor, G. Douglas. (1935 [1929]). *Some Traditional Scottish Dances*. 2nd ed. London: Imperial Society of Teachers of Dancing.

T B.—Dance book. Lowe family: Dance manuscripts. (1826). Ref: MSX-2895. Alexander Turnbull Library, Wellington, New Zealand./records/23231219. http://natlib.govt.nz/records/23231219

Terry, Walter. (1979). *The King's Ballet Master: A Biography of Denmark's August Bournonville*. New York: Dodd, Mead, and Company.

Thomas, Allan, Ed. (1992). *A New Most Excellent Dancing Master: the Journal of Joseph Lowe's Visits to Balmoral and Windsor (1852–1860) to Teach the Family of Queen Victoria*. Dance and Music Series No. 5. Stuyvesant, NY: Pendragon Press.

Thornton, Col. Thomas. Ed. (1804; 1896). *A Sporting Tour Through the Northern Parts of England and the Great Part of the Highlands of Scotland*. London: Arnold. Republished in 1896 in the Sporting Library.

Thurston, Hugh. (1984 [1954]). *Scotland's Dances*. Kitchener: Teachers' Association of Canada.

Topham, Edward. (1776). *Letters from Edinburgh Written in the Years 1774 and 1775*. London: J. Dodsley.

Tubridy, Michael. (2018 [1998]). *A Selection of Irish Traditional Step Dances*, Dublin: Brooks Academy.

UNESCO. (2003). UNESCO's convention for the safeguarding of the *Intangible Cultural Heritage*. https://ich.unesco.org/en/convention

United Kingdom Alliance of Professional Teachers of Dancing. (2012). *The UKA Highland, National, and Hebridean Book*. Blackpool: UKAPTD.

Victorian Scottish Union. (1974). *National Games and Pastimes*. Victoria, Australia.

———. (n.d.). *National Games and Pastimes*. Victoria, Australia. Revised edition, probably from late 1980s.

256   *Bibliography*

———. (n.d. 1980s?). *The Theory of the Irish Jig.* Victoria, Australia. Extract out of a larger undated manuscript, no publication name or date on copy.

Wake, Lady Charlotte. (1909). *The Reminiscences of Charlotte, Lady Wake.* Ed. Lucy Wake. Edinburgh: William Blackwood and Sons.

Wallace, J.F. (1881). *People's Edition of the 'Excelsior' Manual of Dancing, Etc.* Glasgow: W. Watson.

Walker, William. (1883). *The Life and Times, The Rev John Skinner of Linshart, Longside, author of 'Tullochgorum,' etc.* London: W. Skeffington & Son.

Whitta, Kim. (*c.* 1982). *Scottish Highland Dance—Tradition and Style.* MA thesis, Queen's University of Belfast.

Wilson, Thomas. (1811). *An analysis of country dancing, wherein all the figures used in that polite amusement are rendered familiar by engraved lines. Containing also, directions for composing almost any number of figures to one tune, with some entire new reels; together with the complete etiquette of the ball-room. By T. Wilson ...*; London, J. S. Dickson.

———. (1815). *Complete System of English Country Dancing.* London: Sherwood, Neeley, and Jones.

———. (1824). *The Danciad, or Dancer's Monitor.* London: T. Wilson.

Newspapers and Magazines

Aberdeen Press and Journal. 1782, 1783, 1805, 1907, 1909, 1933, and 1948.

Banffshire Journal and General Advertiser. 1850.

Belfast Chronicle. 1841.

Caledonian Mercury. 1745, 1772, 1785, 1795, and 1817.

Clansman. 1993.

Dancing: A journal devoted to the terpsichorean art, physical culture and fashionable entertainments. Facsimile reprint of issues originally published June 1891–May 1893. Toronto: Press of Terpsichore Limited, 1984.

Edinburgh Dramatic Review. 1822, 1823 and 1825.

Edinburgh Evening Courant. 1832.

Elgin Courant and Morayshire Advertiser. 1849, 1850, and 1852.

Falkirk Herald. 1869.

Glasgow Herald. 1830.

Hamilton Advertiser. 1864.

Motherwell Times. 1909, 1919, and 1921.

Newcastle Courant. 1734.

Notes and Queries. 1855.

Oban Times. 1923–1928.

Otago Daily Times. 1874.

Stonehaven Journal. 1871.

The Edinburgh Magazine: Or Literary Miscellany. 1800 and 1824.

Theatre-Royal Edinburgh. 1821.

West Highland Free Press. 1993 and 1994.

Index

General

Académie Royale de Danse 57
Act of Union 77
aesthetics, dance 8, 19, 21, 25, 27, 30–34,
   51–53, 56–58, 65, 131, 134, 139, 146,
   179, 195, 222, 232–233, 235, 237 (*see
   also* stylistic differences/shifts)
aisig-thrasd/aiseag-thrasd 105, **106–107**,
   109
anacrusis 67, 136, **151**, 157, 220–221,
   228
Appalachian dance (*see* Step dancing)
arm positions/movements 18, 35–36,
   51–53, 81, 88, 89, 127, 142, 144, 147,
   149, 150, 168, 169, 175, 193, 194, 204
assemblies 45, 59, 71–72, 78, 80, 86, 90,
   110, 114–115

backstep 126–127, 204, 212, **217**
backstep with a hop 97, 103, 108, **217**
bagpipes 32, 35, 48, 62, 65, 68, 69, 85,
   95, 101, 117, 121, 126, 131, 132, 137,
   138–139, 141–142, 145, 149, 151, 159,
   162, 163–164, 164–165, 168–169,
   176–177, 181, 182, 189, 192, 195, 203,
   205, 219
Ballet 30–34, 56, 70, 105, 110, 126–127,
   134–136, 142, 147, 174, 179, 184, 203,
   231; Romantic 132, 139
Ballroom dancing 27, 32, 45, 163, 165
bare feet 7, 17, 49–51, 61, 159
barns, dancing in 61, 96, 114, 118, 119,
   134–135, 140–141, 147, 149–150, 152,
   159, 178
Baroque dance 57, 133, 222
Basse Dances 71
batter 21, 51, 152, 159, 193, 213 (*see also*
   shuffle)

beat/double beat/beating 5, 13, 18,
   31–34, 41, 56, 85, 97, 110, 118–120,
   122–123, 125–126, 138–139, 140,
   145–146, 152, 154, 156–159, 169,
   174–176, 177, 179, 186, 188, 191, 193,
   195–196, 206, 211, 213, **214–215**, 217,
   220–221
biases/prejudices 3–7, 24, 53, 222
breabaidh (*see* kicking dance)
bridges, dancing on 192, 202, 205
Brig O'Tilt Meeting 132
British Association of Teachers' of
   Dancing (BATD) 29–30, 135–136,
   162
bròg/brògan/brogues (*see* shoes)
brush/brushing 17, 174, 176–177, 207,
   211–212, **214–216**
buckles, silver 2, 45, 53, 169

Caledonian steps 79
Calvinism 96
candles 95–96, 116, 120, 147, 161
Cape Breton Step dancing (*see* Step
   dancing)
capering 71, 99, 124, 128, 132, 158
catch in/catch out **13–14**, 146, 156–158
Ceilidh dancing 27, 48, 163
chassé 186, 188, 226
clappers (*see* shoes)
clapping 17–19, 59, 62, 64, 82, 152, 169,
   176, 190
Clearances, Scottish/Highland 101–102
cleek/cleekit 149, 159, **166**
Clogging (*see* Step dancing)
clogs (*see* shoes)
competitions, dancing 1–2, 24, 31, 37,
   46, 61, 115, 131, 137, 163, 171–172,
   193–195, 207, 211, 223

258   *Index*

complex inferiority 232–233
Comunn Gàidhleach, An 163
Country Dance Society of America 176
Country dances 13, 18–19, 27, 37, 48, 71–75, 78, 80, 81, 86, 88, 90, 97, 104, 106, 108, 118, 131, 158, 163, 178, 208, 220, 229, 233
coupé 72, 146
Court dancing 32, 56–57, 59, 60, 65
cross the buckle step 180
crossover step 180
crossroads, dancing at 202, 205
cuaran (*see* shoes)
cuartag **107**, 128

Dagenham Girls Pipe Band 168
dance, definition of 14–15
dance classes 15, 27, 45, 88, 115, 136, 147, 153–154, 167, 169, 177, 185
Dancie 14, **172**
Dancing Master (term/profession) 28, 58, 79, 103
dancing surfaces 41–42, 97, 205, 212, 214–216 (*see also* flooring)
dannsa breabaidh 15, **95**, 97, 216
dannsa-ceum 15 (*see also* Step dancing)
dialects 7, 21, 22, 29, 77, 143
diaspora, Scottish 25, 184–197
diddling 196 (*see also puirt a beul*)
double beat 31, 174
Double Triangles formation 34
dramatic jigs 78, 103, 115

échappé 133
elevation 15, 31, 41, 71, 110, 146, 199, 215, 218
emasculation 162
embodiment 6, 7, 19–20, 22–23, 39, 51, 220–221, 234–235, 237
emic (insider perspective) 6, 11
Enlightenment, Scottish 77–78
entr'acte 89, 116, 128
entrechats 30, 31, 107, **146**, 214
ethnochoreology 3, 8, 11, 14, 17 33, 56
etic (outsider perspective) 3, 4, 6, 11, 20, 37, 149, 174, 231, 232, 233
etiquette 112, 132

fashions, dance 3, 8, 19, 25, 27, 39, 45–46, 65, 71, 72, 74, 86, 88, 90, 91–92, 95–96, 100, 112–113, 121, 123, 128, 131–132, 165, 168, 175, 184, 189, 202, 232
Fèisean nan Gàidheal 236–238

fiddle 39, 59–60, 61, 83, 88, 91, 93, 112, 113, 118, 120, 121, 126, 140–141, 143, 149, 159, 163, 167, 168, 178, 181, 189–190, 205–206, 218–219, 235–236
Flamenco 19
flap 119, **215–216**
flatter 156, **157–158**, 159, 213
fleg 118–119, 128, **216**
fleup 118–**119**, 128
fling (motif) 38, 112, 137, 177, **216**
Floaters' ball 113
flooring 60, 152; dirt/earthen 7, 49, 61; sand 49, 94, 143, 203; Step-dancing stone 205; stone 7, 49, 61; wooden 7, 51, 59–62, 64–65
folklore **3**, 140, 192
foot anatomy 41–42
footing 97, 106, 138, 141, 166 (*see also* kemkóssy)
footwear (*see* shoes)
fosgladh 105, **107**, 133

Gaelic College (*see* Cape Breton Island, NS, St. Ann's)
Gàidhlig/Scottish Gaelic language (*see* Scotland in Places and Languages Index)
gender roles 31–32, 135
geographical labels 21
ghillies (*see* shoes)
Glasgow City Police Pipe Band 205
Glen Orchy [Orgue] kick 4, 12, 15, **91**, 95–96, 109, 121, 216
globalism 233
Gordon Highlanders 138, 162
grinds 195

hard-soled shoes (*see* shoes)
harmonica/harmonium (*see* mouthie)
harp 166–167
harvest home 91, 113, 119 (*see also* kirn)
Hebridean dancing 22, 171, 201
heel-and-toe steps 56, 112, 123, 216
heels 33, 41–42, 45–46, 48, 51–53, 56, 80–83, 97, 116, 121–122, 128, 139, 147, 151, 159, 163, 168, 182, 195, 212; calcaneus bone 41; heel rattle 123
heuch/heeuch 18, 28, 132, 159, 168, 230, hooch 153, 164, 182, 192, howl 18, 140, screams 178, shouts/shouting 30, 114, 142, 144, 152, 155, 168, 190, 206–207, yeeps 178, yeeuch 168, yelling 18, 132, 165, 166
High Dances 67, **71–73**, 87–89, 132, 153

Index 259

highcuts 31, 70, 108, 128–129
Highland and National Dancers' Association of Victoria 195
Highland dancing 1–2, 6, 22, 24, 27, 29–31, 33–34, 38–39, 41, 45–47, 91–92, 115, 116, 133, 137, 147, 155, 159, 162–163, 169, 174, 179, 187, 190, 193–194, 196, 202–203, 206, 211, 213, 215–218, 225
Highland dancing pumps (*see* shoes)
Highland Games 1, 2, 22, 30, 36, 37, 46, 48, 70, 132–133, 146, 162, 186, 209
Highland Society 112, 115, 125, 132
Highlanders 22, 42–43, 47, 77, 88, 89, 92–95, 110–113, 115, 125, 132, 142–143, 154
hop-brush-beat-beat 174, 179, **215**, 218; shar/*sèarr* 215, 218
hornpipe (tune type/time signature) **68–71**, 241; Jacky Tar 69, 195; double 67, 68–70,87; single 68–71; triple 68, 241
Hyland step 80–81

Imperial Society of Teachers of Dancing (ISTD) 147, 162, 168
improving dances 25, 30–31, 38–39, 175
improvisation 12, 16, 25, 28, 31, 36, 51, 53, 88, 90, 95, 111, 126, 166, 176, 188, 197, 204
Industrial Revolution 78, 101
insider perspective (*see emic*)
inverted positions 31, **155**, 169, 174–175
Irish National dancing (New Zealand) 193

Jacobitism 59, 77, 131
jaw/jew's harp 144
jeté/jetté 33, 117, 122, 146
jig/jigging (dancing) 41, 84, 105, 203, 207, 208; (tune type) 15, 73–75, 80, 90, 97, 121, 122, 174, 187, 221, 224, 226–227, 242 (*see also* Dance Titles Index)

kem Badenoch 107
kemkóssy/*ceum-coisiche* 105, **106**, 107–108
kemshóole/*ceumsiubhail* 23, **105–106**
kick/kick step/kicking dance 15, 64–65, 91, 95, 97, **109**, 117, 119, 127–128, 141, 150, 159, 176, 216, 218 (*see also* Glen Orchy kick)
kirk-shoon (*see* shoes)
kirn 113–114, 140–141, 149, 178 (*see also* harvest home)

knacking (*see* snapping)

Ladies' Step dancing (*see* Step dancing)
Laki haze 79, 98
legacies 23–25
lematrást/*leum-a-trasd* **106**, 110, 123
light/lightness 12, 14–15, 31–32, 49, 53, 73, 97, 112, 146, 151, 199, 207, 214–216, 218, 221, 231

migration 77, 85, 102
mime 103, 175
minuet (tune type) 239 (*see also* Dance Titles and Song/Tune Titles Indices)
motif (movement) 5, 7, **13–16**, 21, 24, 31, 33–34, 95–97, 107–109, 127, 133–137, 146–147, 151, 157–159, 169, 174, 176–177, 179, 196, 206, 208, 211–221, 224–227, **228**, 233, 234, 237
mouth music (*see puirt a beul*)
mouthie 166, 208

National dances 27, 86, 117, 133, 175
neat/neatness 62–63, 87–88, 112, 117, **218**
New Zealand Academy 29–31, 170, 193–195, 218
notation of dancing 6, 57, 58, 69, 108–109, 136, 137, 146, 157–158, 212, 220, 233–234

Old Time/Old Tyme dancing 27, 39, 48, 163
onomatopoeia 6, **211–220**
orthography 3, 47, 106, 122, 133, 161
outsider perspective (*see etic*)

pas bas 34
pas de Basque 19, **33–34**, 109, 146, 177, 191
Pas Seul 67–70, **73–74**, 116, 122, 134
patent leather dancing shoes (*see* shoes)
Pell's Ethiopian Minstrels 152
percussive qualities, 6, 31, 49, 62, 188, 197, 207, 211–217, 237
Peter a Dick's Peatstack 118, 216
pigeon-toed fashion 175 (*see also* inverted positions)
Piping and Dancing Association of New Zealand 195
playbills 59, 70, 90, 116, 139, 224
poetry 62, 78, 93, 125, 140
pointe 31, 33, 127, 139, 203
posture 51–53, 56, 88
puirt a beul/mouth music 49, 114, 188, 191, **218**, 219, 223

260   *Index*

rally/raleigh 213 (*see also* shuffle)
rant (tune type/time signature) 67, 70, **75**
Rant step 75, 221, 228
rattling 14, 19, 71, 123, 124, 128, 168, 182
reel (dance motif/pathway) 6, 13, 14, 18, 25, 35, 61, 64, 72, 73, **74–75**, 86–87, 96–97, 124–125, 142–143, 149, 153, 159, 167–168, 186–187, Quartett 110, Trio 110; (tune type/time signature) 15–16, 35, 70, **74–75**, 83, 114, 121–122, 145, 150, 151, 186–187, 206–208, 217, 221, 223–224, 226–227, 241
Reelers/Reeling 19, 27, 48, 163, 176, 223, **229**
refinement 25, 30–32, 45, 60, 65, 74, 128, 132, 164, 169, 233, 236
rhythm 2, 12, 13, 14, 17, 19–20, 28–29, 41, 42, 51, 57–59, 67–70, 80, 82–83, 86, 108–109, 115, 136–138, 142, 154, 165, 176, 186, 188, 197, 199, 206, 211–221, 230
Riverdance 39
Rob Roy (play) 22, 139
rock/rocking step 123, 146, 169, strocks 80
ronde de jambe 146, 174
Royal Celtic Society 170–171
Royal Scottish Country Dance Society (RSCDS) 1–2, 5–9, 27–28, 32–36, 48, 53, 80, 133–136, 163, 176, 232–233
Royal Scottish Official Board of Highland Dancing (RSOBHD) 1–2, 9, 12, 23–24, 27, 31, 34, 36–38, 53, 134, 162, 175, 193, 233

schools, dancing 30, 49, 68, 72, 80, 88, 90, 96–97, 104, 120, 135, 141, 162, 193, 203, 218, 233, 235–236
Scotch/Scots/Scottish measure (tune type/time signature) 16, **67–69**, 73, 90, 180, 242 (*see also* Scotch Measure in Dance Titles Index)
Scots language (*see* Scotland in Places and Languages Index)
Scottish Country dancing 1–2, 6, 8–9, 12, 18–19, 29, 32–35, 37, 39, 40, 45, 48, 75, 146, 162–163, 164, 179, 231, 232
Scottish Dance Teachers' Alliance (SDTA) 135–136, 162
Scottish Gaelic language (*see* Scotland in Places and Languages Index)
Scottish National dancing 134
Scottish Official Highland Dancing Association (SOHDA) 1, 11, 27, 31, 162

Scottish Step dancing (*see* Step dancing)
Scottish Traditions of Dance Trust (STDT) 160, 180, 208–209, 210, 237
scruffle/scruffling 207–208, 217
seby-trast/*siabadh-trasd* **106**–107, 133
segmentation 15–16, 221–227
shallie **133**, 136
shar/*sèarr* (*see* hop-brush-beat-beat)
shoes: *bròganⁱ*/brogues 15, 42–44, 47, 50, 52, 53, 55, 63, 91–92, 94, 117, 128; clappers 118, 209, clogs 50, 51, 118, 135; *cuaran* 42–43, 44; ghillies 2, 46–48, 136, 180, 211; hard-soled/hard-shoe 2, 5–6, 7, 16, 17, 21, **48**, 50–53, 59, 61, 116, 127, 136, 139, 153, 177, 179–180, 193, 196, 211, 213; Highland dancing pumps 2, 45, 46–47, 169, 211; historical 41–51; kirk-shoon 118; light shoes 46; outdoor shoes 46, 48; patent leather dancing shoes 46; pumps **42–43**, 91–92, 118, 136, 209; slippers, dancing 2, 45, 46, 127, 145, 159, 189; soft-soled shoes 2, 6, 16, 17, 46–48, 50, 53, 61, 92, 134–136, 141, 169, 177, 179, 195, 203, 211; tackety boots 14, 46, 153, 159, 178, 209
shout (*see* heuch/heuching)
shuffles/shuffling 3, 12, **14**, 19, 21, 31, 49, 50, 51, 53, 71, 80, 91, 95, 97, 111–112, 116, 119, 122–123, 124, 127, 132, 138–139, 141, 145, 149, 150, 151, 153, 154, 158–159, 174, 177, 178, 179, 182, 187–188, 195, 196, 203, 204, 206, 208, 211, **212–213**, 217, 220–221
sissonne 106, **110**, 123
skiff **174**, 177, 217
skip/skipping 18, 32, 83, **97**, 99, 116, 140, 217
slide/sliding 45, 56, 138, 146, 174, 214
slippers (*see* shoes)
snapping 3, 18–19, 30, 46, 64, 113, 114, 128, 132, 140, 144, 164, 168, 176, 230; knacking 18, 81, 144
social dancing 2, 6, 8–9, 13–14, 18, 27–28, 32–34, 46, 48, 90, 101, 108, 124, 133, 163, 164–166, 167, 176–177, 179, 181, 197, 223, 233
soft-soled shoes (*see* shoes)
soundscape 17, 28, 41, 50, 92 (*see also* percussive qualities)
stamps/stamping 56, 61, 114, 118, 127, 128, 142, 149, 159, 174, 176, 178, 195, 206, 208, 217
step, definitions 15–17

Index 261

Step dancing **17**, 20–21, 49, 51–53, 73, 80–82, 88, 95, 155–156, 163–164, 167, 169–170, 178–179, 179–180, 230–232, 237; African style 51, 196; Appalachian clogging 51, 196–197; Australian 191, 196; Cape Breton 8–9, 15, 20, 21, 22, 38, 39, 41, 51–53, 95, 108–109, 181, 186, 188–189, 200–201, 202, 203, 210, 213, 216, 217, 218, 219, 231, 235, 236, 237; Clogging 21, 196; English 108, 136, 207, 218; First Nations/Native American 196, 206–207; Irish 51, 56, 108, 136, 193, 213, 228, 231; Ladies' 134; North Kerry 21, 22; Scottish xi, 15, 27, 36–39, 48, 110, 181, 232, 236–237; *Sean nós* 21, 51, 204, 218, 221, 228
stereotypes 3, 18, 22, 31–32, 38–39, 70, 89, 117
stone for Step dancing (*see* flooring)
strathspey (dance type) 16, 18, 35, 73, 97, 108–109, 112, 114, 123, 149, 187, (tune type) 15, 70, 74, 75, 121, 137, 150–151, 187, 206, 223, 225, 226, 240
stylistic differences/shifts 2, 7, 34, 56, 234, labels 21 (*see also* aesthetics, dance)

tacht with the music 143
tackety boots (*see* shoes)
Tap dancing 17, 41, 152, 196, 199–200, 203
tap/tapping 64, 168, 174, 176, 179, 182, 188, 206, 215, 216
tartan 95
tartanism/tartanry 3, 131, 192
Tea dancing 163 (*see also* Old Time/Old Tyme dancing)
teachers, dance 5, 7, 9, 15, 21, 27, 28, 29, 30–31, 33–34, 37–38, 72, 78, 79, 92–93, 104, 126, 129, 134–135, 136, 146–147, 153–154, 158, 160, 162, 163, 164, 165, 166, 168, 170, 171–172, 175–176, 176–177, 179, 181, 185, 195, 200–201, 202, 203, 211–212, 213, 215–216, 217, 230, 231, 235, 237
terminology, dance 5–6, 7, 67, 80, 105, 108, 117, 119, 123, 127, 133, 136, 146, 150, 156, 158, 174, 188, 196, 211–218
thumping 38, 59, 61, 113, 117, 127–128, 145
toe-and-heel 41
tradition/traditions xi–xii, 1, 2, 8, 13, 20, 21, 24, 30–31, 33, 37–39, 41, 44,

48, 55, 95, 111, 117, 120, 122, 128, 131, 134, 136, 147, 162, 166, 169, 176, 180, 181, 184, 186, 188, 189, 193, 194, 195, 196, 197, 199, 204, 207, 211, 213, 215, 216, 217, 219, 221, 222, 225, 230, 231–233, 235, 236, tradition vs. legacies **23–25**
Traditional Dance Forum of Scotland 182
transmission xi, 6, 7, 20, 23, 25, 138, 146, 218, 224, 233, 235
treble 71, 110, 119, 136–**137**, 138, 139, 141, **156–159**, **173**–174, 180, 182, 212, **213–214**, 215, 221, 230, treeple/treepling **13–14**, 19, 48, 71, 118–119, 132, 149–150, 153, 159, 178–179, 182, 186, 213, 230, trible 118–119, triple/tripples 14, 67, 119, 174, 182, 196, 213–214
triple time signatures 68–69, 70, 90, 133, 213, 220–221, 239

UNESCO 24–25
United Kingdom Alliance of Professional Teachers' of Dancing (UKA) 135–136, 155, 162
urbanisation 77, 101–102

vernacular 2, 16, 20–25, 32, 35, 39, 59, 101, 126, 191, 195–196, 197, 215, 218, 220, 221–222, 223, 235, *term* defined **22–23**
verticality, posture 51–53
Victorian Scottish Union 29, 142, 195

Women's Rural Institute 32, 162
wooden floors (*see* flooring)
World Wars 32, 162; First 46, 162; Second 35, 158, 195

yeeps/yeeuch/yell/yelling/yelping 18, 132, 165, 168, 178 (*see also* heuch/heuching)

Dance titles

Aberdonian Lassie 146, 178, 224, 227
Allemande 72, 86
America 85

Baden Powell, The 176, 206
Barn Dance 202
Barracks Johnnie 137–138 (*see also* Wilt Thou Go to the Barricks, Johnnie)
Belile's March 118

262 *Index*

Big Boot Step dancing 170
Blue Bonnets/*Bonaid Ghorm* 70, 133, 165, 217, 223, 225, 227
Blue Bonnets Over the Border 171, 217
Bob-at-the-Bolster/Bobadybouster 168
Bonnie Dundee 174
Borello 118
Boston Two-Step 167
Bride's Reel 167–168
Buck dancing 170, 182
Bumpkin Brawley 118

Cailleach an Dùdain/Old Woman of the Milldust 120, 175
Call to the Piper/Call of the Pipes 176
Canario/Canary 56
Clare Battering 21
Clog Hornpipe 116, 178, 194, 203;
Clog Hornpipe in Real Fetters 166
Clumpie 206, 217
College Hornpipe 132, 277
Cotillon/Cotillion 61, 72, 78, 87–88, 97, 118, 131
Courante 58, 75
Crait an Dreathan/The Wren's Croft 103
Cut the Buckle 113
Cut-Along 61

Dallum's Fancy Footwork 208
Damhsa an Chleoca/The Cloak Dance 102, 120
Damhsa nam Boc/The Buck or Billygoat's Dance 103
Dance of the Bonny Highlanders 133
Dannsa Breabaidh/Kicking Dance 15, 95, 97, 216
Dannsa grad-charach 69, 129 (*see also* Hornpipe)
Dannsa nam Flurs 17, 36, 220, 223, 226–227 (*see also* Flowers of Edinburgh)
Dashing White Serjeant 133
Davonshire Minuet 72
Dirk Dance 108, 138
Double Irish Jig 194
Double-time Jig 193
Drops of Brandy hornpipe 195
Duke of Fife 186
Duke of Perth 27, 229
Dusty Miller 68–69, 132, 136–138, 225, 227

Earl of Erroll 13, 110, 132–136, 151, 180, 212–213, 221, 227
East Fife Clog Hornpipe 178

Eightsome Reel 19, 118, 167, 229
English Hornpipe 123
Esparano 167

Falderallo 118
Fandango 99
Fidh an Gunn/Weaving or Knitting of the Gown 103
Fife Liverpool Hornpipe 178
First of August 13, 16–17, 146, 165, 170, 174, 178, 180–181, 213, 216, 224–227, 234
Fisherwife, The 181
Flora MacDonald's Fancy 134, 212
Flowers of Edinburgh/Flowers of Edinburgh Hornpipe 13, 21, 48, 118, 132, 136, 165, 173, 175, 178–179, 181, 186–188, 213, 220, 223–227
Foxtrot 27

Galliard 65
Gallopade 73
Gay Gordons 177
German Waltz 73
Gigue Brandy/*Grande Gigue Simple* 221
Gille Chaluim (*see* Sword Dance)
Gilli-Callum over a fiddle bow 126
Girl I Left Behind Me, The 186
Graces, The 134
Guaracha 117

Haka 142
Halling 19
Hamilton House 229
Highland Fling/Fling 17, 21–22, 27, 29, 36–38, 61, 70, 73, 89, 96, 110–113, 117–118, 123, 126, 137, 167–169, 175, 177, 180, 186, 192–193, 211–212, 216, 220, 223, 225, 227
Highland Laddie/Hielan' Laddie 67, 123, 133, 146, 155, 165, 169, 174–175, 212, 223, 225, 227
Highland Strathspey 88, 114
Home Style Irish Jig 196
Hooper's Jig 176
Hornpipe 17, 59, 67–75, 80–81, 86–92, 95–97, 110, 116–118, 121–124, 132–139, 159, 163, 172–173, 180, 187, 194–195, 221, 224–227
Hornpipe in Fetters 116
Hornpype from New Zealand, A 181

Imperial Waltz 167
Irish Double Jig 195, 211

Irish Hornpipe 193–194
Irish Jig 12, 22, 133, 158, 167, 170, 173, 182, 193–196, 208, 211, 213, 215, 217, 224, 227
Irish Jig and Reel 195
Irish Reel 195, 211
Irish Shauntreuse 122
Irish Single Jig 194, 211
Irish Washerwoman 186–187

Jack on the Green 118
Jacky Tar/Jacky Tar Hornpipe/Jacky Tar step 27, 48, 64, 70, 173, 178, 186–187, 195, 208

Kerry Jig 194
King of Sweden 36, 110, 119, 132, 134, 136, 180, 227

La Varsovienne 27
Lilt 89, 225
Liverpool Hornpipe 178, 187
Lusan Dhun Èideann 228 (*see also* Flowers of Edinburgh)

Marquis of Huntly's Highland Fling 27, 133, 180, 225
Mary Grey 118
Mazourka 27, 74
Melbourne Clog 194–195
Milanie's Hornpipe 117, 124
Minuet 58–59, 61, 72–75, 78, 86–88, 90, 96–97, 100, 104, 131, 138
Miss Forbes 146, 165, 172, 212
Miss Gayton's Hornpipe 71
Morpeth Rant 221
Mrs. B's Waltz 124

National Pas Seul 116

Over the Hills and Far Away 13, 175, 220, 223, 227
Over the Water 146, 170
Over the Water to Charlie 155, 165 169, 171, 181, 212, 215, 224–227

Parazotti 191
Pas Quatre 123
Petronella 48, 158, 178, 230
Pigeon Wing 113 (*see also* highcuts in the General Index)
Polka 27, 101, 165, 167
Prince of Orange 176
Prince of Wales Minuet 72

Princess Royal 19, 72, 176, 186–187

Quadrille 18, 73–74, 100–102, 114, 118, 135, 153, 163, 167; Caledonian 101; Lancers 101
Quadrille Country Dance, 27
Quickstep 27

Red River Jig 206
Reel 25, 28, 35, 37, 74–75, 80, 85–90, 105, 111, 117, 139, 143, 149–151, 153, 159, 164–166, 186–187, 223–226
Reel of Four/Quartett 35, 101
Reel of the 51st Division 229
Reel of Three/Trio 110
Reel of Tulloch 73, 123–124, 132, 150, 223
Rock and the Wee Pickle Tow 120
Roley Poley 117
Rowly-Powly 61
Ruidhle nam Pòg 50

Sailor Hornpipe Old Style 224
Sailor's Hornpipe 12–13, 69–70, 114, 127, 155, 158, 170, 187, 193–195, 208, 212–213, 217
Sand Dance 49, 170, 182, 203
Sand Jig 49
Schottische 27, 167, 170, 202; German 101; Highland 101, 176–179
Schuhplattler 19
Scotch Blue Bonnets 165
Scotch Blue Bonnets Over the Border 171
Scotch Dance 85, 89, 100, 116
Scotch Four 182, 192, 223
Scotch Measure 67–69, 89–90, 133–134, 146, 178
Scotch Reel 35
Scotch Shauntreuse 123
Scotchmakers 165, 172, 183, 227
Scots Blue Bonnets 227
Seann Triubhas 19, 21, 36–37, 70, 110, 117–118, 123, 168–169, 174–175, 186–187, 191–193, 212–213, 216, 220, 223–224, 227; Shantruish 133, 227; Shantruse 128; Shauntreuse 122–124; Shawintrewse 118; Shean Trews 112
Shetland Reel 207–208
Shillelagh Jig 196
Single-time Jig 194
Skipping Rope Pas Seul 116
Smàladh na Coinnle/Smooring the Candle 147
Strathspey Minuet 59

264   *Index*

Strathspey Reel 59
Strathspey/Straspae 18, 35, 59, 86, 89, 95, 112, 126, 149–150, 223
Strathspeys over a rope 126
Sweden's March 118–119 (*see also* King of Sweden)
Sword Dance 17, 19, 36, 37, 53, 70, 73, 110, 132, 141–142, 154–155, 167, 168, 175, 186, 192–193, 211

Tango 27
Threesome and Foursome Scotch and Irish Reels 197
Top Boot Step dancing 170, 182
Trumpet Hornpipe 132, 136, 227
Tullochgorm/Tullochgorum 150–151, 186
Two Step 101, 167

Universal Two-Step 167

Valeta 167

Waltz 27, 73, 101, 118, 165, 170, 182, 189, 220–221
Waltz Clog 195
White Cockade, The 181
Wigtownshire Liverpool Hornpipe 178
Wilt Thou Go to the Barricks [Berwick], Johnnie 133, 137–138, 225, 227
Wooden-Shoe Step dancing 170
Wooing of the Maiden 119
Wun that Shook the Barley, The 118

Yillwife and her Barrles 118

Song/tune titles

An Gille Crùbach anns a' Ghleann/Miss Drummond of Perth 223, 240
Ap Shenkin/The Tempest 177

Blue Bonnets 70, 223
Bonnie Dundee 174
Bonny Jean of Aberdeen 74
Braes O' Mar 137

Carleton House High Dance 74
Cock O' the North 137
College Hornpipe 69, 241

Dance to Y'r Daddie 69
Dornoch Links 227
Drops of Brandy 195

Durang's Hornpipe 224
Dusty Miller 68–69, 136, 138, 227

Flooers o' Edinburgh/Flowers of Edinburgh 67–69, 242

Gillie Calluin 142
Go to Berwick, Johnnie/Johnny 68, 239

Highland Laddie 67, 227

Inverness Gathering 206

Jacky Tar type hornpipe 69

Kenmure's on an' awa,' Willie 166

Lady Lucy Ramsay 82

Maggie Pickens 70
Minuet 73, 87 239
Miss Ann Cockburn's Fancy High Dance 72
Miss Eliza Low's High Dance 74
Miss Honeyman of Armadale's High Dance 72
Miss Robertson's High Dance 71
Mr Keith's Favorite High Dance 72

Over the Hills and Far Away/*'S truagh nach bu leis &c.* 241
Over the Water to Charlie/*Null air an Uisge gu Tearlach* 241

Pas Seul danced by Miss Francis Urquhart 74
Pas Seul danced by Miss Margaret Burnett of Leys 74
Pas Seul Miss Jane Forbes 74
Polka 16

Quaker's Wife 227

Rock and the Wee Pickle Tow 120

Sabhal Iain 'ic Ùisdean 15, 50
Sailor's Hornpipe (*see* College Hornpipe)
Soldier's Joy 70
Speed the Plough 74
Stirling Castle 227

Tuloch Gorm/Tulloch Gorum 240

Wee Totum Fogg 69
Whistle o'er the Lave o't 70, 227

Index   265

White Cockade/*An Chòcard* 16, 67, 69
Woo'd and Married an A' 75
Wooing of the Maiden 119

People

Aberdeen, Lord 125
Adamson, William (dancing master) 132
Aitken, Mary 160
Albert of Saxe-Coburg and Gotha, Prince Consort 132
Alburger, Mary Anne 75
Alger, John Goldworth 99
Allan, David 52–53
Allan, Sir William 48
Amelia, Princess 128
Anderson, David (dancing master) 132, 153, 156–158, 172, 174, 216, 224
Anderson, Gillin 202
Anderson, Paul 143, 209
Anklewicz, Michael 24
Arbeau, Thoinot (dancing master) 56
Argyll, Duke of 93
Armstrong, John 176

Bain, Anna 203–204
Ballantyne, Patricia 29, 108, 129, 181, 237
Barber, Elizabeth Wayland 220, 222
Barnard (dancing master) 79, 115
Barratti, Maestro (dancing master) 30
Barrymore, Mrs Wm. (dancing master) 124
Barstow, G. 116
Bean Iain 'ic Sheumais 147
Beaton family of Mabou 185
Beaton, Donald 235
Beaton, Harvey 8, 22, 216, 231
Beaton, Mary MacDonald/*Màiri Aoghais Thullaich* 185
Beattie, Julia 209
Beckwith, Lillian 177–178
Bennett, Margaret xi, 9, 189, 191, 201–202, 206, 209, 232
Biggins, H. 170
Boswell, David (dancing master) 89
Boswell, James 78, 83–85, 92
Bournonville, August (dancing master) 92, 126–127
Boyle, Michael 231
Brainard, Ingrid 56
Brande, W.T. 211
Breadalbane, Lord 91, 94
Bremner, Robert 99, 220
Britton, Màiri 9, 49, 66, 182, 237
Brockbank, Ian 228

Brown, William 98
Buchan, Flora Cruickshank 134, 136, 160
Buchanan, Robert 152–153
Buckland, Theresa Jill 4, 23, 29,
Burns, James 158
Burns, Robert 78, 96, 119, 121, 150
Burt, Edward/Edmond 43–44
Byron, Lord (George Gordon) 71, 150

Cameron, Alasdair 139
Cameron, I.D. 30
Cameron, James 93
Cameron, William 23, 175
Campbell, Alexander 100, 102–103, 114, 120
Campbell, Duncan 139
Campbell, John Francis 147
Campbell, W.F. 139
Carleton, William 61
Carolina/Caroline, Princess 128
Caroso, Febritio (dancing master) 56
Carswell, Captain Ranald 172
Carter, Nathaniel Hazeltine 120
Carus, Carl Gustav 141–142
Cattanach, Captain 172
Cecchetti, Enrico (dancing master) 30–31
Charles IX, King 57
Chartrand, Pierre 221
Clark, Heather 191, 196
Clement, William 'Bill' 48
Comrie, Peter 139
Cooper, Danny 209
Cooper, Mr Isaac (music master) 72
Craig, Carol 232
Cramb, Isobel 'Tibbie' 110, 134–137
Cromar, John 209
Cruickshank, George (dancing master) 134
Cruickshank, John (dancing master) 113, 134
Cunningham, Allan 119–120
Currie, Clare MacDonald 187
Currie, James 96–97

d'Egville, James Harvey (dancing master) 79
Dalyell, Sir John Graham 70
Dawney, Mr John (dancing master) 103
Daye, Anne 108
Dembling, Jonathan 236
Dempsy, Mr 88
Desnoyer/Denoyer (dancing master) 104, 128
Devine, T.M. 4–5, 101
Dickson, Joshua 165

266 *Index*

Docherty, *Ciorstaigh*/Christina 201, 232
Doherty, Elizabeth 206, 219
Dòmhnallach, Goiridh 14
Donald, Mr and Mrs (dancing master) 167
Donald, Mr William 172
Douglas, Lewis (dancing master) 113
Downie (dancing master) 79
Downie, John 92
Duff, A. (dancing master) 79
Duff, Archibald (dancing master) 79
Dunn, Margaret MacEachern 187
Durang, Charles 224
Durang, John 224
Dwelly, Edward 25, 54, 161

Elizabeth I, Queen 112
Elizabeth II, Queen 154
Elphinstone, Lord and Lady 154
Emmerson, George S. 5–6, 28, 32, 44–
    45, 55, 58–59, 67, 70, 78–80, 88–90,
    110, 116, 118–119
Eyre, Miss Mary 117, 124; Eyres, Misses 117

Faujas de Saint-Fond, Barthélemy 93–94
Feintuch, Bert 24
Fergusson, Robert 83
Fettes, Mr John F. (dancing master)
    153–154
Feuillet, Raoul Auger (dancing master)
    57–58, 133
Finlayson, James 93
Flett, Thomas 'Tom' and Joan 6, 13–14,
    21, 27–28, 32, 35, 42, 46, 50, 55, 67,
    70, 78, 80, 88, 103, 108, 115–116, 136,
    146–147, 175, 206, 213, 215, 230, 234
Foley, Catherine 8, 17–19, 56–58
Ford, Ruby 195
Foss, Hugh 35, 172
François I, King 57
Fraser, Alasdair 236
Fraser, G.M. 103
Fraser, James (dancing master) 93
Fraser, Mr (dancing master) 73
Fraser, Patrick 93
Fraser, William (dancing master) 89
Frederick Augustus II, King 141
Froment, Monsieur (dancing master) 72

Gallini, *Giovanni-Andrea*/Sir John Andrew
    (dancing master) 79, 90, 99, 155
Galt, John 78
Gareiss, Nic 182
Garnett, Thomas 88
Gaudrau, Michel (dancing master) 57

Gay, John 116
Gayton, Miss Esther Jane 71
Genée, Alexander (dancing master) 30
Gibson, John G. 63, 181, 184, 188, 192
Gillies, Annie 201
Gillies, Lachlan 206
Gillis, Alexander/*Mac Iain ic Alasdair*
    (dancing master) 185
Gillis, Helen 188
Gillis Margaret 185, 187–188, 191, 224
Glassie, Henry 24
Glover, Leach (dancing master) 104, 128
Gordon, Duchess of 112
Gordon, Jock 208
Gow, James 93
Gow, Niel 88
Grant (Smith), Elizabeth 111
Grant, Donald (dancing master) 126
Grant, Snr, Angus 206, 236
Grattan Flood, William H. 70
Gregg, James (dancing master) 79
Grey, Sarah 204
Guillard, Yves 9, 108–109
Guynemer, Monsieur 74
Gwich'in people 206

Hall, James 88
Hamilton, Duke of 114
Harden, John 88
Hardie, Alastair J. 67
Hardie, J. 141
Hay, James, Earl of Erroll 110
Henderson, Joan 179
Henri III, King 57
Hill, Frederick 5, 73, 110, 132–133, 141,
    220, 225
Hilton, Wendy 58,
Hobsbawm, Eric xii, 24
Hogg, James 78, 119
Howat, William (dancing master) 133
Howe, Elias (dancing master) 224
Huat (dancing master) 27, 133
Hume, David 53

Jaffray, Alexander 104,
Jamison, Phil 51, 196–197
Jerdan, William 80
Jodrell, Sir Paul 85
Johnson, James 68
Johnson, John Harald 208
Johnson, Samuel 42, 83–85
Johnston, Ann 203
Jowitt, Deborah 127
Juba, Master 152

Kaltman, Frank 176–177
Kennedy, Michael 38
Kennedy Family, Broad Cove 185
Knox, John 93
Kohl, Johann Georg 142–143
Kydd, Dancie David (dancing master) 135, 208

Laban, Rudolph 3, 9; Labanotation 108–109
Lally (dancing master) 104
Lamb, William 9, 117, 130, 206
Lamotte, Pierre (dancing master) 79
Laughlan, Mr Andrew (dancing master) 93
Laurie, Ronnie 205
Lederman, Anne 207
LePicq, Antoine (dancing master) 79
Logan, James 107, 124–126, 143
Louis XII, King 57
Louis XIV, King 57–58
Lowe brothers (dancing masters) 19, 71, 122–124, 132; James 124; John 124; Joseph 123–124; Robert 74, 124
Lowe, Joe 158
Lowe, John (dancing master) 79
Lully, Jean-Baptiste 56, 58

M'Donald, James (dancing master) 89
M'Donald, Mr James, factor 85
M'Donald of Sleat, Sir Alexander 85
M'Ewan, Tom 153
M'Guigan, W.T. 170
M'Intosh, Duncan 121
M'Intosh, Mr 73
M'Nichol, Mr John 93
M'Pike, J. 158
Mac an t-Saoir, Donnchadh Bàn 93
MacArthur, Allan 191
MacArthur, Frank 210
MacArthur family 189–191, 210
MacCoinneach, Coinneach 93
MacDhughaill, Iain/John MacDougall 62–63
MacDonald, Angus 189
MacDonald, Angus L. 35–36
MacDonald, Christena 187
MacDonald, Dan Alec 62
MacDonald, Donald 'Rcidean'146, 165, 170–172, 234
MacDonald, Gordon 192
MacDonald, Hugh 203
MacDonald, Mary Janet 200–201, 216
MacDonald, Mary Jessie 187

MacDonald, Miss Bella 172
MacDonald, Miss Harriet 172
MacDonald, Miss Sarah 172
MacDonald, Peter 49
MacDonald of Glenuig, Iain 9, 16
MacDougall, Angus Bàn 185
MacDougall, John 61
MacDougall, John of Broad Cove Banks 184–185
MacDougall, Lauchlin 185
MacEachen, Mr Louis 172
MacEachern, Sadie Gillis 188
MacFadyen, Dr Alastair 133
Macgillichallum, MacLeod laird 83
MacGillivray, Allister 9, 185, 187
MacGillivray, Mary 9, 216
Macgregor, Ranald (dancing master) 73
MacInnes, Maggie 201
MacInnes, Sheldon 231
Macintosh, Duncan and Mrs 112
MacIntosh, John 63
Macintyre, Mr Archibald (dancing master) 93
MacKay/M'Kay, Angus 139, 151, 239–242
MacKay, Donald 'Donnie' 205
Mackay, Duncan (dancing master) 92
MacKay, John 42
Mackay, Master Harry 155–156
Mackenzie, Anita 133
MacKenzie, Donald R. (dancing master) 211–212
MacKenzie, Henry 115
MacKenzie, J.L. 37–38
MacLachlan, Ewen (dancing master) 145–147, 172, 174, 234
MacLachlan, Ewen/Eòghann MacLachlainn (Gaelic scholar) 105
MacLachlan, Janet 'Jenny' Thomson 181, 194
MacLagan, Robert 70
MacLean, Calum 147
MacLean, Johnny 'Washabuck'/Johnny 'Red' Rory 189
MacLean, Mairi 202
MacLean, Michael Dan/Mickey 'Red' Rory 189
MacLean, Rory 'Red'/Ruairidh Dearg ic Domnull 189
MacLennan, D.G. (dancing master) 2, 6, 22, 24, 30–34, 38, 46, 111, 146, 162, 168–169, 172, 174–177, 191, 216, 234
MacLennan, Malcolm 69
MacLennan, William 30–31

268   *Index*

MacLeod, Dr Norman 151–152
MacLeod, Jayne 237
MacLeod, John of Iochdar 146, 174, 215, 234
MacLeod, Rev Norman 152, 163
MacLeod, Sandie 83
MacLeoid, Calum 108
MacLeoid, Iain *Breac* 60
MacMhaoirn, Alasdair 219
MacMillan, Allan 185
MacMillan, Calum 147
MacMillan, Don 169
MacMillans 'The Dancers' 185
MacNab, Mary Isdale 37
MacNeil, Fearchar 22, 53, 146–147, 199–200, 215, 234
MacNeil, Flora 201
MacNeil, Jean 216, 235
MacNeill, Seumas 37–38
MacPhee, Kate 165
Macpherson, Alan 133
MacPherson, Archibald 'Archie' 146, 170–176, 234
MacPherson, Iain 'Coddy' 147
MacQuarrie, Abbie 231
MacQueen (dancing master) 79
MacQueen, Canon Angus 147
MacRae, Farquhar 206, 236
MacRury, Rev John 43
MacTaggart, John 70, 118–119, 216
Maltere (dancing master) 79
Manchester, Duke of 112
Maori people 142, 192
Marcoucci, Signora (dancing master) 72
Martin (dancing master) 79, 115
Martin, Martin 42, 44
Maxwell, Herbert 96
McBain, A. 154
McColl, Alexander C. 177
McColl, Jeanetta 176–177
McConachie, Jack 6, 146–147, 174, 176–177, 215, 234
McCormick, Andrew 166
McDonald, Patrick 93
McEwan, Charles 31
McGill, Johnny (dancing master) 79–82
McHarg, Mary 202, 232
McIan, Robert Ranald 143–144
McIntosh, Gordon 208
McIntosh, Robert 208
McIntosh, William 209
McIntyre North, Charles Niven 142, 154–155, 175
McIntyre, Sandy 154

McKay, Sheila 203–204
McKenzie, John 31
McKenzie, Judy 9
McKimmie, J.E. and William (dancing master) 162
McNaughton, J.D. 29
McNeill, Snr., John (dancing master) 30–31, 172, 225
McOwen, Robert 234
Melin, Mats 8, 181, 199–210
Melish, John 99
Menzies, Lady 114
Metherell, Chris 9, 136, 234
Métis people 206–207
Middlemist, Robert (dancing master) 89
Miller, Scotch musician 141
Milligan, Jean 1, 32–33, 134
Milton, John 122
Moffat, Mr (dancing master) 72
Molloy, Maureen 192
Montague, Lady Jane 112
Montgomerie, Alexander 75
Moore, Hamish 236
Moore, Maggie 202–205, 209
Morer, Thomas 44
Morin, Mac 237
Muir, Miss J. (dancing master) 167
Muir, Mr James D. (dancing master) 167
Murray, W.H. 139
Myren, Adam (dancing master) 113, 133

Neat, Timothy 204
Nedderman, Ron 134
Negri, Cesare (dancing master) 56
Neill, Dancie James (dancing master) 158, 172
Nelson, Mr 169
Nevile, Jennifer 55–59, 222
Newton, Michael S. 9, 55, 59–60, 64–65, 93, 182, 219
Nichol, Miss 116
Nicholson, John 139
Nicoll, Miss 116

O'Donnell (Smith), Shiobhan 193–195
Oswald, James 239, 242
Owen, Robert 135

Palmer, Mr 194
Paton, Jeanie 194
Peacock, Francis (dancing master) 12, 32, 35, 78–79, 89, 97, 100, 103–111, 123–126, 133
Pennant, Thomas 95

Index 269

Pforsich, Janis 68–69
Picard, Ludovic 94
Pirie, John 31
Playford, John (dancing master) 67
Pocock, Isaac 139
Poitier, family of dancers 90
Pollock, James (dancing master) 72–73
Purcell, Henry 67, 69

Radestock, Rudolph (dancing master) 107
Rameau, Pierre (dancing master) 58
Ramsay, Allan 48, 78
Raonaid *nighean mhic Néill* MacDonald 64
Rea, Frederick 164–166
Reid, Dancie John (dancing master) 28, 132, 135, 153, 158, 162. 172–174, 177, 208, 225, 230
Rhodes, Frank 6, 21, 36–37, 78, 109, 136, 146–147, 174, 178–179, 185–188, 220, 223–224, 230, 234
Roberts, George 17, 155
Robertson, Colin 9–10, 136, 180
Robertson, James Stewart 242
Robertson, Sandra 148
Robson, Marion 208–209
Ross, Alexander 75, 81
Ross, Provost Alexander 43
Rousseau, F. (dancing master) 57
Russell, Colin 104

Sakurai, Kae 237
Schoonover, Jennifer 8–9, 220, 234
Scott, Edward (dancing master) 107
Scott, James (dancing master) 72, 88
Scott, Sir Walter 78, 96, 139
Scott, William (dancing master) 164
Sealey, Joesph (dancing master) 89
Sharp, Cecil 20
Shelley, J.P. 170
Sibbald, Susan 113
Siddons, Mrs Henry 139
Sinclair, Catherine 132, 159
Sinclair, Sir John 132
Skinner, J. 'Scott' (dancing master) 108, 163–164
Skinner, Rev John 150
Skinner, William (dancing master) 164
Slyde, Jimmy 196
Smith, Mrs Orma 195
Smout, T.C. 77–78
Smyth, W. (dancing master) 74
Snody, Morrison 206
Snow, Miss 90
Spalding, Susan Eike 24, 197

Sparling, Heather 9, 182, 188
St. John, Charles 144–145
Stanley, Mr 116
Stapleton, Anne McKee 28–29, 113, 150
Stearns, Marshall 51, 197
Stenhouse, William 68
Stephenson, Sophie 237
Steward Burt, Mr D. 195
Stewart, Charles (Bonnie Prince Charlie) 18
Stewart, Charles, musician 68
Stewart, Essie 204
Stewart, Grannie 166
Stewart, Ysobel 1, 33
Strange, David (dancing master) 68, 79, 89, 110
Struthers, Miss Peggy 170
Stuart, James 103

Taglioni, Filippo (dancing master) 127
Taglioni, Marie 92, 127, 138–139
Tait, Crauford 113
Taylor, George Douglas (dancing master) 31, 168–169
Taylor, James (dancing master) 27, 133, 141
Taylor, John (dancing master) 133
Taylor, T. (dancing master) 141
Terry, Walter 127
Thornton, Colonel Thomas 4, 12, 15, 20, 50, 90–96, 121, 126
Thurston, Hugh 35–36, 225
Topham, Edward 35, 59, 78, 85–90, 108, 110, 115, 125, 166
Traveller/s 166, 204
Turtle Mountain Band of Ojibway and Métis people 206

Vestris (dancing master) family 79, 91
Vestris, Auguste/Marie-Jean-Augustin 92, 98, 126
Vestris, Gaétan/Gaetano Apolline Baldassarre 98
Victoria, Queen 19, 123, 131, 143, 145

Wadsworth, Winnie 48
Wake, Charles 113
Wake, Lady Charlotte Murdoch Tait 113–114
Walker, Miss Annie 172
Wallace, J.F. (dancing master) 132
Wallace, Joseph (dancing master) 71
Wallace, Ron 234
Walsh, John 99

270   *Index*

Watson, Robert 'Bobby' (dancing master) 135, 137
Weaver, John (dancing master) 58, 133
Whitta, Kim, 30, 162
William of Orange/William III and II, King 44
William, King of the Marshall Gang 166
Williamson, Alec John 204
Wilson, Thomas (dancing master) 18, 34, 100–102, 128

Young, David (dancing master) 99

Places and languages

Aberdeen 12, 31, 32, 35, 72, 73–74, 78, 79, 89, 103–111, 125, 129, 135, 137, 138, 152, 160, 164, 167, 168, 181
Aberdeenshire 13, 29, 73, 81, 110, 131, 132–138, 143, 145, 163–164, 181, 208–209, Abergeldie Castle 123; Alford 5, 133; Arbeadie near Banchory 164; Auchinblae 154; Balmoral Castle 123, 131, 145; Braemar Gathering (Highland Games) 46, 145; Cairn O' Mount 143; Clachnaben 143; Clatt near Alford 133; Corriemulzie 145; Dunnottar 154; Fetteresso 154; Finzean 209; Fyvie 113, 134; Howe o' Cromar near Tarland 209; Kildrummy 209; Laurencekirk 208; Lumphanan 208–209; Marykirk 79; Peterhead 110, 134; Portsoy 162; Stonehaven 154; Stoneywood 164; Torphins 209; Turriff 110, 133; Banffshire 145; Banff 72, 113; Mortlach 113; Kincardineshire 79, 154; Morayshire 113; Barnhill Farm 141; Dallas 113; Elgin 133, 141; Fochabers 113, 133; Urquhart 126
Angus 8, 17, 28, 81, 135, 153–154, 158, 163, 172–174, 208–209; Alyth 172; Arbroath 139; Brechin 73, 153–154, 156; Forfar 158, 172; Glenesk 208–209; Kirriemuir 172; Lochlee 81; Montrose 73, 79, 103; Newtyle 28, 162, 172–174
Argyll/Argyllshire 1, 12, 70, 90–95, 121, 122, 148, 163–164, 166; Ardrishaig 33; Arrochar 121–122; Bridge of Orchy 122; Campbeltown 163–164; Crear 148; Dalmally 90–95; Glen Orchy/Glen Orgue/Glenurchy 4, 12, 15, 91, 93, 95, 96, 109, 120, 121, 216, 237; Inveroran

120–121, 122; Kenmore near Inverary 93; Kilmartin 92; Loch Tulla 120; Oban 22, 93, 170, 171, 205
Australia 142, 184, 191–192, 195–196; Victoria 29, 195–196
Ayrshire 79, 80, 110; Arran, Isle of 114; Ayr 139; Girvan 80

Borders 113, 137; Dunse 80; Roxburghshire 158, 178, 186; West Berwickshire 158, 178, 186

Canada/Canadian 7–9, 142, 181, 207, 208
Cape Breton Island, NS 7–9, 13, 21, 36–39, 182, 184–189; Broad Cove, NS 185; Creignish, NS 185; Dunvegan, NS 35–36, 185; Framboise, NS 62; Inverness County, NS 184–185; Judique, NS 185; Mabou Coal Mines, NS 185; Maple Brook (Glendale), NS 188; New Waterford, NS 187; South West Margaree, NS 185; St. Ann's (Gaelic College), NS 36–39, 40; Washabuck, NS 189; West Lake, NS 185
Central Scotland: Clackmannanshire: Harviestoun near Alva 113–114; Falkirk 95, 139, 152–153, 178, Feeing Fair 152, 178; Larbert 202; Stirling 139, 180, 202; Killin (formerly Perthshire) 142

Dumfries & Galloway 140; Annandale 96; Dumfries 80, 96, 139, 140, 166; Dumfriesshire 96, 119; Galloway 118–119, 139–140, 166; Keir 119; Kirkcudbright 118–119, 139; Kirroughtree 167; Newton Stewart 166
Dunbartonshire 118
Dundee 17, 99, 139, 155–156, 156–158, 172, 174, 224

England/English/British 1, 3, 4, 5, 7, 8, 14, 18, 19, 20, 21, 22, 23, 26, 28–29, 34, 35, 42, 47, 51, 57, 58, 59, 67, 68, 69, 70, 71, 77, 79, 83, 85–86, 88, 89, 90, 92, 93, 97, 98, 100–102, 104, 105, 106, 107–108, 110, 112, 114, 119, 121, 122, 123, 133, 136, 141, 143, 144, 147, 151, 152, 158, 163, 165, 166–167, 176, 179, 186, 190, 194, 195, 196, 199, 207, 215, 217–219, 200, 221, 228, 232; Bath 143, Bristol 143; Bowness;

Bushey 169; Carlisle 166; Cumberland 166; Cumbria 88; Derbyshire 113; Hammersmith, Middlesex 133; Hampstead 143; Hexham, Northumberland 72; Lakeland 21; Lancashire 22, 77; Leeds 158; Lichfield, Staffordshire 83 (*see also* London/ Londoners)
Europe 8, 14, 20, 31, 42, 51 55–61, 65, 100–101, 184, 196

Fife 158, 202–204, 208; Dunfermline 139; Glenrothes 203, 72; Kirkaldy 139; Leslie 203
France/French 14, 18, 25, 30, 32–33, 34, 37, 55–60, 65, 73, 74, 79, 85, 90, 93, 98, 100–101, 108, 111, 117, 120, 122, 129, 156, 162, 207, 214; Brittany 220; Coutances 59; French chalk 178; French Revolution 58, 79, 98; Loos, Battle of 169; Paris 79, 87, 90, 92, 98, 126–127; St. Lô 59

Germany/German 14, 19, 25, 55, 73, 100–101, 143, 215
Glasgow 4, 20, 29, 31, 37, 61, 63, 74, 79, 138–139, 152, 172, 174, 177, 205; Royal Conservatoire of Music/Royal Academy of Music and Drama 237

Hebrides, Inner and Outer: Barra, Isle of 22, 53, 145–148, 170–172, 179, 186, 189, 199–202, 210, 215, 217, 234; Barra *Fèis* 200–201; Castlebay 199–202; Eoligarry 202; Benbecula, 43; Bernera, Isle of 205; Canna 185, 186; Easdale 93; Islay 130, 139, 147; Lewis, Isle of 179, 203, Barbhas 205; Callanish 203; Siabost/Shawbost 205; North Uist 62, 114–115; Lochmaddy 114, 172; Raasay 83–85; Skye, Isle of 8, 64, 83, 85, 177–178, 231, 236; Armadale 72, 185; Dunvegan 60; *Sabhal Mòr Ostaig* (Sleat) 15; Snizort 43; Soay, Isle of 177–178; South Uist 16, 22, 24, 60, 145–147, 147–148, 163, 164–166, 170–172, 174, 175, 179, 215, 234, 236; Askernish Highland Games (South Uist and Barra Highland Gathering) 146, 165, 170–172; Bornish 147; *Ceòlas* festival 236, 237; Daliburgh, 165, 170, 172; Garrynamonie 164; Iochdar 146, 170, 171, 172, 174; Ormaclete 147

Highland/Highlands 3, 4–8, 12, 17, 18, 22, 42, 44, 49–50, 55, 59, 78, 80, 83, 91, 102, 105, 106, 114, 117, 120–121, 125, 127, 129, 131, 143, 145, 148, 149, 159, 170, 171, 204, 231–232, 233, 235, 236; Advie 73; Alness 204; Arasaig/Arisaig 62, 206; Ardgour near Inverlochy 61; Aviemore 111; Badenoch 95, 107; Ballachulish 121; Balmeanach 73; Black Isle (Ross-shire) 61, 205; Brae Lochaber 63; Breadalbane 141–142; Carron 146, 174; Cromdale 73; Cromarty 93; Dingwall 203, 204; Durness 206; Fort William 93; Grantown on Spey 73; Invermoriston 49; Inverness 43, 139, 151, 168; Kingussie 95; Lochaber 44, 95, 105, 151, 185, 186; Moidart 172, 185, 186; Morar 21, 185, 186; Rogart 205, 111–113; Roshven 206; Scourie 144–145; Spey 95; Speyside 111–113, 146, 149–150; Strathspey 73, 95, 113; Sutherland 8, 61, 176, 191, 192, 203, 204, 205–205, 219; Tongue 206; Torcroy 201
Holland/Dutch 25, 75, 215

Ireland/Irish xi, 8, 18, 21, 38, 40, 51, 58, 59, 61, 120, 142, 144, 193, 194, 195, 201, Clare 21; Connemara 22, 204; Cork 193; Dublin 53, 58, 88; Irish Gaelic 68–69; Kerry 21, 22, 193, 194; Limerick 8, 193, 230
Italy/Italian 25, 55–57, 59, 60, 72, 79, 90, 99, 102, 120, 139; Cremona 57; Florence 98, 99; Milan 57; Rome 59

Lanarkshire (North) 170; Airdrie 139, 149; Coatbridge 139; Craigneuk 170; Motherwell 139, 167, 169–170; New Monkland 149; Lanarkshire (South) New Lanark 135
Lithuania 102
London/Londoners 4, 18, 19, 20, 22, 26, 31, 44, 46, 58, 70, 71, 74, 79, 87, 88, 89, 91, 92, 96, 99, 100–101, 104, 118, 119, 124–125, 126, 128, 133, 139, 143, 147, 154, 158, 168–169, 174, 176–177, 179, 184; Bow 158; Covent Garden 90; Drury Lane 70, 71, 128, 133; King's Theatre 18, 79; Lewisham 154; Northumberland/Northumbrian 69, 75; Pitsford, Northamptonshire 113; Royal Academy of the Arts 125;

272 *Index*

St. James's 95; Tonbridge, Kent 154; Worcestershire 113; York 85

Lothian: East Lothian 158, 178, 186; North Berwick 172; Edinburgh 22, 30–31, 46, 58, 68, 72, 74, 78, 79, 80, 83, 85–89, 101, 103, 104, 105, 110, 111, 113, 114, 115–116, 116–117, 119, 129, 130, 132, 146, 162, 172, 174–176, 225; Edinburgh Assembly Rooms 79; Leith 72, 89; School of Scottish Studies 206, 231; Theatre-Royal 124, 139; Midlothian: Newbigging near Inveresk 154

Lowland/Lowlands 3, 4–5, 43, 44, 55, 56–57, 69, 77, 78, 88, 90, 102, 118

Manitoba, Canada 207

New Brunswick, Canada 181

New Zealand 8, 29, 30–31, 123, 162, 170, 181, 184, 191–195, 211, 215, 218; Auckland 192; Dunedin 193–194; Dunedin Caledonian Games 194; North Island 191; South Island 195; Timaru 195; Waipu, 191–193; Waipu Caledonian Games 192–193

Newfoundland, Canada 181, 183, Codroy Valley, NL 189–191, 206

North America 77, 79, 85, 150, 175, 184–191, 196–197, 224, 235

Northwest Territories, Canada 206

Nova Scotia, Canada xi, 12, 35, 36, 38–39, 45, 108, 148, 184, 186; Antigonish, NS 36, 185; Antigonish Highland Games 36 (*see also* Cape Breton Island, NS)

Ontario, Canada 181, 194; Glengarry, ON 231, Ottawa Valley 22

Orkney/Orcadian 8, 129, 167–168, 206–207, 217, 233; Kirkwall 206

Perth and Kinross 8, Aberfeldy 93; Birnam 203; Blair Atholl 52, 93, 132, 159; Comrie 139; Dunkeld 88, 203; Foss 139; Kenmore, near Aberfeldy 93; Kincraigie 93; Loch Lubnaig 103; Perth 139, 154, 165; Perthshire (historic designation) 142, 166, 172, 208

Poland 142

Prince Edward Island, Canada 181, 184

Quebec, Canada 207, 221

Renfrewshire: Paisley 139; Inverclyde: Greenock 139

Russia 100, 142; Crimean War 150; St. Petersburg 74

Scandinavia 59; Copenhagen, DK 126, Denmark/Danish 25, 30, 126, 127; Faroese 220; Finland 59; Norway/Norwegian 19, 25; Sweden/Swedish 8, 25, 139

Scotland/Scottish xi–238, map 10, Cant (Romany) 166; Gaeldom 4–5, 143, 235; *Gàidhealtachd* 4, 95, 232, 236; Scots language 4, 18, 53, 77, 81–83, 118–119, 152–153, 161, 213, 220, 236; Scottish Gaelic/*Gàidhlig*/Erse 14–15, 21, 25,36–39, 42–43, 47–48, 50, 53, 55, 59–65, 69, 77, 93, 95, 105, 107, 110, 121, 122, 124–126, 128, 147, 154, 161, 165, 166, 168, 181, 182, 184, 186, 187, 189, 191–192, 197, 199–202, 205, 206, 210, 215, 216, **217–220**, 225, 228, 231, 236, 238

Shetland 8, 61, 108, 126, 129, 163, 207–208, 217, 233; Lerwick 208

Spain/Spanish 14, 19, 25, 55, 56, 57, 59, 74, 85, 101; Basque Country 33, Valladolid 59

Switzerland/Swiss 85, 120

United States 8, 101, 128, 142, 184; Alaska, 206; American Civil War 150; American War of Independence 77; Appalachia (region) 51, 196–197; Boston, MA 8–9, 176, 224; Canton, MA 231; Concord, NH 120; North Dakota 206; Plymouth, MA 176; Virginia 37, 150

Wales 21; Wrexham 79

Yukon, Canada 206